Copy-editing

Other titles by Barbara Horn

Copy-editing by Distance Leaning

Editorial Project Management with exercises and model answers

Editorial Project Management by Distance Learning

The Effective Editor's Handbook

Copy-editing

with exercises and model answers

Barbara Horn

HEB

The PUBLISHING TRAINING CENTRE
AT BOOK HOUSE

HORN EDITORIAL BOOKS *and* THE PUBLISHING TRAINING CENTRE
London

First published in Great Britain in 2008 by Horn Editorial Books,
32 Greenway Close, London N20 8EN, and The Publishing Training
Centre at Book House, 45 East Hill, London SW18 2QZ.

© Barbara Horn 2008
Index © Christine Shuttleworth and Barbara Horn 2008

Barbara Horn has asserted her right to be identified
as the author of this work in accordance with the
Copyright, Designs and Patents Act 1988.

All rights reserved. No part of this publication may be reproduced,
stored in a retrieval system, or transmitted, in any form or by any
means, electronic, mechanical, photocopying, recording, or otherwise,
without the prior written permission of the publisher.

ISBN 978-0-9553404-1-3

A CIP record for this work can be obtained
from the British Library

Editor: Enid Barker
Proofreader: Margaret Aherne

Typeset in 11/14 Sabon by M Rules
Printed and bound in Great Britain by
Biddles, 24 Rollesby Road, King's Lynn, Norfolk

Contents

Preface	ix
Acknowledgements	xi
The copy-editor's world	xiii
Our colleagues	xv
Stages of production	xvi
Copy-editing tools	xxi
Copy-editing marks	xxi
House and book style	xxiii
Writing queries for authors	xxiv
1 Marking up	1
Designers and typesetters	1
How to mark up	3
What to mark up	5
2 Grammar and punctuation	34
Correct is not always appropriate	34
The author's voice	35
The house voice	36
Grammar	36
Punctuation	50
3 Cover to cover	77
Covers and binding	77
In the beginning	80
The body of the book	94
Endmatter	95
Running heads	100

vi *Copy-editing*

	Copyright	103
	Other legal issues	112
	You are responsible	114
4	**Style and level**	**115**
	Capitals	115
	Italics	125
	Numbers	134
	Purpose and level	145
5	**Specialist texts**	**157**
	Poetry	157
	Plays	165
	Manuals	173
	Jacket or cover copy	181
6	**Tables, technical figures and copy-fitting**	**188**
	Tables	188
	Technical figures	204
	Cutting and expanding	219
7	**Endmatter**	**230**
	Notes and reference systems	230
	Indexes	270

Have toolkit, can travel — 286

Glossary — 288

Model Answers — 295

Resources — 415
 General — 415
 Style manuals — 417

English usage and writing style	418
Copyright guides	419
Production	419
Organizations for editors in Europe	420
Organizations for editors outside Europe	421
Training organizations in Britain and Ireland	421
Other useful websites	422

Index 423

Preface

This book is based on *Copy-editing by Distance Learning*, which was launched by the Publishing Training Centre in September 2005, and on my many years of working as a copy-editor and trainer. The text, which has been revised and expanded, reflects British practice and explains some of the important differences in American usage.

Copy-editing is aimed at both aspiring copy-editors (sometimes called 'subeditors') and those with some experience who want to improve, consolidate or add to their skills. It is a starting point, not the final answer to every question you will have. No book has all the answers, partly because any manuscript can raise new, unique questions and partly because the appropriate answer in one circumstance will not be the same in another. Copy-editing is as much about judging what is appropriate for the reader as it is about applying technical skills. There are, of course, many manuals and reference works that will help you, and some of them are listed in Resources.

Ideally, you will have some knowledge of, and experience in, proofreading. It is common practice for people to learn to proofread before they learn to copy-edit because, in addition to being a skilled job in its own right, proofreading helps to familiarize them with what copy-editors do and the environment in which they work. The symbols used for correcting proofs (BS 5261-2: 2005) are also used for editing on paper. Whether or not you are an experienced proofreader, be sure to read 'Copy-editing marks' (p. xxi) before beginning Chapter 1. No other prior knowledge of publishing is necessary.

Copy-editors use the same basic copy-editing skills to work on fiction and non-fiction, and on many kinds of publications, including books, journals, magazines, newsletters and reports. This book will explain how to apply these skills in paper-based and electronic media, although it is not about specific on-screen editing techniques and the model answers show handwritten, rather than electronic, changes. In addition, you will learn particular aspects of copy-editing that are relevant mainly to books and journals, so that you have the tools needed to work in any of these fields.

The introductory text, 'The copy-editor's world', introduces you to the publishing environment. It explains the role of the copy-editor, the purpose and composition of house style, and the stages of producing a publication. Reading it first will help you to understand the rest of the book. You might want to familiarize yourself with the terms and the diagram of type in the Glossary, too, before beginning the first chapter as well as refer to them later.

Chapter 1 is about marking up the elements in, and structure of, a publication for design and typesetting. Chapter 2 concentrates on grammar and punctuation, and Chapter 3 outlines the material between the covers of a publication and explains the basic rules of copyright. Style issues – when to use italics and how to represent numbers – and getting the level right for the reader are covered in Chapter 4. Editing specialist texts is the focus of Chapter 5, while editing tables and drawn illustrations, indicating their position in the text, and copy-fitting text are dealt with in Chapter 6. Chapter 7 is about endmatter: indexes and references.

Several exercises are interspersed in each chapter to help you test your understanding. You can work on them in the book or photocopy them to keep separately. While focusing on a specific aspect of copy-editing, each exercise also builds on what has been learned in preceding exercises and chapters, so that you constantly practise and strengthen your skills, consolidate what you are learning, and get used to dealing with the kind of material you are likely to encounter in the workplace. Compare your work to the model answers at the back of the book, then read the text following each exercise. This will help you to confirm what you have learned or will indicate what you might need to review. In some cases the model answers show one way, not necessarily the only way, to handle a particular issue. Occasionally, an exercise includes an element that is explained in detail at a later point.

There is a lot of information in each chapter. You cannot absorb it at one reading any more than you can edit a book by working through the text only once. Be prepared to reread the text – even several times if you are working through the book, and at any time in your career when you need to check on specific points. Make sure you understand what each exercise has taught you, so that you really learn and, just as important, do not repeat mistakes. This will increase your confidence and make each following step easier.

Acknowledgements

This book has greatly benefited from feedback from the tutors of *Copy-editing by Distance Learning*: Enid Barker, Lionel Browne, Linda Cayford, Caroline Drake, Solveig Gardner-Servian, Elaine Leek, Kate Salway and Elizabeth Teague. I am grateful to them and to the following individuals who helped on the original course. My thanks go to John Whitley of the Publishing Training Centre and to all the staff there for their support throughout the years; to Gillian Clarke for invaluable help and advice; to Solveig Gardner-Servian for reviewing all the early drafts; to David Bann, Alison Baverstock, Michele Clarke and Andrew Steeds for important improvements to specific chapters; and to Richard Johnson, who provided technical information and help. I will always be grateful to the late Elizabeth Bland and to Nicola Harris for paving the way with the first distance-learning course on this subject, and to Judith Butcher for writing *Copy-editing*, which has helped me throughout my career.

My deepest thanks to Enid Barker for her careful, thoughtful and patient editing, and to Margaret Aherne for her meticulous proof-reading, excellent queries and uplifting enthusiasm, and to both of them for their positive contributions to the text; these two professionals exemplify the standard to which all editors should aspire. I am also extremely grateful to Christine Shuttleworth for her work on the index, and to Mike Hauser and the team at M Rules for the design and typesetting.

And more than thanks to Bob, my husband, whose faith in me has given me confidence, whose love has given me joy, and to whom I dedicate this work.

The Publishing Training Centre and I are grateful to the following authors, publishers and other organizations for giving their permission, on the most generous terms, to adapt and reproduce copyright material. Errors in the extracts have been introduced for the purpose of the exercise and are not attributable to the original source.

Anne Baring and Jules Cashford, *The Myth of the Goddess: Evolution of an Image*, Harmondsworth, Penguin Books, 1991; Joanne Edwards, N. Sarath Krishna, Rono Mukherjee and John M. S. Bartlett, 'The role of c-Jun and c-Fos expression in androgen-dependent prostate cancer', *Journal of Pathology*, October 2004, vol. 204, no. 2, pp. 153–4, Copyright Pathological Society of Great Britain and Ireland, reproduced with permission, permission is granted by John Wiley and Sons Ltd on behalf of the PathSoc; Roy Goode, *Commercial Law*, 3rd edn, London, LexisNexis Butterworth, 2004; Philip J. Lankester, 'Two maces from Henry VIII's arsenal?', *Royal Armouries Yearbook*, 2000; Dick Leonard, *The Economist Guide to the European Union*, rev. edn, London, Profile Books, 1994; Kate Lewis, 'Larks Recovering', *Birds*, vol. 19, no. 8, Winter 2003, pp. 26–32; Nigel Lewis, *Channel Firing: The Tragedy of Exercise Tiger*, London, Viking, 1989; Lesley Milroy, *Observing and Analysing Natural Language: A Critical Account of Sociolinguistic Method*, Oxford, Blackwell, 1987; 'New Screen Technologies on the Horizon', *Spindrift*, vol. 2, no. 8, Dec/Jan 2004–2005, pp. 5–6; Peter Ridley Waste Systems, *Using a Compost Bin*, Saxmundham, Suffolk, 2000; Scottish Wildlife Trust, 'Creature Feature: the Common Frog', *Wildwatch Scotland*, Spring 2004; Claire Tomalin, *Samuel Pepys: The Unequalled Self*, London, Viking, 2002; Michael van Straten, *The ORACle Diet*, London, Kyle Cathie, 2002; Linda B. White and Steven Foster, *The Herbal Drugstore*, London, Rodale Books, 2000; Andrew Wilson, *Beautiful Shadow: A Life of Patricia Highsmith*, London, Bloomsbury, 2003.

Exercises that are unattributed were created by me.

Every effort has been made to obtain permission to reproduce copyright material, but if there have been any inadvertent oversights, we will be happy to correct them in future editions.

The copy-editor's world

Put most succinctly, the role of the copy-editor is to make the author's message clear and accessible for the readers and to mark up the manuscript for the typesetter. That might sound simple, but it's a complex job, involving an understanding of not only language and grammar but also production processes, typography and design conventions, and the extent – and limits – of responsibility and authority. It requires an enquiring mind, attention to detail, organization and good communication skills.

The author's message may be fiction or non-fiction, an article, company report, newsletter, or book, and may include editorial and source notes, tables and diagrams or other forms of illustration. To make it clear, the copy-editor must first know who the intended readers are. They can be children, adolescents or adults; their reading level may be below, commensurate with or above their chronological age; and they may have no knowledge, some knowledge or a great deal of knowledge of the subject. Always keeping these readers in mind, the copy-editor endeavours to ensure

- accurate and consistent information in text, tables and illustrations;
- appropriate and consistent structure and level of text and other elements;
- appropriate and consistent literary and typographic style;
- appropriate and consistent spelling and punctuation;
- appropriate grammar.

It is the author's responsibility to provide accurate information, and the copy-editor's job to check it when necessary. That means we need to know when it is necessary, how to check information efficiently, and when and how to bring questions to an author's attention (see 'Writing queries for authors', p. xxiv). All copy-editors need to have these skills to be competent. How much subject knowledge a copy-editor needs varies. To work across a wide range of materials, copy-editors need a good general knowledge. To work in some areas of publishing – for example, educational, technical and legal – we might need special knowledge that can be acquired on the job. We can copy-edit documents above the level of our own subject knowledge if the text is peer-reviewed and the information is confirmed to be accurate, but in other cases we might need to bring extensive knowledge of the subject to the work.

Copy-editors talk about 'appropriate' because there is often more than one way to do something. It is not a matter of an absolute right way and a completely wrong way, but the way that we think works best to convey the message of the publication to its readers. We need to understand the principles of grammar and style so that we can bend the rules when necessary. We impose consistency in structure, style and spelling to help guide the reader through the work; inconsistency distracts and confuses. Consistency in information is essential for the clarity of the message; inconsistency confuses, and undermines the reader's confidence in the work as a whole. But we agree with Emerson that 'A foolish consistency is the hobgoblin of little minds' and use our understanding of a text to allow *appropriate* inconsistency.

Copy-editors work with the author to resolve ambiguities, fill gaps, determine whether seemingly irrelevant text can be made relevant or should be deleted, and whether repetition is essential, desirable or to be eliminated. We strive to enhance the clarity of the author's message and strengthen the author's voice, or style, not impose our own. It is essential that we raise our queries clearly, concisely and politely.

Part of our job is to follow the brief: on some manuscripts we might be asked to do a minimal edit – just imposing house style and ensuring basic consistency and clarity; on others we might be asked to do more, from minor revision to major rewriting.

We prepare the prelim pages – those that precede the text – for books, and for all publications ensure that acknowledgements are made and permissions cleared for the use of other people's copyright materials, and we eliminate material that would contravene any law, including libel.

We might be responsible for preparing briefs for artwork, picture research, photography and indexes, and, for books, we may have some responsibility for preparing the jacket or cover.

We understand, and keep up to date with, relevant production processes and typographic conventions so that we can work effectively with our colleagues in design and production to make sure that typographically and physically the publication is appropriate for the

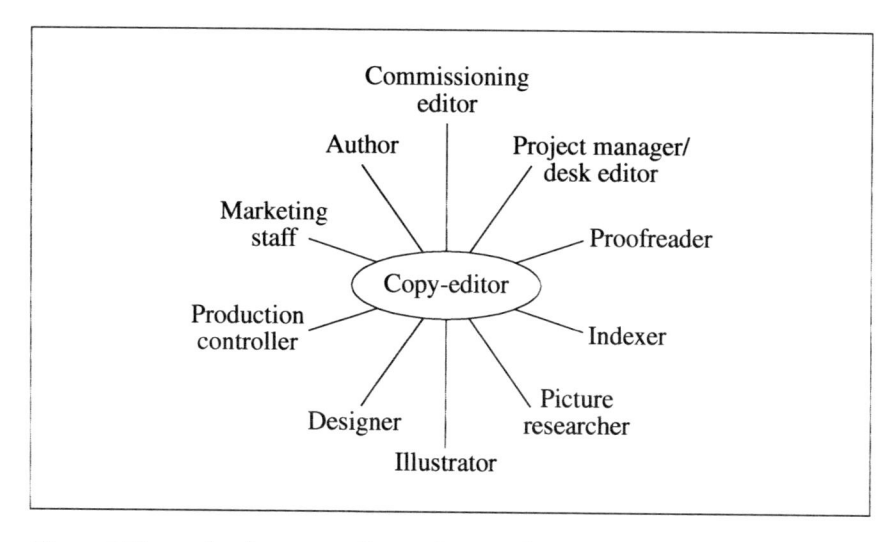

```
                    Commissioning
                        editor
            Author          │    Project manager/
                  \         │    / desk editor
     Marketing     \        │   /
        staff  ──           │      ── Proofreader
                     ┌─────────────┐
                     │ Copy-editor │
     Production  ──  └─────────────┘
     controller     /       │    \   ── Indexer
                   /        │     \
                            │      \  Picture
                Designer    │       researcher
                        Illustrator
```

Figure 1 Network of contacts. Depending on the type and structure of the organization in or for which a copy-editor works, he or she might work with some or all of the people shown.

intended readers – the target market – and that it is finished on schedule, within budget and to the required quality.

Our colleagues

Figure 1 shows the jobs done by people in a range of publishing environments. How many of these jobs are done by different people, whether they are in-house or freelance, and which ones we work with depends on the kind of publishing environment in which we work.

There must be an author, whether he or she is an in-house colleague or an external novelist or non-fiction specialist. In publishing companies a commissioning or acquisitions editor is responsible for contracting the author. Sometimes commissioning editors work with authors to develop the text. In some publishing houses this is the job of a development editor; in others, the authors might not get any editorial help until they submit the finished text.

When the text is submitted, it may be passed to a managing editor, project manager or desk editor or to a copy-editor. How many distinct types of editor there are, what they are called and what their specific functions are varies from house to house. In some cases, in book publishing, the copy-editor might perform all the functions.

Some copy-editors, particularly those working freelance, may be in contact only with the editor who briefs them. Others might also be in contact with the author, might brief the indexer and picture researcher, might brief an illustrator directly or through a designer, and might brief a photographer directly or through a picture researcher or designer. Similarly, some copy-editors, often called production editors, deal directly with the typesetter and printer, whereas others work with the company's in-house or freelance production manager. In publishing houses and in the publishing department of many other organizations our colleagues include people working in marketing, sales and publicity.

No matter how few or how many people are in our network of contacts, we must be good communicators. The copy-editor knows more about the manuscript than anyone else, even the author, and must be able to pass information to the appropriate people at the right time. Being a good communicator means being a good listener too, understanding and responding to what other people say.

Stages of production

Technically, 'production' refers to the manufacturing stages of producing a publication, from typesetting to printing and binding. Preparing the material before that point is called 'pre-press'. Figure 2 outlines the pre-press stages of book and journal publishing, and the production stages that are common to all publications.

The first pre-press stage is the proposal. In journals, articles may be commissioned or submitted and peer-reviewed before acceptance for publication. The journal as a whole, rather than the individual articles, is budgeted.

In book publishing, an outline of what is to be published and sample text, or a complete manuscript, accompanied by an estimate of the costs, is presented to a committee. The outline or manuscript can be submitted by an author or agent or might be commissioned by someone in-house. The commissioning or acquiring editor is responsible for presenting the estimate of costs and the reasons for publishing. The combined information is called the proposal. The committee to which the proposal is presented, which usually includes people from editorial, production, finance and marketing, decides whether the proposed material is appropriate for the company's list –

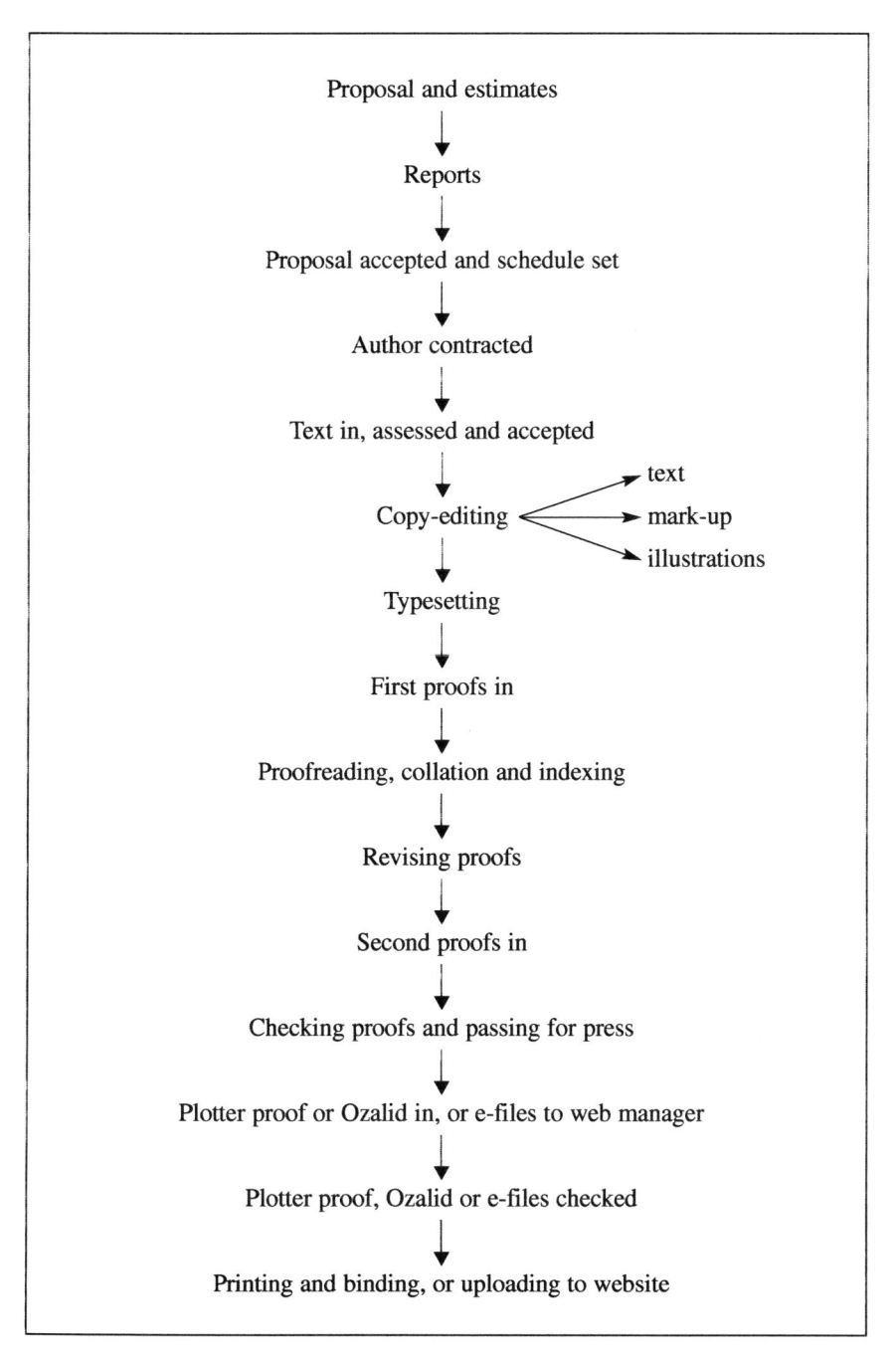

Proposal and estimates
↓
Reports
↓
Proposal accepted and schedule set
↓
Author contracted
↓
Text in, assessed and accepted
↓
Copy-editing → text, mark-up, illustrations
↓
Typesetting
↓
First proofs in
↓
Proofreading, collation and indexing
↓
Revising proofs
↓
Second proofs in
↓
Checking proofs and passing for press
↓
Plotter proof or Ozalid in, or e-files to web manager
↓
Plotter proof, Ozalid or e-files checked
↓
Printing and binding, or uploading to website

Figure 2 Pre-press and production stages

its product line – in terms of subject, focus, level and quality, and might get reports from external consultants to help it make that decision. It also determines whether the proposal is financially viable: the cost of producing a commercial publication must be at least equalled – and, preferably, exceeded – by the money that will be received from sales. In-house publications, where the text is written by people within the organization and the publications are not necessarily for sale, also have budgets but do not have to prove their financial viability.

In book publishing, when a proposal is approved, a date for publication is set and the author is contracted. In all kinds of publishing, authors' contracts stipulate the number of words, remuneration and various responsibilities of the publisher and the author, and the date when the final text and any other materials are to be submitted.

When a typescript arrives, the commissioning editor decides whether it is of acceptable quality and, if so, hands it over for editing. A book text might go to a development editor, who deals with substantive issues, or to a project manager, who prepares a brief, or directly to a copy-editor. In all kinds of publication the copy-editor does the work indicated on pp. xiii–xv, following the brief and making sure that the author accepts all changes, marking up the text and keying in any illustrations. Sometimes freelance copy-editors do not have contact with authors but it is essential for all copy-editors to know when and how to raise queries.

Copy-editors can work
- only on hard copy (i.e., a paper-based document), which the typesetter will rekey or use to make the changes to the author's electronic document (e-file);
- on hard copy first, making the changes and marking up the e-file on-screen and sending the e-file to the typesetter, with the hard copy as a back-up;
- on-screen only, sending only the e-file to the typesetter.

The editorial skills are the same in each case, but as publishers move to a completely electronic workflow it is important for copy-editors to have good basic computer skills.

After the typescript has been copy-edited, it is sent into the first stage of production: typesetting, which is done by either a typesetter or a designer using a typesetting program. Although some authors think that they have typeset their work, the e-files they produce are word-processed documents. Typesetting processes this data in different and more precise ways affecting the characters, attributes, styles, spacing and layout.

The output of the completed typesetting, as either a printout or PDF files, is a proof. In the past it was usual for the first proofs to be in the form of galleys – unpaginated text without illustrations – but this is rare now and the first proofs are in the form of pages, sometimes with illustrations in place and sometimes with spaces left for them.

First proofs are used to check that the typesetting reproduces the copy (text) accurately and is consistent with the mark-up, and to correct any errors missed or made by the copy-editor; they are not intended as an opportunity for authors to rewrite or copy-editors to re-edit. Most publishers employ proofreaders, who are usually freelance, to read proofs because they are more likely than authors and copy-editors, who are familiar with the text, to find mistakes. When more than one person reads the proofs, the different sets of corrections need to be collated onto the one set of the proofs that will be returned to the typesetter for correction. The proofreader might be asked to collate the proofs, or it might be the responsibility of the copy-editor or project manager, particularly if the author has asked for more changes than are budgeted, so that decisions must be made on which changes to allow. The copy-editor might also have to resolve queries that have been raised by the proofreader.

When a publication is to have an index, it is usually, but not always, compiled at the same time as the first proofs are being read. Indexing is a skill and therefore it is ideal for the work to be done by an appropriate, trained professional indexer (a point I will repeat later), although some authors, particularly academics, are often expected to do it. The reasoning is that authors know their works intimately and know what readers will want to look up in an index. There is more to indexing than this, and while some authors are good indexers, many others are not. When a professional indexer is used, the copy-editor briefs the indexer and edits the index when it is submitted, taking into account any proof corrections that the indexer would not have known about. The index is sent for typesetting when the first proofs are returned for correction.

The second proofs are checked to see that the changes asked for have been made correctly and without introducing new errors. The first proof of the index is often sent at the same time. Ideally, there are no changes, or only very minor ones, to the second proof and it is 'passed for press'. However, it is possible and, in some types of publishing, common to need a third stage of proofs. While proof stages beyond this are not unknown, they should be necessary only in exceptional circumstances.

The typesetter prepares PDF files of the final approved pages and sends them to the printer, usually on a CD or electronically, if the publication is to be printed, or to the web manager if the publication is to be published on the Internet.

Printers use the computer files to make printing plates when the document is to be printed by lithography, or to print from directly if the publication is to be printed digitally.

How the pages are laid out on the printing plates is shown by a plotter proof. The printer sends this proof to the client for a final check that all the pages are present, complete, the right way up and in the right order. This job is often done in the production department, but sometimes in-house copy-editors are asked to check these proofs too. Because the proofs are intended not to be read but only to be looked at for the factors mentioned, very little time is allowed. After this stage of proof is passed, printing and binding can begin.

The cover of a report, journal or direct-mail publication must, obviously, be ready by the time printing the text is to begin. In book publishing, however, the cover or jacket is an essential selling tool and therefore must be ready months in advance of publication. It is the project manager's – and sometimes the copy-editor's – responsibility to schedule work on the cover/jacket to ensure it is ready on time.

Welcome to the copy-editor's world. Have a look at the information on pp. xxi–xxviii as you cross the threshold.

Copy-editing tools

Copy-editing marks

Copy-editors in many countries use the British Standard *Marks for copy preparation and proof correction* (BS 5261-2: 2005) to show changes on hard copy. (We hope that when the revised international standard ISO 5776 is published, it will be used everywhere.) If you are familiar with the use of the standard marks in correcting proofs, you will find it easy to use them in editing; if you are not familiar with them, now is the time to become so. The current marks are presented on a laminated A5 fold-out card that can be purchased from the Publishing Training Centre at Book House or the British Standards Institution, and are reproduced in *Butcher's Copy-editing* and *New Hart's Rules* (see Resources). A sample of their use is shown in Figure 3, and the result is shown in Figure 4.

If you are a proofreader, you will see that the main difference in using the marks in copy-editing is that you do not make corresponding marks in the margins except when indicating that characters typed in italics or bold should be changed to roman (i.e., not italic or bold). You also have to show additions to the copy in the margin when there isn't enough space to do so clearly in the text. The model answers to the exercises will reinforce how the marks should be used.

Obviously, copy-editors who edit only on-screen do not use the marks. It is a good idea to know them nonetheless: you might occasionally work on hard copy, and you might collate proofs.

In book publishing, editorial work divides into two broad areas, the first of which is deciding what to publish. The 'glamour' of our supposedly glamorous industry lies in the image of the editors who 'discover' new authors, ask them to lunch, nurture them into writing bestsellers, mingle with celebrities at launch parties, and go to lunch some more. Complete manuscripts or synopses and sample chapters can be submitted to publishing houses by authors or agents, and certain editors have the job of deciding which ones should be published by their firms and negotiating the terms for the right to do so. The majority of new fiction is acquired in this way. Some editors have the job of originating ideas for books, and finding and commissioning authors to write the manuscripts. The majority of non-fiction is commissioned. From this description you might think that one kind of editor is called an <u>acquisitions</u> editor and the other is called a *commissioning* editor. However, the first kind of editor also commissions and the second kind sometimes selects a complete manuscript that been has submitted, and both types might buy the rights to publish a paperback edition of a hardback book published by another house or the right to publish a translation of a book from another language. The distinction between the job titles is mainly national rather than functional.

Like many perceptions of the world of glamour, this one is composed of solid fact and wishful thinking.

Figure 3 How to mark editorial changes

> In book publishing, editorial work divides into two broad areas, the first of which is deciding what to publish. The 'glamour' of our supposedly glamorous industry lies in the image of the editors who 'discover' new authors, ask them to lunch, nurture them into writing bestsellers, mingle with celebrities at launch parties, and go to lunch some more. Like many perceptions of the world of glamour, this one is composed of solid fact and wishful thinking.
>
> Complete manuscripts or synopses and sample chapters can be submitted to publishing houses by authors or agents, and certain editors have the job of deciding which ones should be published by their firms and negotiating the terms for the right to do so. The majority of new fiction is acquired in this way. Some editors have the job of originating ideas for books, and finding and commissioning authors to write the manuscripts. The majority of non-fiction is commissioned. From this description you might think that one kind of editor is called an *acquisitions* editor and the other is called a *commissioning* editor. However, the first kind of editor also commissions and the second kind sometimes selects a complete manuscript that has been submitted, and both types might buy the rights to publish a paperback edition of a hardback book published by another house or the rights to publish a translation of a book from another language. The distinction between the job titles is mainly national rather than functional.

Figure 4 Result of editorial mark-up

House and book style

To help maintain consistency throughout their publications, organizations establish a list of preferred styles for such issues as spelling and capitalization, lists, numbers, dates, abbreviations, quotations, displayed matter, and notes and references. This is called 'house style' because we refer to companies whose business is publishing as publishing houses, and the term is now used generally by other organizations – commercial and non-commercial – that publish on paper or online.

For an organization that produces a limited range of publications, house style is a sufficient guide for maintaining consistency. But any book might include words, names or other elements that are not used in another publication. Therefore, copy-editors working on books create an additional style guide as they work, noting specific style issues, such as how particular words and names are spelled and punctuated, whether words or phrases are in italic, bold or roman type, and what abbreviations are used. A simple way to make a book style sheet is to divide a piece of paper into boxes, labelling each one with a letter of the alphabet, or to make a similar electronic file. Each time a style point occurs, we put it in the appropriate box, where we can find it quickly, to help us maintain its consistent use (see Figure 5).

Working on fiction, we will include, or make a separate style sheet for, the description of characters and places, to help us ensure that we keep these elements consistent throughout the work (see Figure 6).

Writing queries for authors

Raising queries with authors is one of the most important skills to master. Here are points to remember, followed by some examples of queries and comments.

Mark the location

When you find material in a text that you want to query or need an author's agreement to change, write AQ in pencil in the margin and circle it, so that you can find it again easily when you receive the author's reply, and erase it when it has been dealt with. If you are working on-screen, you can highlight the text or use the software's comment facility, which marks the position.

Type your queries and comments to authors separately from the text. Queries are shown on the model answer sheets, rather than separately, only to save paper; and with continuous line numbers, rather than line numbers per page, only for ease of reference in this book.

Help authors locate the place in the text quickly

Referring to page, paragraph and line numbers is fundamental. However, since authors' copies of the text might not be the same as

A AD
    anglophone
    Anglophile
	H

B BCE	I *-ise*
C *Chernobyl*	J
	K
D	L *Lavoisier, Antoine* *Leiden*
E *electric-blue*	M *medieval*
F	N *Neo-Darwinism*
G *grand siècle*	O

Figure 5 An example of a project style sheet

yours line for line, and very few publishers return the edited hard copy to authors with the queries, it is best to also quote the word or part of the phrase to which the query or comment relates. This is helpful even when working on-screen.

A Adam Brown: blond, green eyes, 27	H
B Bootsy: Jack's black lab Birdie Davis: blonde, blue eyes, 22	I
C	J Jack Deeve: brunette, blue eyes, scar on right cheek, 27
D	K
E	L
F Franny Deveux: tall, long red hair, green eyes, freckles, 24	M
G	N

Figure 6 An example of a character style sheet

Help authors work with you

Whatever you think of the quality of the text, you are working *with* authors. Check that the way you phrase your queries will not offend them or make them feel defensive.

- Make your queries polite, focused, as concise as clarity allows, and objective. Never write 'Surely, you meant...' or even 'You wrote ...'. Instead, refer to the issue in the text – 'The text states ... and para X (or source A) states ...' – and ask whether the text should be altered. There may be times when your author is right and the other sources are wrong.
- Check statements when you think the information is not clear or might be inaccurate. Use up-to-date and authoritative sources, whether printed or online, and cite them in queries to the author.
- Ask authors questions you cannot answer yourself, e.g. because the text is ambiguous or you are not a specialist in the subject.
- Ask authors to confirm suggested changes, particularly small ones that might alter the meaning or nuance.
- Do not ask authors about issues you can decide for yourself or can refer to your line manager (if you work in-house) or to the publisher (if you are freelance) for guidance, e.g. typographic style; basic spelling, punctuation, capitalization and grammar; house style.

Examples: Non-fiction

Chapter 4

p. 89, para 3, l. 10	'We have come ... inquisition': should this be 'inquisitio', as in Chapter 1, p. 14?
p. 91, para 1, l. 7	'records of temperatures': suggest add Celsius equivalents in square brackets, as many readers are not familiar with Fahrenheit.
p. 93, para 4, l. 9	'By 1802 the Speenhamland system': could the text include a brief statement of when and where this system originated?
p. 93, para 4, l. 13	'at the Easter vestry of 1803': text above refers to 1802; is there evidence of the system in this area in 1802 or should that date be changed to 1803?

Examples: Fiction

Chapter 4

p. 210, para 1, l. 2	'She barged through the door and': seems rather a long and fluent speech for this character, who has just run a long distance and up a flight of stairs; should there, perhaps, be some pauses or gasps for air?
p. 212, para 2, l. 8	'Max left through the side door': the building has been described as mid-terrace, so there won't be a side door; could he 'sneak out' through the front or back?
p. 212, para 2, l. 9	'got into his car': Max parked around the corner, so to avoid impression of immediacy, suggest include reference to making his way back to his car.
p. 214, para 1, l. 5	'Climbing to the top of the wall': Marissa would have a difficult time in the outfit described on p. 212; suggest equally alluring trousers are substituted for pencil skirt there.
p. 214, para 1, l. 16	'noted dogs were no longer there': no dogs mentioned before this; should dogs be mentioned at this site in chapter 3, p. 189, or deleted here?

1 Marking up

Copy-editors provide designers and typesetters with the information they need in order to typeset the edited material to the agreed design. This is called marking up.

Designers and typesetters

Designers give publications their visual appearance. They can do this after the copy-editing is done but, to save time in the schedule and sometimes for sales purposes, it is usual to do it before the complete work is ready for typesetting. Commissioning editors can supply all the information designers need to create the initial page design:

* the work's specifications – for example, the size of the page, the number of pages (extent), number of words, and number and types of illustrations
* the subject
* how many levels of heading and what structural elements, such as lists or tables, the work will have
* the age and knowledge level of the intended reader
* in what countries the publication is to be distributed

Designers use this information first to create the framework (the grid) for the text and illustrations on the page (see Figure 1.1). The grid can be a single column or multiple columns, and it can be a mirror image or it can be the same on both the left (verso) and right (recto) pages (see Figure 1.2). Then designers choose the typefaces, sizes and styles (the fonts), and decide the length of the line (the measure) for different elements in the text; these details are known collectively as the type specification (the spec). Together, the type spec and the grid form the complete typographic design.

Because each issue of a journal, magazine or newsletter usually contains the same range of headings and structural elements, a designer creates a single typographic design for that publication based on information supplied by the publisher. For the same reason, some book publishers have a small number of typographic designs for their

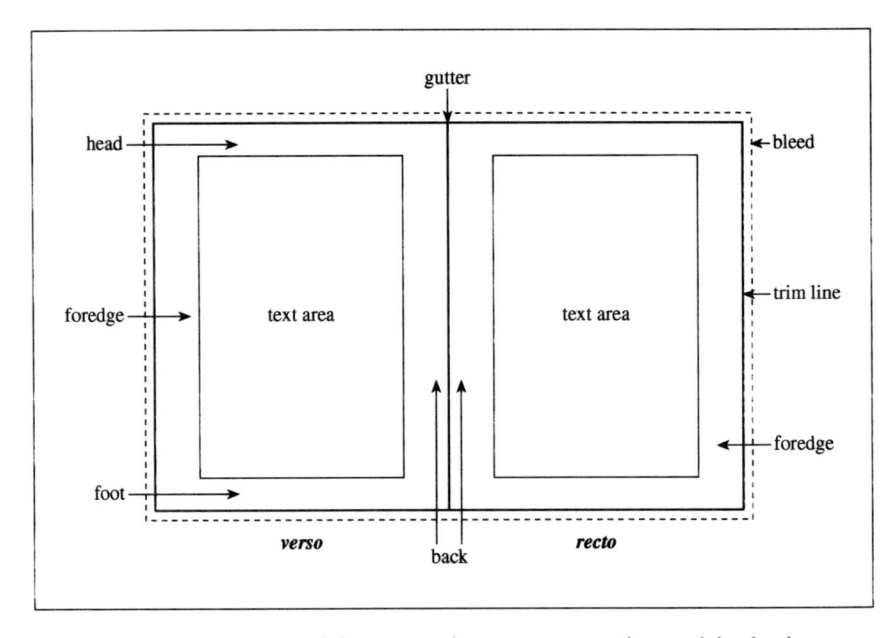

Figure 1.1 The elements of the page. The text area can be used for both text and illustrations. When illustrations extend beyond the text area to the edges of the page, we say that they 'bleed'. The design for a book that bleeds allows an extra 3 mm of paper beyond the trim marks. This ensures that no unprinted border will appear between the illustrations and the page's edges. Running heads go in the head margins or, occasionally, in the foot margins, when they might be called running feet. Page numbers can be in the foot or head margins.

range of publications; this is often referred to as format publishing. In other cases, commissioning editors provide the information needed to design each book or series individually.

Designers do not need to read the copy in order to create the typographic design, and typesetters do not need to read the copy, or even understand the language in which it is written, in order to set it. Both depend on copy-editors to tell them what they need to know by marking every structure in the copy with a very simple code for each one. This marking up enables the typesetter to set all parts of the document consistently in the fonts, sizes and styles specified by the designer, regardless of how the author has presented them. As the copy-editor, you do not need to know anything about the page design or typography in order to mark up text, although you will be expected to know certain typographic conventions in order to do your job.

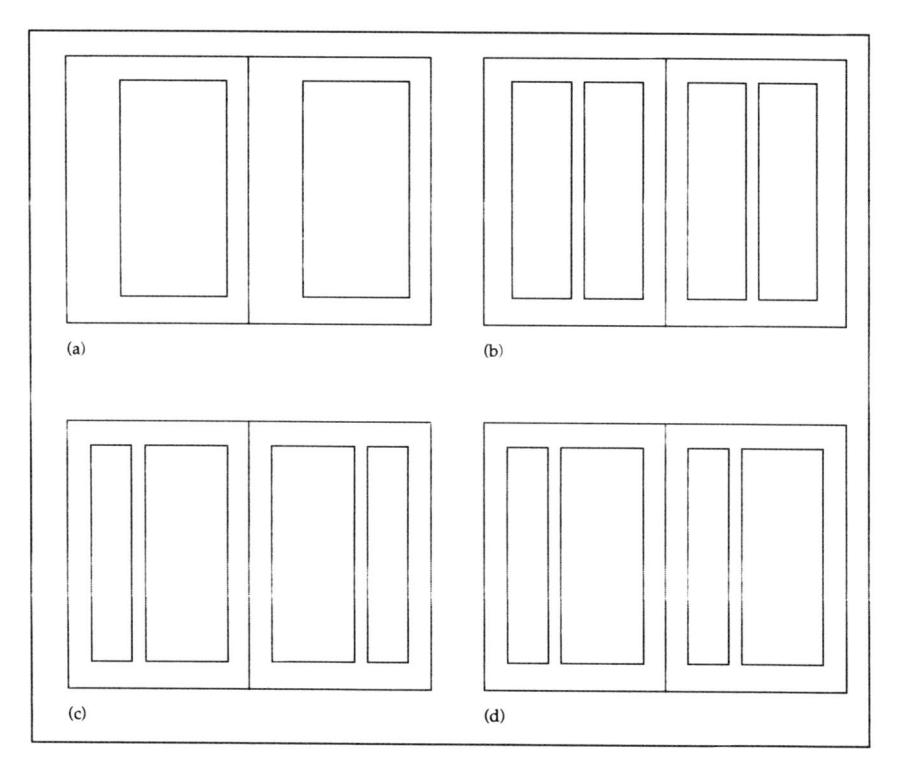

Figure 1.2 Some common grids. (a) One-column, one-page; compare it with the one-column mirror-image design in Figure 1.1. (b) Two-column, mirror image; the two columns are the same dimensions. One + one column (c) mirror-image and (d) one-page; the two columns are different widths and the narrower one is used for captions and special features rather than main text.

How to mark up

Hard copy

On hard copy you mark up structures in the left margin in red ink. This distinguishes the instructions from the changes to the text, which are made in blue ink on the line or in the space above the line. The codes are capital letters. When you are marking up a single line of type, simply put the circled code in the margin next to it:

(A) This is a Heading

When you are marking up more than one line, draw a vertical line in red in the margin next to the lines affected, with a horizontal bar at the top and bottom, and put the circled code to the left of it:

> (Q) These lines are marked up to show that they are to be treated as a 'long' quotation. Why and when we do this will be explained later in this chapter. At this point we are simply showing how to mark up multiple lines.

When the multiple lines span pages of the hard copy, leave the bottom bar off until the last line of the copy. For example, if the first two lines were on one page and the last two on the next, the mark-up would look like this on the first page:

> (Q) These lines are marked up to show that they are to be treated as a 'long' quotation. Why and when we do this will be explained later in

and like this on the next:

> (Q) this chapter. At this point we are simply showing how to mark up multiple lines.

Notice that you repeat the code, so that it is always clear what is intended, no matter how many pages the coded material occupies. Just as your job is to make the author's message clear to the ultimate readers, you must make *your* messages clear to *your* readers: designers and typesetters.

Electronic copy

You mark up electronic files (e-files) in the text. Publishers might have their own sets of codes or they might use those specified by a typesetting program. In word-processed files for use in the typesetting program QuarkXpress, for example, the codes are typed in a specific way:

> @A:This is a heading

> @Q:These lines are marked up to show that they are to be treated as a 'long' quotation. Why and when we do this will be explained later in this chapter. At this point we are simply showing how to mark up multiple lines.

In ASCII files the codes are in square or angle brackets at the beginning and end of the affected text:

> [a1]This is a heading[a2]

<q1>These lines are marked up to show that they are to be treated as a 'long' quotation. Why and when we do this will be explained later in this chapter. At this point we are simply showing how to mark up multiple lines.<q2>

Another mark-up system puts the codes in angle brackets, too, but uses a solidus at the beginning of the end code:

<a1>This is a heading</a2>

In all these coding systems there is no space between the code and the text. Publishers can also use or define the 'styles' provided in a particular word-processing software. These don't appear as codes but are revealed in a separate list, sometimes called a document map.

What to mark up

You mark up everything other than main text, which means headings and structural elements, of which long quotations, lists and notes are the most common. You can give a general instruction on how to set new paragraphs. However they have been typed by the author, the usual style in books and journals is for the first line after a heading to be ranged left (also called 'full out') and subsequent paragraphs to be indented, with no line spaces between them. The instruction to the typesetter is simply 'First paras under headings full out, subsequent paras closed up and indented'. Then you need to mark new paragraphs only when it is not clear where they begin, for example when the last line of one ends at the margin and the first line of the next is not separated by a line space or is on the next folio (typescript, rather than typeset, page), or after a table or figure.

In other types of publications, such as newsletters, internal reports, leaflets and brochures, all paragraphs might be ranged left with a line space between them. This style is not used in books and journals because it wastes space and, therefore, paper, which is the most expensive part of a printed publication.

The hierarchy of headings

Headings are an outline of the text and show how the parts relate to one another. An article in a periodical or a chapter in a book might have a single heading or it might have a main heading and one or more levels of subheading. Look at 'The copy-editor's world': it has a chapter heading and one level of subheading. The chapter you are reading now has a chapter heading and three levels of subheading. Correct coding ensures that a specific level of heading will be in the same typeface, size and style (for example, bold, italic and capitals), and will have the same space between it and the text, whether on a separate line or run into the text, throughout the publication.

When you begin work on a typescript, look through it first to familiarize yourself with the style of writing and content, and to assess the work that you will need to do. Look at how many levels of heading there seem to be. Authors might be asked not to style their headings visually, or they might try but not get the hierarchy right or consistent, so do not assume that the typescript is correct. If there is only a chapter heading and one level of subheading, you can mark them up as you edit. When there is more than one level of subheading, it is best to mark up all the headings after you have edited the chapter, when you will really understand the structure and how the sections within it relate.

Books are sometimes divided into parts. The part headings can be a number or a title or both, and the word used might be 'Part', 'Book' or 'Volume'. Regardless of the word used, we code these headings (PT). Whether or not they are divided into parts, books are usually divided into chapters or units. Like parts, these headings can be a number or a title or both, and in multi-author books they might include the authors' names. We code all this information (CH), whether or not the word 'chapter' is used. The titles of articles can also be coded (CH), although (AT) can be used instead.

Stories and novels don't usually have subheadings, but non-fiction articles and books often do. The first level of subheading divides the chapter into a smaller, more precise part. We code it (A) and, even though it is a subheading, we call it an A heading, or A head. When you look at the next subheading, you have to decide what level it is.

- If it is a subdivision of the text in A, you mark it (B).
- If it is another division of the chapter as a whole, like the first A head, you mark it (A) too.

Similarly, when a heading subdivides the text under a B head, you mark it (C), and when a heading subdivides the text under a C head, you mark it (D). Usually, only publications for academic or professional readers, which may require the information to be divided into very precise parts, use more than four levels of heading in main text.

It is one of your responsibilities to make sure that the number of levels is appropriate for the intended reader. Ideally, this will be part of the brief from your line manager or client, but if it isn't mentioned, ask.

A chapter or an article might have only A heads. There must be an A head before there can be a B head, but there does not have to be a B under every A, and there can be more than one B head under a single A head. Similarly, there must be a B head before there can be a C, but there does not have to be a C under every B, and there can be multiple Cs under a single B. The number of headings at each level does not have to be consistent, so one A head can have no Bs, another can have three, and yet another can have four if the content requires. You might want to read this paragraph again before you continue, to be sure you understand it rather than feeling you have just followed Alice down the rabbit hole.

The headings reflect the structure of a work. Although the number of subheadings can vary, you must ensure that the variation is essential, not a sign that the material is inconsistent in the level of detail. Articles in a journal can differ from each other in structure because each one is a complete work by a different author or authors. The same can be true of the chapters in a multi-author book (one in which the chapters are attributed to different authors). But in a book by one author or by joint authors (one in which the chapters are not attributed individually), variation in the number of heading levels – for example, if some chapters had only A heads and some had A, B and C heads – would indicate an inconsistent structure.

NUMBERING

In some academic books the headings are numbered. Thus the first A head in Chapter 1 would be prefixed 1.1, the second A head would be prefixed 1.2, and so on. The B heads would add another decimal place: 1.1.1, 1.1.2, 1.2.1; and the C heads would add still another: 1.1.1.1, 1.2.1.1, etc. Other academic books do not number the headings but do number each paragraph. These styles enable authors to cross-reference to sections or paragraphs as they write rather than having to wait until the text is set to insert the cross-references on the page proofs, which is very time-consuming – for the typesetter as well as the author – and, therefore, expensive. In both cases you still have to mark the headings A, B, C, etc., because they will be set differently.

You must also check that the numbering sequence is consistent (always the right number of decimal places for each level) and sequential (no numbers duplicated or skipped).

Exercise 1.1, marking up headings

Brief
The following is a list of headings from an article on food. Mark up the headings. In each case, ask yourself 'Is this heading on the same level as one of those preceding it or a subdivision of the one immediately preceding it?'

Food

Dairy
Milk
Full-fat milk
Semi-skimmed milk
Skimmed milk
Cream
Single cream
Double cream
Whipping cream
Butter
Fresh butter
Salted butter
Clarified butter

Cheese
Hard cheese
Pecorino
Parmesan
Firm cheese
Cheddar
Emmenthal
Leicester
Soft cheese
Brie
Camembert
Gorgonzola
Mozzarella
Apples
Dessert apples
Cox

Delicious
McIntosh
Cooking apples
Bramley
Rome Beauty
Royal Russet
Grapes
Green grapes
Red grapes
Black grapes
Berries
Strawberries
Blackberries
Raspberries

EXERCISE FOLLOW-UP

When you compare the headings in the exercise, you see that each A head is a food group (you needed to add 'Fruit'), and each B head is a type of food in that group. The adjectives in the C heads indicate that these are particular kinds of the food in the B heads, and the D heads are all names of varieties. So far, the headings are consistent.

Notice that not all the C heads are followed by D heads. It is your job to check whether the framework is balanced or needs amendment. The C heads under 'Milk', 'Cream' and 'Butter' cannot be broken down into varieties like those under 'Cheese', but the C heads under 'Grapes' and 'Berries' could be. You might notice this while editing the text, in which case you would either add the appropriate headings or, if the information was not in the text, ask the author to supply it. If you had missed this while editing, checking the mark-up would alert you to the imbalance and you would query the author then. If you mark up on-screen, the 'document map' or 'outline' feature in the 'View' menu of some word-processing programs shows you the headings in outline form for easy checking. It cannot be said too often or too strongly: it is essential that all queries are resolved before a text is sent for setting, to reduce the time and cost of making changes at proof stage.

Marking for capitals

The type spec for each level of heading includes instructions for capitalization, which can be:
- all caps
- initial cap for the first word and all subsequent words other than articles, conjunctions and prepositions (i.c.)
- initial cap for the first word and all the remaining characters in small caps (i.c.s.c.)
- initial cap for the first word and proper nouns only (i.c.l.c.).

Journals usually follow the last style. They and some, mainly academic, book publishers brief their authors on how to type headings. Many publishers don't, and, even when they do, authors do not always follow this aspect of a brief; they are focused on the content rather than the typographic style. When you know what the spec is for each level of heading, you can check the typing and correct the capitalization if necessary. When you don't know what the spec is, you should mark the first word and proper nouns for capitals. Although you use the proof-correction symbol to do this, you mark in the text only, not in the margin (see Figure 1.3).

(a) THE FIRST EXPLORATION OF JUPITER'S SURFACE

(b) The First Exploration Of Jupiter's Surface

(c) THE FIRST EXPLORATION OF JUPITER'S SURFACE

(d) The First Exploration Of Jupiter's Surface

(e) The First Exploration Of Jupiter's Surface

Figure 1.3 The simplest way of marking for capitalization is shown in (a) and (b). An alternative method, shown in (c) and (d), marks caps to be lower case, and might be more appropriate when you are sure the letters are to be set that way. The stroke through the top of the caps is an adaptation of the BS negating mark commonly used by copy-editors. Another alternative, shown in (e), is to mark for essential caps, as in (a) and (b), and essential, not optional, lower case.

Exercise 1.2, marking up headings and checking the structure

Brief
Here is an excerpt from a book on herbal remedies. Read the text first, correcting any misspellings and punctuation errors (writing your corrections within the text, not in the margins), then mark up the headings. Latin plant names have an initial cap for the first word only and are in italics. Check the mark-up to make sure the hierarchy is consistent. Add any headings that are missing and, separately, list queries to the author about inconsistency or omissions in the text.

Part IV Herb Profiles

A Look At The Most Common Herbs

In this chapter you'll read more about the herbs most frequently used for treating a variety of conditions. The herbs are listed alphabetically by their common names, with their Latin names in brackets. You'll find basic information on each herb: its other common names, where it is harvested, the plant parts used, available forms of the herb, the conditions it is used for, and any cautions or reasons you should take it. Some herbs are now endangered in their wild form and should be purchased from reputable sources that specify that the herb was harvested from cultivated plants. Therefore, when applicable, there is 'conscientious consumer' information to guide your buying decisions.

There are mo dosages in this chapter, which is mainly for readers who want to compare information on different herbs. If you see that a herb is use to treat a particular condition, you should read that chapter before purchasing or taking the herb. Sometimes those chapters offer additional cautions for specific conditions, such as possible bad interactions of herbs and drugs. It's also important not to self-treat some disorders but to be advised by a professional herbalist or doctor

AGNUS CASTUS (*VITEX AGNUS-CASTUS*)

Also called

Chaste tree, monk's pepper, vitex.

Source

Native to south-western Europe, naturalized in the south-eastern United States, grown commercially in Europe.

Parts used

Fruit (berries).

Forms available

Capsules, tablets, teas, tinctures, combination products.

Uses

Premenstrual tension, heavy or frequent menstruation, spotting, impaired menstrual flow, swelling and tenderness of breasts infertility, menopausal symptoms, and other women's conditions requiring hormone regulation.

Caution

Do not use agnus castus if taking hormone replacement therapy or birth control pills. Generally not recommended for use when pregnant; however, in cases of progesterone deficiency, it has been administered under medical supervision to prevent miscarriages in the first trimester. Some minor skin irritations have been reported.

ALOE (*ALOE VERA*)

Also called

Cape aloe.

Source
Native to Africa; grown commercially in southern Texas and Mexico.

Parts used
Leaf gel, juice.

Forms available
Various concentrations of the gel, powdered dry juice. The gel is incorporated into ointments, creams, lotions and the like. Some of aloe's active compounds deteriorate in storage, so use the fresh gel for maximum potency.

Uses
Externally, aloe gel has long been valued for healing minor burns, wounds and abrasions, and reliving associated pain and inflammation. Aloe juice may hold promise for treating diabetes and reducing the level of triglyserides and blood sugar.

Caution
Don't use this herb if you have intestinal obstruction, abdominal pain of unknown origin, diarrhoea, inflamed intestines (colitis, Crohn's disease, irritable bowel syndrome). Aloe juice may produce a laxative effect if taken in a higher does than recommended. Don't use for more than 10 days.

ARNICA
Also called
Leopard's bane, mountain tobacco.

Source
Native to Europe; most species occur in the mountains of North
America.

Parts used
Whole plant, flower.

Forms available
Creams, ointments, gels, tinctures, homopathic preparations.

Uses
Externally as an anti-inflammatory, pain reliever and antiseptic for sprains, bruises, acne, injuries and swelling caused by bone fractures, insect bites, rheumatic pains and chilblains. seldom used internally because its primary active constituents are considered toxic.

Avoid if you're pregnant. Use only on a short-term basis for acute conditions. May cause allergic dermatitis in sensitive persons or with prolonged use. Do not apply to open wounds or broken skin, except under the advice of a health-care practitioner. Taken internally, low does can cause gastroenteritis; high doses may damage the heart and in rare cases can induce cardiac arrest.

Conscientious consumer information
Protected in the wild in parts of Europe. May be at risk in the wild elsewhere; needs further study.

ASTRAGALUS (*ASTRAGALUS MEMBRANACEUS*)

Also called

Huang qi.

Forms available

Capsules, extracts, tablets, tinctures and in many traditional Chinese formulas.

Uses

Colds, flu, minor infections. Many studies confirm immune boosting, antiviral, antibacterial and tonic properties. Shows promise in restoring T-cell function in cancer patients and preventing growth of cancerous cells.

Caution

None known

Adapted from Linda B. White and Steven Foster, *The Herbal Drugstore*, London, Rodale Books, 2000, pp. 546–550.

EXERCISE FOLLOW-UP

There were only a few spelling errors in the text, and most of them would not have been caught by a computer spell-checker, a useful tool as long as you are aware of its limitations. The part title declares itself, and if you weren't sure what the chapter title was, the first line of the text tells you. The subheadings follow a very simple pattern, so in checking your mark-up you should have spotted the missing ones.

Notice that under Astragalus the information for 'Caution' is 'None known'. Sometimes authors omit a heading because, as here, there is no information or none that they think is useful to the readers. However, readers need to know why a heading is missing or they will assume it is a mistake; they will not only be annoyed but also feel that the entire work loses some credibility. It is your responsibility to make sure this doesn't happen.

Other structures

A document can have many structures that are distinct from the main text. Some have a specific function at a particular point, such as formulas, lists and quotations; others are relevant to the entire text, such as exercises, project work or technical explanations or tips. You mark up each of these structures, including the headings, to be displayed: typeset in a way that distinguishes it from the main text. Thus formulas would always be displayed in one way and lists in another. The style of the heading for exercises or project work would be distinct from the style of the hierarchical headings, and general information relevant to the entire text might be set within a box or on a tinted background. This makes it easier for the reader to identify the structures and to see their relationship to the main text.

You mark the structures using capital letters that cannot be confused with those used for the main text headings or proof-correction symbols: therefore no X, which, when circled, means 'wrong font'. Although you can choose any other letters you like for these codes, use those that seem to relate to the purpose, when possible, because it makes them easier to remember. So although F would be too close to the headings codes, you could use FO for formulas. Technical tips, handy hints and other items that relate to the entire text can be marked H (headings never get this far in the alphabet!) or T or any other letter you choose. Make a list of these codes as you work so that you can maintain consistency, and pass on the list to the designer and typesetter with the document. You can put general instructions on this code sheet too. (see Figure 1.4).

DISPLAYED QUOTATIONS: PROSE

It is common practice to display prose quotations that are more than sixty words, although some house styles make the distinction at forty words. The number of words is not meant to be absolute but to indicate that the displayed quotation (also called an extract or a block quotation) will occupy a minimum of four or six lines when typeset.

We might not follow this general style convention
* when a quotation is an integral part of the narrative and to display it would be to disrupt the author's flow;
* when a quotation is shorter than, but of the same kind as, those of forty or sixty words, and to display it would make it easier for readers to understand its purpose or to compare the quotations.

Codes for *A Big Book*, An Author

Global style

1st paras under heading full out; subsequent paras indented

PT	=	part title
CH	=	chapter title
A	=	subhead level 1
B	=	subhead level 2
C	=	subhead level 3
EP	=	prose epigraph
EPV	=	verse epigraph
FN	=	footnotes
H	=	helpful hints feature
HH	=	helpful hints heading
L	=	list
LB	=	bullet list
LN	=	numbered list
N	=	endnotes
Q	=	displayed quotation
T	=	table
TH	=	table heading
TA	=	table column headings
TB	=	table subhead level 1
V	=	verse, line for line and space for space

Figure 1.4 A sample code sheet

Displayed quotations might be set in a smaller size, or with less leading (space between the lines), which is why they are sometimes said to be 'set down'; or they might be set in a different font or style, justified or unjustified. In addition, the entire quotation might be indented or centred, but the first line is not indented on its own unless it is like that in the original. Because the typographic treatment serves the same purpose as quotation marks, the latter are not needed.

Ⓠ is the code most commonly used for displayed quotations in the text. On hard copy the line showing the extent of material affected is a simple vertical when the quotation begins at the beginning of a line and ends at the end of a line, as shown on p. 4. However, sometimes the author has typed the quotation embedded in the main text. Then you draw the line from the beginning of the quote, down its length and to the point where it ends, but not completely encircling it (see Figure 1.5). In an e-file you will put the code at the beginning and end of the material affected, as shown on p. 5.

> Many people are familiar with Samuel Johnson's remark 'When a man is tired of London, he is tired of life' but a smaller number know the rest of it is 'for there is in London all that life can afford'. I particularly like the aspects that Boswell mentions in his diary. On 5 December 1762 he wrote 'The liberty and the whim that reigns there occasions a variety of perfect and curious characters. Then the immense crowd and hurry and bustle of business and diversion, the great number of public places of entertainment, the noble churches and the superb buildings of different kinds, agitate, amuse and elevate the mind. ... Here a young many of curiosity and observation may have a sufficient fund of present entertainment, and may lay up ideas to employ his mind in age.' I was in my early twenties when I read this and, having arrived in London only weeks before, I felt a kindred spirit, though more than 200 years separated us.

Figure 1.5 How to mark up for display a long quotation embedded in the text. Note that the line, which would be red, does not encircle the quotation and that the quotation marks are deleted.

DISPLAYED QUOTATIONS: POETRY

Lines of verse can be embedded in the text, with a spaced vertical line or solidus to mark line-ends, if context or space requires. However, it is more usual to display even a single complete line of verse. Although quoted poetry may be centred on the page or set with a uniform indent, the indentations and other spaces within or between lines must be the same as in the original. When the first line quoted omits the beginning of the line, you mark the first word shown to be indented so that it is in approximately the same position as in the original.

When the lines do not follow a recognizable pattern and you cannot be certain that the author's text shows the original layout of the poem – sometimes authors like to play with the 'centre' button on the computer – check it yourself *if you can do so quickly* or ask the author to confirm or send a photocopy or scan of the original. Then mark up the quotation, coding it Ⓥ or Ⓟ on hard copy, and perhaps <v1> or <p1> at the beginning and </v2> or </p2> at the end in an e-file. Next to the code on the list for the designer or typesetter, write 'set line for line and space for space'.

EPIGRAPHS

Quotations at the beginning of a book, part, article or chapter and intended to indicate the theme of the text are called epigraphs. They can be prose or poetry, and are set in a style distinct from quotations within the text. The source note, or attribution, is on a separate line and ranged right – usually aligned with the right margin of the quotation, not the main text, or on the longest line in the case of poetry. It includes the author and title of the work; the act, scene and line number if it is from a play; or only the book, chapter and verse if it is from the Bible. If the source note has been typed ranged left, mark it up on the hard copy to range right:

  Stella Gibbons, *Cold Comfort Farm* ┈┈┈┈┈┈┈┈┈┈┈┈┈┈┈┈→

or format it for ranged right in the e-file.

This way of acknowledging a source is sometimes also used for displayed quotations in the main text, although, because the full bibliographic details would be required, it is more common to refer to the source in the text itself or in a reference note.

The mark-up for an epigraph includes the source note and could be (EP) for a prose epigraph and (EPV) for a verse epigraph. Mark up the title of a poem, if included, with the letter of your choice, prefaced by EP, being sure to put it on your style sheet for the typesetter and to use it consistently.

FOOTNOTES

Authors are often asked not to include automatic footnotes in their e-files, but it still happens. Use (FN) to mark up the notes even if you or the typesetter will move them to another location – which we will discuss in Chapter 7.

Exercise 1.3, marking up headings and other elements

Brief
The following extracts are from a book intended for readers with some knowledge of the subject. They will, for example, be familiar with the names of any deities mentioned. Read the text first, correcting spelling, punctuation and grammatical errors, and listing any queries for the authors. Then mark up the copy and make a list of the codes.

House style
- small caps for AD and BC

---

10 Cybele, Great Goddess of Anatolia and Rome

For O, I know, in the dust where we have buried

The silenced races and all their abominations,

We have buried so much of the delicate magic of life.

D. H. Lawrence, 'Cypresses'   5

The Bronze Age myth of the mother goddess and her son–lover did

not die out in spite of the formal worship of the great father god. It persisted in various forms in Egypt, Anatolia, Syria, Palestine Greece and Rome until it found a new expression in the Mystery cults of the Egypt, Greece and Rome. As spirit and nature were driven further and further apart in the religions of the Iron Age, this myth continued to hold them together in their original relationship. It is no coincidence that Anatolia and Syria, as well as Alexandria and Rome were the areas most receptive to both the Orthodox and Gnostic traditions of Christianity.

Cybele is far familiar to us than other goddesses, and the liturgies and hymns addressed to her in the pre-Roman era are very sparse in comparison with the many poems and songs arising from the worship of Inanna and Isis. Nevertheless, it is through her, as well as through the Sumerian or Egyptian goddesses, that the myth of the goddess can be traced from the Neolithic era through the Iron Age and far into the Christian era, for, amazingly, it hardly changes throughout this immense period of time.

The lion is inseparable from the image of the goddess. In Anatolia this relationship can be traced as far back as Çatal Hüyük, where the mother goddess in the act of giving birth sits between two felines, and a miniature lion or leopard rest on the head of the Minoan goddess, who may have come to Crete from Anatolia. In Greece statues of Cybele show her with a lion resting on her lap. After the cult of Cybele moved to Rome early in the third century AD, her chariot, harnessed to lions, was drawn through the streets in her yearly procession.

Like all great goddesses, Cybele was guardian of the dead and goddess of fertility and wild life. Her connection with the goddesses of Greece is clear, for Artemis, the great goddess of wild, untamed nature, was one of her names, and Aphrodite, in the Homeric Hymn, also comes to Mount Ida, with its many springs, followed by wild animals. Another Homeric Hymn, to the nameless 'Mother of the Gods', sings of her in these words:

Mother of all the gods
the mother of mortals

  Sing of he
 for me, Muse,
daughter of mighty Zeus,
  a clear song

  She knows
 the clatter of rattles
the din of kettle drums
  and she loves
the wailing of flutes.[1]

Another hymn of the second to third century AD addresses Cybele as the mother of the gods:

Rightly thou art called the Mother of the Gods
Because by thy loyalty
Thou hast conquered the power of the Gods.[2]

The cult of Cybele spread from Anatolia to Greece. In the fifth century BC a magnificent seated statue of Cybel flanked by lions and with a tambourine in her hands were placed in her temple, the Metroon, in Athens. The Emperor Julian in the fourth century AD told the story of how Cybele's temple was first established in Athens: 'The Athenians are said to have insulted and driven away the gallus [priest of Cybele] … not understanding how important the Goddess was … from that followed the wrath of the deity and the attempt to appease it … The Metroon, they say, was set up for this purpose – the place where all the official documents of the Athenians used to be kept.'[3]

The Hittite Invasion
Anatolia endured a devastating series of invasions by Indo-European tribes between 2300 and 1700 BC. At least 300 cities and villages were sacked and buried during this time. The most powerful of these tribes were the Hittites, who conquered Anatolia about 1740 BC and, overthrowing the dynasty of Hammurabi in Babylon about 1600 BC, established an empire that lasted until about 1170 BC, shortly after the Trojan War.

Names and places
The earliest form of Cybele's name may have been Kubaba or Kumbaba. The root of the name may be *kuba*, meaning a cube, which suggests the connection with the cube-shaped stone worshipped as the goddess in Anatolia. The five ideograms of Kubaba's name in Hittite writing were a lozenge or cube, a doubled-headed axe, a dove, a vase and a door or gate.

1 Translation Jules Cashford, *Harvest*, vol. 35, 1989–90, p. 209.

2 G. B. Pighi, *La Poesia Religiosa Romana*, Bologna, 1958, quoted in M. J. Vermaseren, *Cybele and Attis* (trs. A. M. H. Lemmers), London, Thames and Hudson, 1977, p. 10.

3 Julian, *Orat.*, (ed. G. Rochefort), V, 159a, Paris, 1963, quoted in Vermaseren, *Cybele and Attis*, p. 32.

Adapted from Anne Baring and Jules Cashford, *The Myth of the Goddess: Evolution of an Image*, Harmondsworth, Penguin Books, 1991, pp. 391–5.

EXERCISE FOLLOW-UP

Some changes in the text are so obviously necessary that you don't need to query them, for example deleting the unnecessary 'the' in the first paragraph, inserting the 'less' in the first line of the second paragraph, correcting plural verbs to singular to agree with the nouns, and inserting missing punctuation. You might feel reasonably certain of others but still want the author to confirm your decision, for example, about changing 'or' to 'and' and the capitalization of 'Hymn'. You must always ask the author to confirm *any* changes you suggest for quoted matter. You could ask the question about the layout of the hymns just once, before the line-by-line queries, if the document is short and has only a few verses. However, if it is a long publication in which poems are scattered throughout, it is better to make the author at least think about the query in relation to each one.

When you see quotations, you need to check that their sources have been acknowledged – they are in the footnotes in this exercise – and either check that the author has obtained permission for their use from the copyright owners or prepare to do so yourself. Copyright issues and when and how to clear permissions are discussed in Chapter 3, so don't worry if you didn't raise this query, and give yourself an extra pat on the back if you did.

The mark-up of the chapter heading and the A heading should have been obvious. Coding the verses should have been easy too, but there was more to be done. Even though the copy has line spaces between the stanzas of the first poem, a 'more space' mark (⊃–) is used to emphasize to the typesetter that this is intentional, not just a typing error. At the foot of a page where it is not clear whether or not there is a break, it is essential to mark the space, if there is one, or to use the close-up mark hanging down from the last line to indicate there is no break.

If you didn't figure out that 'Names and places' wasn't just another A head, look at the text again: it relates to the name of the goddess who is the subject of the entire chapter and refers to that name in reference to places discussed under different headings.

Coding the footnotes was essential, but if you didn't know how to mark up the information there, don't worry: it is dealt with in later chapters. When to mark end-of-line hyphens is explained in Chapter 2.

LISTS

Lists can be presented embedded (i.e., run on) in the sentence structure or displayed. You have to consider the context and the author's style, and which way works best for the reader. For example, in a story for children this structure would be appropriate:

> The children were told they would need a piece of heavy paper, coloured pencils, string, glue, a ruler and scissors.

In an article showing children how to make, say, a greeting card, the same information would be better presented like this:

> You will need:
>
> | a piece of heavy paper | glue |
> | coloured pencils | a ruler |
> | string | scissors |

In fiction, lists are usually embedded and should be in the order that makes sense in the context; if the order is irrelevant, you should keep it as the author wrote it. In non-fiction an embedded list of items that are each up to a few words long and require no specific order can be kept as the author wrote them or arranged alphabetically. For example, in the newsletter of a wildlife organization, the random list sounds natural:

> Our landbased lives make us familiar with the woods, fields, rivers and hedgerows of the countryside.

whereas in a company report on refurbishment, the more formal, alphabetical style is appropriate:

> Each work-station has been equipped with a new computer, monitor, printer and scanner.

An embedded list of phrases that has no essential order can also be kept as the author wrote it; then you need to ensure that if the items are subsequently dealt with in more detail individually, it is in the sequence in which they are listed. The items or phrases can be prefixed by a number or lower-case letter in parentheses when they have an essential sequence:

> To begin, (1) tilt the sander back, (2) switch it on and (3) lower it gently to the floor.

or to emphasize the points:

> The contract would provide (a) improved working conditions, (b) shorter working hours and (c) longer holidays.

or to make later reference in the text easy:

> The two sides took longer to agree the terms of (a) than of (c).

Embedded lists are, by definition, part of the main text and therefore are not marked up. (That sentence is really very important, so you might want to highlight it so you won't forget it.)

When you decide to display a list, you need to choose a style that carries the author's message clearly to the reader in an appropriate way. Short items may have no required order, but to display them on the page in random order will distract the reader, who will instinctively look for the reason for the *apparent* organization. Alphabetical order carries the message that sequence is not relevant. Such lists are usually displayed in columns, because a long list of relatively short measure (line length) wastes space, and therefore paper, which, as mentioned earlier, is the most expensive part of the publication.

Items that are to be used in a particular order – for example, in manuals and cookery books – should be listed in that order. Whether they are in one or more columns will depend on the page design: for example, the list might be in two columns if the instructions for use are below, or in a single column if the instructions are in parallel, in the second column.

Like their embedded counterparts, displayed lists composed of phrases or sentences can be prefixed by numbers or letters to indicate a sequence, or for emphasis or easy reference later in the text. House style may determine whether numbers or letters are used and whether they are capitals or lower-case, and how they should appear, but sometimes it is the editor's decision. If the style the author has used works well for the reader and is consistent, use it. Otherwise, choose the most appropriate style and impose it consistently. Numerals followed by a space are clear, so do not use parentheses or full points unless house style demands. Letters, however, might require parentheses or a full point to avoid their being read as part of the listed items.

Symbols can be used to call attention to each point in a list when sequence and emphasis are irrelevant. Bullets, and alternative versions such as diamonds and squares, are common for general use, and icons of telephones, cups, planes and so on are used to indicate the nature of the information.

Lists can also start with subheadings rather than symbols:

To support recycling, the council is providing:
black bins for household waste only
green bins for garden waste
black boxes for paper and newspaper but not cardboard
blue boxes for glass bottles and jars and for cans

When a list is a series of phrases, each one must be constructed to fit grammatically with the introductory phrase (as in the example above) and, where relevant, with the concluding part of the sentence. Check this by reading each point in the list with the introductory and concluding phrases.

Displayed lists can include subordinate lists, and the style can then be a combination of numerals and letters, or either of these and bullets, or bullets and other symbols. Again, house style might stipulate the sequence of numerals and letters, or authors might follow a particular pattern. If you have to create your own system, look through all the lists to see the maximum number of levels and use a sequence that will be easy for the reader to follow. Common systems are lower-case letters followed by lower-case roman numerals, and arabic numerals followed by lower-case letters followed by lower-case roman numerals, with each succeeding level indented (see Figure 1.6).

There are several categories of ownership.
1 Equitable ownership may be acquired
   a by an agreement to transfer a legal or equitable title; or
   b by a present transfer that is defective at law; or
   c by creation of a trust either
      i by the intended transferor declaring himself to be a trustee for the intended transferee, or
      ii by transfer of the asset to a third party to hold as trustee for the intended transferee.

Equitable ownership may be acquired
1 by an agreement to transfer a legal or equitable title; or
2 by a present transfer that is defective at law; or
3 by creation of a trust either
   (a) by the intended transferor declaring himself to be a trustee for the intended transferee, or
   (b) by transfer of the asset to a third party to hold as trustee for the intended transferee.

Equitable ownership may be acquired in any of the following ways:
a. by an agreement to transfer a legal or equitable title;
b. by a present transfer that is defective at law;
c. by creation of a trust either
   i. by the intended transferor declaring himself to be a trustee for the intended transferee, or
   ii. by transfer of the asset to a third party to hold as trustee for the intended transferee.

Pupils should be taught:
1 to recognize how arguments are constructed to be effective through
- the expression, sequence and linking of points;
- the provision of persuasive examples, illustrations and evidence;
- pre-empting or answering potential objections;
2 to discuss the way standard English varies in different contexts.

> Pupils should be taught:
> - to recognize how arguments are constructed to be effective through
>   – the expression, sequence and linking of points;
>   – the provision of persuasive examples, illustrations and evidence;
>   – pre-empting or answering potential objections;
> - to discuss the way standard English varies in different contexts.

Figure 1.6 Styles of lists

> (LN) Wipe the surface with a clean cloth, then cover your work area with a large sheet of a white or light-coloured paper. Arrange the paper cut-outs in front of you in the following order: [1] small circles [2] large circles [3] small squares [4] large squares [5] small triangles [6] large triangles.

Figure 1.7 Marking up a run-on list for display

When a list is embedded in the copy and you want it to be displayed, draw a red line to indicate the text affected as you would for a quotation, and then use the symbol ⌐ to indicate the start of each subsequent new line. When each item is to be preceded by a letter, number or symbol and it isn't in the text, write it in the text where you want it to appear. If there is not enough room on the line, write in the space above the line, using the insert mark to show the typesetter exactly where the character belongs (see Figure 1.7).

When a list has letters and you want it to have numbers or bullets, or vice versa, delete the existing characters with a single stroke in each case and replace them with the new characters in the space above the line.

Displayed lists are marked up, and L is the code most commonly used. You can refer to different kinds of lists as L1, L2 and so on, or as L for alphabetical list, LB for bulleted lists, and LN for numbered lists. Remember to put the codes on your list for the typesetter.

Exercise 1.4, marking up lists

Brief

Read each text, making any necessary corrections to spelling, punctuation and grammar, then mark up the list in the most appropriate style. Remember to consider the author's intentions and style, the context, and the reader's needs. Do not worry about indents or columns, as the typesetter knows what is required in each case.

1 Excerpt from a cookery article

For an elegant sweet at a midsummer party, try this variation on a traditional pavlova. Its easy to make with prepared meringue nests from the supermarket. You will need: 250 g grape, 250 g raspberries, 2 ripe pears, 2 ripe peaches, 2 oranges, 500 ml whipping cream, 12 meringue nests. Wash the grapes and raspberries and peel the pears, peaches and orange. Slice the grapes in half and chop al the other fruit except the raspberries. Put the fruit in a bowl and mix. Whip the cream to soft peaks and fold into the fruit. Fill the meringue nests with the mixture. The meringues are so sweet that you don't any sugar!

2 Excerpt from a computer guide

Setting text attributes

Text attributes determine how characters appear in Browse and when you print. Text attributes include font, size, style and colour; alignment of text characters in a field; text line spacing.

In Layout you can set text attributes for field so data in that field, in all records, appears as you specify. Follow these four steps to set text attributes: (a) in Layout, select the field you want to modify (click once in the field); (b) from the submenus on the Format menu, choose the text attributes you want; (c) choose Browse to resume data entry.

ClarisWorks User's Guide, Santa Clara, CA, Claris Corporation, 1993

3 Excerpt from a guide to copyright

Criminal proceedings The provisions of the Act regarding penalties and summary proceedings in respect of dealings which infringe copyright are set out in sections 107–110. Section 107 provides that any person who makes for sale or hire; or imports into the United Kingdom otherwise than for his private and domestic use; or possess in the course of business with a view to committing any act infringing the copyright; or in the course of business sells or lets for hire, or offers or exposes for sale or hire, or exhibits in public, or distributes; or distributes otherwise in the course of a business to such an extent as to effect prejudicially the owner of the copyright an article which he knows or has reason to believe is an infringing copy of a copyright work shall be guilty of an offence

Michael F. Flint, *A User's Guide to Copyright*, 4th edn, London, Butterworths, 1997, p. 82

4 Excerpt from an article on building materials

Photovoltaic (PV) cladding can be considered as a new building material that not only serves as a source of energy but also protects buildings from the elements. It will not be suitable in all situations, such as sensitive historical areas subject to planning restrictions. However there are many circumstances in which it is appropriate, especially where glass walls are used, such as curtain walling, rainscreen cladding and roofs.

Rainscreen cladding has been identified as a prime site for the exploitation of PV cladding technology. Such a location is particularly useful because rainscreens naturally permit ventilation behind the cladding, which encourages cooling and improves PV performance.

Curtain walling is another location in which PV cladding might be used, but care must be taken to avoid the visual intrusion of wiring and junction boxes.

Pitched roofs offer opportunities for mounting PV arrays, and atria roofs, where the view out is often less important than the general light level, also offer potential sites.

Peter F. Smith and Adrian C. Pitts, *Energy: Building for the Third Millennium*, London, Batsford, 1997

5 Excerpt from a story

Fleet Street was choked with red-headed folk, and Pope's Court looked like a coster's orange barrow. I should not have though there were so many in the whole country as were brought together by that single advertisement. Every shade of colour they were: straw, lemon, orange, brick, Irish-setter, liver, clay; but, as Spaulding said, there were not many who had the real vivid flame-coloured tint.

Sir Arthur Conan Doyle, 'The Red-Headed League'

EXERCISE FOLLOW-UP

Ingredients lists are simple to mark up: they don't require numerals or bullets. Did you check that the ingredients were listed in the order of use? If they hadn't been, you would have had to correct the order. When you are working on hard copy and only one ingredient needs to be moved, you can transpose it with the ⌐ symbol or by circling it and drawing a line to where it belongs. However, when a list is really jumbled, you can use circled numbers to show the correct order, or retype it so that the typesetter can rekey it. When you are working on-screen, it is easy to move the text into the correct order, of course.

Bullets are appropriate for the first list from the computer guide because it is composed of phrases that do not have a necessary sequence. The semicolons show which items belong together, but notice how the new-line symbols are drawn through the punctuation to delete it when the list is displayed. Deleting the punctuation is not essential; it is a style choice. There was room on the line to write in the bullets, although you could have put them in the space above the line. The second list from the computer guide is numbered to show the sequence of the actions. Did you correct the text to 'three' rather than 'four steps'? Whenever the text states the number of items in a list, count them, whether they are to be numbered or not. Sometimes when the numbers in the text and list do not agree, you will know how you should correct the text, as in this exercise; at other times you will have to ask the author whether there is something missing from the list.

The excerpt from the copyright guide was complex. It does not matter whether you used lower-case letters and roman numerals as in the model answer, or used arabic numerals and letters, as long as you got the pattern right. Parentheses work better than full points in this long, complex list, clearly separating the indicators from the text.

You could have made a bulleted list in Excerpt 4, but it isn't essential. It is necessary, however, to ensure that the order in the list and the order of further discussion of each item are the same.

The last excerpt in the exercise was just to make sure you remembered what I've said about leaving lists embedded in fiction.

2 Grammar and punctuation

The aim of copy-editing is to make the text not simply grammatically correct but also appropriate for its purpose, so that it fulfils the intention of the author and serves the needs of the reader. A copy-editor must be fully competent in grammar. For most, if not all, of us, maintaining that competence is a continuing process of review – particularly as attitudes towards usage can, and often do, change over time. Obviously, this chapter cannot be, and is not intended as, a comprehensive course in grammar. For more information about, different views on, or other ways of explaining aspects of grammar, look at the books recommended in Resources.

When you understand the basic rules, you will know how and when they can be bent to achieve an effect desired by the author.

Correct is not always appropriate

There are rules about how sentences should be constructed and punctuated, and many of them can be, and often are, bent or broken to good effect. The purpose of the work and the type of reader it is aimed at determine how formal and how grammatically correct the text needs to be.

The purpose of non-fiction is to convey information. Following the rules of grammar will help the text to do so clearly and make it accessible to readers whose own speech may be quite different. While adhering to the rules, the style of the language can range from very formal, as in company reports and articles and books aimed at professionals, through less formal, as in company newsletters, books for the non-specialist reader and schoolbooks, to relatively informal, as in sales brochures and popular magazines.

The purposes of fiction are many and varied. Some fiction intends to convey information; some wants to convey messages about life, society, politics, or the universe; some aims to thrill, frighten or amuse, or present mysteries, dramas or romance. The way characters in a story think and speak should reflect who they are and the world in which they live. Their world might be anywhere in the real world at any time in its history or at a future time of the author's creation, or in another world of the author's imagination. The way people spoke in, say, the eighteenth century is different from the way they speak now. The way educated adults speak is different from the way uneducated adults speak, and even highly educated people do not speak perfectly grammatically all the time – speech is informal. The way adults speak is different from the way children speak. There are differences in speech depending on the region in which people grew up. There are differences that can reveal whether people are speaking a language that is not their mother tongue, and how well they know it. Even people with the same background speak differently from each other in some ways. Vocabulary is the foundation of speech. Spelling can provide an accent or reflect a dialect. Grammar can be used or bent to indicate age, class, period, and regional background. The way the author uses these tools can create an individual voice for each character. You have to understand the context so that you can ensure that the grammar and style for the work and, if relevant, the characters in it are appropriate and consistent.

The author's voice

Authors also have their own voice, or style, which will be the only one in a work of non-fiction and may be that of the narrator or protagonist in a work of fiction. When an author is credited with a publication, **your job is to convey that author's voice(s) clearly and consistently, not substitute your own.** That clause is in bold because it is, in effect, a warning. On the editorial path there is a long muddy stretch created by the tears of authors frustrated by, distraught at and enraged by the thoughtless transformations of meaning and style imposed by misguided individuals. As you would expect, this book is designed to help you avoid slipping in it and adding to it.

There are authors with strong, clear voices, and others who mumble or whisper. It may be a matter of innate talent or experience. You might need only to impose house style on the strong voices and perhaps resolve the occasional ambiguity or hiccup; you will need to make the mumblers and whisperers clear and audible. Copy-editors should be given a brief telling them what to do on any document, but this doesn't always happen, and even when it does, it isn't enough.

You have to *hear* the author's voice for yourself. Before you begin any editorial work, always read some of the text. *Listen* to it to get a feeling for the rhythm of the sentences and paragraphs. Look at how the author uses nouns and pronouns, modifiers and conjunctions. When you feel that you don't *like* a word, phrase or sentence, ask yourself why. Is it just a question of your style versus the author's, or is it something that does not work well to convey the author's message to the intended readership? Try to identify generally which aspects of the writing work well and which don't. Then when you begin to edit you will be better able to change the aspects that don't work into those that do in a way consistent with the author's own style.

The house voice

Some publications are not credited to specific authors and are not intended to have a personal voice. Organizations can create their own voice, a style that is imposed on the work of many individuals so that they all sound the same:

- where the information is more important than the writer's view, as in brochures and instruction leaflets
- where the publication needs to have a consistent style over successive issues, as in newsletters
- where there needs to be a consistent style throughout large works with text written by many contributors, such as encyclopedias.

Grammar

Now that you understand how the context determines what is appropriate, we'll look at some of the major issues of grammar. There are people who get worried or even frightened at the mention of 'grammar', maybe because they were never taught it and think it's a very difficult subject, or maybe because they were taught it badly. Grammar is simply the system of our language; you use it every day. From time to time you might need to think about certain points more than others, or consult a colleague or a reference book, but, happily, every grammatical problem has a solution. Often it's more important that it should be appropriate than 'right', and it can't bite. Reassured? Read on.

Rules that aren't rules

1 You must not use a conjunction at the beginning of a sentence.

Do not deprive your authors of this useful means of emphasis, but make sure they do not overuse it, as then it loses its impact.

2 You must not split infinitives.

Sometimes a split infinitive is necessary for clarity or to avoid an awkward or overly formal construction. For example, 'I want to closely observe the various ways in which the task is completed' is clearer than 'I want to observe the various ways in which the task is completed closely' and it overcomes the awkwardness of either 'I want closely to observe …' or 'I want to observe closely …'. However, 'I want to closely observe you' is not an improvement on 'I want to observe you closely'. Listening to the text will often guide you to the appropriate decision.

3 You cannot end a sentence with a preposition.

Yes you can. Prepositions are words that express a relationship, usually of time or place, between a preceding noun or pronoun and another word or phrase. The category includes *above, across, after, among, at, before, below, for, of, off, on, over, to, under, with*. You can allow a sentence to end with a preposition when it is appropriate for the tone of the document or the language of a character in a piece of fiction. For example, whether to allow 'Who are we doing this for?' or change it to 'For whom are we doing this?' will depend on the tone of the document: the former is more immediate and even urgent, and a reflection of the way many people speak; the latter is formal and impersonal.

Sentences

Sentences start with a capital and end with a full point, question mark or exclamation mark. They usually have a subject and a verb, unless they are representing dialogue or are single words or phrases used as imperatives or for emphatic effect. There is no minimum or maximum length for a sentence. There is no law against a mixture of long and short sentences; indeed, the variety reflects a natural speech pattern and avoids the monotony that sends a reader to sleep. Consider the reading ability of the target market. Listen to the author's voice, particularly its rhythm, and use punctuation to guide the reader, combining or separating sentences where grammar, clarity and the reader's ability demand.

Subject–verb agreement

Here are the points I'm sure you know, each followed by a perhaps lesser known related one.

- Singular or plural, the subject and the verb in a clause or sentence should agree:

   This apple is red but those apples are green.

Certain nouns can be singular or plural: 'government', 'family' and 'team' are just a few examples. In British English the way these nouns of multitude, also called collective nouns, are used depends on whether the author is emphasizing the unity of the subject:

   The company is having a celebration.

or the separateness or individuality of the parts of the unit:

   The committee are determined to come to an agreement.

In the latter case, you can imagine 'the members of' preceding the subject. Whichever way it is used, you must ensure that the verb and any related, or attendant, pronoun in the same sentence are in agreement with it. This is referred to as 'agreement in number'. In American English collective nouns are usually singular.

- When singular nouns are linked by the conjunction 'and' or by a comma substituting for 'and', they form a plural subject and so need a plural verb:

   The apple, the pear and the peach are on the table.

A singular noun that is followed by a clause introduced by a linking phrase such as 'as well as' or 'together with' and set within paired commas requires a singular verb:

   The leader of the council, together with other council members, was standing on the stage.

It's as if the clause between the commas were within parentheses.

- When singular nouns are separated by the conjunction 'or', each one remains a singular subject and needs a singular verb:

> An apple or a peach is a good snack.

But if a singular noun and a plural noun are each the subject, do you use a singular or plural verb?

> The cats or the dog was [or were?] to blame.

Here's the answer: use the verb form that agrees with the subject nearest to it:

> The cats or the dog was to blame.

or

> The dog or the cats were to blame.

Most often, the plural subject is placed nearest the verb, so that there appears to be a logical increase from singular to plural.

The only time you can allow authors to break these rules is when they are writing dialogue for a child or an uneducated adult.

INDEFINITE NOUNS AND PRONOUNS

Of course you know that the pronoun must agree with the subject noun in number and gender. The one issue that is frequently debated is which pronoun and possessive to use when the subject is a non-gender-specific noun – for example, 'an author', 'the patient', 'a client', 'a person' – or an indefinite pronoun, such as 'everyone', 'anyone', 'no one'. It has long been deemed sexist to use the masculine singulars – 'he', 'him', 'his' – and using both the masculine and feminine singulars – 'he and/or she' etc. – repeatedly can make the text sound stilted and awkward. There are people who defend using the third-person plural – 'they', 'their', 'theirs' – even though it obviously does not agree in number, on the grounds that instances of its use in that way go back to the sixteenth century. If you think for a moment of some of the truly awful things people have been doing for centuries, you will realize that time alone is not reason enough. As a copy-editor you must always think about the most appropriate usage in the context.

Using both the masculine and feminine singulars is clumsy if done repeatedly, but it is a good solution when the occurrence is occasional. Be careful, however, because there are contexts where gender is relevant. Medical texts are a good example: some conditions occur only in men and some only in women. In many texts, changing singular nouns to plurals does not affect the author's voice or meaning, and precludes problems with pronouns and possessives: notice how often 'authors' is used in this text for just that reason. And notice, too, that the noun can be used in both the singular and the plural, just not in the same sentence.

The indefinite pronoun may seem more difficult, but think how the author is using it. For example, whereas 'every one' written as two words is always singular, 'everyone' and 'everybody' are usually singular but can be used as a plural:

> Everyone [i.e., all the people] found their way out of the tunnel.

Similarly, 'no one' is always singular, but the context – both the surrounding words and the intended meaning – will determine whether 'none' should be singular or plural:

> None of the money was lost. None of the men and women were forgotten.

Every time you are faced with the issue of an indefinite noun or pronoun think until you find the best solution; it will not always be the same one.

'WAS' OR 'WERE'?

Both 'was' and 'were' are the past tense of 'to be'; they indicate something that has happened and, as we have seen, must agree in number with the subject. However, when 'to be' is used to indicate something that has *not* happened – a hypothesis, or something imagined or wished – only 'were' can be used and it agrees with both singular and plural subjects.

> Don was a guest at the party. Mark and Simon were guests at the same party.

It happened.

> Don wished he were at the party. He wished Mark and Simon were there too.

It hasn't happened.

When a hypothesis is introduced, the conclusion uses the conditional form:

> If all politicians were pacifists, there would be fewer wars.

In the last two examples the first use of the verb 'to be' is in the subjunctive mood. Many people are unaware of the subjunctive mood and use 'was' in their speech, and some people argue that since this is the way people speak, we should allow it in writing. By now you know that is not reason enough. By all means, let authors use 'was' in their characters' dialogue, but elsewhere make the distinction between what has and has not happened. As editors, we are trying to make the text clear to the reader, and we should use all the means available. If an author questions such a change, explain that you are merely correcting the grammar. To authors of English Language Teaching books, you could tactfully point out that it makes no sense to ignore the subjunctive when students understand its use in their native language.

The dangling participle and similar constructions

Starting a sentence with a present participle (the '-ing' form of a verb) can help the rhythm of a paragraph, but there are dangers. The first is that authors sometimes neglect to connect the verb to the subject:

> Being afraid of heights, a holiday in the mountains was not what I wanted.

The holiday is not afraid of heights, I am:

> Being afraid of heights, I did not want a holiday in the mountains.

The second danger is that authors start lots of sentences with participles and the text becomes as monotonous as a ringing bell – ing, ing, ing – and difficult to understand because too many sentences are inverted from their usual order. Do not fall into the trap of changing the structure of all such sentences – that would be monotonous too; allow such inversions occasionally, so that they help to create a balanced rhythm in the text.

The same displacement can occur between other verb forms and the subject.

> Based on the latest information, we drew an accurate map.

'We' are not based on the information, the map is:

> We drew an accurate map based on the latest information.

I found this next example in a cookery book, and it is now my favourite example of disjuncture between a prepositional phrase and the subject:

> Of all the countries in the Middle East, allspice is used most in Turkey.

Misplaced modifiers

It is not uncommon to misplace modifiers when speaking, and authors may make their characters do this to give them verisimilitude. In other circumstances, ensure that adjectives and adverbs are placed so that they modify the right word or phrase. For example:

> He only signs cheques on Thursday

means he doesn't do anything else on that day.

> He signs cheques only on Thursday

and

> He signs cheques on Thursday only

mean that Thursday is the only day on which he signs cheques.

> Only he signs cheques on Thursday

means that no one else signs cheques on Thursday.

Exercise 2.1, focusing on the types of grammatical issues explained above

Brief
This text is from a wildlife newsletter for children aged 8–10. Read it to get a feeling for the author's style and to assess the problems it presents so that you can determine how to handle them. You should, of course, edit for consistency, spelling and punctuation as well as basic grammar.

The common frog grows up to 8 cm in length and has a smooth moist skin. Usually a yellowish brown, skin colours vary a lot, often including oranges, greens, red or even blue. A frog has an obvious

hump of their back and moves by hops, jumps and leaps. Toads have
rougher, drier, warty skin and tend to crawl.

A frog has distinctive large eyes that stick up so they can see out of the water while their bodies are submerged. They have very good eyesight and can detect even the slightest movement from a unsuspecting creature. Using their long sticky tongue at high speed, their prey is quickly snapped up, they will eat almost anything that moves but their favourite food are snails and slugs. Frogs don't really have teeth, just small pegs in their jaws to stop their prey escaping. When they have an animal in their mouths, they squash it between their tongue and eyeballs (which can be drawn down into the head) to make them easier to swallow.

When it's warmer and the days are getting longer, frogs emerge from hibernation, crawling out from the bottom of ponds and from under rocks. In the relative safety of the pond a male tries to attract a mate. Slightly smaller and darker than the females, you can identify the males by the bluish tinge to their throats. Males climb on to a female's back and hang on with their front legs until she is ready to lay her eggs. The wait may be days or even weeks, and the male has special rough black swellings (called 'nuptial pads') on their thumbs that help them to hang on. Only a few of the 2,000 eggs the female lays will hatch into tadpoles.

The mass of black eggs, called frogspawn, have a jelly coating and and are a very tasty and nutritious meal for fish, water beetles and dragonfly nymphs. The frogspawn floats on the surface of the water, warmed by the sun, and the tadpoles finally hatch after two to four weeks. Insects or fish not only eat frogspawn but also tadpoles, which try to hide among the weeds.

Tadpoles start life as vegetarians, mainly eating algae and plants, but after about seven weeks they start eating insects. It has gills so that it can breathe underwater. Until they are about four weeks old, the gills can be seen on the outside of the tadpole's body. Then the gills are absorbed into the body. The tadpole grows hind legs, then front ones, and finally looses its tail. After 12 weeks, with all four legs and the ability to breathe air, the tiny froglet climbs out of the pond to find a safe place on land to spend the rest of the summer.

From *Wildwatch* Scotland, Scottish Wildlife Trust, Spring 2004

EXERCISE FOLLOW-UP

Readers of this age will understand the use of the singular or the plural noun to represent all the individuals in the species, so you can use both forms – just not in the same sentence. A frog has, and frogs have, eyes and legs, but you had to decide whether 'frogs' have 'mouths' and 'throats' or 'a mouth' and 'a throat'. The model answer shows the fewest changes to the author's text that are compatible with clarity.

There were some errors that had to be corrected. The change to 'and can be' in lines 2–3 makes it clear that the other colours are not part of the yellowish brown, and 'oranges' and 'greens' are made singular for consistency with the form for all the other colours mentioned. After you solved the problem of the dangling modifier in lines 9–10, you needed to divide the run-on sentence into two. Changing 'really' in line 11 to 'real' and moving it to precede 'teeth' in line 12 improves precision, and changing 'them' to 'it' in line 15 makes the pronoun agree with the noun to which it refers.

The third sentence in paragraph 3 (line 19) begins with a dangling adverbial phrase; the reader is, presumably, not smaller and darker than a female frog. You could have revised this sentence in different ways, but it is easy to dispose of the phrase 'you can identify', as the author does not involve the reader directly elsewhere.

In the fourth paragraph, as well as making the verbs in lines 26–7 agree with the singular 'mass', you needed to delete the repeated 'and' at the end of line 26 and ensure that in line 30 'not only' modifies the noun, not the verb. For the same reason, you should have transposed 'mainly' and 'eating' in line 32. Replacing the pronoun 'they' with the noun 'tadpoles' at the beginning of the next sentence resolves the problem of the dangling prepositional phrase.

There was no problem with the subjunctive in that exercise, but it will occur in others.

Relative pronouns

Relative pronouns introduce a clause that qualifies the preceding noun or pronoun. 'That' is called the defining, or restrictive, relative pronoun: it introduces a clause that defines, restricts the meaning of, or identifies the preceding noun:

> There are many books in this room. The books that are on the table belong to the library.

Some of the books belong to the library, and the clause introduced by 'that' identifies them. Used as a relative pronoun, 'that' cannot be preceded by a comma; it can, however, often be omitted from a sentence without affecting the meaning:

> The book that he was reading belonged to Mike.
>
> The book he was reading belonged to Mike.

'Which' is called the non-defining, or non-restrictive, relative pronoun. Preceded by a comma, it introduces a clause that adds information about the preceding noun or pronoun. The clause must be followed by a comma when it comes between the subject and the remainder of the sentence.

> The books, which are on the table, belong to the library.

This sentence tells us that all the books belong to the library, and the clause introduced by ', which' adds information about their location. The clause is not essential to the identification of the books or to the grammatical structure of the sentence; it can be dropped without changing the meaning of the main clause:

> The books belong to the library.

Many people use 'which' instead of 'that' and claim that the context makes the meaning clear. Sometimes it does, but why make the reader work any more than necessary to receive the author's message? 'That' and ', which' give the desired precision instantly, and avoid ambiguity. Most rules can be bent, and you need to be flexible in applying them too. For example, if 'that' appears nearby in the sentence as a determiner, an author might want to use 'which' as the relative pronoun:

> The work that he did on that project ...

or

> The work which he did on that project ...

When there is no ambiguity and it makes the sentence flow better, it is an acceptable choice. Copy-editing is about thinking and making appropriate choices, not merely following rules.

These relative pronouns are used for objects and animals. In introducing clauses referring to people, 'who' is the defining relative pronoun – the equivalent of 'that' – and ', who' is the non-defining relative pronoun – the equivalent of ', which'.

> The men who had worked hard were given a holiday.

Only those men got a holiday; the men who had not worked hard did not get a holiday.

> The men, who had worked hard, were given a holiday.

All the men were given a holiday; they all had worked hard. Another way of introducing this clause would be:

> The men, all of whom had worked hard, were given a holiday.

When a preposition precedes the relative pronoun, use 'whom'.

Exercise 2.2, focusing on relative pronouns

Brief
Read or skim the article first to hear the author's voice and to assess the problems before you edit and mark up the text. The exercise focuses on the use of relative pronouns, but you must also correct errors in grammar, spelling, punctuation and consistency.

House style
- -ise for verbs
- i.c. for headings

THE STATE OF OUR HEALTH

The NHS is always in the news. There is a cycle of articles about the seemingly endless reorganisations and restructurings; the long hours and the poor pay which results in people not entering the medical profession or leaving it quickly for private practise or better conditions abroad; the closure of wards because there aren't enough doctors and nurses; the lack of beds; the patients on trolleys in corridors where they lie untended for hours; the waiting lists; the post-code lottery. People can hardly be blamed for wondering whether you can get into a hospital if you need to and whether they'll get good care if they do.

Not As Bad As We Feared?
Visiting a close friend in hospital recently, he told me how hard everyone had worked to treat not only his medial condition but also to make him feel comfortable. There was the consultant who tried to alay his fears before the surgery by explaining what was about to happen. It had been the middle of the night and my friend was very

weak from the loss of blood, he said, and could only remember what she said vaguely but her manner comforting. She came to see him the next day to reassure him that the operation had gone well. The nurses who, of course, gave him to his medications and the aides who saw to all his other needs, from smoothing the bedclothes to bringing his meals, were all efficient and personable. Everything was great, he told me, until our mutual friend Ted had turned up and started on about the resurgance of MRA, an infection which had been rampent in the early 2000s and could kill you. My friend hadn't known about it before and now was watching the cleaners like an eagle, checking that the nurse was wearing gloves when they changed his bandages, wondering if the plates had been sterilized and the aides washed their hands. Instead of believing the hospital was the right place for his recuperation, he now wanted to go home as soon as possible. His situation is so far from unique that action is finally being taken.

Are We Dreaming?
The government which knows it stands to lose many of its supporters if they don't produce a strategy to cope with the current problems has made a number of important decisions. Hospitals which fail to achieve the minimum standard will be told not only what their failings are, but also given funding to remedy them. Recognising that the rise in the spread of infections is a result of poor hygiene, money will be earmarked for employing additional cleaners. Other new policies which apply to all hospitals were announced by a man who had earned the public's confidence as

Minister for Scientific Advancement and is the new Minsiter for
Health: Robin Natiramas. Signs will be placed in appropriate places
to remind all staff, including doctors and nurses, to wash their hands
and to wear and dispose of gowns and gloves appropriately. Senior
staff in all departments will check that the proper procedures are
being followed, particularly by new or temporary staff who might
not be familar with the new guidelines. A expert team of public-
health inspectors will make unannounced visits to inspect kitchens
where dirty surfaces, inefficient dishwashers and unrefrigerated
food could lead to major disasters. Funds will be provided for
rebuilding every hospital which is more than forty years old this
year so that they will come up to the standard set out in the NHS
Reform Act 2035.

EXERCISE FOLLOW-UP

The headings could have been marked A and B rather than in the way they are shown on the model answer, as long as you got the relationships right. The list is left embedded. If you did extract it, it should have been bulleted rather than numbered because the sequence of points is irrelevant and there is no indication that they will be referred to later.

There were choices elsewhere too. You could have decided to use the second-person singular throughout the last sentence in the first paragraph, but there are fewer changes the way I've done it. Perhaps you found another way to make the subject agree with the verb in line 13 (e.g. 'I visited . . . and he') and you may have decided to use 'thinking' or 'feeling' instead of 'believing' in line 30. You might have chosen to keep the present participle in line 40 and alter the second clause to 'the government will earmark'. There were, of course, no choices in correcting spelling, making tenses agree, or using the relative pronouns correctly – with one exception: you could have queried the author to find out if Ted was the only friend he or she shared with the man in hospital; if so, you would need commas around 'Ted'.

Punctuation

Were you taught at school to put a comma where you pause for breath? Well, forget it. Punctuation is not a function of the respiratory system. It does not equate to breathing; it guides the reader through the sentence, signalling groupings of words, changes of tone, and relationships between clauses. The application of punctuation is, as you would expect, governed by rules, but personal taste also plays a role. When you edit, apply the rules in a way that's consistent with the author's style. A lot of information follows, and I suggest that you read it and reread it so that you absorb as much as you can; it'll always be here for review.

The comma

Of all punctuation, the comma has the greatest number of jobs. It helps readers navigate through sentences by separating words, phrases and clauses to avoid ambiguity, and by acting as a substitute for words that would otherwise be repeated. We will examine its use with numerals in Chapter 4; here we will concentrate on words.

LISTS AND THE SERIAL COMMA

The comma separating items in a list is a substitute for 'and' or 'or'.

> **He could buy apples, pears, bananas, peaches and [or] oranges.**
>
> **We went swimming, rode horses, walked in the woods and played tennis.**

Some authors always use the conjunctions instead of the comma, and it would be wrong to alter their style. Sometimes authors who usually use commas in lists use conjunctions instead, for emphasis, and it would be wrong to change their intended tone.

To use a comma before 'and' in a list seems redundant, but sometimes it is necessary to avoid ambiguity.

> He bought books published by Hammer, Steel, Iron and Tack and Nail.

Is one publisher Iron and Tack and the other Nail, or is one Iron and the other Tack and Nail? The handy little comma will make it clear.

The comma before the final 'and' in a list is called the serial comma. It is sometimes called the Oxford comma, because it is the house style of Oxford University Press, one of the oldest publishers in Britain. Some authors and some organizations use it whether or not it is needed to avoid ambiguity; it's their individual or house style. Their argument seems to be that if you always use it, you won't have to think about using it to avoid ambiguity. Of course, if the serial comma is the house style of the organization you are working for, or the consistent style of an author, use it; but remember that thinking is what you should be doing all the time.

A list of adjectives preceding a noun should be separated by commas if each adjective modifies only the noun. The test is whether the sense permits you to put 'and' between them:

> The Martins were a cheerful, musical family.

The Martins were a cheerful family and a musical family.

Do not use a comma after one adjective in a list that modifies subsequent adjectives combined with a noun:

> The director advocated a radical economic policy.

The economic policy was radical.

MAIN CLAUSES

A main clause has a subject and a verb, and can stand on its own as a sentence, which is why it is also called an independent clause. Often, two independent clauses joined by a conjunction do not require any punctuation:

> You will go to the north and I will go to the south.

> He was out of breath but at least he was not late.

There is no change of tone, no added emphasis in the second clause.

However, a comma is used to separate such clauses when it is necessary to avoid ambiguity:

> He took care of the sales, and his brother took care of the purchases.

or to sharpen contrast:

> They tried every possible solution, but it was to no avail.

No comma is needed before a conjunction when the subject of the first clause is implied in the second:

> The cat jumped out of the window and chased the dog.

But when the verb or a modified noun is implied, it is replaced by a comma:

> The children were frightened; the parents, calm.

> Their first choice was a trip to the seaside; their second, a day by the pool.

SUBORDINATE CLAUSES

A subordinate clause cannot stand on its own, which is why it is also called a dependent clause. Just to add to the terminology, it is also a parenthetical clause and can be separated from the main clause by parentheses or dashes. We'll stick to commas for the present.

> The car was relatively new, purchased only five months earlier.

In this sentence 'the car was relatively new' is the main clause and 'purchased only five months earlier' is the subordinate clause.

When a subordinate clause follows the main clause, as above, it is preceded by a comma; when it interrupts the main clause, it needs a comma at the end too:

> The car, purchased only five months earlier, was relatively new.

Commas are often used after a subordinate clause that precedes a main clause:

> Purchased only five months earlier, the car was relatively new.

This is also the case when the subordinate clause begins with an adverb (an adverbial clause):

> When she burst into the room, David looked surprised.

A comma is not needed after a dependent phrase beginning with a preposition:

> Under his management the company increased productivity.
>
> In 2005 we had a holiday in Italy.

except when it is necessary to avoid even momentary ambiguity:

> In the valley below, the farms were well protected.
>
> In the morning, news of the truce reached the final outpost.

However, a comma is usually needed after a dependent clause beginning with a preposition:

> If it continues to rain, the village will be flooded.
>
> On reaching the station, she sighed with relief.

As we have seen above, a comma is used before a non-defining relative pronoun introducing a clause:

> He chose the earrings, which matched the colour of her eyes.

and before and after the clause when it interrupts the sentence:

> She asked the child, who was standing next to her, to open the door.

But a clause introduced by a defining relative pronoun does not have any commas:

> He chose the earrings that matched the colour of her eyes.
>
> She asked the child who was standing next to her to open the door.

APPOSITES

Like subordinate clauses but without the verbs, apposites are words or phrases in a sentence that add information about a preceding noun or noun phrase.

> Anne Boleyn, the daughter of Elizabeth Howard and Sir Thomas Boleyn, was the second wife of Henry VIII.
>
> My brother, Michael, will be best man.

This construction means that I have one brother and his name is Michael.

> My brother Michael will be best man.

This construction means that I have more than one brother and I am identifying the one who will be best man.

There can be a succession of apposites, each set off by commas:

> Mr Weatherby, collector of medieval glassware, well-known philanthropist, amateur sleuth, was photographed arriving at the celebration.

ADVERBS

Commas usually should not be used to separate adverbs and short adverbial phrases from the subject:

> Today it rained.
> During the interval we had a drink.
> Slowly flows the Don.

That said, there are some adverbs that need a comma when they begin a sentence, such as 'moreover' and 'already'. 'However' is set off by a comma or commas at any position in a sentence when it is used to indicate contrast:

> However, he tried to reword the report to make it sound more positive.
>
> He tried to reword the report, however, to make it sound more positive.

but not when it is used to mean 'in whatever way':

> However he tried to reword the report, the negative result was clear.

INTERJECTIONS

We all do it when we speak: add words and short phrases that express emotion or are verbal pauses, ranging from 'oh' and 'well' to 'you see', and 'ya know whad I mean'. When authors do it in their text, use commas to set off these interjections:

> 'Well, Herbie was really tired, you see,' said Raj, 'so I said I'd do the job.'

ADDRESSEES AND SPEAKERS

Commas are usually used to set off the character addressed from the rest of the dialogue at any position in the sentence:

'Mrs Adams, someone left this package for you.'
'C'mon, dog, let's go for a run.'

although there are times when the sense – and the sound – preclude them. Look at and listen to the differences here:

'Hey, you!'
'Hey you, get outta there!'
'Hey, you get outta there!'

Commas are also used in dialogue to separate the speaker from the speech:

The ticket seller said, 'The train for Brighton is waiting on platform 12.'

'The train for Brighton', the ticket seller said, 'is waiting on platform 12.'

Notice that the comma after 'Brighton' is outside the quotation mark, as it is not part of the quoted sentence. This will be explained further in the section 'Quotation marks' below.

Although some authors like to use the colon to separate speakers from their dialogue, this can be done only when the speakers are identified before the dialogue begins, as in the first example above. There would then be an inconsistency in style when the speaker is interposed in the speech, as in the second example above. You can point this out to an author, but if he or she prefers the inconsistency, perhaps arguing that the colon adds more emphasis or simply that it is a stylistic choice, you must accept it.

The semicolon

After all the ways to use a comma, it is a relief to encounter the semicolon. It has only two functions.

- Stronger than a comma, it separates lists or phrases that are already punctuated by commas:

    She bought vanilla, chocolate and mint ice cream; raspberry, strawberry and blackberry sorbet; and macaroons and vanilla wafers.

    There were suits of mail standing like ghosts in armour here and there; fantastic carvings brought from monkish cloisters; rusty weapons of various kinds; distorted figures in china, wood, iron and ivory; tapestry and strange furniture that might have been designed in dreams.

I like to quote Dickens, as well as more recent authors, when people say sentences have to be short to be understood. The example above and the two below are all from *The Old Curiosity Shop*.

- Weaker than a full stop, the semicolon joins independent clauses that are not joined by a conjunction. A full stop could be used, but the author is emphasizing the close relationship of the two clauses by holding them together.

> The haggard aspect of the little old man was wonderfully suited to the place; he might have groped among old churches and tombs and deserted houses, and gathered all the spoils with his own hands.

When a semicolon is used between independent clauses joined by a conjunction, it indicates more of a separation, change of tone or emphasis than a comma in this position would.

> But her dwarfish spouse still smoked his cigar and drank his rum without heeding her; and it was not until the sun had sometime risen and the activity and noise of the city day were rife in the street that he deigned to recognize her presence by any word or sign.

The colon

The colon, as mentioned above, can be used to introduce dialogue, and is usually used for this purpose in scripts:

> Juliet: O Romeo, Romeo! wherefore art thou Romeo?

It can introduce a list or example, which is done so frequently throughout this text I don't need to do it again here.

When it is used between two main clauses, it establishes a causal relationship, moving from cause to effect, from premiss to explanation or conclusion, from stimulus to response:

> Dr Pavlov rang the bell: the dogs salivated.

It is never necessary to use a dash after a colon in modern texts.

Full stop, exclamation mark and question mark

A full stop ends a sentence, even if it is only a single word intended as a complete statement. Really.

Full stops are rarely used in abbreviations composed of capital letters, whether they are acronyms (UNICEF, OPEC) or initialisms (BBC, UK, EU). In British usage a full stop is placed at the end of an abbreviation: a word that has been shortened by omitting the ending: 'abbr.', 'co.', 'inc.'. It is not used at the end of a contraction (a word shortened by using at least the first and the last letters): 'Mr', 'Mrs', 'Dr', 'Ltd'. In American practice the full stop is still commonly used after both abbreviations and contractions.

Exclamation marks are used appropriately after words, phrases or sentences that express surprise, strong feelings, or raised voices. In non-fiction and literary works there is no reason to use more than one at the end of any sentence; a practice common in comic books. Scattered too freely through a text – in other words, overused – exclamation marks fail to express anything but may succeed in annoying the reader.

When doesn't a question mark come at the end of a question?

- When it's an indirect question, one that is incorporated into a statement:

  He asked why cats like cream.

- When it's a rhetorical question, one that doesn't require an answer because it presupposes that there is only one possible answer:

  What cat doesn't like cream.
  Will you please leave by the nearest exit.

Here, an author might choose to use a full stop instead of the question mark to emphasize this point or to indicate a tone of voice.

Similarly, sometimes authors use question marks with what appear to be statements to reflect the character's tone of voice:

You didn't eat the pie? You gave it to the dog?

After all that, I bet you're just aching to do an exercise.

Exercise 2.3, focusing on baseline punctuation

Brief

As usual, read through the text first to get a feeling for the author's style. Then punctuate and correct any errors in grammar and spelling. When you are finished with the first paragraph, read it to see if your punctuation has given you a better understanding of the author's rhythm, then continue. Read the entire text over and make any final corrections before checking the model answer.

House style
- Use the serial comma only to avoid ambiguity.

On a fine summer morning when the leaves were warm under the sun and the more industrious bees abroad diving into every blue and red cup which could possibly be considered a flower Anne was sitting at the back window of her mother's portion of the house measuring out lengths of worsted for a fringed rug that she was making which lay about three-quarter finished beside her the work though chromatically brilliant was tedious a hearth-rug was a thing which nobody worked at from morning to night it was taken up and put down it was in the chair on the floor across the handrail under the bed kicked here kicked there rolled away in the closet brought out again and so on more capriciously perhaps than any other homemade article nobody was expected to finish a rug within a calculable period and the wools of the begining became faded and historical before the end was reached a sense of this inherent nature of worsted-work rather than idelness led Anne to look rather frequently from the open casement

The gril glanced at the down and the sheep for no particular reason the steep margin of turf and daisies rising above the roofs chimneys apple trees and church tower of the hamlet around her bounded the view from her position and it was necessary to look somewhere when she raised her head. While thus engaged in working and stopping her attention was attracted by the sudden rising and running away of the sheep squatted on the down and there suceeded sounds of a heavy tramping over the hard sod which the sheep had quitted the tramp being accompanied by a metallic jingle turning her eyes further she beheld two cavalry soldiers on bulky grey chargers armed and accoutred throughout ascending the down at a point to the left where the incline was comparatively easy the burnished chains buckles and plates of their trappings shown like little looking-glasses and the blue red and white about them was unsubdued by weather or wear

The two trooper rode proudly on as if nothing less than crowns and empires ever concerned their magnificent minds they reached that part of the down which lay just in front of her where they came to a halt in another minute there appeared behind them a group containing some half dozen more of the same sort these came on halted and dismounted likewise

Two of the soldiers then walked some distance onward together when one stood still the other advancing further and stretching a white line of tape between them two more of the men marched to another outlying point where they made marks in the ground thus they walked about and took distances according to some preconcerted scheme.

At the end of this systematic proceeding one solitary horsemen – a commissioned officer if his uniform could be judged rightly at this distance – rode up the down went over the ground looked at what the others had done and seemed to think that it was good and then the girl heard yet louder tramps and clankings and she beheld rising from where the others had risen a whole column of calvary in marching order at a distance behind these came a cloud of dust enveloping more and more troops their arms and acoutrements reflecting the sun through the haze in faint flashes stars and streaks of light the whole body approached slowly towards the plateau at the top of the down

Anne threw down her work and letting her eyes remain on the nearing masses of cavalry the worseds getting entangled as they would said 'Mother, mother come here here's such a fine sight what does it mean what can they be going to do up there'

From Thomas Hardy, *The Trumpet-Major*

EXERCISE FOLLOW-UP

I really enjoyed the phrase 'up the down' and hope you didn't change it to 'downs'; if you had been in doubt, you should have checked in a dictionary. You would not have been technically wrong if you used full stops where the answer shows colons or semicolons, but compare the differences in the rhythm of the paragraph and the relationship between clauses and you will understand Hardy's choices. You could make a case for commas around 'rather than idleness' but they are not essential and change the tone. I left the dashes in the text because we have not yet discussed them. We're approaching them now.

Hyphens and en and em rules

These three mid-line punctuation marks have some similarities and, as you would expect, major differences. First, learn to distinguish them visually. Their relative sizes are the same in any typeface:
- the hyphen is a short, relatively thick mark;
– the en rule is longer and thinner; it measures an en in a given type size, so an 8-point en is shorter than a 14-point en;
— the em rule is twice as long as the en and the same weight (just as thin), and its length is also relative to its type size.

THE HYPHEN

If you are a proofreader, you won't be surprised to hear that there are two kinds of hyphen: the soft and the hard. They look identical but have different uses. The soft hyphen is used for word breaks at the end of a line of justified type. Because authors are usually asked not to justify type, editors should not see any soft hyphens. However, authors don't always do as requested. If you have the e-file, you can unjustify the type before you begin work and all the soft hyphens will disappear. If you don't have this opportunity and have to work on hard copy of justified text, mark soft hyphens for deletion because you cannot be sure whether they are in the e-file as soft or hard.

The hard hyphen is so called because it remains wherever the word comes on the line. If a hyphenated word has to be broken at the end of the line, the break comes at the hyphen. This type of word break can appear in an unjustified typescript; when it does, you mark it with the 'leave unchanged', or stet, symbol. You can use the dotted line under the hyphen but I prefer the circled tick above it (used only as a margin mark in proofreading), as I think it stands out more clearly.

When you need to add a hyphen to hard copy, just draw it in between the words if there is space, with a caret mark (∧) under it, or above the line with an insert mark between the words. Draw only the hyphen, not the proof-correction symbol, as you are marking up a manuscript, not a page proof. Unless a rule between words is marked otherwise, the typesetter assumes it is a hyphen.

Hyphenation can change from the time a word first enters the language. 'To-day' was common until the 1940s, and 'co-operate' and 'co-ordinate' were widely used until the 1990s. British English differs from American English, and house styles of various organizations differ from each other. The basic rules are stated below. Always remember that, like all punctuation, the hyphen is used to help clarify the text, so the context will often tell you where to use it. When you are uncertain, refer to your house style, a current dictionary, *NODWE* for various terms and names, or a biographical dictionary for names.

A hard hyphen connects words in the following circumstances.

1 When two or more words are used as a unit preceding a noun to modify it – a compound adjective – the hyphen makes this construction clear:

   a five-star hotel
   a ten-year-old child
   up-to-date statistics

and prevents ambiguity or absurdity:

   twenty-odd people
   a live-wire fence
   a little-known writer

When the words are transferred to the predicate (the part of the sentence following the subject and containing a verb), they do not need the hyphens:

   the hotel has five stars
   the child is ten years old
   a fence with a live wire

When a compound adjective is repeated in succession with different first elements, the latter can appear with space after the hyphen until the last mention – the so-called hanging hyphen:

   The book was about sixteenth- and seventeenth-century Flemish paintings.

2 A hyphen can be, but is not always, used to connect the elements of compound names. People in the same family can decide to adopt it or drop it, so you may need to check:

William Douglas-Home
David Lloyd George

3 A hyphen clarifies a word where successive vowels are doubled or consonants tripled after a prefix:

anti-inflationary
co-opt
re-edit
bell-like

4 A hyphen distinguishes a word from its homograph: a word spelled the same way but having a different meaning:

re-creation
re-cover
re-form
un-ionize

5 A hyphen connects the numerator and the denominator in a fraction that is spelled out in words:

two-thirds

except when another part of the fraction is already hyphenated:

three twenty-fourths
thirty-two hundredths

6 Despite the frequency with which you see them like this in newspapers and magazines, hyphens are not needed – and therefore should not be used – between adverbs and the words they modify:

It was a beautifully designed room by a tremendously talented individual.

THE EN RULE

The en rule has three uses.

1 It is used to join two words or numbers that form a range, replacing 'from' and 'to', and 'between' and 'and':

The sign said: Open Monday–Friday 9.30–3.15.

Notice I said 'replacing': consider each of those pairs of words inextricably linked, like handcuffs, and never allow a text to say 'from X–Y' or 'between A–B'.

2 It replaces 'to' or 'and' between words of equal importance. You can transpose the words, reflecting a different perspective, without affecting the nature of the relationship:

> patient–doctor confidentiality or doctor–patient confidentiality
> Edinburgh–Glasgow road or Glasgow–Edinburgh road

3 The en rule, spaced on both sides, is the standard British style for a dash, although some house styles prefer the em (see below). Dashes separate a word, phrase or clause from the main clause, as do commas and parentheses. But whereas commas indicate a slight subordination, a slight lowering of tone, and parentheses contain more of an aside, dashes call more attention to the words or phrase so separated. (I think of this series as quiet, whisper, shout.) The dash can be used singly or in pairs to emphasize the information, to indicate sarcasm or to create humour.

> He testified to the committee – not once but several times – that he had never seen the report.
>
> The journalist said that the story must be true – the source was a politician.
>
> On Saturday the children helped – or so they thought – to tidy the house.

The single dash can often be replaced by a colon. Consider this option when the text is so littered with dashes that clarity is affected.

To mark up an en rule or dash, or to change a hyphen to an en rule, just write a circled N above it; the circle is important, telling the typesetter that the N is an instruction, not a character to be set. If a closed-up en rule needs to be spaced either side, insert the 'more space' marks:

> On Saturday the children helped – or so they thought⌣to tidy the house.

THE EM RULE

The em rule resembles the en rule only in its first function.

1 Closed up to the text on both sides, the em rule is the standard American style for the dash, and is used by some organizations in Britain:

> He testified to the committee—not once but several times—that he had never seen the report.

> The journalist said that the story must be true—the source was a politician..

2 Spaced, the em rule is used to replace a word, and closed up, it replaces part of a word. Unlike the use of any initial to hide an individual's identity, for example in a court case, the initial followed by an em rule indicates that the person's name really begins with that letter.

> Max saw the — in the room, muttered 's—t' and ran to tell Mr B—.

3 The em rule can be used in dialogue closed up to indicate the breaking off of a word:

> 'Look out, you're going to spill the cof—', but my warning was too late.

or spaced to indicate the interruption of a sentence:

> 'I think I hear someone in —' A crashing noise interrupted her.

This is different from the ellipsis, which is described later.

4 In works for an academic or professional audience the spaced em can be used in indexes to replace a repeated entry, and a 2- or 3-em rule, according to house style, can be used in bibliographies instead of repeating an author's name.

To change a hyphen or an en rule to an em, write a circled M above it and use the 'close up' or 'more space' symbol as appropriate.

The apostrophe

There is hardly any excuse for misplacing the apostrophe, but it still happens. It has two functions.

1 It indicates missing letters and numbers generally:

> 'Ah, 'twas a fine mornin' in the summer of '68,' he began.

and in contractions particularly:

> can't = cannot
> he'd = he had, he would
> it's = it is, it has

Without the apostrophe 'its' is a pronoun. Your authors might be confused, but you mustn't be.

2 It indicates the possessive:

> Mrs White's appointment was at two.
>
> The adults' and children's libraries were on different floors.

The possessive pronouns 'its', 'hers', 'theirs', 'ours' and 'yours' do not have apostrophes.

Quotation marks

Whereas it makes no difference whether you call them 'quote marks' or 'quotation marks', I see no point in calling them 'inverted commas', since they do not function like commas. Happily, no one has thought of using this term for an apostrophe, or calling quotation marks 'facing apostrophes'; it would make about as much sense – none – so let's stick with the most descriptive term.

You read about displaying quotations in Chapter 1, and here you will find guidance on how to use quotation marks generally and with other punctuation marks. The rules cover quite a few situations, some only subtly different from others, so take your time and be sure you really understand each of the following points before you read the next one. First, here are some rules about what authors can do with text from other sources.

EDITORIAL TREATMENT OF QUOTATIONS

The main rule is that the *words* quoted must be the same as in the original. Authors can:

Grammar and punctuation 67

- omit text from quotations, which will be discussed under 'The ellipsis' below;
- italicize parts of the text as long as they add 'my italics' or 'my emphasis' in square brackets at the end of the words affected;
- insert 'sic' (Latin for 'so' or 'thus') in square brackets after text to indicate that the apparent error or archaic usage is in the original source;
- correct typographical errors, unless it is necessary to produce a facsimile;
- add missing letters or words, clarifications or comments in square brackets:

> 'Stu[y]vesant lost a leg in the attack on St Martin [later New York] but survived to rule for another twenty years before surrendering to the English.'

When a quotation has such insertions in parentheses (round brackets like these), and you are certain they are your author's own additions, change them to square brackets. When you cannot be certain but suspect they are not part of the original source, check with the author. In addition, you can impose house style on quotation marks and dashes, but not on other punctuation, spelling or the use of italics or bold.

FUNCTIONS AND EXCEPTIONS

Quotation marks are used around quotations that are not displayed but run on in the text, which are referred to as 'embedded'. They are also used to enclose direct speech, including unspoken thoughts if the author wishes.

> I said, 'I will be there in an hour.'
> He thought, 'This really is the best route.'
> Scott asked Maria, 'Have you found your keys?'

They are not used for indirect speech (a report of what someone has said). In indirect speech the sentences can be paraphrased or introduced by an actual or implied 'that', the verb form reflects a greater past tense, and pronouns change in accord with a third-person tone:

> I said [that] I would be there in an hour.

> He thought that this really was the best route.
> Scott asked Maria if she had found her keys.

Quotation marks can be used around words that are being introduced to the reader or to identify them as technical terms. This is a matter of style only, for such words can just as appropriately be shown in italics, bold or a different font from the rest of the text.

Quote marks can also be used around words that are not to be taken literally, which can otherwise be prefaced by 'so-called'; Judith Butcher calls these 'sneer quotes', but they are also known as 'scare quotes'.

The titles of songs, chapters, articles, episodes of broadcast programmes, and short poems referred to in the text are enclosed in single quotes; the titles of the larger works in which these appear are shown in italics, which will be discussed in Chapter 4.

BASIC STYLES

The British convention is to use single quotation marks and then double quotation marks for quotes within quotes.

> Sally said, 'I overheard him say "I'll be there at once" and then he put down the phone.'

Some house styles follow the reverse pattern: double quotes with single quotes within, which is also the American convention. The given pattern alternates for however many levels of quotes there are. Your job is to follow the given house style and maintain consistency. To make a change from double to single quotes on hard copy, cross out the former and write the latter above it. When you are making the change from single to double, you can write in the extra mark if there is enough space to do so *clearly*; otherwise, strike out the single and write the double above it.

CONVENTIONS FOR DIALOGUE

You know that quotation marks enclose speech and that a new paragraph starts when there is a change of speaker. However, the speech itself does not have to begin the paragraph; it can, if the author chooses, be run on after introductory narrative, as in this excerpt from John Le Carré's *The Secret Pilgrim*:

> He was feeding on me with his eyes. He reminded me of my dog Lizzie when she watches me for a signal – unblinking, body ready to go. 'Shall we start, then?' he said.

Please note: *if the author chooses*. This aspect of style does not have to be consistent throughout a work; an author might choose to run on speech in some places and to separate it from the narrative in others to affect the pace. If you think the author has not chosen the most effective or appropriate style, you can explain why and suggest the alternative, but in the end it is still the author's choice.

When an individual's speech continues for more than one paragraph, an opening quote mark is used at the beginning of each paragraph and a closing quote mark is used only when that individual stops speaking.

WITH TERMINAL PUNCTUATION

To determine where other punctuation goes in relation to quotation marks see whether the text concerned is a complete sentence, exclamation or question. When it is not, the punctuation goes outside the quotation marks:

> The critic described the production as 'breathtaking'.

When the quotation is a complete sentence, the final punctuation is inside the marks:

> She said, 'You'll be pleased to know that there is an easy way to do this.'

> He asked, 'What will you do if, or should I say when, you get caught?'

> In his script for *This Happy Breed* Noel Coward wrote 'We know what we belong to, where we come from, and where we're going.'

When a sentence is quoted in order to illustrate or explain a statement, it is effectively incorporated in the longer sentence, and the full stop is placed outside the quotation mark:

> You may say 'He is economical with the truth' but you mean 'He is a liar'.

> She based her communications on the old Chinese proverb 'The strongest memory is weaker than the faintest ink'.

The punctuation is also outside the quote mark when a single sentence is introduced by the conjunction 'that':

> In his script for *This Happy Breed* Noel Coward wrote that 'we know what we belong to, where we come from, and where we're going'.

The punctuation is placed inside the closing quote mark when more than one sentence is quoted, because the subsequent sentences are independent of the conjunction:

> In his script for *This Happy Breed* Noel Coward wrote that 'we know what we belong to, where we come from, and where we're going. We may not know it with our brains, but we know it with our roots.'

Notice that the sentence quoted after 'that' loses its capital letter. In scholarly works only, the letter is sometimes placed in square brackets, to indicate that this is not how it was in the original:

> Noel Coward wrote that '[w]e know ...

When either the main sentence or the quoted sentence ends in a question mark and the other sentence ends in a full stop, only one mark of terminal punctuation is needed and the question mark will rule out the use of the full stop:

> He kept repeating to himself, 'Where did I put it?'

> Was it Marx who wrote 'The workers have nothing to lose but their chains'?

However, the exclamation mark and the question mark can be used together at the end of an embedded quotation, according to sense:

> Did the accused shout 'Let him have it!'?

> Don't you dare ask 'Are we almost there?'!

What if the speech or quotation precedes the source? Technically, the sentence does not need any punctuation and in narrative text gets none:

> 'We know what we belong to' wrote Noel Coward.

In representing speech, however, the practice is to use a comma within the quote mark:

> 'You'll be pleased to know that there is an easy way to do this,' she said.

Why? No one ever used to give a reason for this usage – because there isn't one. It's just a convention. Some manuals say that the comma in this case is a substitute for a full point. Why should it be? There is no other circumstance in English where one kind of punctuation substitutes for another one that has a distinctly different function. The comma does not indicate a particular tone of voice here – without any punctuation the reader knows it's a statement. I repeat, it's just a convention, and one so firmly entrenched that change is unlikely.

It is essential to retain the original punctuation within the quotation mark if it is an exclamation mark or question mark, because it represents the tone of voice:

> 'What will you do if, or should I say when, you get caught?' he asked.

WITH INTERNAL PUNCTUATION

When the speech or quotation is interrupted by the source, commas are used around the latter and thus are outside the quotation marks:

> 'You'll be pleased to know', she said, 'that there is an easy way to do this.'

> 'Outside every fat man', wrote Kingsley Amis, playing on a well-known phrase, 'there was an even fatter man trying to close in.'

In each case if you drop the source and its punctuation, the original sentence remains as originally punctuated. Following this logic, you can see that if the sentence quoted has its own internal punctuation, it will appear inside the quotation marks when interrupted by the speaker of the source:

> 'What will you do if,' he almost sneered, 'or should I say when, you get caught?'

> 'It is a fine thing to be honest,' Churchill wrote in reference to Baldwin, 'but it is also very important to be right.'

When you are uncertain about the original punctuation, ask the author to tell you how it appears in the source.

As with terminal punctuation, internal punctuation goes outside the quotation marks when the quoted text is not a complete sentence:

> The report criticized the action taken on the basis of 'weak intelligence',

'poor communication' between the agencies involved, and a 'failure of imagination'.

The ellipsis

Dot dot dot, you might say. Yes and no. The three dots are, in fact, a single character on the keyboard (you might find it at alt + ;). The ellipsis is used to indicate pauses in or the trailing off of speech or thought:

> I wonder … I wonder if … no …

and to indicate the omission of text in a quotation:

> In an article in *Impecunias* Gillian Thomson wrote 'Colleagues in the Justice Department are at present working on proposals for a draft bankruptcy and diligence bill … It is proposed that any changes to the Bankruptcy Act will not come into effect until the autumn of 2006.'

How much text has been omitted: a clause, an entire sentence, or the end of one sentence and the beginning of another? The position of the final full stop, if correct, means that there were at least two sentences in the original text (if you don't remember why, reread the text above about quotations introduced by 'that'). The capital letter after the ellipsis does not necessarily tell us that this is the beginning of a sentence, for it is acceptable to alter the capitalization for grammatical reasons. A full stop here

> diligence bill. … It is proposed that

tells readers that there is a complete sentence before the omission and that some subsequent text has been dropped, but even Sherlock Holmes couldn't work out how much. Although with the ellipsis closed up to the text like this

> diligence bill. …it is proposed that

readers can see that text has been omitted that includes the beginning of the second sentence, they still cannot know how much.

A full stop here

> diligence bill … . It is proposed that

would reveal that the first sentence was unfinished and nothing had been dropped from or before the second.

Grammar and punctuation 73

Confusing? Sure. And because it can be, coupled with the knowledge that authors might use anything from four dots upwards and not indicate whether the first or last of them is a meant as a full stop, very few organizations insist on a full stop with the ellipsis. Now, isn't that a relief! However, when authors make a clear distinction between an ellipsis and a full stop, keep the text as shown. Ask authors who use four or more undifferentiated dots which is the full stop; if they don't know, use only the ellipsis.

Exercise 2.4, focusing on hyphens, rules and quotation marks

Brief
This is an extract from a well-known story. As usual, skim the text, paying particular attention to how the different characters speak. Edit for spelling, consistency and, of course, for punctuation.

House style
- -ise verb endings
- spaced en rules for dashes
- single quotes and double quotes within

Close to the rude landing stage was a small brick house, with a
wooden placard slung out through the second window. Mordecai
Smith was printed across it in large letters and underneath Boats to
hire by the hour or day. A second inscription above the door
informed us that a steam launch was kept - a statement which was   5
confirmed by a great pile of coke upon the jetty. Sherlock Holmes
looked slowly round and his face assumed an ominous expression.
This looks bad, said he. These fellows are sharper than I expected.
They seem to have covered their tracks. There has, I fear, been
preconcerted management here.   10
He was approaching the door of the house, when it opened and a
little curly-headed lad of six came running out followed by a stoutish

red faced woman with a large sponge in her hand.

You come back and be washed, Jack she shouted. Come back you young imp, for if your father comes home and finds you like that, he'll let us hear of it.

Dear little chap! cried Holmes, strategically. What a rosy cheeked young rascal! Now, Jack, is there anything you would like?

The youth pondered for a moment.

I'd like a shillin' he said.

Nothing you would like better?

I'd like two shillin' better the prodigy answered after some thought.

Here you are then! Catch! — A fine child Mrs Smith!

Lor bless you, sir, he is that, and forward. He gets a'most too much for me to manage, 'specialy when my man is away days at a time.

Away, is he? said Holmes in a disappointed voice. I am sorry for that, for I wanted to speak to Mr Smith.

He's been away since yesterday morning, sir, and truth to tell, I am beginning to feel frightened about him. But if it was about a boat, sir maybe I could serve as well.

I wanted to hire his steam launch.

Why, bless you sir, it is in the steam launch that he has gone. That's what puzzles me, for I know there aint more coals in her than would take her to about Woolwich and back. If he'd been away in the barge I'd ha' thought nothin', for many a time a job has taken him as far as Gravesend, and if there was much doin' there he might ha' stayed over. But what good is a steam launch without coals?

He might have bought some at a wharf down the river

He might sir but it weren't his way. Many a time I've heard him call out at prices they charge for a few odd bags. Besides I don't like that wooden legged man, wi' his ugly face and outlandish talk. What did he want always knocking about here for?

A wooden legged man? Said Holmes, with bland surprise.

Yes, sir, a brown, monkey faced chap that's called more'n once for my old man. It was him that roused him up yesternight and, whats more, my man knew he was comin', for he had steam up in the launch. I tell you straight, sir, I don't feel easy in my mind about it.

But my dear Mrs Smith, said Holmes, shrugging his shoulders, you are frightening yourself about nothing. How could you possibly tell that it was the wooden legged man who came in the night? I don't quite understand how you can be so sure.

His voice, sir. I knew his voice, which is kind o thick and foggy. He tapped at the winder - about three it would be. Show a leg, matey, says he, time to turn out guard.

And was this wooden-legged man alone?

Couldn't say, I am sure, sir. I didn't here no one else.

I am sorry Mrs Smith for I wanted a steam launch and I have hear good reports of the - of the - let me see, what is her name?

The Aurora, sir.

Ah! She's not that old green launch with a yellow line, very broad in the beam?

No, indeed. She's as trim a little thing as on any river. She's been fresh painted, black with two red streaks.

From Sir Arthur Conan Doyle, *The Sign of Four*.

EXERCISE FOLLOW-UP

You should now be getting used to seeing the difference between hyphens, ens and ems. The ones in this exercise are straightforward. You could have made inserting the hyphen in 'wooden legged' a global change, as shown, whereas the other hyphens ('red-faced', 'rosy-cheeked', 'monkey-faced') had to be inserted individually. In line 23 the em dash should be replaced by an en dash. The speaker is not being interrupted, which would make an em dash appropriate; instead, he is turning his address quickly from one person to another. In line 58 the hyphens should be replaced by ellipses: the speaker is pausing, as if trying to remember the name.

The quotation marks are rather simple too. It is common to use them to identify signs, as in lines 2–3. You might have marked these for display instead, but that would place too much emphasis on them. The only place where double quotes are needed is in lines 53–4, and you needed to remember to use a closing single quote after the double.

Commas are needed to set off the person being spoken to from what is being said to them, as in line 14.

Did you pay attention to how the characters speak? Then you noticed that the syntax and pronunciation show that Sherlock Holmes is educated and Mrs Smith and Jack are not. Elementary, my dear reader. For consistency, you should have knocked the final letter off 'morning' (line 28), 'beginning' (line 29) and 'knocking' (line 42).

3 Cover to cover

All types of publication have some components in common. In this chapter we look at covers and styles of binding, explain the pages that precede and follow the text in a book, and show you how to create or check contents pages and running heads. Here you will learn what copyright is, how it is protected, the basic rules about using copyright material and how to obtain permission to do so. Even if you do not work, or plan to work, in book or journal publishing, having this basic knowledge will keep your options open for the future.

Covers and binding

The pages of a publication are bound or held between covers, which vary in form and content depending on the quality and price of the work and the market for which it is intended. Hardback, paperback, and limp or softback publications can be sewn, glued (perfect bound), wire-stitched, spiral- or comb-bound. Looseleaf is also considered a form of binding, although the pages are not bound to the covers.

Hardback covers

The front and back covers of a hardback, or cased, book are made of board (thick, stiff cardboard) and covered with a fabric (leather, cloth, imitation cloth) or paper (varnished or matt- or pvc-laminated) that joins them at the back, leaving sufficient space in between for the pages. This expanse of material between the covers is the spine. Hardback picture books for children, which typically have printed-paper board covers and 'pages', are referred to as board books.

When a book is fabric-covered, the back is usually blank and the volume has a jacket (see below). The front might be blank or carry the title of the work, the full names of the authors, the number of the edition if other than the first, and the publisher's name and colophon (graphic icon, like Penguin's penguin in the oval) or logo (icon including letters, such as Faber & Faber's 'ff'). The spine usually shows the authors' surnames at the top, the title of the work and the number of the edition other than the first, and the publisher's name and/or colophon or logo at the bottom. Printed-paper covers (PPC) will carry this same information on the front and spine, and might include 'In association with . . .' and that organization's logo or colophon on the front if the book is sponsored. They can be illustrated, and the back usually carries sales blurb in addition to the International Standard Book Number (ISBN – you know better than to say 'ISBN number').

JACKETS

A hardback might have a removable paper jacket, which can duplicate the design of the cover or be more elaborate. Originally, a jacket was intended only to protect the cover – it is sometimes still referred to as a 'dust jacket' – but now it is also a major sales tool. The front and spine contain the same information as the cover, but the design and typography are often different, as their purpose is not merely to identify the work but to attract the attention of potential readers. The front might announce the author of the foreword or that the book has been shortlisted for or won a prize, or that it is by the author of another well-known or best-selling title.

The flaps, which hold the jacket around the cover, carry blurb about the book and may include a brief biography of the author, a recommended selling price, and credits for the design and for illustrations on the front and back unless this information is placed on the back of the jacket.

The back might be illustrated too, will list major selling points or extracts of reviews for this work or for previous works by the same author, and will carry a barcode incorporating the ISBN.

Paperback, trade paperback and softback covers

A publication of any format (trimmed page size) may be bound between soft covers. Books that are 180 × 110 mm are called paperbacks; those that are 198 × 128 mm are called B format or trade paperbacks; and all other formats are described as limp bound or softback. They all have printed, flexible card covers, which can be varnished or laminated and have other special finishes, such as foil-embossed lettering. The front, back and spine, if it is wide enough, carry the same information as a jacket, and some soft covers even have flaps.

The front cover of a journal states the journal title and the volume and/or issue number or date. If the journal has an International Standard Serial Number (ISSN), it will appear in the upper right-hand corner. (Not all journals have an ISSN, as it does not have the same stock-control and retail imperatives as an ISBN does for books – no shop will stock a book without an ISBN.) The front cover might indicate the price, the titles of the articles and the names of authors, and it might be illustrated, but it will not carry the name of the publisher.

The spine states the title of the journal and the volume and/or issue number or date. The back cover can have information about the contents of the present issue or might refer to the contents of forthcoming issues, acknowledge the source of illustrations on the front or back, and state the price if that is not on the front.

Binding

A small proportion of hardback books still have a sewn binding. The individual printed sections of the book (signatures) are sewn through the spine, gathered in the correct sequence (collated) and sewn together at the back, forming a 'block'. A paper or gauze 'liner' is glued to the spine, and endpapers are glued to the first and last signatures 3 mm deep down the spine edge. The block is trimmed to the final page size at the head, foot and foredge. It is then placed between the covers, to which the endpapers are glued; it is not attached to the spine of the cover. Have a look at some hardback books to identify these elements.

Most paperbacks, journals, magazines and hardbacks are now perfect bound. The signatures are gathered, and trimmed and roughened at the spine to help hold the glue. The roughened edges are glued to a strip of gauze, which is then glued to the spine of the cover. The covered publication is then trimmed at the top, foot and foredge.

Brochures, magazines, and some limp-bound books of a single signature may be stapled, or wire-stitched, down the gutter to the spine of the cover (saddle-stitched). The spine is usually too narrow to carry any printed information. Limp-bound publications of more than one signature can be wire-stitched down the side about 6 mm in from the spine (side- or stab-stitching).

Spiral- and comb-bound books have front and back laminated-paper board covers, which carry the same information as front and back jackets. The gathered signatures are trimmed on the spine edge as well as on the margins, so that the block is, in fact, a stack of individual sheets. The spine margin is punctured with a series of holes, through which a plastic-coated wire spiral, or a series of slits, through which the flat teeth of a plastic band, or comb, slot. In both types of binding the individual sheets can be opened flat.

Looseleaf binding is used for publications that need to have parts updated regularly or are delivered to the readers in sections. The pages are printed individually, not as signatures. They are punched with holes corresponding to the rings in the binders being supplied, and bound with a narrow paper wrapper. The binders have printed-paper board covers, often with a pvc or plastic lamination. The front cover and spine will carry the same information as a jacket. Although the work might have an ISBN or an ISSN, it is not carried on the cover because the pages and the cover are not bound together.

In the beginning

'Prelims' is an abbreviation for 'preliminary pages', the pages that precede the main text and are also called 'front matter'. In a journal this is usually the masthead, which lists the staff, with their contact details; basic copyright notices; volume and/or issue number. It may include details for submission of articles, subscription information and other information about the journal, and a contents list. These items can occupy the same page or several pages.

Books tend to have more extensive prelims. What follows is neither a minimal nor an exhaustive list. It covers the most commonly used features, but which of them are included in the prelims in a particular publication depends on its level and intended market. They are presented here in the order in which they usually appear. They may be put in a different order or combined to save pages to fit an even working.

In books other than children's books and schoolbooks, the prelim pages are usually numbered in lower-case roman numerals. Although the numbering begins with the first printed page, no page numbers (folios) appear before the contents page or on any following page that has a chapter-weight heading. All pages are included in the numbering sequence whether or not a folio appears on them.

In journals the pages are usually numbered consecutively within volumes; for example, issue 1, pages 1–240; issue 2, pages 241–480.

Half-title

This is the first printed page in many books and is always a recto. In hardbacks and some paperbacks it states only the title of the work – not the subtitle, author or publisher. Why do we bother, you might ask; we put that information and more on the title page. Here's the story. When the printers and binders were in separate locations, the printer would stick a piece of paper on top of the gathered signatures to ensure that the binder put them into the correct covers. Often these pieces of paper were bound with the rest of the book, and so the convention of the half-title evolved. Because the half-title is not essential and because paper is a very expensive component of a book, the half-title is omitted from price-sensitive publications, such as children's books and schoolbooks. In paperbacks the half-title is now often used for biographical information about the author, which would have appeared on the flaps of a jacket, saving the back cover for blurb.

When you are marking up this page, check that nothing other than the main title appears and write '1/2 title, p. i' in red and circle it so that the instruction does not get typeset. If you are marking up on screen, put the information between angle brackets and inform the typesetter that information represented in this way is for identification only.

Half-title verso

It used to be common to put an illustration – the frontispiece – on the reverse side of the half-title, but it is relatively rare now. There is no information that must appear on this page, and it can be left blank. When a page is to be blank, put its number and 'blank' on the blank page, in red and circled on hard copy, and between angle brackets on an e-file, to ensure that this information does not get typeset.

The marketing department might sigh, groan or weep if this is all you do. It would prefer to see this otherwise wasted space used to help promote sales. It's a good place, for example, to list other titles by the author or other titles in the series, or the names of esteemed contributors or consultants.

Title page

The minimum information on this page is the title, the name of the author – 'by' is unnecessary – or literary or general editor and the name of the publisher. Stating the city of publication or cities in which the publisher has offices is common but optional. Here are other items to be included when relevant:

- Series title
- Subtitle
- The name of the translator of a literary work; the usual phrasing is 'Translated from the [language] by [name]'
- The number of the edition if other than the first; a second edition might be called 'revised edition', but the next edition will be called the third
- The name of an illustrator; this occurs when the illustrator is famous or, as in many children's board books, is as important to the work as the writer, in which case credit on the title page will be stipulated in the illustrator's contract
- The name of the author of the foreword
- The volume number
- The publisher's colophon or logo
- 'In association with …' if the book is sponsored

Mark this page 'title, p. iii', in red and circled on hard copy, between angle brackets on an e-file.

Imprint page

The imprint page is also called the biblio (short for 'bibliographic') page, because it carries the printing history of the book. Publishers usually have a template for the imprint page that lists all the standard information, but you still need to know what to do when the information required is more than the bare minimum. Don't try to rearrange the information already on the template, as that will be the publisher's preferred style. In books, you are expected to check that all the essential elements have been included, to fill in the template with the information that you have and to query your project manager about missing elements or information.

The imprint information for journals does not alter from issue to issue, so you usually do not have to do anything to it, except perhaps alter the issue number if it is given there.

The imprint page is usually the title-page verso in book publishing in English-speaking countries. When that is the case, mark it 'imprint, p. iv' in red and circled on hard copy, and between angle brackets on an e-file. However, some publishers in English-speaking countries, and many in other countries, put this information at the very end of the book; and journals and magazines include the relevant parts of it in the masthead on the contents page. Wherever the information comes, it is the most important in the publication – even, or especially, if the text contains something as important as the cure for the common cold. Can you think why? Well, let's see what's included.

PUBLICATION HISTORY OF A BOOK

Publishers can put the information in any order they like; what follows is just one way of doing it.

There is a statement of the publication of the present edition. The usual wording is

First published in [country] in [year] by [imprint/publisher]

although 'first' is optional. This is followed by the full registered address of the publisher – the street and number, the town or city, and the postcode. Many publishers also include their website address. This information is followed by, if relevant,

- a statement of publication of a simultaneous co-edition, giving the same information about the other publisher, i.e.

  First published in [another country] in [year] by [publisher],[city or town]

  but not the street address or postcode;
- a statement of previous publishing history, which might be a reference to the title's publication in part or in whole in the same language, starting with the most recent date and working back. For example, it might say

  Chapters 2 and 3 first appeared as articles in [X journal or magazine] in [year(s)]

  and a paperback might state

  Originally published in hardback in [country] in [year] by [other publisher] or give the name of the imprint if the hardback and paperback imprints belong to the same group;

and a translation would explain

First published in [language] as [foreign title] by [publisher] in [year].

Reprint information usually follows, although, like the remaining information, it can be positioned anywhere on the page. It might be a list of the relevant years or a line of numbers from 1 to 10, which are deleted in ascending order to signify a reprint.

COPYRIGHT NOTICE

Copyright notices inform people that the right to use the material identified is protected by law. Therefore they should identify all the owners of copyright material in the publication – such as text, illustrations and index – and state the year of publication. The form required by the Universal Copyright Convention, one of the two main copyright organizations to which most of the countries in the world belong, is '© year, owner'. Many publishers use '© owner, year' (the commas are optional) because it is then easier to add another year to cover new material in subsequent editions: '© A.N. Owner, 2004, 2006'. Copyright, explained in greater detail below, is what makes the page on which the notice appears the most important in the work.

The 'All rights reserved' clause, which might be this brief or longer to make the meaning of the phrase explicit, indicates that no part of the publication can be reproduced without written permission, usually from the publisher but sometimes from the author(s) and the publisher.

MORAL RIGHTS

British and European copyright laws incorporate four moral rights. The first one is the right to be identified as the author of a work that is covered by copyright whether or not the individual still owns the copyright. So, since 1 August 1989, when the Copyright, Designs and Patents Act 1988 came into effect, the authors of text, artwork, photographs or indexes, for example, have retained the right to be acknowledged on the work and at any mention of the work even if they have sold their copyright. All they have to do is assert this right in writing. Most publishing contracts make this assertion for authors, and editors have only to complete the statement on the imprint page appropriately. It usually reads something like this:

> The moral right of [name as on title page] to be identified as the author of this work has been asserted in accordance with the Copyright, Designs and Patents Act 1988.

The other moral rights will be discussed below.

AGENCY NOTICE

Plays and books of music carry a notice of the agency to which to apply for permission to perform the work publicly. People don't need permission to perform songs or even act plays in the privacy of their own home, but do need permission to do so in public if the work is still in copyright.

CIP AND STANDARD NUMBERS

Many countries require that a copy of every book published there is sent to the national library. Thus a copy of every book published in the United Kingdom must be deposited with the British Library. Information about the work is provided to the library in advance of publication so that it can provide, in return, the Cataloguing in Publication Data (CIP). In Britain, when publishers choose not to print the full CIP – it is of interest to a minority of readers, and sometimes there isn't space on the page – they print a statement that a CIP record is available from the British Library. However, they must always print the ISBN, which is part of CIP. Every book published for retail sale carries an ISBN.

The ISBN identifies a specific edition of a book. From its inception in 1967 until 1 January 2007, the ISBN had ten digits, arranged in various groupings separated by hyphens, which are required as part of the standard established by the International Organization for Standardization (ISO):

0-907706-??-?

The first part, from one to five digits long, is the group identifier – the language, geographical or national area in which the work was published. British and many other English-language publishers are in groups 0 and 1. The next group, of between one and seven numbers long, identifies the publisher. The third group, of one to six digits (determined by the number of preceding digits), is the title identifier, which is specific to that title from that publisher in a particular format and edition. Thus different numbers will be given to the same title published in hardback and paperback, and to the abridged edition, the large-print edition, the revised edition and for every new edition thereafter. The last part, which is always a single digit (0–9 and X for 10), is called the check digit, because it is calculated to check that all the preceding numbers are correct.

When it became apparent that the numbers would run out, a new standard of 13 digits was devised, and had to be used after 1 January 2007. Publishers who still had 10-digit numbers could add the prefix 978, but when all the 10-digit numbers run out, all ISBNs will be prefixed 979. Too much to remember? Well, don't worry. The numbers are given to you. Your job is to ensure that the appropriate ISBN appears on the imprint page and that the same number appears on the back cover or jacket of the publication and any other relevant documentation for which you are responsible.

ISSNs are used by periodicals, in print and online. The eight digits are arranged in two groups of four, separated by a hyphen. The eighth numeral (0–9 and X for 10) is the check digit. The ISSN identifies the title of the periodical, not the publisher or country of publication.

ISMNs are used for printed music. The form is the letter M followed by nine digits, the last of which is the check digit. The first eight numbers are the publisher identifier and the item identifier; the number of digits for each is variable.

CREDITS

In books printed and published in Britain the name and address of the printer must be stated on the imprint page, but the name and address of the typesetter are optional. Most publications carry the information about all relevant suppliers, for whom this is useful free advertising. While only some book publishers credit all the individuals who have worked on the volume, this is common practice in periodicals.

Financial assistance or sponsorship for a publication is acknowledged on the imprint page. The wording of the acknowledgement is often specified by the awarding body or sponsoring organization and may include a colophon or logo.

Some publishers also state the typeface and size, and provide information about the composition of the paper.

CONDITIONS OF SALE

This standard paragraph appears in some books, particularly paperbacks, and prohibits alterations to the binding or cover.

Exercise 3.1, compiling basic prelims

Brief
Use the information below to compile the prelims from half-title to imprint page. You might find it useful to make yourself a checklist of items to be included on each page.

Bitter Lemon Press, which has established itself in London's fashionable Notting Hill district at 37 Arundel Gardens, W11 2LW, publishes literature, and particularly crime novels, in translation. Among the works it has brought to English-speaking audiences is Friedrich Glauser's first Sergeant Studer mystery. Originally serialized as *'Wachtmeister Studer'* in the journal *Zürcher Illustrierte* in 1936, just two years before Glauser's death, it was published in book form as *Schlumpf Erwin, Mord (Wachtmeister Studer)* 59 years later by the Zurich-based publisher Limmat Verlag, which owns the copyright. Called *Thumbprint* in English, the translation of this German cult masterpiece by Mike Mitchell received the financial assistance of Pro Helvetica, the Arts Council of Switzerland, and was published in 2004. Continuing the international flavour, the book was printed and bound by W S Bookwell of Finland, although the typesetting was done by RefineCatch Limited of Bungay in Suffolk. You can order *Thumbprint* from your local bookshop by citing ISBN 1 904738 00 1. Other titles under the distinctive Bitter Lemon logo include *Holy Smoke* by Tonino Benacquista, *The Russian Passenger* by Günter Ohnemus, Rolo Diez's *Tequila Blue*, *Goat Song* by Chantal Pelletier, and *The Snowman* by Jörg Fauser. You can read summaries of these titles and keep up to date with the complete list at www.bitterlemonpress.com.

EXERCISE FOLLOW-UP

The half-title, its verso and the title page were really straightforward; the only item you had to think about adding was the logo.

On the imprint page you had to give the publication history in the right order, acknowledge the source of financial aid, and show the copyright for the German edition and the English translation. Stating 'All rights reserved' is sufficient, but good for you if you included a longer version. Mike Mitchell is the only person entitled to assert his moral right, because Friedrich Glauser died long before the Act came into effect. There was no CIP data, so you needed to say that a record was available from the British Library. You had to add the hyphens to the ISBN because they are required by the ISO standard.

Dedication

Dedications can be included in any type of book but are rarely found in schoolbooks, or in dictionaries, encyclopedias and similar reference works of multiple authorship. Ideally, dedications are on a recto, so the manuscript page would be marked 'dedication, new recto' in red and circled on hard copy, between angle brackets on an e-file. Sometimes, however, when it is necessary to save space to fit the book into an even working, a dedication is squeezed on to the imprint page or even on to the half-title verso to make better use of a blank page, in which case, mark it up accordingly.

Epigraph

The epigraph was explained in Chapter 1, so you might want to review that text. The point here is that the epigraph for a book is usually on a new recto. The mark up would be 'epigraph, new recto' in red and circled on hard copy, between angle brackets on an e-file. To save space, the epigraph might be placed on the same page with the dedication, and both might be placed on the verso facing the first page of text.

Contents

You may have to create, and will certainly have to check, the contents pages for journals and books. Although we often say 'contents page' or 'table of contents', the only heading this page should have is 'Contents'. Like other prelim and endmatter headings, it is not a chapter as such but its heading is marked up and treated as one: it is a chapter-weight heading. The Contents lists everything that follows it that has a chapter-weight heading, from the remaining prelims to the final element in the endmatter. The only exception in books is that the Contents will list the frontispiece if there is one but there is no list of illustrations. The usual way is to state the title on the left and 'frontispiece' in place of a page reference.

In books the Contents may list only part titles and chapter-weight headings with their page references, or may include A (and other) heads, with or without page references. If there is no house or series style, decide whether including these headings is appropriate to the length and complexity of the book and is helpful to the target reader. Contents pages in multi-contributor books may also include authors with or without their affiliations under the relevant chapter titles.

The titles in a book may be prefixed by the words 'Part' and 'Chapter' and by a number. The words can be dropped in the Contents or they can be repeated for every part and chapter; the numbers must always appear, and they must be in the same form as inside the work: as a word, roman numeral or arabic numeral. When a book has both numbered parts and chapters, the numbering style of each must be different to help the reader distinguish between them, e.g., Part I, Chapter 1, Part 1, Chapter One, or Part One, Chapter 1. Books that have only chapter numbers, not titles, do not have a contents page. In all publications the wording, spelling, punctuation, and capitalization of proper nouns of the titles should be identical to that within the work, but the styling can be different; for example, the title can be roman inside the work and italic in the Contents, or small caps in the Contents and initial and proper-noun caps only inside the work.

Some journals are divided into parts when they have a significant number of items of different kinds. Then the Contents lists the article titles, their authors and their academic or professional qualifications or affiliations in sequence under the relevant headings, such as 'News', 'Features' and 'Regulars'. Some journals do not use category headings in the main body of the text but gather the entries under appropriate category headings in the list of contents. Then the sequence is relative to each heading, and articles unique to an issue usually precede regular features. Other journals simply list their contents in order of appearance without part or category headings.

Creating or checking a contents page is a useful way to check that the headings within the publication are consistent in spelling, punctuation, and capitalization too. Here's how to streamline your work: in books, first check just the numbering of the parts, if relevant, and then the numbering of the chapters on their opening pages: are they all there, no numbers repeated or omitted? Check for consistency of use of the word 'chapter' and the way numbers are presented. In all publications you will have checked the spelling of the chapter or article titles when you were editing, so now check that the spelling is consistent between them (-ise or -ize verbs, etc.). Check again for capitalization. And once more for punctuation. Breaking the job down into separate tasks like this helps maximize accuracy and speed.

It is easy to create a contents page: just copy the information from the text in the correct order. Leave it for a day or so, then check it and mark it up as you would if it had been supplied by the author. Break down the checking into discrete tasks too. First read it and correct obvious errors in spelling and capitalization. Check that the part numbers, if relevant, are consistent and consecutive. Then do the same for the chapter numbers. Now proofread the titles on the contents page, in order, against those in the text. In journals, also proofread the information about the contributors. Check that all expected prelims and endmatter appear in the Contents even if they have not been created yet: for example, the index won't be created until the page proofs are available but it should be listed in the Contents. This is often when copy-editors realize that there is something missing – in books, perhaps the preface or acknowledgements, or perhaps the foreword because it doesn't come from the author; in journals, the copy for a regular feature such as the book reviews.

Next, mark up the page. 'Contents' is a chapter-weight heading, so code it 'CH'. When publications have only chapter-weight heads, you don't need to code them in the Contents. Otherwise, use codes to show the hierarchy; for example, code part titles CA (Contents A head) and chapter-weight titles CB, and decide whether or not to use the word 'Chapter'. Then code the next level – perhaps author attributions or chapter A heads – CC.

Now attend to the page references. The numbers are those of the first page of the item listed. They can precede the headings, as is often the case in magazines and journals, or follow them, as is the usual practice in books. You don't know the page references when you send an edited text for typesetting, so you mark them all '00'. Unpaginated sections of illustrations are listed in the Contents as 'between pages 00 and 00'. If the author has supplied a contents page referenced to the manuscript pages, circle those numbers and mark 'do not set', and write the 00s next to them on the hard copy. The 00s remind the proofreader to insert the page numbers at first proof, and having the manuscript numbers can make it easier to check information. When you work on e-files, you can keep a copy of the contents page before replacing the numbers with 00s. Nowadays some typesetters will program their computers to complete the numbers on the contents page. However, this is not a foolproof method: on one of my projects the typesetter, for reasons he could not explain even to himself, began numbering Chapter 19 seven pages before the end of Chapter 18. Definitely a White Rabbit day. If this mistake had not been caught, it would have been reflected in the Contents too, so it is always essential to check.

Finally, mark the first page 'new recto', with the page number if you know it, in red and circled on hard copy, between angle brackets on an e-file. The following prelim pages do not have to begin on new rectos, so on hard copy mark them for setting as new pages; on an e-file ensure that they are new pages.

Lists of illustrative material

When a publication contains many photographs, maps, tables or diagrams that readers might want to refer to independently of the text, they are listed under the relevant heading, which is marked up as a chapter heading and does not include the words 'list of'. Although shortened versions of the captions or table headings are acceptable, make sure that they are otherwise consistent in numbering, wording, spelling, punctuation, and capitalization of proper nouns with those in the text. Acknowledgement of permission to reproduce copyright material is often included here too.

There is no rule about where in the prelims such lists should be placed, nor in what order if there are several of them. Decide what is most helpful to the reader, and make sure that the order is the same in all volumes in a series.

List of contributors

In works where the many authors have not contributed individual chapters, such as dictionaries and encyclopedias, they are listed here in alphabetical order, usually with their academic or professional qualifications or affiliations, and sometimes with brief biographies.

When authors have contributed individual chapters, their names appear below the chapter title. However, their qualifications, affiliations and, if desired, brief biographies are presented here rather than with the chapters or in the list of contents.

Foreword

The foreword is by someone other, and better known, than the author(s) of the book. Its purpose is to praise the author(s) and the work, and by so doing enhance the credibility of the former and increase the sales of the latter. A foreword writer's name can appear under the heading or at the end, and usually appears on the cover, jacket, title page and contents page.

Preface

Written by the author of a non-fiction book, the preface might explain the nature or perspective of the work, why the author wrote it or the experiences he or she has undergone in researching and writing it, what is or isn't included and why, and how the reader might approach it. Novelists aside, it is exceedingly rare for a person to produce a text completely single-handedly, so the preface might also include the names of organizations, colleagues, friends and relatives the author wants to thank for their help if there is not a separate acknowledgements section. Do not scoff at authors who are grateful to their family or even their pets for supporting them; writing for publication can be an ordeal. Sometimes authors even thank their copy-editors and proofreaders here, or in the Acknowledgements.

Sometimes, particularly in reference books and manuals, this page is replaced by notes on how to use the book.

Acknowledgements

This is where authors thank individuals and organizations for their help and support if they haven't done so in the preface. Schoolbooks and children's books often do not include such acknowledgements, but in other cases when authors haven't provided any, you can ask them if they want to; it would be awful for them to realize too late that they have missed this opportunity.

Acknowledgements of permission to use copyright material can follow the personal ones, separated by a line space, or be the only information under this heading, or can appear instead in the notes and references to the text. Acknowledgements for permission to use photos can appear in a list of illustrations or, as is common practice for integrated illustrated works, at the very end of the book – yes, after the index – under the chapter-weight heading 'Picture Credits'. In publications other than books it is usual to acknowledge the source of illustrations in the captions or under or at the side of the images.

Tables

Don't be confused. These 'tables' are particular to law books and refer to the indexes of cases, legislation, statutes and similar legal instruments that are cited in the text. The people who collate them are often referred to as tablers rather than indexers.

Chronology, genealogical diagrams, list of abbreviations

These headings are self-explanatory. The point is that they go close to the text to make it easy for readers to refer to them.

Introduction

When the introduction is not intended as part of the main text, it is included in the prelim page numbering. When it is part of the main text, it is numbered accordingly (see below). There is no law that an introduction has to carry a chapter number, although the heading is marked up as a chapter; and although 'Introduction' is an accurate descriptive title, you might be able to help an author find a more interesting one.

The body of the book

The main text of most books starts on a recto, is the beginning of the use of arabic numerals for the page numbers (folios), and should be clearly marked for the typesetter. The exceptions are spread-by-spread books, in which each pair of facing pages (a double-page spread) is a complete unit or chapter. Such books are usually for children and have few prelims, so the numbering is in arabic numerals from the beginning.

As you saw in Chapter 1, books may be divided into parts, which can also be called 'books' or 'volumes' when separate publications are brought together in a single publication. The numbering can be in words or roman numerals, and should be a different form from the chapter numbering. Where space permits, part titles are on a recto and usually have a blank or illustrated verso. Although they are counted in the pagination, these pages do not carry folios. Where there isn't enough space, part titles are placed above the title of the first chapter of the part, with ample space between the two.

The chapter numbering is consecutive throughout the work – it does not start from 1 for each part. Roman numerals are rarely used for chapters; even in academic books they seem pretentious. Chapters can have numbers and titles, but in many books they have only numbers or only titles, and in some novels they have neither. The first chapter usually starts on a recto, but space will determine whether subsequent chapters do too. If each chapter must start on a recto, mark it 'new recto' in red and circled on hard copy, and between angle brackets above the chapter title in an e-file. Otherwise, mark it 'new page' on hard copy and ensure it is a new page on an e-file.

Each chapter can begin with an epigraph, and when some do, then all should. To maintain the structural consistency of works, ask authors to provide epigraphs for any chapters that do not have them, and check that each one acknowledges the author and title.

Endmatter

Please laugh at anybody who calls them 'endlims'. 'Endmatter' refers to everything that comes after the main text, the order of which is determined by the relationship with the text.

Appendices

When there is only one, use 'Appendix' before the title, and mark them up together as a chapter-weight heading. Where there is more than one appendix and the text itself is divided into parts, create a part title, and number or letter each appendix. Where there is more than one appendix and part titles are *not* used in the book, you can – but do not have to – list only the number or letter and title of each one on the contents page under a heading 'Appendices' or 'Appendixes', according to house style, to avoid repeating 'Appendix' each time.

Glossary

Check that the spelling and definitions in a glossary are consistent with the information in the text. Mark down the page reference for each definition as you copy-edit the text, then check the spellings and definitions as a separate task.

When you have blank pages at the end of a non-fiction book for children, a glossary is a relatively inexpensive way to use them and enhance the quality of the publication.

Notes and references

In Chapter 7 you will learn about the different ways of presenting editorial comments and citing references to quoted matter, but here you need to know that both can be printed as footnotes on the relevant page, collected at the end of chapters or gathered at the back of the book; in the last case they are listed on the contents page.

Bibliography and further reading list

'Bibliography' is always more specific than just a list of books: it can be a list of books by a particular author or on a particular subject or of a particular type. A bibliography in a book is the list of the sources the author consulted in writing his or her own work, and is to be expected in most works of non-fiction, but particularly where there are notes and references.

The author is recommending the titles on a further reading list but may not have used them as reference material. This is commonly the case in schoolbooks and other books for children, and many non-academic books for the general adult market. These lists can be placed at the end of chapters or at the end of the book, grouped under chapter headings or not. Further reading lists can be organized alphabetically by author, in which case the names are listed surname first. Otherwise the books can be presented in order of importance, in which case the authors' names are not inverted.

Index

There can be more than one index in a book – for example, a subject index and a name index – and they must all be listed in the Contents. If there are several indexes and the book has part titles, create a part title for the indexes and reflect this on the contents page.

Exercise 3.2, creating contents pages

Brief
Below are descriptions of three publications and information about the contents. Bearing in mind the subject matter and the level of readership, create and mark up the Contents for each publication, checking spelling, imposing consistency, and, for the book only, adding any prelims or endmatter that you think would be appropriate and expected.

---

1 *Geriatric Medicine*, which uses its GM logo predominantly, is a monthly peer-reviewed journal for clinicians practising geriatric

medicine. In every issue, in an introductory section called Commentary, there is an article by the editor, Alison Boyle. In the current issue, for August 20—, the article is 'A new era for statin use in CHD prevention'. The other regular features, at the back of the journal, are 'Writing for Publication in GM', a page setting out in detail how to prepare, present and submit articles; and 'Advance Reports', short articles previewing the results of reports that will be treated in depth at a later date. There are four other articles for the current issue. 'The social theories of ageing' is by joint authors Dr A.B. Michael, a Specialist Registrar in Geriatric Medicine at Queen's Hospital in Burton on Trent, and Dr B. Rowe, who is a Senior Lecturer in Social Gerontology at the University of Keele in the Department of Geriatric Medicine. Julie Hutton works at Ramyard Dowe House, in Blackheath, London. The Nursing Sister there, she has contributed 'The Role Of Catheter Valves In Urinary Incontinence'. The author of 'CVD and the GMS contract' is Dr George Kassianos, who is a General Practitioner in Bracknell Forest, Berkshire. Dr Christopher Beer, a Senior Lecturer at the University Department of Geriatric Medicine, Perth, has written 'The Challenge of Medical Management in PD'.

2 *Birds*, the journal of the Royal Society for the Protection of Birds, is published quarterly and supplied free to the society's members. The hard copy for the Spring 20— issue has been organized in two piles. The headings of the items that appear in every issue are 'the RSPB view', 'Mailbox', 'The news', 'Learning about Birds', 'Enjoying

your wildlife garden', 'Action pages', 'birdbox', 'Classified Adds' and 'RSPB PEOPLE'. There are five special articles featured in this issue. 'Members weekend' highlights an opportunity for members to enjoy a weekend in York, where they can learn more about birds and the RSPB. Mike Shrubb, who, by virtue of being an ornithologist and farmer, is ideally placed to reflect on how agricultural alterations have affected British wildlife, does just that in 'Birds and Combines'. As part of a year-long celebration of the society's working for wildlife in Scotland, Rob Hume visited Frosinard and reports the results in 'Priceless Peatlands'. 'Beating a retreat', by Andre Farrar, leader of the society's conservation team at The Lodge, expresses his worry that snipe, lapwings and redshanks are declining in the countryside. Artist Dafila Scott, who won the RSPB Award in the show, comments on her favourite pictures in the Society of Wildlife Artist's Exhibition in 'Bird Art At The SWLA'.

3 *Exploring the Weather* is a book for children 10 to 12 years old. Each chapter is divided evenly between text and illustrations, both photographic and drawn. The author has typed the chapter titles as 'The Global Circulation', 'The Atmosphere', 'Oceans, currants and Climates', 'Weather on the move', 'Jet streams', 'Climates', 'Seasons', 'Daily Whether', 'Extreme Conditions', 'Energy From The Weather', 'Measuring the weather', 'Who uses Forecasts?', 'Weather Lore', Weather and our bodies', 'Climate and Cops', 'Are We Changing the Weather', 'The Future of Forcasting'.

EXERCISE FOLLOW-UP

The first journal is for a professional readership, so the credentials of the authors should be shown with the titles of their articles. These needed to be edited to make them concise and consistent in order. There are only three regular features, so on the Contents it is appropriate to place them in the order of appearance indicated, not divide them into parts. The titles of the two items at the end are self-explanatory and not attributed to an author, so do not require any copy under the titles. Marking the titles as CA and the authors as CB makes it easy for the typesetter to impose the relevant styling without having to read a word.

The second journal is for a general readership, and has a large enough number of regular features to divide the Contents into parts. You might have chosen different part titles, which is fine as long as they clearly identified the two types of material, and you needed to correct a few spelling or typing errors. The blurbs about the author and the article under each title are used to attract the readers' attention and inform their choice of which articles to read and in what order. You needed to make these consistent in style as well as short and informative. The mark-up reflects the extra tier in the structure.

In both cases the titles are presented with initial and proper-noun caps only, which is how they are likely to remain in the professional journal; it is always the way to mark titles when you do not know the specific style that will be applied. It does not matter whether you put the 00s for the page references before or after the titles, as long as you put them in consistently in each journal.

The author of the book on weather seems to need help with spelling; a Contents supplied by an author can inform you of some of the issues you will need to deal with in the text. After correcting the spelling and punctuation, and showing the titles consistently with initial caps, which is usual in children's books, you needed to think what other items might be in the text. As it is a book for children, neither a foreword nor a preface is likely, but an introduction is a possibility. Similarly, appendices and a bibliography are not expected at this level, but a glossary and further reading list would be appropriate. An index and picture credits are required. Because there is no differentiation in the chapter titles and no subsidiary information, the only mark-up is for 'Contents', a chapter-weight heading.

Running heads

These headings get their name because they usually appear throughout a publication in the head margins. They can remind readers what they are perusing – for example, when they resume reading after a long break – or be used to help them locate a particular part of a publication. When they are placed in the foot margins, as they are in some journals and books, they are called 'running feet' – a good enough reason not to call this part of the page the bottom. They can also be designed to run down the foredge margins. The folios can appear with the running heads or separately.

Books

In general non-fiction books, decide what kind of running heads will be most useful to the readers. The most common variations are:

verso	*recto*
book title	chapter title
part title	chapter title
chapter title	most recent A head
contributor's name	chapter or article title

In dictionaries and encyclopedias that have a single-column grid the verso running head is the first new entry on that page, and the recto running head is the last entry on that page. However, most such reference works are on a two-column grid, and then on each page the running head over the left column is the first entry on the page and the running head over the right column is the last entry on the page.

Running heads do not appear in prelims before the contents page. After that they are usually the chapter-weight heading on both versos and rectos: for example, 'Contents', 'Foreword'. Although 'List of' does not appear in the titles of lists in the prelims, it has to be used in their running heads: for example, 'List of Contributors'. The same pattern is followed in the endmatter for a single appendix, a glossary, bibliography and index. If there is more than one appendix and each is lettered or numbered and titled, 'Appendix X' goes on the verso and the title on the recto. The most precise, and therefore most helpful, running heads for notes at the end of a book state the pages to which they refer: for example, 'Notes to pages 75–76'. However, this can usually be completed only at proof stage, and can be time-consuming and expensive, so the alternative is to state the relevant chapter number(s): 'Notes to Chapter X'.

Fiction often follows the pattern of book title on the versos and chapter or story title (in collections of short stories) on the rectos. Novels in which the chapters do not have titles can use the book title as the running heads on both versos and rectos, or can dispense with running heads; it is usually safe to assume that people reading a novel know what it is called.

In all books running heads do not appear on

- prelims preceding the Contents
- part titles
- chapter openers (the first text page of a chapter) or pages with chapter-weight headings
- turned pages (typically, a portrait page on which matter has been printed landscape, so you have to turn the page 90° to see it)
- blank pages
- pages where tables or illustrations extend into the relevant margin

Journals

In journals the running heads may be, in relevant sections,

verso	*recto*
journal title, volume, issue or date	regular feature title
author and article title	author and article title

Some journals, including *The Bookseller*, the weekly journal of the British book trade, make their feature or article titles the running heads and the journal title and date running feet.

Length

Some titles are too long to fit in the margin as running heads or feet. If you do not have sample pages or a design specification, ask the designer or typesetter how many characters are allowed for the running heads.

When you have to shorten the titles, retain the words that convey the essence of the subject. An opening definite or indefinite article can usually be sacrificed. Sometimes dropping a phrase after a conjunction does the job; at other times it might be best to omit an initial prepositional phrase. For example, in a book on law these chapter headings:

> Duties of the Buyer and Remedies of the Seller for Misrepresentation or Breach
>
> The Characteristics and Organization of International Sales Transactions

were abbreviated to these running heads:

> Duties of the Buyer and Remedies of the Seller
> International Sales Transactions

Always send the abbreviated titles to the authors for confirmation or amendment before sending them for setting.

Marking up

You need to tell the typesetter what the running heads will be. When the titles are to be used in full, you can usually state the title levels for the pages: for example, 'versos, part title; rectos, chapter title'. Check with production or the typesetter first, however: the typesetter might need a full list to be supplied if the running heads are not going to be generated by the computer typesetting program. When the titles are to be abbreviated, you need to add a list of all the titles, not only the abbreviated ones.

Exercise 3.3, determining running heads and feet

> Brief
> Use the information in Exercise 3.2 to create running heads and running feet, if appropriate, for those publications. The maximum number of characters, including spaces, for each running head is 47. List them as *verso* and *recto*.

EXERCISE FOLLOW-UP

The running heads for the professional journal should have the authors' names and article titles, and most of them needed to be abbreviated to fit. There is no running head for 'Writing for publication in GM' because it is only one page and has a chapter-weight title. The running feet are a suggestion of how they might appear, with the logo always on the foredge so that the folio and the date are separated to avoid confusion. The folios could be in the running heads, but there is already a lot of information there and the extent of the line is limited.

No abbreviations or authors' names are necessary for the RSPB journal, so an instruction to use the article or chapter-weight headings should be sufficient. The folios might be used here too; otherwise they can appear in the running feet. In a journal like this, where the articles might be only a page or two, it is also likely that only the journal title and date will appear, in either the head or foot margins.

Similarly, the children's book needs only a generic instruction. Although typesetters should know the conventions about running heads in prelims, endmatter and on chapter openers, check with production whether this information should also be stated.

Copyright

Copyright is a huge and complex field. You aren't expected to be an expert but you do need to know the basics. It will be your responsibility to keep up to date with changes in the law, for example by reading the trade journals or using the Internet, or even asking a colleague who specializes in rights. Similarly, when there is an issue beyond your knowledge, you should consult a senior or more knowledgeable or experienced colleague.

What it is and how it is protected

Copyright is the legal right to control the use of original intellectual property, and is one of the intellectual property rights. Each country has its own copyright law, which exists to protect and regulate the use of such material for the benefit of copyright owners and their beneficiaries. The duration of copyright can vary from one country to another, which can cause complications when producing an international edition. To minimize such problems, copyright law was harmonized in countries that were members of the European Union before 2004; the laws in new member states are harmonized in due course. In addition, there are more than a dozen international agreements to protect some aspect of copyright. The United Kingdom, like a majority of other countries, is a member of both main international conventions for literary works: the Berne Convention for the Protection of Literary and Artistic Works and the Universal Copyright Convention (UCC). Both set a minimum duration of copyright and require their member states to give the same legal protection to copyright works by the nationals of other member states as they do to the copyright works of their own nationals. There are two important differences between the conventions:

1 Berne does not require a particular format for the statement about copyright ownership in a work to ensure protection of copyright, but the UCC requires the use of the © with the year of publication and the copyright holder's name in a sufficiently prominent place to give 'reasonable notice' of ownership to consumers.

2 Duration of copyright is a minimum of 50 years after the end of the year of an author's death under the Berne Convention, and a minimum of 25 years after the end of the year of an author's death under the UCC.

In Britain copyright is protected under the Copyright, Designs and Patents Act 1988, which came into effect on 1 August 1989 and has been amended by subsequent EU directives. The Act states what kinds of works have copyright and for what period of time, and sets out guidelines for when and how different types of copyright work can be used by other people. Here is a short guide to these main points.

Ownership

Copyright exists in original artistic, dramatic, literary, and musical works as defined by the Act. Initially, it belongs to the person who creates the work (called 'the author' in all cases), unless he or she is an employee and creates the work as part of his or her job – in which case the copyright belongs to the employer. Authors can part with the physical form of their work – a text, artwork or photo, for example – and still retain the copyright, or they can contract to assign (i.e., sell) the copyright or license it for use.

Moral rights

Even if authors sell their copyright, they retain the four moral rights stated in the Act:
1 The right to be identified as the author whenever and wherever the work is used. It is hard to understand why the authors of the Act referred to this as the 'paternity right'; the 'right to be identified' says it all in a non-gender-specific way. This is the only one of the four rights that has to be asserted in writing, and that assertion is now a standard clause in most authors' contracts and is shown on the imprint page. Other authors – indexers and illustrators, for example – can assert their right by stating it in a letter to the publisher.
2 The right of integrity prohibits treating the work in a 'derogatory' way, one that would damage the author's reputation. Even if this were not the law, copy-editors should not distort or in any other way make an author's work worse. Yet it happens, and, yes, authors do complain and insist that such derogatory treatment is rectified.
3 The right not to have a work falsely attributed to you (compare 'passing off', p, 112). Since people would not have copyright in a work falsely attributed to them, this is the only one of the moral rights that does not last as long as copyright; it continues for 20 years after the end of the year in which a person dies.
4 The right to privacy of photos and films commissioned for private and domestic purposes is relevant to everyone, not just authors. The photographer retains the copyright but cannot make the work public in any way – not in his or her shop window or advertising materials, for example – without the permission of the person who commissioned it. The people in the images have no say in the matter either – only the person who commissioned the work can give or withhold permission.

How long it lasts

The duration of copyright in literary, dramatic, musical and artistic works differs according to who owns the copyright. At present,
- when a person owns the copyright, it is 70 years from the end of the calendar year in which the author or the last of joint authors dies;
- when a corporate body owns the copyright, it is 70 years from the end of the calendar year in which the work was published;

- when the Crown owns copyright, it is 125 years from the end of the calendar year in which a work was made, unless it is published commercially within 75 years of being made, in which case copyright lasts for 50 years after publication;
- when Parliament owns the copyright, as it does for Acts of Parliament and Measures of the Great Synod of the Church of England, it is 50 years from the end of the calendar year in which the Royal Assent is given.

There are different rules and variations depending on whether the author is anonymous; whether the work is a 'published edition' (i.e., copyright is in the typographical arrangement rather than the content) or computer-generated; and when the work was published. You will find all these details and more in either of the two handbooks on copyright law listed in Resources.

Acknowledgement

Authors who use *any* copyright material belonging to another party must acknowledge the source, stating at least the author and the title of the work, and, ideally, the publisher or, if the borrowed material is from an article, the name of the publication.

Fair dealing and permissions

As long as acknowledgements are made, authors can use extracts from other people's work for the purposes of criticism or review, a circumstance known as 'fair dealing'. In other cases authors might need permission from copyright holders to use their work. Some publishers require authors to obtain, or clear, permissions themselves. Where this is the case, you need to get the documents from the author to check the details and the wording of the acknowledgements. In other cases you might be required to clear permissions, and you'll find out how to do it on pp. 107–9.

The Act says authors have to ask permission if they use a 'substantial' amount of someone else's copyright work, and that is seen in qualitative as well as quantitative terms. Because the law is complex and does not state in finite terms or numbers what 'substantial' is, publishers developed a general guideline: up to 400 words from any source in a single extract or up to 800 words from a single source in multiple extracts can be used in a single work with acknowledgement but without permission. This is still a useful rule of thumb when authors are quoting from works that are tens of thousands of words long. Otherwise, think what the law means.

If, for example, an article is 2400 words long, 400 words is quantitatively a substantial part. Even a smaller number of words that embody the main principle or essence of the article can be qualitatively substantial. A poem or a song might be far less than 400 words long, and even a phrase or two might be a substantial part. The music industry is very diligent in protecting the copyright of its members, and here the rule of thumb might be: if the lyrics can be recognized, get permission.

The general guideline also does not make clear that an author cannot claim copyright in a work that is composed mainly of extracts from other people's copyright works. The editor of an anthology of stories or poems, even if they are all in the public domain (i.e., out of copyright), can have copyright in the original 'published edition' – the typographical arrangement – but not in the content other than that which he or she wrote. Copyright in such a published edition lasts for 25 years from the end of the calendar year in which it is published.

Permission is needed to reproduce any entire work that is in copyright: for example, an entire poem, chapter or article, no matter how short; a table, even if it is only one of hundreds in another publication; a drawing, a map or a photograph. All copyright material that is to appear in an anthology must be cleared.

Two illustrators could be given the same verbal information and create remarkably similar original images, and each would have copyright. However, when an illustration is based on a copyright image and closely resembles it, the source must be acknowledged and permission cleared. When the acknowledgement is prefixed by 'after' (for example, 'After Fig. 3 The diagram of a power station in ...'), it indicates that substantial changes have been made to the original, perhaps to update it, correct it or simplify it. Depending on the nature, extent and result of the alterations, permission might still be required, and it is generally safest to seek it.

REQUESTING PERMISSIONS

When you need to request a permission, write to the publisher. If it does not have the right to grant permission, it will forward your

request to the appropriate person or agency, or tell you to whom to send it. Enclose a photocopy of the material concerned with your request and cite the:
- author or editor
- title of the work
- date of publication and
- pages on which the text or illustration appears,

which will form the basis of the acknowledgement that you will prepare if the publisher does not specify any wording.

Provide all of the following information that is relevant about the publication you are working on:
- name of the author or editor
- title of the work
- extent
- publisher
- planned date of publication
- proposed selling price
- proposed print run
- rights required

You might want rights to reproduce the material in print and/or on a recording, database or website. The rights may be for a specific language and/or for publication in a particular territory or in a particular format. For example, you might need English-language rights for the United Kingdom only or for the UK and Commonwealth, or you might need world English-language rights if the publication is going to be sold throughout the world. Similarly, you might need, only or in addition, rights for other languages, which can be limited to a single country or all the countries where that language is used. For titles that are to be published in more than two countries, it is usually more economical to request world rights (all languages and all territories) rather than to ask for each one separately. If your publication is a book, find out whether you need to ask for volume rights for all editions (which covers revised editions, book club editions, and different bindings), and whether the quoted material is likely to be included in an extract or serialization in a newspaper or periodical, so that you can request those rights at the same time.

Fees vary and usually are lower for educational publications – schoolbooks – than for others. The fees are paid on publication: it is always possible that some material for which permissions have been requested will not be used.

Permissions must be in writing. When sources specify the wording of the acknowledgements, it must be followed exactly: it is part of their terms and conditions. Otherwise, the usual phrasing introducing a list of acknowledgements is: 'The author [and/or publisher] wishes to thank the following for permission to reproduce copyright material.' A single item might have its author, title and date listed first and be followed by 'is reproduced by the kind permission of …'.

Disclaimers in the publication that every effort has been made to find copyright owners will stand up in law only when it can be proved that those efforts were indeed made. You must show that you have written to the appropriate sources at their known addresses. An unanswered e-mail or letter is not proof of anything. If your first efforts fail, send a registered letter to the last known address. Whether it is accepted and unanswered, or returned as not at that address, you have evidence that you tried.

Infringement and plagiarism

Infringement is using copyright material without acknowledgement or, where required, permission, and is a criminal offence. It is easy to avoid infringing copyright when authors reveal that they are copying, for example by using quotation marks in text or providing details of the sources of illustrations. If authors do not provide sources, you must simply request them. When it is clear that quotation marks are missing, perhaps because the author has mentioned the source or the wording is obviously not in the author's own style, ask where they belong.

It has been known for authors to rearrange someone else's words, to paraphrase extensively, and present the result as their own work: this particular form of infringement is plagiarism, and it's against the law too. Although there is no copyright in an idea, if the execution of that idea is remarkably similar in detail to an existing work, a case for plagiarism might be made. Many song composers refuse to listen to unsolicited tapes sent to them by other musicians so that they cannot later be accused of copying, knowingly or not, from those works. On rare occasions accusations of literary plagiarism have, after investigation, turned to acknowledgement of amazing coincidence in creation of characters and story lines.

It is possible to infringe copyright by not taking sufficient care to avoid copying source material, and it can be a very expensive mistake, as the Automobile Association found out. The Ordnance Survey sued the AA for infringement of copyright on maps that the latter had used as source material for its atlases without permission or acknowledgement. The case began at the end of 1996 and was settled out of court in 2001, when the AA agreed to become a licensee and to pay the Ordnance Survey £20 million to cover backdated royalties, interest, legal costs, and an advance on future royalties. It was said at the time that all the other publishers of atlases immediately, and perhaps with some trepidation, investigated what source material had been used, and in what way, in creating their own publications. In addition to the financial costs, the negative publicity can be very damaging to a company's reputation and, therefore, its business.

Plagiarism can be difficult to spot, but if you do suspect it, you should notify the commissioning editor or your supervisor.

Exercise 3.4, sorting out permissions

Brief
- Stirling Jones is preparing an anthology of short stories to be published by Greenway Books in October 20—.
- Greenway, which has offices in London, Sydney and New York, publishes all its titles in trade paperback only, with an initial print run of 3000.
- Jones's book, provisionally titled *Sting in the Tale: An Anthology*, will be 240 pages long and have a recommended selling price of £8.99.
- Mr Jones has sent you a list of some of the titles he is planning to include and will send you the publication details when you tell him which of them need copyright permissions.
- Do some simple research to find out which story or stories listed below need permission and draft the permissions request letter(s), using generic terms for the missing information.

Vernon Lee, 'The Virgin of the Seven Daggers'

Sir Edward Bulwer-Lytton, 'The Haunted and the Haunters'

Thomas Hardy, 'The Withered Arm'

Guy de Maupassant, 'The Case of Louise Roque', translated by Stirling Jones

Edgar Allan Poe, 'The Tell-Tale Heart'

F. Marion Crawford, 'Man Overboard!'

Mary Braddon, 'Eveline's Visitant'

Ambrose Bierce, 'The Middle Toe of the Right Foot'

Isabel Allende, 'Revenge', translated by Margaret Sayers Peden

M. R. James, 'A Warning to the Curious'

J. S. LeFanu, 'Green Tea'

Bram Stoker, 'Dracula's Guest'

EXERCISE FOLLOW-UP

Probably the quickest way to find out which authors are still in copyright is to check in a companion to English literature or a dictionary of biography. You could also investigate them on the Internet. When you discovered that only Allende is still in copyright, you might have been tempted to use the Internet to find out in which of her collections of short stories 'Revenge' appears, but it is a better use of your time to ask Mr Jones for this information, as he already has it.

Even if Allende had been out of copyright, the translation might have been in copyright. It is also possible for there to be translations of the same story into the same language by different translators. In each case, the copyright in the translated text belongs to the translator. Publishers usually control licensing permissions for the editions they publish, and will either check and, if necessary, correct the detail of the acknowledgement you suggest or provide their own wording.

The fact that Greenway Books publishes in New York, London and Sydney indicates that world English-language rights are needed. Because it publishes only in paperback, there is no need for volume rights for all editions, as there will not be any others; and because this is an anthology, there will not be an extract or serialization.

You could have used other wording in your letter and put the information in a different order. It just needs to be complete, concise and clear. It saves time to create a form letter with the basic information that is repeated each time and headings to remind you of the details to include for each request. This approach also helps you keep the letter brief, which makes it easier for the recipient to quickly understand what you want.

Other legal issues

The following is a brief overview of areas you need to be aware of, based on British law. If you live or work elsewhere, you should find out about similar laws in that country. As always, when in doubt about the status of any material, refer it to a more senior colleague. Remember, ignorance is not a defence in law.

Passing off

Passing off is not part of copyright law, but it is logically related. It refers to misrepresenting to consumers the work of an individual or company as the work of a better-known person or company and, by succeeding in doing so, inflicting financial loss on, or harming the goodwill of, that better-known party. Close copies of designer clothes and accessories are a well-known example. In publishing, passing off would occur if

- the main character could be confused with an established one: for example, if a comic book featured a spiky-haired, yellow-skinned boy called Brat, or a story about a young wizard was titled 'Henry Potter and ...'
- a book in a particular genre bore a name remarkably similar to that of a well-known author: for example, a natural history book by David Bellemy or a romantic novel by Katherine Cookson
- a periodical used a title similar to that of another in the same field, which might be confused with or imply a relationship to the original: for example, *New Economist* or *Teen Tatler*
- the design of a publication cover was a close imitation of another.

Libel

Libel is a printed defamation, an *untrue* allegation that damages the reputation of a person or an organization. It does not have to be a direct statement; an innuendo or implication can be damaging. Nor does the libel have to be deliberate; it can be an accident, a mere coincidence. This is why authors try to ensure that the names of their characters are unlikely to be those of real people of the same description doing the same or similar jobs in the same place, and why they make up names for towns and villages if the stories they are telling would cast aspersions on anyone or any organization there. Such efforts must be made for disclaimers, which appear at the front of the book, that the characters and events are all fictitious to be considered reasonable in law.

A falsified photo or an untrue caption can also be libellous. Repeating a libel, even when using the word 'alleged', is also a libel.

Although authors indemnify their publishers against libel, this will not stop a lawsuit from being brought, nor save a publisher from paying damages if the author cannot. The publisher tries to protect the author as well as itself. If you suspect a statement could be libellous, refer it and any related material to your project manager.

Statements made or photographs taken in confidence – such as in the course of medical examinations or consultations with legal counsel – cannot be published without the written permission of *both* parties. This is why photos in medical journals and books blank out the eyes and mouths or do not use the faces of subjects.

Obscenity and indecency

Obscenity would seem easier to define than to prove. An item is obscene if 'taken as a whole' it would 'tend to deprave and corrupt persons' – not just one or two, but a reasonable number of its intended audience – 'who are likely' to come into contact with it. It is an offence to publish such an item. Although many people may think of obscenity only in relation to sex, the glorification of violence and the encouragement to use drugs can also be judged obscene.

Indecency applies usually to photographs and computer-generated images of children under the age of 16, and is determined by a jury, whose attitudes will be influenced by the mores of the times.

Blasphemy

Under current English law, it is an offence to say anything indecent or offensive about the Christian religion only. This is so restrictive as to be offensive itself. The law might not treat all religions with equal respect, but, wherever you are, you can ensure that your authors do. Analysis and criticism are acceptable; being offensive is not. The great difficulty, of course, is determining what is offensive. When in doubt, consult your project manager.

Incitement to racial hatred

The Public Order Act 1968 makes it an offence to publish material that is 'threatening, abusive or insulting' to people 'defined by reference to colour, race, nationality (including citizenship) or ethnic or racial origins' *and* intends, or is likely, to stir up racial hatred.

You are responsible

It is your responsibility throughout your career to be aware of changes in the law concerning intellectual property rights and other laws that affect your work. Newspapers and trade journals report changes in the law when they are under discussion and when they have been made. Using up-to-date reference works is essential.

4 Style and level

The use of capitals and italics, and the representation of numbers as words or numerals are house-style issues. There are rules and guidelines in each case, but every copy-editor has to learn how to interpret them and what to do when they don't seem to apply to a particular document. There are also some guidelines for adjusting the level of text, which might be necessary to make it consistent or appropriate for the intended readership.

Capitals

Sentences and phrases used as sentences start with a capital letter, although there are authors who have eschewed this practice. That should be enough to remind you that even when you are imposing house style on authors' texts, you should discuss any differences between it and their consistent usage before you alter the text.

Nouns

In German all nouns start with a capital letter, which must make life easier if you copy-edit German texts, but in English only proper nouns are capitalized. Many nouns can be common or proper. A dictionary and *NODWE* are useful references, and here is some general guidance.

Use an initial cap for the names of *specific*
- individuals: so 'Eve' but 'woman';
- organizations: 'the Liberal Party' but 'a liberal party' (a description);
- religious denominations: 'Catholic faith' but 'catholic taste'; 'the Protestant Church' (an organization) but 'a Protestant church' (a building) and 'St Andrew's Church' (a specific building);
- historical eras and events: 'the Middle Ages' but 'people who reach middle age'; 'the Second World War lasted from 1939 to 1945' but 'it was feared there would be another world war'; the 'Naughty Nineties' but 'in the nineties';

- places: 'Glasgow' but 'city'; 'the Royal Borough of Kensington and Chelsea' but 'a London borough'; 'the City' is correct in reference to the financial centre of London;
- brand and trade-marked names: 'Xerox' but 'photocopy', 'Hoover' but 'vacuum cleaner';
- things: 'Apollo' but 'spacecraft'.

Context can make a difference. Although technically 'Earth' (the name of the planet), 'Sun' (the name of our sun) and 'Moon' (the name of Earth's satellite) should be capitalized, they usually are only in fiction that concerns space travel, and in non-fiction texts about astronomy and related subjects. Similarly, 'heaven' and 'hell' are capitalized, as being specific places, in theological works but are lower-case in general usage.

Titles and ranks can be used as proper nouns and as common nouns, and, again, context is the key to knowing which it is. They are lower-case when used in a general sense:

> Sorry, mister, but all the tickets have been sold.
> He found a professor in the office.
> Jones spoke to the sergeant on duty.

> At a gathering of international government leaders a reporter approached a prime minister.

> A king of England and an earl of Leinster were in conflict.

and when accompanying a name as a job description, however elevated:

> He found Rosemary Patel, a professor of English, in the office.

> Jones spoke to Jason McNally, the sergeant on duty.

> The reporter approached Gordon Brown, a European prime minister.

> Henry, the king, and Richard, an earl, were in conflict.

Titles and ranks are capitalized when they accompany a name and are used as part of the name:

> Sorry, Mr Ling, but all the tickets have been sold.

> He found Professor Patel in the office.

> Jones spoke to Sergeant McNally, who was on duty.

> The reporter approached Prime Minister Gordon Brown.

> Henry II, King of England, and Richard, Earl of Leinster, were in conflict. It was clear that King Henry would prevail, as he had in the case of Thomas Becket, Archbishop of Canterbury.

When a specific person is addressed in direct speech by his or her title only (excepting civil titles: Mr, Mrs, Ms), the title is capitalized:

> He found Professor Patel in her office. 'Good morning, Professor', he said.

> Jones spoke to Sergeant McNally, who was on duty. 'Look, Sergeant, I found this bag on the street.'

> The reporter approached Prime Minister Brown. 'Tell us, Prime Minister, will you win the next election?'

Capitals are also used when a full or shortened title or rank that identifies a specific holder of that title is used in narrative:

> Henry II, King of England, and Richard, Earl of Leinster, were in conflict. It was clear that the King would prevail, as he had in the case of Thomas Becket, Archbishop of Canterbury. This time the King would openly overpower the Earl, not merely be the indirect instrument of his destruction, as he had been in the case of the Archbishop.

Some historians and some house styles do not follow this rule and would use lower-case initials for all the titles in the last example. Their reasoning is that in works concerned with such historical figures, the page would have a lot of capital letters. So what? If the texts used the names of the people instead of the titles each time, the page would have a lot of capitals too. A page with a lot of sentences has a lot of full stops – is that a 'reason' to omit full stops? Of course not. Are capitals an impediment to reading? No. When they avoid ambiguity and differentiate the individual from the general – this king, not any monarch; that person, not the office – then they should be used. You must, of course, follow the house style you are given, but remember that house styles are created by individuals and therefore may not necessarily be correct or appropriate in every detail. They can and do change, and understanding the principles of any aspect of house style enables you to make informed contributions to discussion about these issues. A good copy-editor questions the illogical or unreasonable.

Pronouns

Pronouns other than 'I' are lower-case in text, even in reference to the monotheistic deity unless the author or house style states otherwise.

> Dharma found her gloves on the table.
>
> God works in mysterious ways his wonders to perform.
>
> Stella and Roshan took their children to the park.

They are capitalized in the titles of books, songs, plays and other works of art.

> 'He Has the Whole World in His Hands'
>
> *Twelfth Night, or What You Will*

Adjectives and verbs

The rules about whether and which adjectives and verbs derived from proper nouns should be capitalized have changed from time to time and may vary according to house style. When the house style does not answer your question, check in *NODWE* or a general English dictionary. Here are some guidelines.

There is agreement that names of peoples and languages are capitalized: he is Australian, she is Irish, they speak Italian, the text was Americanized.

Names of foods and beverages that originate in a particular place – for example, Champagne, Cheddar cheese, Brussels sprouts – are capitalized, although it is a rule that is not followed in all publications, particularly fiction. The principle underlying whether to capitalize other terms, such as French polish and Indian ink, used to be that if the association with the country was remote or merely conventional, the word should be lower-case. It is not clear what has caused a reference book such as *NODWE* to change its policy and reinstate caps, but not all house styles agree.

Similarly, when names associated with objects or processes are registered or trade-marked, they are, as stated above, capitalized, but otherwise, when they become generic, they are lower-case: thus wellington boots, pasteurized milk and so on.

Compass points

The points of the compass and words derived from them are lower-case when they are used to indicate direction – 'he travelled south', 'the wind came from the east', 'the sun sets in the west'. The same words are capitalized when they are part of a place name – South America, Northern Ireland, South-east Asia, West Sussex – and when they are used in a geo-political sense – Western industrialized countries, Eastern philosophy, the peoples of the North.

Titles of works

The first word of a title is capitalized no matter what part of speech it is. Subsequent articles, prepositions and conjunctions are lower-case – *All About Eve* might be the only title where this rule is sensibly ignored – and all other parts of speech are capitalized. This rule applies to the titles of complete works in English: e.g., books, journals, newspapers, films, plays, songs, works of art. It does not necessarily apply to article or chapter titles, which might be lower-case throughout after the first word, depending on house style or the design of a particular document. If a poem does not have a title but is referred to by its first line, capitalization follows the usage in the poem.

All style guides agree that the definite article is capitalized and italicized in citing *The Times* and *The Economist*, and in foreign-language periodicals, such as *La Stampa*, *Die Welt* and *Le Monde*. They disagree about its use with other periodical titles in English. Increasingly, house styles have chosen to simplify the rules, so that '*The*' is used with periodical titles consisting of the definite article and only one other word: *The Times*, but the *Sunday Times*. This is an easy convention to follow unless your house style stipulates otherwise. The definite article is lower case and roman when the periodical itself is not the subject of the sentence:

> He was the *Economist* theatre critic.

and where the sentence structure would be awkward:

> Yesterday's *Times* was on the floor.

120 *Copy-editing*

Exercise 4.1, focusing on capitalization

Brief
The following text is an extract from a biography of Samuel Pepys, aimed at educated adult readers. The electronic file has suffered a glitch and all the capitals have been removed. Edit the extract. Although the focus is on capitals, there may be other issues to consider. List any queries for the author, and make a book style sheet and list of global changes as you work.

House style:
- -ize verbs
- no serial comma except to avoid ambiguity
- single quotes with doubles within

---

the two passions fuelling parliament and the people were religious fervour and the fear that the king, egged on by his catholic wife, was aiming to become an absolute ruler. the religious rollercoaster of the previous century when successive tudor monarchs first overthrew the catholic church, set up protestantism, restored catholicism and   5
then settled into uneasy compromise under elizabeth, had left a legacy of fierce hatred of the catholics and a burgeoning of protestant sects. the movement came to be called puritanism an the puritans, disliking the established church with its bishops and tithes that bore harshly on the poor who had no money to pay them became the allies   10
of the political opponents of the king. margaret pepys, like a great many of her neighbours, seems to have veered towards puristanism, although she still attended st brides church and had her own pew. her boys grew accustomed to hearing puritan preachers in the street. in 1640 a local leather-seller called praisegod barebones set up his   15

baptist congregation right outside in fleet street. baptist ministers saw no need for church buildings, supported themselves by working at other jobs and welcomed women as preachers, and more baptist congregations were begun in other parts of town. the city apprentices who gathered in westminster in 1641 shouted 'no bishops!', there was some fighting and in the days after christmas the same boys blocked the river stairs to prevent bishops newly appointed by the king from taking their seats in the house of lords and went on to attack them in their coaches. when they protested, parliament found grounds for impeaching them and sent them to prison, at which the apprentices rang the city churchbells joyfully and made bonfires in the street. the king then moved to impeach his chief enemies in parliament.

pepys was quite old enough to be on the streets when on 4 january 1642 the king pursued the five mps he was trying to arrest from the house of commons into the city. he was mobbed by huge numbers of tradesmen, apprentices and seamen, all shouting 'privilege of parliament, privilege of parliament' - a difficult mouthful for a mob, but they made it sound frightening. although the king was not harmed, he was thoroughly scared. this was a spectacular moment in english history and a week later charles left london with his family. he was not seen again until his execution in whitehall, seven years later in 1649, when an approving pepys was by his own account standing in the crowd.

on the day after the king left, the five mps he had threatened made a triumphal journey on the thames from the city to westminster, escorted by a flotilla of beribboned boats loaded with cheering and waving londoners while citizen soldiers marched along the strand with drums and flags to meet them as they came ashore. these soldiers, known as the trained bands, were ordinary townsmen organised into fighting groups, their effectiveness depending more on enthusiasm than discipline. the next big street show was the execution in late january of two catholic priests in front of an approving crowd. in march parliament began to raise its own army, and in may the city's regiments were reviewed on finsbury fields in front of the mps assembled. in june londoners were asked for money by parliament and they responded generously even though times were hard for tradesmen in the absence of the court. john pepys's lawyer customers had fewer clients and less to spend and the prospect of civil war promised worse to come as their one-time neighbour lawyer whitlocke now in parliament warned saying the country was "at the pit's brink, ready to plunge ourselves into an ocean of troubles and miseries … what the issue of it will be no man alive can tell.' in july the royalist mayor gurney was impeached in parliament and sent to the tower where he remained almost until his death five years later. a puritan was appointed as mayor in his place. milton called the city 'the mansion house of liberty,' and as such it had to prepare to defend itself against the gathering forces of the king, who raised his standard at nottingham on 22 august 1642.

This was the official start of the civil war between the opposing factions. It was brought about essentially by the king's refusal to accept the limitations parliament was determined to set upon his power, and by parliament's refusal to accept his supremacy. The war split the nation, dividing families cities, counties and social classes as well as the great bodies and institutions, the navy, the universities, the legal and medical professions; and the religious rift between those who held to the established church of england and those who rejected it sharpened the bitterness of the fight. Within seven years the country would rid itself of king, lords and bishops, and though these reforms were reversed, it was never again ruled for any length of time without the cooperation of the elected house of commons. From the revolution inengland came much of the inspiration for both the american and the french revolutions of the next century. The intellectual revolution that accompanied the war was as important as the war itself.

meanwhile parliament ordered the digging of trenches and building of ramparts ad forts to close all the main roads into london. islington, the fields around st pancreas church, mile end, rotherhithe and wapping were the sites of some of the twenty-four forts. a huge workforce was needed. it was found among the people of the city and the suburbs, women and children included. sam and tom pepys may well have taken part. when announcements were made in the churches citizens turned out with 'baskets, spades and such-like instruments, for digging of trenches and casting up of breast works from one fort to another.' more than 20,000 people were said to have worked on the defences, a sixth of the population. they were directed by sailors and officers of the trained bands, and their affectiveness was observed with surprise and respect by the venetian ambassader among others. john evelyn, a supporter of the king, also came to view the 'much celebrated line of communication'. the work was in full swing in the autumn of 1642, the season of edward montagu's marriage to jemima crew in westminster and of prince ruperts sacking of brentford which inspired john milton to write his sonnet 'when the assault was intended to the city'. it was addressed to the expected royalist invaders, and suggested they would be well advised to spare a poet.

miltons' plea proved unnecessary. the royalists were kept from london. the london troops had good supplies, including the baskets of food brought to them by their wives and sweethearts. the royalists were tired after a long march, and short of supplies, and their nerve failed. the earl of essex, with 24,000 of the trained bands, held turnham green for parliament.

Adapted from Claire Tomalin, *Samuel Pepys: The Unequalled Self*, London, Viking, 2002.

EXERCISE FOLLOW-UP

It becomes clear before the end of the extract that 'the king' refers to a specific monarch – Charles I – in all but one mention (line 74). You could make the change to a capital K global and mark the exception for the typesetter's attention. When working on e-files, it is faster to make changes to spelling and capitalization from a list, even for words that are mentioned only once. When keying all the text from hard copy, it is faster to have all the changes marked throughout the copy.

Words beginning a sentence, personal names, the names of political and religious institutions and the names of buildings require capitalization. You might have referred to *NODWE* and/or a dictionary if you were uncertain about 'royalist' (lower-case, although 'Cavalier' –

royalist specifically in this conflict – is upper-case) and 'Puritan' (upper-case to distinguish the historical movement from the general meaning).

As well as these technical corrections, you should also be on the lookout for grammatical problems and the kinds of unnecessary repetition and poor organization that are evident in this exercise. You should have deleted the phrase 'who had no money to pay them' (line 10), because it is tautological, which is also the reason for crossing out 'between the opposing factions' (lines 65–6). Changing 'they' to 'the bishops' (line 24) and 'he' to 'the King' (line 31) clarifies the subjects in these sentences. You can delete 'in 1649' (line 38) (or 'seven years later', line 37) because the reference to 1642 earlier in the paragraph (line 30) is close enough to make this combination of passage of time and date unnecessary. Transposing 'MPs' and 'assembled' (line 51) is a more natural formation and is in keeping with the author's style, and changing 'revolution in England' to 'English Revolution' (line 77) makes the construction parallel and consistent with the reference to the other revolutions in the same sentence. The logic of the last paragraph is clearer when the sentences are reordered as shown, although you could also have moved 'the London troops … sweethearts' to the end of the paragraph.

You should not spend a lot of time checking points that the author can clarify for you, such as whether 'city' was used generally (lower-case) or to refer to the City of London specifically (upper-case) and whether the reference to the poem by Milton is a first line or a title; and you should make your queries as concise as is consistent with clarity and courtesy, to save your time and the author's.

Italics

Italics can be, and often are, used to indicate emphasis, but that's not essential; house style can allow caps, bold or exclamation marks, or you can just adjust the syntax instead. Similarly, italics can be, and often are, used for the cross-references 'see' and 'see also', particularly in indexes, but these can also be in bold or small caps. However, there are some elements for which italics are always used: the main ones are titles and subtitles of works, parties to legal cases, names of ships and other means of transport, biological names, and foreign words. Punctuation that is part of the text affected is italicized, but punctuation before, after or between separate italicized elements is not.

When text is set in italics for design reasons – as is sometimes the case for extracts and captions – characters that would normally be italicized are set in roman type.

Titles of works

Figure 4.1 shows that the titles and subtitles of some works are italicized and others are not. You can see that there is a pattern to the categories: the roman items – some in quotes, others not – are smaller parts or unofficial counterparts of the italicized items; series titles are an exception to this rule. And although the titles of articles are enclosed in quotation marks when mentioned in texts, in the final chapter you will learn how and when they are treated differently in references.

Legal cases

The title of a legal case is composed of the names of the parties: the plaintiff, complainant or appellant versus the defendant. Before computers were commonly used, the names of the parties were italicized but the 'v' (for 'versus') was roman. Highlighting the entire title to italicize or apply a format is faster than singling out the names, so now this is the accepted practice, a small example of how technology can influence our work.

In a table of cases – an index that appears in the prelims of law texts – the case titles are in roman type.

Means of transport

All means of transport have manufacturers', marque or model names, e.g. White Star ships, Boeing aircraft, a Renault Clio. These, as well as preceding articles, prefixes (such as P&O, HMS) and the possessive indicator ('s), are set in roman type. However, ships and some trains, planes, spacecraft and other means of transport have individual names, and these are italicized: *Titanic*, *Orient Express*, *Spirit of St Louis*, USS *Enterprise*.

Italics	**Roman**
Publications	
books	sacred or revered texts of all religions, 'chapters', 'entries' in encyclopedias
brochures, pamphlets	
epic poems and collections	'cantos', 'sonnets', 'odes' and other 'short poems'
journals, magazines, newspapers, company reports, conference proceedings	'articles', sometimes without the quote marks
series title of books/journals without individual volume titles	series title of individually titled books/journals
Dramatic and musical works	
ballets and other dance	
broadcast series or unique programme	'episode in series'
films and plays	
musicals, song cycles, albums and CDs	'songs'
official titles of symphonies, concertos and suites	'movements', overtures, unofficial titles and descriptions
operas, oratorios	'arias'
Works of art	
official titles of paintings, sculptures and other works of art	unofficial titles and descriptions

Figure 4.1 Styling of titles and subtitles

Biological names

The names of plants and animals are classified according to kingdom, phylum or division, class, order, and family, all of which are set in roman type; and genus and species, which are set in italics, with the genus capitalized. For example, people are *Homo sapiens*; the poinsettia is *Euphorbia pulcherrima*, a delightfully musical name.

When a genus name is used in the plural or in a general way, it is set in roman type:

> There were many magnolia trees in the park. Denise liked most magnolias and was particularly fond of *Magnolia grandiflora*.

Subspecies and varietal names are also italicized, preceded by the abbreviations 'subsp.' and 'var.', respectively, in roman type. Cultivar names, which can be preceded by the abbreviation 'cv.', are in roman type and single quotes:

> *Rosa floribunda* 'Peace'

The same pattern applies to the names of bacteria:

> salmonella, an ailment
> *Salmonella*, a genus
> *Salmonella typhi*, the genus and a species

The names of hormones are roman, lower-case. The names of diseases and other ailments are roman, and lower-case except when they are, or incorporate, the name of a person, as in Alzheimer's and Parkinson's.

Foreign words

English is replete with words of foreign origin that have been assimilated over the centuries; they are now English – we'd hardly be able to communicate without them – and so are printed in roman type. Proper nouns in a foreign language – the names of people, places, streets, institutions and organizations – are also printed in roman type. Foreign words that are not in either of these categories are set in italics.

Some words are assimilated quickly, others take a long time and still others remain foreign. Some that are considered foreign by the 'general' reader are accepted as everyday language by particular audiences. So, when you encounter a word that seems foreign, how do you know whether it has been assimilated generally or only by your target readers? If the word or phrase is in roman type in a general English-language dictionary, that dictionary thinks it has been assimilated generally. Dictionaries also include in italics some foreign words and phrases that are frequently used but not assimilated. If, like most people, you use a concise dictionary, remember that a word is not automatically foreign just because it doesn't appear there, and remember too that not all dictionaries agree. *NODWE* is another useful reference, which might have some terms not in your concise dictionary. House-style guides, particularly those for specialized lists, such as law and the social sciences, might also indicate which frequently occurring terms of foreign origin are to be italicized and which not.

Of course, references can be out of date: house-style guides are not revised very often, and there is usually a five-year gap between editions of a dictionary – and words can cross over in a lot less time than that. Online dictionaries are revised more often – quarterly, in some cases – but require a subscription for access to the entire work. Your firm might not subscribe, and if you are freelance you might find the subscription uneconomic. When you are in doubt about the status of a word or phrase in the text – whether you think it has been assimilated by the target readership but the reference works don't agree, or vice versa – discuss it with the author. If the decision is to go counter to the dictionary or house style, let your line manager know; it might be unique for this title or it might mean a change to house style to maintain consistency throughout the list.

Exercise 4.2, focusing on the use of italics

Brief
Edit the piece below, underlining words that should be italicized. Although this is the newest skill you are practising, it is not the only one. You must also, where necessary, correct capitalization, spelling, grammar and punctuation, and ensure consistency. Check for single spacing between words and after punctuation, and give global instructions to the typesetter where appropriate.

Rita was tired. She had stayed up late the night before practicing her

shorthand by taking notes as she watched one news programme after

another, as she had been doing for two weeks. Her well-thumbed

copy of A Career in Journalism told her shorthand was the only way

to keep an accurate account of every word and every action and was   5

an essential skill for a reporter. Rita was more of a general assistant than a reporter at the Five Villages Gazette, occasionally being allowed two write a short report on a village fete or flower show. This evening she had been to a local council meeting. There were no major issues on the agenda, certainly nothing really newsworthy, but her editor said it would be good experience for her to attend and report. And now stiff from the tension of sitting in the council chamber straining to hear everything that was said and write them down at the same time, her hand was cramped from having gripped the pencil so tightly. But tired, stiff and cramped, she was still in high spirits. The meeting had begun in the usual dull way – attendance, apologies for absence, reading and approval of the minutes of the last meeting – and look like it would continue in that vein with a discussion of a report on road maintenance and repairs. Then Councillor Beauregard had made a comment that Rita didn't hear and Councillor Stally had screamed at him 'How dare you! Apologise! Apologise at once or I'll– ' 'You'll what?" retorted Beauregard, clenching his fists and looking menacing. The other councillors had had to intervene to prevent a fight. The meeting was adjournd and the two near combatants ushered out separately, each surrounded bya few colleagues. OK, rita thought, not earth shattering, but it would certainly make an interesting article.

She had put her notebook into her shoulderbag, grabbed her jacket from under the bench and headed out of the council chamber in pursuit of a strong coffee to revive her before the trip home. La Stella d'Italia was across the street, which was cleverly split into a coffee bar at the front and a traditional Italian trattoria at the back. It had been there as long as Rita could remember and was as popular as any of the fancier establishments that had opened more recently. Rita's father, a regular at La Stella from the early days – his and its – had recently commented on how the décor had changed but the menu had not. This was only partly true, and perhaps a reflection of the fact that he usually ordered exactly he same meal. The dark red walls had been repainted a mediterranean gold, a scattering of original paintings had replaced the hanging fishnets adn baskets and faded prints of Guardi's Santa Maria della Salute and the Dogana and Canaletto's Piazza San Marco and other views of Florence and the chianti bottles covered in candle wax had been banished in favour of frosted glass bowls that radiated the candle light. Dust catching chandeliers had gone and small downlights now provided bright light when needed during the day and a warm glow in the evenings. The old menu, however, had not been discarded. The classics in every category had been retained while changing tastes had allowed the addition of other Italian dishes that would once have been too daring for the residents of the town and surrounding villages. So as well as the familiar minestrone and zuppa di verdura, the menu now offered ribollita and zuppa garmugia, the pastas included not only spaghetti bolognese and ravioli with tomato sauce but also capelli d'angelo neri con capesante and the vegetarian's delight, maltagliati al sugo di melanzane. When Rita went out for a meal there with her parents, her father always ordered osso buco while her mother could be counted on to choose veal escalopes in mushroom sauce, although they both claimed they would soon try coniglio al forno, or the fagiano in salmi or perhaps the carciofi ripieni, all of which had appeared on the menu in the last couple of years. Rita would always try one new dish and encourage her parents to have a taste but they always declined.

As she made her way through the door and to a small table at the front the aromas were so tantalizing that Rita, who had had only a cheese sandwich – brie and halved grapes, her own invention –before the meeting knew she would have to have just a little something, perhaps just a couple of biscotti, with her coffee. And which coffee would she have. Ah, it would definitely be a latte. Waiting for her coffee and, oh dear, a little selection of crostini, Rita pretended to read an article in the current week's Economist which someone had left behind while she eavesdropped on the conversations around her. Actually she thought it looked like a very interesting article and if the café had been empty she really would have read it. As it was, however, the place was rather full, the tables were fairly close together and by concentrating on one or another she could clearly hear everything being said. The two boys and a girl to her left were discussing the songs on Dumb Noise, the latest album by The Raw Deal. This was not the kind of music Rita chose to listen to but some of her friends like it and she had to admit that the lyrics of Too Many Drums, the hit single from the album, made her laugh. As she listened to trio discussing the merits of the lead singer she could hear the Winter movement of Vivaldi's Four Seasons playing quietly in the tratorria at the back. As the coffee and bruschetti arrived Rita transferred her attention to two middle-aged women discussing advice they had heard about growing bougainvilleas on

Gardeners' Question Time. Rita's Aunt Millie had a fabulous bougainvillea glabra in her little conservatory but before she could pick up any tips to pass along she was distracted by an agitated voice speaking just above a whisper at the table slightly behind her.

'… not to phone me. It can be traced.'

'Well, meeting in public's not a great idea either, is it?'

'We just bumped into each other, that's all. Decided to have a coffee in the same place. Now, whats so damned important? And keep your voice down!'

Rita was riveted. Why should two men be worried about being seen together? Why did they need to whisper.

'Drake says the goods are arriving tonight and he wants us to help him move them.'

'Move them? Move them where? When?"

'The Burgo will dock unseen after –

'Shut up! Haven't either of you got any brains?' Even at a hoarse whisper the familiar voice sound exasperated.

Rita's curiosity got the better of her. She took out her compact and appeared to be checking her hair as she moved the mirror so she could see the men behind her. It was Dan Reynard, the defendant in Anser v Reynard! She had seen his photo in the national press. "Rusty" Reynard, so called because of his orange tinted brown hair, was accused of embezzaling funds from his business partner, Guillaume Anser. What was he doing here? And who was that rather rough looking man with him? As the waiter bringing coffees to Reyanrd's table blocked her from view, Rita took her notepad and pencil out of her handbag as discretely as possible. Feeling like a character in a film – like that old black-and-white one she'd seen on TV last year, The Big Scoop – Rita brushed her hair away from her ear and casually leaned back in her chair hoping to her more.

EXERCISE FOLLOW-UP

Where to use italics in this exercise was probably clear for everything except food names, because some are assimilated and some are not. Here, consistency takes second place to usage. You might have decided to use italics for emphasis in one or two places, but remember to do this sparingly or it will lose its impact.

There were, of course, quite a few other points that needed editorial attention, particularly changes to make the text accurate and consistent. Review the relevant text for any that you missed or misunderstood, as this will help you to remember it or them in the future. Learning is like editing in this respect: we often have to review the text several times to really do the job.

Numbers

The central style issue about numbers is when they should be represented as words and when as numerals in text (Chapter 6 will look at numbers in tables). The four main rules are:
1 use words for numbers up to and including nine *or* ninety-nine (which I call the cut-off point), depending on house style, and use numerals thereafter; but, regardless of the cut-off point,
2 use words for all numbers at the beginning of a sentence, or revise the sentence so that the number is not the first element;
3 use numerals with precise units of measurement and percentages;
4 use numerals for labels on graphs, charts and other figures.
Simple, isn't it? Well, now come the exceptions and variations, so be prepared to think – and always bear in mind that the goal is to make the text clear for the intended reader. Remember, too, that fiction is more informal than non-fiction, and take this into account in making your decisions.

Matching and mixing for consistency

When a sentence contains numbers that are both below and above the cut-off point, use numerals for all of them:

> The children were aged 5, 7 and 11.
> He counted 110 cows and 60 calves in the fields.

When numbers refer to two categories, use numerals for one and words for the other:

> There were five 2-seater cars, seven 4-seaters, and two 10-seater vans.

Round numbers in the millions and above can be given as a numeral and a word combined:

> 1 million, 2 billion, 3 trillion

Notice that the word is in the singular. On hard copy mark a fixed space between the numeral and the word, as if the word were zeros. This will prevent the number being split across lines.

Imprecise numbers

For generalizations and estimates, and when units of measurement are not meant to be precise, use words:

> The chances of winning are one in a thousand.
>
> He figured they would have to travel a hundred and fifty kilometres by nightfall.
>
> I bet that case weighs twenty kilos.
>
> There were two thousand delegates at the conference.

But when there is a succession of large numbers being used for comparison, consider whether numerals would be clearer to the reader:

> Transitional *Homo sapiens* forms appeared about 250,000 years ago, but completely modern *Homo sapiens sapiens* did not appear before about 40,000 years ago.

Precise numbers

UNITS OF MEASUREMENT

When the measurement is precise, and always when the unit is abbreviated, use numerals:

> Add 25 g butter to the pan.
> The car exceeded 80 mph.
> B format is 198 x 127 mm.
> The bleed is 3 mm over the trim line.

Some house styles require the numerals and the abbreviations to be closed up; others stipulate a fixed, thin space between them. I think the latter works better, as a space would be used if the unit were spelled out. The fixed space means that the numeral and the abbreviation are not spaced out as separate words in a line of justified type, and cannot be split across lines.

Abbreviations of metric units are always in the singular: mm, not mms. Abbreviations of imperial weights and measures are also in the singular, although some house styles might still use plurals.

Units that are spelled out are plural in general use and singular when preceded by a number:

> There were thousands of people at the game.
> There were thirty thousand people at the game.

Words are used for numbers and units in general contexts:

> He turned the telescope forty degrees to the right and saw the comet clearly.
> The temperature in the room fell about ten degrees.

In mathematical, scientific and technical contexts, the degree symbol is used and closed up to the numeral for degrees of angle, latitude and longitude:

> A right-angle is 45°. Land's End is about 50° N, 5° W.

but closed up to the abbreviation for degrees of temperature:

> The thermometer read 20 °C, which is 68 °F.

PERCENTAGES AND FRACTIONS

It is standard practice to use numerals, no matter how small the number, to indicate percentages. Use the symbol (%, closed up to the numeral unless standing alone in a column heading) in tables, charts and graphs, and in documents that have a consistently heavy reference to percentages – for example, company reports and annual accounts, and texts on statistics and economics. In other, general texts, even if there is an occasional clustering of references to percentages, use the words 'per cent'.

Fractions can be expressed as words (Chapter 2 explained how to hyphenate them); as cased numerals: 1/2, 2/3; or as decimal numbers: 0.5, 0.66. The decimal fractions are easier to set and more precise. Of course, fractions can be used with whole numbers – e.g., 3.75 – but when the number is less than one, there must usually be a zero before the decimal point, so that the reader knows nothing has been omitted accidentally and that the decimal itself is not a mistake. The zero is omitted when the quantity is never more than 1, as in levels of probability and ballistics.

Cardinal and ordinal numbers

Use words for cardinal numbers in names:

Ten Commandments; Thirty Years War

and when expressing hours generally or with 'o'clock':

It was five o'clock. We were meeting at five-thirty.

Use numerals for cardinal numbers in dates and addresses, for road numbers and for expressing time with 'a.m.' and 'p.m.':

23 August 2010   23/8/10
45 East Hill   Flat 3
A414   M6
7 a.m.   4.15 p.m

and for numbering paragraphs, sections, clauses and pages.

Dates are given in the order of day, month, year, and do not require any punctuation when the month is spelled out. In the United States, where the order is month, day, year, a comma is used to separate the numerals for day and year. Even when the year is omitted, the day remains a cardinal number, but when the month is omitted in subsequent references, the day is given as an ordinal number in either words or numerals, according to house style or the context of the work:

> The first interview took place on 4 October. His lawyer visited him again on the 8th, 9th, and 15th.

When the date is written entirely numerically, it is a matter of house style whether the numerals are separated by soliduses or hyphens, and whether or not the single-digit months are preceded by a zero. It is best to avoid an all-number style when the publication is likely to have an international audience: 6/10 is 6 October to a European audience, and June 10 to an American readership.

Decades can be words or numerals:

> 1980s *or* the eighties; in their 60s *or* in their sixties

Use the full date if there could be any doubt about the century. There is no reason to capitalize the words, unless your house style does – and that would be unfortunate. The only exceptions are named decades, such as the Naughty Nineties and Swinging Sixties. Do not use apostrophes with the numerals: *not* 1960's or '60s. When the text refers to both the time and people in term of decades, use numerals for one and words for the other, e.g.:

> They were in their sixties in the 80s

Use words for ordinal numbers in names and for periods of time:

First World War	first year
fourth estate	second decade
fifth columnist	third century
Sixth Avenue	fourth millennium

However, when periods of time are mentioned frequently, particularly for comparative purposes – as in history and art history texts – or the text is set in narrow columns, it can be clearer to use the numeric form: 1st, 2nd, 3rd.

Use numerals for ordinal numbers referring to editions in references, and to nobility and monarchs:

> Judith Butcher, Caroline Drake and Maureen Leach, *Butcher's Copy-editing: The Cambridge Handbook for Editors, Copy-editors and Proofreaders*, 4th edn, Cambridge: CUP, 2006

Henry VI
Frederic, 1st Baron Leighton

Style and punctuation of numerals

Numerals can be lining – aligning at the top and bottom: 123456; or non-lining (also called 'old-style') – having ascenders and descenders: 123456. Non-lining numerals are all right used sparingly in texts, but lining numerals are better for frequent use in a document and should always be used in tables. Think about which style works best for the targeted reader. When the text must use lining numerals, state this clearly on your handover form or setting instructions, or write it on top of the first page of the hard copy. Then even if the work had been designed to use non-lining numerals, the designer or typesetter knows to change the style.

Four-digit numerals in text can be set closed up: 2882; with a comma separating the hundreds from the thousands: 2,882; or with a fixed thin space instead of a comma: 2 882. By now you are expecting me to remind you of the need for consistency, so it might come as a surprise that a particular inconsistency is accepted: four-digit numerals can appear closed up in text even though they must be separated in tables in the same document so that they align with figures of five or more digits.

When there are more than four digits preceding the decimal point, the separation usually must be shown by either a comma or a space. It is usual for schoolbooks and other books for children to use the comma. It is increasingly common for other documents to use a space: it is visually clear and avoids confusion for European readers, for whom the comma acts as a decimal point. House style rules, as you know by now.

When the comma style is used, numerals following the decimal point are not separated:

12,345.33333

When the fixed space style is used, numerals following the decimal point are separated in threes from the left:

12 345. 333 33

Four-digit years, page numbers, library and shelf numbers, and address numbers are not grouped into threes. Telephone numbers and ISBNs have their own systems of grouping.

House style states how to present numerals in a range. You remember about using the en rule (of course you do, it's in Chapter 2), but here we're concerned with elision. The numerals in a range can be given in full: 34–35, 223–226, as is usual in children's books; or elided to the fewest digits possible: 34–5, 223–6. Some house styles require the repetition of the numeral that precedes a zero or zeros in the first part of the range: 30–34, 920–24, 200–214.

Of course, you will realize the minute you look at an example that the teens can never be elided: 11–19, not 11–9. The same applies to
- BC dates: 850–848 BC, not 850–48 BC;
- other ranges that go down: 140–120, not 140–20;
- ranges that include letters or symbols: £120–£130, not £120–130;
- the first set of digits in a range: 2000–3000, not 2–3000;
- four-digit ranges in which three of the digits change: 1845–1923.

Dates in a two-year range that are other than calendar years (such as financial years, academic years or seasons) are written with a solidus: 2004/5. Even when house style requires elision, numerals in headings, which are usually dates, are not elided.

Exercise 4.3, providingmore practice in applying correct punctuation, capitalization, italics and style for numbers

Brief
The following extracts are from an account of events preceding the D-Day landings in the Second World War. It is a British publication aimed at an adult market. Skim through the piece first, to understand the context and hear the author's voice, then edit the text.

Style:
- numbers up to 99 spelled out
- numbers in names of military divisions and corps spelled out; those in names of military companies are numerical
- four-digit numerals closed up
- elision to the fewest digits
- serial comma only to avoid ambiguity

- use full points in 'a.m.' and 'p.m.'
- abbreviations 'LST', 'LCT', etc. have been explained earlier in the text

---

In 1939 the United States had a regular army of only a hundred and ninety thousand men; by the end of the was it would be 8.5 million. Over the second half of 1943 and the first half of 1944, the D-Day build-up period in which this story opens, new American soldiers sailors and airmen were pouring into Britain in their 1000's every week, to make a total of some 1,600,000 British based American troops by the eve of the Normandy invasion. A vast quantity of American life was being committed to the crucible of the war in North-west Europe and the Second Front, which Russia, to relieve the pressure upon itself, had asked the western allies to open against Germany. Every one of those hundreds of thousands of men had family, friends, or sweet hearts back home; naturally there was unease, and some reassurance was in order.

In the first half of 1944 Time, Life and Newsweek carried profiles of 'the Doughboy's General', Omar Bradley, commander of the US Army in northwest Europe. "Most of them,' Bradley noted, 'stressed that I valued the lives of my soldiers and would not spend them recklessly." In December 1943 General Dwight D. Eisenhower had been appointed Supreme Commander of the Allied Expeditionary Force. Eisenhouer's attitude was that his relationship with the American soldier was 'sacred.'.

In the United States there was patriotism and even enthusiasm for the war. There was scarcely a house that did not display the flag of one of the services, meaning a husband, brother, father or, most commonly, son serving in it. But there were houses, too, in whose windows gold stars and the words 'Gold Star Mother' were displayed, meaning a life lost, perhaps in the pacific ocean campaign against Japan on in the north African or Italian campaigns of 1942-43. more gold stars — many more – could be expected from the opening of the Second Front; but America had the word of its military leaders that deaths would be kept to the minimum possible in war.

There would be no unnecessary, wasteful, superficially glorious heroics of the kind that seemed to abound in the military histories of the European countries. No 'noble 600' would ride, as in Tennyson's poem about the charge of the Light Brigade, 'into the valley of death'.

The Plymouth section of Convoy T-4 put to see at 9.45 on the morning of April 27. The 515 would lead the line of LSTs and as the ship slipped its mooring in Plymouth Harbour the loud hailer system crackled into life with Doyle's voice saying 'This is a drill, but we're going into enemy waters'. The ships cleared the harbour easterly and then, in Plymouth Sound, formed themselves into a convoy of five, the 515 at its head, followed by the 496, 511, 531 and the 58 towing it's two platoons. Also waiting in the Sound was the Royal Navy flower-class corvette Azalea, which would precede the 515 as escort.

With u-boats in mind, the Azalea was equipped with hedgehog and depth charges. But she had other armament too; fewer guns than the average LST but of heavier calibre. Perhaps, as with Commander Skahill, the experience of T-4 would later colour how those on the convoy perceived Azalea. A number of survivors have said that they thought the corvette was an anti-submarine trawler. For example, Elson Hendrick, Doyle's communications officer on the 515: 'As convoy T-4 was forming up off Plymouth I got a look at our escort through binoculars. She looked more like a converted trawler to me than a corvette.' (In what must be a slightly mistaken memory, Henderick recalled that 'as we were forming up outside Plymouth I took a blinker message from her: 'My best speed ten knots'.) Likewise, someone on another LST would recall that 'we were reported to have more fire power than the trawler' when, in fact, the Azalea was armed with four-inch cannon forward and a 2-pounder on the bridge, with two anti-aircraft Oerlikons and a two pounder about the bridge and funnel.

But the Azalea was not intended as the T-4s only or chief escort. The bulk of the convoy's fire power protection was to be provided by the twenty-six knot destroyer Scimitar; in common British escort pattern of the time, it would steam along T-4's flank while Azalea took the bow position. Scimitar however had the small hole in her side and at seven fifty-two that morning had signalled Plymouth to that affect.

The Scimitar was ordered into port for dockyard repairs which could not begin until 28 April. At some point after 10 a.m. as the first five ships of t-4 were lining up in Plymouth Sound, the Scimitar, their second escort ship, steamed past them in the opposite direction. The first five sips of T-4 were about to sail out into 'enemy waters' deaf, dumb, virtually blind (few of the LSTs had radar), and defenceless.

So were the three LSTs in Brixham, but perhaps because they ahd less far to go before meeting up with the Plymouth section off Bery Head, the eastern tip of Start Bay, they left Harbour later, on the afternoon of the twenty-seventh. The first of them in line was the 499, followed by the 289 and 507. 250 soldiers of 1048 UDT Company were, according to records, among the 395 on the 289.

Now all the ships are at sea, sailing into the dusk of British double summer time, and at 8.30 p.m. meeting off Berry Head to form T-4. In the same order as before the Brixham section attaches itself to the ships from Plymouth, Azalea a mile ahead, six hundred yards between the LSTs – although their station-keeping would prove shaky.

Now it is between nine and 10 pm. The sky is dark, with a setting quarter moon. Visibility is good. The air is chilly and the ships intake valves are registering sea temperature of 42 degrees Farenheit. Led by their solitary escort the eight large LTSs are about to embark on another of that night's 'endless meanderings'. The idea is that the ships should stay at sea for as long as they will on D-Day. Off Torquay and the promontory called Hope's Nose they start a long slow turn to starboard. From here their course to the transport area 12 miles off slapton Sands is shaped like a perfect question mark.

The transport area is full of ships as T-4 starts its turn. Rear-Admiral

Moon would report that at the close of 27 April his Force U had 221 ships and boats of all shapes and sizes under its protection in Lime Bay, 'awaiting unloading and sailing empty at daylight'. There were twenty-one LSTs, 28 LCIs, 65 LCTs and '14 miscellaneous and 92 small landing craft.' Moon also referred to an APA, or attack   100
transport: the USS Bayfield, cmmand ship for Tiger, as it would be for Utah. On board the Bayfield with Moon were General Collins of the Seventh Corps and Major-General Raymond O. Barton commander of the Fourth Infantry Division which that morning had made the assault on Slapton Sands.   105

Adapted from Nigel Lewis, *Channel Firing: the Tragedy of Exercise Tiger*, London, Viking, 1989, pp. 3–4, 73–4, 75, 76, 78–9.

EXERCISE FOLLOW-UP

You could easily check the spelling of Bery Head/Berry Head and Eisenhower/Eisenhouer if you were not sure, but you would have to query the author about Hendrick/Henderick. LSTs are identified as ships, so their names have to be italicized even though they are numbers. There is more than one way to revise the sentence starting '250 soldiers' in line 79 so that it does not begin with numerals; the model answer shows the way the author actually wrote it. All the numbers in line 99 must be numerals because some of them are above the cut-off point (see p. 135). As usual, there was plenty of editing to do to correct spelling, capitalization and punctuation – did you distinguish the roman punctuation from the italicized terms?

Purpose and level

By now you know you need to keep the intended readers in mind while you work so that you can make appropriate decisions about punctuation and styling. Being always aware of the intended audience and the purpose of the publication is also important so that you can ensure that the language and content level of the text are appropriate.

The purpose may be, broadly, to inform, to instruct, to entertain or to promote, and the level is determined by the readers' age range, reading ability, and extent of subject knowledge or interest. For example, the purpose of a dictionary is to inform; its level may be simple if its intended audience is young, or is older but has a reading ability below its age range, or is foreign and beginning to learn the language; the more advanced, in age or knowledge, the intended audience, the more complex the dictionary can be. A monthly or quarterly company newsletter may assume that the readers are familiar with current company structure, policy, activities and personnel, whereas an annual company report to shareholders assumes the readers have no previous knowledge and will provide background to these references. A cookery book instructs its readers how to prepare food; it can be aimed, for example, at children, at adults with no knowledge or experience of cooking, adults who have some knowledge, and adults who are highly proficient. A product leaflet, say, for a camera, instructs the reader on how to operate that particular model without knowing whether – and therefore without assuming that – the reader has ever used a camera or has any skill. There are many genres of stories and novels – romance, fantasy, thriller, mystery, science fiction, slice of life – and their plots, characters and vocabulary are designed to appeal to and entertain specific audiences. The purpose of blurbs, catalogues and publicity leaflets is to sell, and what they are selling and to whom will determine their tone and level.

The same idea or concept can be conveyed at varying levels. Level is determined by

- vocabulary: which words are understood by the readers and which need to be defined or explained;
- structure: the complexity of the document as a whole and of each paragraph and sentence; and
- the nature of information: what it is assumed the reader knows and what needs to be stated.

Authors do not necessarily write evenly. In a single document you might have to raise the level in some places and lower it in others, increase the pace here and slow it down there, and adjust the tone in different places. The text that needs to be changed, as well as the changes, might be obvious or subtle.

When you think you need to alter the level of a document and you have not been briefed to do so, check with your project manager first. Remember that the changes you make are, in effect, suggestions to the author. Consider the reason for every change: it should never be because you don't 'like' what the author wrote or you prefer it to be said another way, but only because the text doesn't *work* for the reader in a specific way that you can explain. There are some basic techniques you can use to get text to the appropriate level.

Lowering the level

When the level is too high, you might
* use simpler vocabulary or explain terms the reader cannot be assumed to understand;
* make sentences simpler and shorter by using fewer subordinate clauses, taking care not to create a monotonous, boring tone:
* make paragraphs shorter by dividing a topic into smaller units;
* organize the text to move forward logically, ensuring no gaps in information and no tangents;
* repeat information to help the reader understand or remember;
* make sure that there is a clearly stated transition between the information in one sentence and the next, and between one paragraph and the next;
* in non-fiction, use fewer levels of heading and more examples of concepts;
* apply the active rather than the passive voice.

The active voice, in which the subject precedes the verb, is more direct, lively and forceful than the passive, in which the verb precedes the subject:

active

> The editor made many important improvements to the text.

passive

> Many important improvements to the text were made by the editor.

The active voice can help to lower the level of a text, although it can also be used effectively in texts at any level. There are times, of course, when the passive is necessary:

> Politicians are distrusted by many people now

is appropriate when the topic is politicians, whereas

> Many people now distrust politicians

is appropriate when the topic is people's attitudes.

Raising the level

To raise the level, you might

- use more conceptual, consolidated or technical vocabulary and remove unnecessary explanations;
- create compound and complex sentences with a variety of syntax and subordinate clauses;
- make longer paragraphs by combining related ideas about a topic;
- delete information that the reader is assumed to know;
- avoid repetition;
- allow the reader to extrapolate the transition between sentences and paragraphs;
- use more levels of headings for complex, detailed non-fiction text.

Changing the tone

The author's style, or voice, also plays a role. Whether it is formal or informal, objective or subjective, restrained or excited, it, too, should be appropriate to the purpose and the market. To make a text more informal, you can use:

- contractions
- the active voice
- the first and second persons
- incomplete sentences

To make it more formal, avoid contractions and incomplete sentences.

Choice of vocabulary is the key to whether statements are objective or subjective. Because the copy-editor needs to query any statement that is subjective when the purpose is to be objective, you have to read text carefully and make sure you understand the nuances of the vocabulary and construction.

Vocabulary and the rhythm of the text convey emotion, from restraint to excitement. Using emphatic modifiers and varying the length and complexity of sentences – particularly making some very short – can enliven a plodding text. But whereas enthusiasm can be a wonderful tool to excite the reader's interest, excessive hyperbolic language and structure can have the opposite effect.

Exercise 4.4, adjusting level and tone

Brief
Below are extracts from the first draft for an instruction booklet to accompany compost bins for small gardens. Adjust the level and/or tone to make it appropriate for the intended purpose and reader, list any queries or suggestions you have for the author, and mark up the text for setting.

USING A COMPOST BIN

This booklet will take you through the process of setting up your composting bin and using it to make high quality compost. It will tell you how to use the compost in your garden and how to tackle any composting problems that might arise. 5

How To Start

Selecting The Best Site

The bin should be placed in your selected position in the garden on soil but never on concrete or paving. Ideally, the site should be in the shade and far enough from the house to prevent any odours being 10 detected but not so far that it becomes arduous to carry kitchen and garden waste to it. Sites exposed to winds should be avoided if possible.

Installation

Firstly, to help drainage from the bin and allow worms to enter the compost, the soil on which the composter is to be placed should be broken up. Recessing the bottom of the composter into the soil seals the base which increases stability and reduces excessive air flow in bins without a base. If particular problems with vermin are expected and there is no base, the bin can be set up on top of a sheet of narrow gauge wire mesh which has been dug in and you should be prepared to replace this if broken or corroded. The composter should be checked to make sure it is level.

Kitchen Bin

Use a pre-sorting bin to sort kitchen materials easily and hygienically on a daily basis. The kitchen bin should be kept in a convenient place and the lid kept shut. The contents of the kitchen bin should be transferred to the compost bin every day or at least every other day.

Which Organic Material Can Be Composted?

There are many organic materials in the kitchen and garden that can be used to make excellent compost. Although inn principle any organic material can be composted, for reasons that will be discussed, you should select what you add to your composting mixture with great care.

Kitchen Materials

Fruit and vegetable peeling and salad scraps are excellent for composting. Large or fibrous stems, such as those of cabbage and brussel sprouts, should be cut up or crushed before use. Bread, teabags, coffee grounds and filters, small amounts of vegetable oils and fats and crushed egg shells can be used.

Garden Materials
Grass cuttings are excellent for composting. Large amounts of grass should not be added alone but should be mixed in with other feedstock such as leaves and shredded woody material. This will prevent the cuttings from producing an offensive smell. Leaves should be shredded before use as they can take a long time to compost. Dead flowers and finished annuals should be cut up before use.

Other materials
Human and pet hair and feathers provide good sources of nitrogen. Animal manures, such as rabbit, bird and guinea pig manures, and the sawdust or wood chip bedding from these animals, can help a composting considerably through the addition of nitrogen. For health reasons do not use cat or dog faeces , or cat litter which absorbs moisture. Horse manure, with wood chips or straw as bedding, can be excellent components in a composting mixture, providing useful nutrients and helpful micro-organisms

Newspaper can be added in small quantitites as long as it is first finely shredded, but cardboard, except perhaps shredded egg boxes, is best avoided.

Which Wastes Should Not Be Composted

There are a number of wastes that should never be added to a compost mixture. The following wastes should be avoided for the reasons given.

Non-Organic Materials

Glass, plastics, plastic bags and metals will not break down in a compost heap and will reduce the quality of the compost if present. They should be separated from waste for composting and recycled or reused whenever possible.

Meat, Fish And Bones

Although fish and meat will break down in a composter it is best to avoid their use. They can attract dogs, cats, hedgehogs, foxes, rats and flies, and produce offensive smells.

Disease Carrying Plant Material

The microorganisms causing many plant diseases are not always killed by the typical garden composting process and should be excluded from the feedstock. Problems can particularly arise if, for example, compost made from waste including diseased tomato plants is then applied to the next crop of tomatoes. This can lead to a build up of disease affecting these plants.

Other organic wastes

Leather and rubber should not be added, as they will not break down to any significant extent, and the same is true of synthetic textiles. Wool, linen and cotton will only break down very slowly and may contain undesirable dyes. It is probably best to exclude textiles completely. The contents of vacuum cleaner bags, coal ash, soot, cigarette ash and cigarette stubs should not be added and treated or pained wood should be avoided. Plants treated with herbicides or pesticides should not be used, as these chemical may prevent composting from taking palce and make the finished compost unusable in the garden. Mineral oils such as oil from a car should never be used.

Remember – if in doubt leave it out!!!

Making Compost In The Composting Bin

Composting is a natural process carried out by micro-organisms such as bacteria and fungi. An efficient gardener carries out this process in a controlled way to produce weed-free, sweet smelling compost. Excellent results can be achieved by following the few simple suggestions outlined below.

Use Good feedstock

A list of feedstock suitable for composting is given on pages 00–00.

Not too Wet

Do not allow the mixture of feedstock to be too wet or too soft. If you attempt to only make compost from vegetable peelings, salads or grass cuttings, you will find that the compost tends to collapse into a stick mess that is likely to produce offensive odours. It is important that some drier, woody or fibrous material are mixed in with the soft vegetable matter. This will prevent the compost from becoming too wet and give it a good structure.

Not too Dry

Do not allow the mixture of feedstock to be too dry. If you attempt to make compost from just shredded wood or straw or tree trimmings, you will find that composting will be very slow or may not take place at all. Mixing in grass cuttings, horse manure or some other suitable green materials usually ensures there is sufficient moisture and nitrogen present to encourage the micro-organisms to start composting.

Not too Woody

Do not attempt to make compost with large pieces of material such as unshredded woody branches, large pieces of fibrous roots or stems, or unshredded leaves.

Mix and Match In Batches

The materials to be composted should be mixed, after shredding if necessary, before placing the mixture into the bin. Do not put in large amounts of a single type of feedstock at any one time.

Keep it Loose

Do not allow the mixture to become compacted. Never stand on or press the compost down but keep the structure loose so that air can easily penetrate through the compositing mixture.

How to fill the Composting Bin

Open the lid of the composting bin and add a first layer of shredded stems and trimmings to a depth of about 5 – 10 cms. Then, using the principles outlined above, add feedstock on a daily basis until the bin is full. You will find that the level of material will drop considerably in the first few days. Continue to fill with a suitable mixture of material until the bin is full again.

How Long Does it Take to Make Compost?

Depending on the ingredients used to make the compost and how often the compost is turned, composting can take ten to twenty weeks. During this time the weight of the material in the bin will drop by about 50% while the volume will reduce by 33% to 66%.

Turning the Compost

The composting process can be accelerated and the quality of the compost considerably improved if the composting material is turned on a regular basis. When turning, make sure the composting material in the outside regions of the heap goes into the centre and that the material in the centre is moved to the outside. Continue this process until all of the compost is uniformly turned adding moisture if necessary.

<small>Adapted from Peter Ridley Waste Systems, *Using a Compost Bin*, Saxmundham, Suffolk, 2000, and reproduced by kind permission of the publisher.</small>

EXERCISE FOLLOW-UP

The readers are adults, who are presumably interested in gardening but not assumed to have any special knowledge. The average adult reader is assumed to have been educated only to the age of 16 and to have the reading age of an even younger person.

Changing the voice to active throughout imposes a welcome consistency on the text, and makes it more concise, direct and friendly. In this piece it also helped to keep the level consistent, as did changing a word or phrase. Correcting the punctuation helped improve the clarity. When a text is this heavily edited or rewritten, it is usual to send the author a clean copy of the revised text, not the edit itself, to read and approve or change. In this exercise, most of the changes are to adjust the level. You would still need to have a dialogue with the author about the substantive changes. For example, you might have understood what the author meant at line 21, but you should have asked him or her to confirm your suggested change. Similarly, you should have asked for the author's agreement if you wanted to move the text in lines 54–5 to the section on wastes that should not be used. The author might have responded that it is important to make this exclusion clear when saying which manures to use, in case readers read or reviewed only this section, and that it would be best to repeat the information in the section on what to exclude. Because reasons for exclusion are explained more clearly for other substances, you should have asked the author to explain the health reasons in this case. Some of your changes and queries might be different from those in the model answer, of course, but the point is to have achieved the same result.

5 Specialist texts

As a copy-editor you might work on fiction or non-fiction prose texts that include extracts from poems and plays in an epigraph or in the body of the work, or on drama scripts or anthologies of poetry. In most cases your role will be mainly to mark up rather than closely edit the copy, but there's still plenty to do. This chapter explains what to do and how to do it, as well as the principles of editing and marking up the kind of instructional text that appears in manuals, from cookery to car repair. Forget the old adage 'Don't judge a book by its cover' – many people do, so this chapter also covers the principles of editing blurbs and checking cover or jacket copy.

Poetry

Poets, rather than copy-editors or designers, decide how to lay out their verse. They might start all lines ranged left, indent alternate lines, or centre all lines. Those who write concrete poetry arrange the lines to create shapes, or space each line and the words or characters within it individually. Poets might start each line with a capital letter, use capitals at the beginning of a sentence only, or use only lower-case letters. They might well use different styles for different works.

You may think that this doesn't leave you much to do, but you'd be wrong. The copy-editor must ensure that the poet's intentions are respected when verse is quoted. When poetry follows the normal rules of the English language, you should be prepared to correct spelling, punctuation and capitalization. When you are unsure whether the quoted extract or entire poem is an accurate copy of the original – because of erratic capitalization, inconsistent indentation or rhyme scheme, or incorrect punctuation, for example – check with the author on the specific point; if there are many such quotations, ask the author for scans or photocopies of the original material so that you can assist him or her by checking for accuracy.

To indicate the pronunciation of '-ed', some poets use a grave accent (èd) and others use an acute accent (éd). Impose consistency when poems appear in an anthology, following house style if it covers this point, unless the general editor says that each poet's style should be used.

Extracts of poetry can be set in the text (embedded) or displayed. You need to consider which is the preferred option in each project. It might seem that displaying verse is always clearer for the reader, but consider whether there is sufficient space to do it and whether it is necessary or even desirable in the context of the work. It might seem less visually disruptive, for example, to embed a single, short extract of a few lines, whereas it wouldn't be possible to convey the essence of a line of concrete poetry this way. It would also be better to display multiple extracts of varying lengths, particularly if they are to be compared.

Remember that, as explained in Chapter 3, the poems must be acknowledged and those in copyright need to have permissions cleared. As with all quoted material, do not alter the spelling to conform to your own house style.

Embedded

House style might indicate the maximum number of lines of poetry that can be embedded, and whether a vertical line or a solidus is to be used to mark line breaks: the end of one line of verse and the beginning of the next. A double vertical line or double solidus can be used to mark the break between stanzas. If the house style is silent on these issues, you make the decisions and apply them consistently, of course.

Instruct the designer/typesetter that the line-break marks must be spaced either side and that such a mark cannot be at the beginning of a line of type. Although this is standard procedure, never assume that everyone knows: if you tell people what is needed and they already know, it is just confirmation; if you don't tell them and they don't know, it becomes your mistake.

Use quotation marks around the verse as around any quotation. If words are omitted from an extract, use an ellipsis; put it in square brackets if the verse itself includes ellipses to indicate pauses. Check that the acknowledgement is in the text or in a note.

Displayed

Ensure that all verse has been typed exactly as in the original, and mark it up with a code, remembering to encircle it, as for all instructions. On the list of codes, give a general instruction that this code means 'to be set line for line and space for space', which covers spacing on a line and spacing between stanzas. When the quotation begins other than at the beginning of a line, check that the first word in that line is shown in its correct position relative to the following line. As in prose quotations, do not enclose displayed verse in quotation marks, unless, of course, they are part of the verse itself.

Displayed verse is generally set in a smaller size than the text, although this is not obligatory. It can be centred *as a block* on the page, optically or using the longest line in the poem to determine this position, or it can be indented from the left uniformly. The latter gives a consistent visual appearance when there are likely to be a number of displayed quotations on a single page.

When you are working on hard copy and the verse is embedded but you want it displayed, mark the beginning of each line. When the verse has been displayed in the typescript, mark any turnover lines with the run-on mark. If the line is too long for the typeset measure, the typesetter may indent the turnover further from the left than other indentations, or even indent it from the right to avoid disrupting a centred pattern. Check that the pattern of indentation for the beginning of lines is consistent. When you edit on-screen, you can embed verse or display it, but, of course, you must still code it. In an e-file, the return symbol shows the end of a line.

Instruct the typesetter not to separate paired lines or break short stanzas, and mark intentional breaks between stanzas with a line space. When lines are to be numbered, usually in 5s or 10s, write the numerals in the right margin and instruct the typesetter to set them ranged right within the text area. When the line is too long to accommodate the numerals, number the line above or below.

If the acknowledgement is not in the text, mark it to be set under the verse, ranged right on the longest line of the verse or full out to the margin, according to house style. When there are repeated extracts from the same source interspersed with text, work a mention of the source into the text. Then place a reference to the book, canto or line numbers in parentheses on the last line of each extract if there is space or on the line below, ranged right as described above.

160 *Copy-editing*

Exercise 5.1, editing and marking up poetry

Brief
Edit and mark up this extract from a short story.

House style
- -ise verb endings
- single quotes
- numbers as words up to ninety-nine

What was going on? He used to be able to recite the entire poem as easily as say his name. Now all he could recall was 'if thou must love me, let it be for nought/except for love's sake only'. He knew that was right, he knew it, but that was cold comfort when there were another twelve lines to the sonnet. Which one was it? It was in the teens – number 13 or 14 perhaps. Yes, yes, that's right, it was the fourteenth of Elizabeth Barrett Browning's Sonnets from the Portuguese. OK, OK, let's not just give into this stupid business of losing one's memory; think how you're going to fight it. 'Old Sanjay, now he'd be a great help. What's his phone number? Damn, what *is* his phone number?

'Sanjay? Hi, it's Pete, how are you? Listen, remember a couple of months ago when we were having coffee and talking about the old days? And Abe remembered how you won that competition for reciting poetry?

'Yeah, I wasn't sure if hed finally got over coming second. So?'

'It was a long time ago; he's over it. And you'll recall that I came fourth. Anyway, how good are you now?'

'What, at reciting poetry?'

'Poetry or anything. Not so much reciting as just remembering.'

'Hmm, probably not as good as I used to be. You know, I kept it up – memorizing poetry – for a long time after school. It really impressed the girls, and Reeta said it was one of the most romantic things about me. But I haven't done it for a long time now. Why?'

'I've been trying to remember that Barrett Browning sonnet, the one that starts 'If thou must love me let it be for nought/Except for love's sake only.' Only I can't get any farther than that.'

'Have you tried looking it up in a book? Or on the web? You didn't really ring to see if I remembered it, did you?'

'Yes and no. Do you?'

There was silence, and Pete figured Sanjay was just combing through his memory, so he didn't say anything either. He was right.

'Got a pen?'

Then Sanjay spoke not only the words but also their meaning, pausing occasionally, and Pete wrote them down even as he rejoiced in its familiarity. Later, after he'd explained his idea to Sanjay and they'd agreed to meet the following week, he found his anthology of Victorian poetry and looked up the sonnet. Sanjay had been word perfect, although since he had spoken so expressively, Pete's version didn't have the line breaks or capital letters as they were on the page:

If thou must love me let it be for nought
Except for love's sake only. Do not say

'I love her for her smile … her look … her way
Of speaking gently … for a trick of thought
A sense of pleasant ease on such a day' –   45
For these things in themselves , Belovèd, may
Be changed, or change for thee, – and love, so wrought,
may be unwrought so. Neither love me for
Thine own dear pity's wiping my cheeks dry, –
A creature might forget to weep,   50
who bore thy comfort long, and lose thy love therby!
But love me for love's sake, that evermore
Thou mayst love on, through love's eternity.

    Pete really loved that poem. In fact, like Sanjay, Abe and Mark, he loved poetry, and he wasn't willing to lose it. He had spoken to Abe and Mark too. They had remained friends since school, when they had worked together to memorise poems and then competed against each other for the school prize. They didn't often meet as a group, but they were all retired now and the revival of their poetry trio seemed a good way to fill some of their time.

    'Not a bad idea', Abe had said. 'I don't have anything pressing to do and I suspect Becca will be glad to have me out of the house for a while. You make the coffee and I'll bring some biscuits.'

    'Good, but bring some poetry too.'

    Mark had not only been enthusiastic, he guessed that Abe would offer to bring something to eat. 'Don't you remember how he always brought biscuits or chocolates or a bag of sweets in the old days? Said it helped him to concentrate. Maybe that's why he didn't win, Mark laughed, 'he didn't have anything to eat during the contest. Sure, I'll come. I'll bing some modern stuff, 'cause I know you'll supply the golden oldies.'

They would each bring a book of poetry or at least a few of their favourite poems: they would read them all and then choose a few to memorize for their next meeting. Sanjay had said that for this first session at least none of the poems should be very long or they might get discouraged. So they had agreed on nothing longer than a sonnet. Pete decided to type out two of his favourites in addition to the Barrett Browning. He would do it from memory and then look them up to correct the errors and fill the gaps. He started with Shakespeare's first sonnet:

When forty winters shall besiege they brow
And dig deep trenches in thy beautys field

He'd done rather well with that one, missing just a few words here and here. He started to type another – 'My glass shall not persuade me that I am old,/ So long as youth and you are of one date' – but he decided one poem about old age was enough. Still, he checked what he had typed so far and then continued to read. He read, dozed, got up for a cup of tea and found other things to do. A few days later he pulled some books off the shelf and began to browse. He needed to find another poem for the meeting. Nothing too obvious. Aha! Here was Maria's copy of Flame and Shadow, a collection of poems by Sara Teasdale. There must be something in there. Yes, 'Meadowlarks' would do: not about old age or death, not gloomy at all, not really.

He typed it out:

In the silver light after a storm 95
  Under dripping boughs of bright new green,
I take the low path to hear meadowlarks
  Alone and high-hearted as if I were a queen.

What have I to fear in life or death
  Who have known these things: the kiss in the 100
    night,
The white flying joy when a song is born
  And meadowlarks whistling in silver light

EXERCISE FOLLOW-UP

There were some errors of punctuation and grammar to correct – keeping tenses consistent in the narrative is important, although you should always remember that characters can be allowed to speak ungrammatically. You are not expected to check every quotation an author uses, but you should know that a sonnet is 14 lines, so in checking the Barrett Browning poem you could either have pencilled a query to the author or looked up the sonnet: it's so well known that it is easy to do. If you did look it up on the Internet, you might have found versions with the alternative spelling of 'naught' for 'nought' and with different layouts, which should have prompted you to query the author.

The complete works of Shakespeare should be part of every copy-editor's reference library, as authors of all kinds of works are fond of quoting the plays as well as the poems. Many authors quote from memory and they won't always do so accurately. Don't depend on your memory either: check. Be aware that any differences you find might be because the author has used a different edition, so be sure to query, not simply change, them.

In the Teasdale poem, you needed to mark the turnover line in the second stanza to be run on, so that the typesetter will put it on the correct line if space allows.

Plays

The main elements of a script are the speakers' names, the dialogue and the stage directions, and they are typographically styled to keep them visually distinct. There are many ways to style play texts, so once again the guiding principles are house style and consistency.

Numbering

In classical plays the acts and scenes usually have roman numerals. Mark these up as A and B level headings, and let the designer decide on the typographic style. Modern plays can follow the same pattern or use arabic numerals, and some are divided into scenes only. See below for how to acknowledge the sources of extracts.

Characters

A complete play will have a list of characters, which can also be titled 'dramatis personae' or 'cast list'. It *can* be on a recto after the prelims, but it is a common practice to have a part-title on the recto and the cast list on its verso so that it faces the first page of text. Keep the cast list where you can see it throughout the editing to help you maintain consistency in the spelling of names and in the attributes of the characters.

Speakers' names are usually set in small caps (LEAR) or in initial cap and small caps (LEAR), and can be followed by a colon, full point or space. The same style is used for the characters' names when they appear in the stage directions, so that the actors can quickly and easily find all references to themselves. A certain inconsistency is allowed: the names of the major characters might be abbreviated and those of the minor ones spelled out. Of course, the names of all the characters might be spelled out or all might be abbreviated. Whatever the choice, impose it consistently.

Dialogue

The dialogue, in a roman serif face, starts on the same line as the speaker's name, and turnover lines are usually indented 1 em under the speaker's name. Again, this is designed to make it easy for the actors to find their own parts. Nonetheless, there are examples with the speakers' names indented.

When a line of verse is split between speakers, the beginning of the second and subsequent parts aligns with the end of the preceding one. You will have to mark this clearly on the hard copy or e-file. When such a subsequent part is too long to fit on a single line, the turnover is indented from the right. The typesetter should know this, but you can include a global instruction to be sure.

Stage directions

Italic type is reserved for stage directions, excepting the characters' names. The other style attributes depend on the nature and position of the directions in the play, whether the play is classical or modern, and, of course, house style. For example, the description of the scene can be set without brackets, centred or full measure, or, if very long, indented 2 ems. Entrances and other action following the scene directions and before the first speech can run on or be broken off, in which case they are either centred or full measure, like the scene description. Other entrances are on a separate line, often without terminal punctuation unless they are composed of more than one sentence.

There is greater unanimity on setting the directions between the speaker's name and speech: in square brackets, all lower-case, without terminal punctuation. Directions while a character is speaking are set in square brackets with an initial cap, and terminal punctuation only if they are complete sentences. They are set within the dialogue if the action refers to the speaker but on a separate line if the action refers to another character or comes between speeches.

When exits come at the end of a character's speech, they are ranged right – on the same line if there is space, on the next line otherwise – with an opening square bracket but no terminal punctuation. Use the word 'exit' only for a single character; use 'exeunt' when more than one character leaves the stage.

Marking up

If you are working on the hard copy of a text that has not been typed in the appropriate styles, it is simplest to highlight all the characters' names instead of coding or marking them up individually. (However, if the hard copy is going to be scanned, this might not work, so check with the production department or typesetter first.) Because they are short and within lines of dialogue, it is most efficient to mark up individually stage directions after a speaker's name and within his or her speech. You can use a mark-up code, for example 'SD', for stage directions before and between speeches, and another code, perhaps 'SDE', for exits. Then list the codes and highlighter colours and the styles they represent for the typesetter or designer. On an e-file, you can use the style menu to mark up in a similar way. In all cases, mark up the text for caps, lower case, punctuation and square brackets as required.

While your main job on a play text is likely to be the marking up, you must still correct spelling and punctuation, and check, as you would with any fiction, that the action is consistent with the stage directions: for example, that no one uses the phone after the wire's been cut, or speaks before an indication that he or she has entered or after an indication that he or she has exited.

Extracts in text

The reference to the source can be worked into the text or appear ranged right under the extract, as in an epigraph. The source should include the playwright's name, the title of the play, and the act, scene and line numbers. For classical works it is still common to:
- capitalize 'Act' and use an upper-case roman numeral
- capitalize 'Scene' and use a lower-case roman numeral
- use lower case for 'line' and use arabic numerals

References to modern plays are styled like this or with only arabic numerals, according to the style in the play itself.

Commas separate the elements in the reference in running text – Act I, Scene ii, lines 45–50 – but full stops are used and words omitted in short references – I. ii. 45–50 and 1.2.45–50.

168 *Copy-editing*

Exercise 5.2, marking up a play script

Brief
Edit and mark up this extract from Act IV of Shakespeare's *Romeo and Juliet*, which an author has typed out for inclusion in a schoolbook. Make a list of queries for the author.

House style
- centre scene descriptions and entrances without brackets
- spell out characters' names
- use a colon followed by a single space after a speaker's name
- indent turnovers 1 em from right

Scene Iv Hall in Capulet's house

Enter Lady Capulet and Nurse

Lady Capulet: Hold, take these keys, and fetch more

spices, nurse

Nurse: They call for quinces and dates in the pastry.

Enter Capulet

Capulet: come stir, stir, stir! The second cock hath

crow'd.

The curfew bell hath rung, 'tis three o'clock:

Look to the baked meats good Angelica:

Spare not for cost.

Nurse: Go you cot-queen, go,

Get you to bed; faith, you'll be sick tomorrow

For this night's watching.

Capulet: No, not a whit: what! I have watch'd ere now
All night for lesser cause, and ne'er been sick. 10
Lady Capulet: Ay, you have been a mouse-hunt in your time;
But I will watch you from such watching now. [*Exit Lady Capulet and Nurse.*
Capulet: A jealous-hood, a jealous hood! – Now fellow
What's there/

Enter servants, with spits, logs and baskets

First Servant Things for the cook, sir, but I know not what.
Capulet: Make haste, make haste [Exit first
Servant] Sirrah, fetch drier logs:
Call Peter, he will show thee where they are.
Second Servant: I have a head, sir, that will find out logs,
And never trouble Peter for the matter.   [Exit.
Capulet: 'Mass, and well said; a merry whoreson, Ha! 20
Thou shalt be logger-head – Good faith, 'tis day:
The county will be here with the music straight
For so he said he would. *Music within* I hear him near. –
Nurse! – Wife! – What, ho! – what, nurse, I say!
                              Re-enter Nurse.
Go waken Juliet, go and trim her up;

I'll go and chat with Paris: — hie, make haste,
Make haste: the bridegroom he is come already:
Make haste, I say. [*Exeunt.*]

Scene v Juliet's chamber; Juliet on the bed

Enter Nurse

Nurse: Mistress! what, mistress! Juliet! fast, I warrant
  her, she:
Why, lamb! why, lady! fie, you slug-a-bed!
Why, love, I say! madam! sweet-heart! why, bride!
What, not a word? you take your pennyworths now;
Sleep for a week; for the next night, I warrant,
The County Paris has set up his rest
That you shall rest but little — God forgive me,
Marry, and amen, how sound she is asleep!
I needs must wake her. Madam, madam, madam!
Ay, let the county take you in your bed;   10
He'll fright you up, i'faith. Will it not be?
What, dress'd! and in your clothes! And down again!
I must needs wake you! Lady! lady! lady!
Alas, alas! Help, help! My lady's dead!
O well-a-day that ever I was born!
Some aqua-vitae, ho! My lord! My lady!

Lady Capulet: What noise is here?
Nurse   O lamentable day!

Lady Capulet: What is the matter?

Nurse: Look, look, O heavy day!

Lady Capulet: O me, O me! My child, my only life,

Revive, look up, or I will die with thee, 20

Help, help! Call help!

Enter Capulet

Capulet: For shame, bring Juliet forth; her lord is come.

Nurse She's dead, deceased, she's dead; alack the day!

Lady Capulet Alack the day, she's dead, she's dead, she's dead!

Capulet: Ha! Let me see her. Out, alas! she's cold;

her blood is settled and her joints are stiff;

Life and these lips have long been separated.

Death lies on her like an untimely frost.

Upon the sweetest flower of all the field.

Nurse O lamentable day!

Lady Capulet O woeful time! 30

Capulet: Death hath ta'en her hence to make me wail,

ties up my tongue and will not let me speak.

Enter Friar Laurence and Paris, with Musicians

Friar Lawrence : Come, is the bride ready to go to church?

Capulet: Ready to go, but never to return.

O son, the night before they wedding-day

Hath death lain with thy wife: see, there she lies,

Flower as she was, deflowered by him.

My daughter he hath wedded: I will die

And leave him all; life, living, all is Death's   40

Paris: Have I thought long to see this morning's

   face,

And does it give me such a sight as this?

Lady Cap.: Accurst, unhappy, wretched, hateful day!

Most miserable hour that e'er time saw

In lasting labour of his pilgrimage!

But one, poor one, one poor and loving child,

But one thing to rejoice and solace in,

And cruel death hath catch'd it from my sight!

Nurse O woe! O woeful, woeful, woeful day!

Most lamentable day, most woeful day,

That ever, ever, I did yet behold!

O day! O day! O day! O hateful day!

Never was seen so a day as this:

O woeful day, o woeful day!   50

Paris: Beguied, divorced, wronged, spited, slain!

Most detestable death, by thee beguiled,

By cruel thee quite overthrown!

O love! O life! not life, but love in death!

Capulet: Despised, distressed, hated, martyr'd,

   kill'd!

Uncomfortable time, why camest thou now   60

To murder, murder our solemnity?

O child! O child! my soul, and not my child!

Dead art thou! Alack, my child is dead;

And with my child my joys are buried!

EXERCISE FOLLOW-UP

Seeing the text like this reminds me that even the best playwrights need talented acting to make some dialogue work.

  Never assume that an author has copied from a source accurately: read quotations for sense and raise queries where necessary. Shakespeare is easy to check, particularly when you have been given the precise location of the text. Reading through the author's version, you should have been prompted to check a source to see how Lady Capulet's second entrance is described and when. You would also have to look at a source to check capitalization and find the words occasionally missing from the copy. If the edition you consulted had differences in the words, capitalization or punctuation from the author's copy, you should have made it a query for the author. You need to be certain whether the author is using a different edition or has merely made a typing error. The marking up was simple: codes for speakers' names – including the use of a colon instead of just space – and for characters' names (the model answer uses highlighter) and stage directions; individual mark-up for alignment of partial lines and run-ons. You needed to give a global instruction about turnovers, because the typesetter might not have realized the dialogue is verse.

Manuals

Books or looseleaf binders that give instructions on how to do something are manuals, although it's not how we usually think of cookery and craft titles. Such publications on gardening, training, DIY and car repair, on the other hand, may have the word 'manual' in the title. The common features of these publications are a list of materials and instructions for using them.

Because the aim is to make the author's message clear for the reader, the list of ingredients or tools and materials should be in the order of use in the instructions (often referred to as the method). When it is, it also helps you to check that every item in the list is used in the instructions and in the stated amount, and that every item used in the instructions is given in the correct quantity in the list. Items for which amounts are not specified, like 'salt and pepper to taste', 'box of pins', 'turps or white spirit for cleaning brushes', 'flipchart' or 'copies of handouts', are put at the end of the list no matter where they are mentioned in the instructions. You would, of course, query the author about any discrepancies between the list and the instructions.

Although you are not expected to test the instructions, you are expected to check that they are clear, logical and complete, and can work. For training manuals, for example, visualize yourself doing the exercise from the point of view of both the trainer and the participants. Thus you would query the author, for example, if it is not clear that materials can be used in a particular way without further explanation or will fit together as described or are the right amounts or proportions, or that the tasks can be completed in the time stated.

The house style should state whether metric or imperial units are to be used, or, if both, which is to be first and how the second one should be shown. In cookery, house style might also dictate whether units in the list are spelled out or abbreviated, although it is common practice to spell out 'teaspoon' and 'tablespoon' in the method even when they are abbreviated in the list, to avoid any confusion between the two. Numerals are always used for the listed items, no matter how small the amount, and most prepositions and articles are omitted. In the method, words are used for the number of bowls, plates and other containers. Brand names are generally avoided, unless, of course, the article or book is promoting particular products.

The items can be listed in a prepared state: '225 g green beans, rinsed and trimmed' or 'angle grippers, cut to stair width'; or the preparation can be stated as part of the instructions: 'Rinse the green beans, then trim ends'; 'Measure width of stairs and cut grippers to size'.

Check for information that might appear with every set of instructions, such as number of portions or items, preparation and cooking

Specialist texts 175

times, or duration of the exercise or course. Materials that may be photocopied from a training manual should have a copyright line on each page, and a statement that copies may be made only for training purposes should appear on the imprint page in the prelims.

Instructions can be written in normal prose or in 'headline' style, omitting all unnecessary articles and prepositions. They can be divided into paragraphs as appropriate or arranged step by step, in which each step is restricted to one action. Steps can be numbered, lettered or bulleted. How the instructions are written can vary from author to author, and project to project, but should, of course, be consistent in a single publication.

Exercise 5.3, editing text for a manual

Brief

Edit and mark up the following recipes. Consistency is very important, of course, so look through all the material before you begin working on it, and keep a style sheet. When preparing your queries, make sure that the point to which each refers will be clear to the author.

House style
- metric (imperial) for ingredients: 'equivalents' are not always exact; query only if significantly different
- use 'tsp' for 'teaspoon' and 'tbsp' for 'tablespoon' in the ingredients list; spell out both in the instructions
- C/F/gas mark for oven temperature
- fixed space between numerals and abbreviations
- ingredients listed as prepared
- ingredients for which there are recipes elsewhere in the book have initial caps

ORAC stands for 'oxygen radical absorption capacity' and is the premise of the book.

Fish risotto

This is one of our family favourites for a light nourishing late supper on Fridays after a long and busy week. Sally has the recipe down to a T and the delicious crunchy texture of the mangetout, with the softness of the rice and fish, blend perfectly with the Asian flavour of curry. Excellent nutrition and a good ORAC recipe too.

2 tablespoons rapeseed oil – preferably organic but certainly GM-free
1 garlic clove, finely chopped
1 onion chopped
2 tsp curry powder
1 small red pepper
225 (8 oz) arborio rice
450 ml (16 fl oz) Basic Stock
450 ml (16 fl oz) coconut milk
350 ml (12 oz) cod fillet or other firm fish such as hake, halibut, monkfish, haddock, fresh tuna or swordfish – or 225 g (8 oz) fish and 110 g (4 oz) cooked, peeled prawns
75 g (3 oz) young mange tout, cut into ½ in lengths
225 g (8oz) canned sweetcorn, rinsed and drained
leaves of 6 sprigs flat-leaf parsley, coarsely chopped

1 Heat the oil in a deep frying pan or saucepan and gently sauté the onion and garlic until soft – about 5 minutes.
2 Stir in the curry powder, mix thoroughly and cook for 2 minutes.

3 Add the red pepper, stock, coconut milk and rice, and simmer for 20 minutes, until the rice is tender and nearly all the liquid has been absorbed.

4 Break the fish into bite-sized chunks, stir into the rice mixture, mix well and put back on a gentle heat for five minutes, adding more stock if the risotto looks as if its drying out. Check that the firm fish is cooked: fish with denser flesh, monkfish and tuna particularly, may take a few minutes longer.

5 Add the mange-tout and sweetcorn, and heat through for 2 minutes. Serve the risotto with the parsley on top.

Beef and Couscous Pilaff

Distinct flavours of North Africa enhance this substantial dish. The unique combination of pistachios, beef and spices is what produces the taste, but it's the addition of the peas ad dried fruits that bump up the ORAC score. Including generous amounts of fresh mint improves digestion and offsets any fatiness in the beef.

Scant ½ tsp ground cumin

Scant ½ tsp ground cinammon

1 tsp ground coriander

225 g (8 oz lean braising steak, cut into small cubes

2 tbsp rapeseed oil – preferably organic

225 g (6 oz) couscous

75 g (3 oz) no-need-to-soak apricots, each cut into six pieces

75 g (3 oz) sultanas

700ml (1½ pints) Basic Stock (see page 00)

75 g shelled pistachio nuts

Leaves of 4 large sprigs of mint, chopped

1 Mix the ground cumin and cinammon and half the coriander

2 Coat the meat with the spice mixture and set aside.

3 Heat half the oil in a large frying pan, pour in the couscous and cook, stirring continuously, for 2 minutes. Take off the heat and stir in the remaining coriander.

4 Add the dried apricots to the couscous.

5 Boil the stock and add half to the couscous, stir, cover and leave to stand for 10 minutes.

6 Meanwhile, dry-fry the nuts gently for 5 minutes.

7 Fluff up the couscous with a fork and add the rest of the stock.

9 Cook the peas in boiling water for 2 minutes, sprinkle them on top of the couscous and set aside.

10 In another pan, seal the steak, turn down the heat slightly and continue cooking for 8 minutes, or until as well done as you like it, stirring continuously.

11 Add the meat and nuts to the couscous and stir thoroughly.

12 Sprinkle with the mint and serve.

Steamed fish in foil

A brilliantly easy way to cook fish ad the healthiest way to cook the vegetables, this produces a finished dish that is high in essential nutrients and has a simple clean flavour.

Serves 4

4 steaks of salmon, halibut of hake

2 small carrots thinly sliced with a vegetable peeler

1 orange pepper, deseeded and cut into very fine strips

4 spring onioins, sliced lengthways into strands

juice of 1 lemon

150ml (5 fl ozs) dry white wine

50 g (2 oz) unsalted butter

4 sprigs dill

1½ lb mixed green leafy vegetables – spinach, chard, cabbage, kale, etc. – coarsely chopped

2 leeks, very finely sliced

freshly ground black pepper

1 Cut 4 pieces of kitchen foil large enough to envelop each piece of fish comfortably. Put each fish steak into the middle of a piece of foil. Add the strips of carrots, pepper and spring onions.

2 Pull up the sides and pour in the wine and lemon juice. Dot each parcel with butter, lay the dill on top, add a twist of freshly ground black pepper and seal the parcels.

3 Preheat the over to 200° C and bake the parcels for 20 minutes.

4 Meanwhile, put the leafy green vegetables in a steamer and cook until they're just tender but with bite.

5 When the fish is done, pile the green vegetables on individual serving plates. Carefully open one end of each foil parcel and pour

the juices over the vegetables. Use a fish slice or spatula to lift the fish, with the vegetables on top, on to the green vegetables.

Recipes adapted from Michael van Straten, *The ORACle Diet*, London, Kyle Cathie, 2002.

EXERCISE FOLLOW-UP

You don't have to know how to cook to edit these recipes. Checking the list of ingredients against the method would trigger most of the queries. Comparing the recipes would lead you to add the page cross-reference for the stock recipe and the additional phrase in the reference to rapeseed oil, and would prompt you to ask the author about the number served in the first two recipes. In two of the recipes there needed to be some reordering of the ingredients. The order in which they are used determines the order in the list, but in these recipes the ingredients concerned are used together, so you could have changed the order in either the list or the method. Always check the numbering of steps in the instructions (as in lists in general) as a separate task, to make it easier to catch mistakes. When this happens and you are not sending a copy of the renumbered text to the author with the queries, use the author's original numbers in the queries.

In the first recipe you should have noticed the inconsistency in 'mangetout'. Whether you made all the mentions one word or hyphenated does not matter – dictionaries differ – but consistency is essential.

In the introduction to the second recipe the deletion of 'the addition of' makes the text more concise and ensures noun–verb agreement.

In the third recipe you had to convert the imperial weight for the vegetables and find the equivalent oven temperatures in Fahrenheit and gas mark. Thinking about the logic of the instructions leads to putting the preheating instruction first ('pre-' indicates that this action must be done before another), so that the oven temperature will be reached by the time the reader has prepared the foil parcels. Asking how long the vegetables need to cook is important too: start them too soon and they'll be either overcooked or cold by the time the fish is done.

You may have had more or fewer queries than those shown, depending on whether you were able to work out some answers for yourself from the text.

Jacket or cover copy

Copy-editors are usually responsible for checking that all the copy on the jacket or cover is complete and correct, that is, matches the text. The minimum copy on the front panel is the author's name and the book title. Other copy can include a subtitle; a series title; 'Foreword by —'; an edition number; a 'strap line' about the content, the sales (if good) or a prize the book has been nominated for or won; and, if the publication is sponsored, 'in association with …' and that company's logo.

The spine has the book title, the author's name and the publisher's name and/or logo or colophon.

Generally, the front flap of a jacket has copy about the contents of the book, and the back flap has information about the author. When there are no flaps, the back cover contains the 'blurb' about the book and a brief note about the author. Otherwise, it may have a list of features – selling points – or quotations from reviews of this or the author's previous work or from testimonials. (Reviews can be gathered for the first publication by sending text to reviewers at an early stage.) It should have the barcode and ISBN in the lower right corner, usually 10 mm from the bottom and 10 mm from the spine. Why so exact? So that staff doing stock-taking in bookshops can pull the books just a little off the shelf and use an electronic scanner to read the data in the barcode.

House style determines where the publisher's name and logo/colophon appear other than on the spine, and where the price, if printed, and the credit for the design and any illustrations appear.

Blurb

A word we now accept at face value as meaning the sales copy for a book, 'blurb' was coined in the early twentieth century by the American humorist Gelett Burgess to describe hyperbolic advertisements. Of course, blurb doesn't have to be hyperbolic to do its job.

Blurbs might be written by commissioning editors, copy-editors or publicity copywriters. It is customary for copy-editors to check or edit blurbs they have not written themselves. Obviously, blurbs are aimed at the same market as the books they describe, but they serve a different purpose. Before you write or edit a blurb, think about how you approach books in a shop, and watch other people do it. People read the blurb first. If it doesn't arouse their interest, they put the book down. No sale. When the blurb does arouse interest, people look inside the book to see if it reinforces the message of the blurb, and then make their decision.

So the blurb has to be an appealing and accurate representation of the book. It achieves this by conveying the tone of a novel or the nature of the material in an anthology, or by highlighting the features of a non-fiction work. Listen when you read blurb out loud: it should not be excessively effusive, nor should it be turgid or plodding. It can repeat information that is seen as an important selling point. Varying the length of sentences and the syntax, stripping out unnecessary words, using phrases for greater impact, focusing on one point and combining others are techniques to help create the right pace. Clichés, hyperbole and giving away the ending of a story are all to be avoided.

Exercise 5.4, editing jacket and cover copy

Brief
Edit the jacket copy and the cover copy below, rewriting if necessary, but not exceeding the length. Ensure that all the information is included in the appropriate place and query any that is missing.

House style
- initials with full points and spaced
- -ize spelling for verbs, where appropriate

1

Front panel:

The Standard Guide to Cats

Consultant Editor:O. P. Elliott

General Editors: Katrina Brown and Dr Tom Korat

Spine:

Elliot, Brown, Korat

The Standard Guide to Cats

Zoo House [and logo]

Front flap (single photo of cat):

The Standard Guide to Cats

This book has been produced with the cooperation of the Governing Council of the Cat Fancy in Great Britain and the Cat Fanciers' Association Inc. of the United States.

There has been no standard cat reference book that meets the needs of pedigree breeders as well as all those people who have cats as pets until now. To meet this need *The Standard Guide to Cats* has been produced in cooperation with the paramount breed-recognition organizations in the world. The Standards of Points are given for all recognized breeds and colour variations. They include the precise wording of the official British and American standards. Each Standard is accompanied by a short descriptive, historical article, photographs of top quality show cats and line drawing to illustrate specific points.

The book also includes an up-to-date guide to feline genetics, an chapter on health care and research, boarding cattery and stud quarters standards, and a chapter on development and behaviour in kittens and adult cats. A unique feature is the specially commissioned Eye Colour Guide. The light values of colour photography frequently distort the true shade of a cat's iris, due to its high reflectivity, and there can be confusion about the true colour that is laid down in official standards. Therefore the correct shades are reproduced in this section from artwork, prepared under guidance from the governing bodies. A similar Coat Colour Guide and Coat Pattern Guide are also included.

There is a full index to every breed, colour and veterinary term used in the book.

Back flap:
O.P. Elliott is on the Council of the Cat Fanciers' Association Inc., and is a well known breeder and judge.

Katrina Brown has been organizing world-class cat shows for more than twenty years. She has written many books and articles and contributed to many encyclopedias in that time, She is a breeder and a stud owner, and an internationally renowned judge. She is also on the Governing Council of the Cat Fancy, a member of the International Committee of the Cat Fanciers' Association Inc. and a patron of the Cat Clubs in Australia and South Africa.

Dr Tom Korat is a specialist in cat genetics and behaviour and has written several popular books on these subjects, as well as articles for scientific journals. He is also a highly regarded international cat judge.

Zoo House
901 The Enclosure
Big City BC 1 2EM
www.zoohouse.com

Back panel (5 photos):

The first complete guide to the Standards of Points of more than 300 breeds and colour variations in cats produced in cooperation with the world's top breed-recognition bodies, the Cat Fancy in Britain and the Cat Fanciers' Association Inc. of the United States. 350 illustrations include colour guides to eyes and coats, line drawing of points and coat patterns, and photos of every breed as a kitten and adult. This is a best reference book for pedigree breeder as well as for countless pet owners.

2

Front cover:

Holy Smoke

Tonino Benacquista

Winner of France's Grand Prix de la Littérature Policière and the Prix Mystère de la Critique

Spine:

Holy Smoke

Tonino Benacquista

Bitter Lemon Press [and logo]

Back cover:

The Mafia was only the first one of Tonio's problems

Some favours simply cannot be refused, which is why Tonio Polsinelli agrees to write a love letter for a guy named Dario, an old school friend who has become a Paris gigolo. Some time later Dario is found murdered, with a single shot in the head, and Tonio is surprised to find that his friend has left him a small vineyard somewhere in the area east of Naples. When he investigates further he finds that the wine is so bad, it's undrinkable but an elaborate scam has been set up. Thre is the smell of easy money, which attracts the attentions of not only the Mafia but also powerful people at the Vatican and arouses the unbridled hatred of the local people. Mafiosi are not choir boys and, it turns out, monsignors can be very much like them.

A darkly comic and iconoclastic tale told by an author of great verve and humour.

'A story of wine, miracles, the mafia, fascists an even love … Benacquista improves at every outing' Libération

"Energy, humour, fast-paced action and florid storytelling" Le Nouvel Observateur

Holy Smoke won the Grand Prix de la Littérature Policière. It also won the 813 Trophy and the Prix Mystère de la Critique in the same year.

[logo]
Bitter Lemon Press
Crime Paperback Original
£8.99

[barcode attached]

EXERCISE FOLLOW-UP

In blurb, as in so many other areas, fewer words are more effective, which, for some people, makes them more difficult to write. Your edited version may well be different from the model answer and no less successful. The model answer for the non-fiction book repeats information about the governing bodies because it is a vital selling point, and deletes unnecessary and distracting detail about the eye-colour chart. Read all the copy before you begin and you will find it faster and easier to see what needs to be moved, what needs to stay, and what needs to be deleted.

Deleting repetition, unnecessary information and transitional narrative tightens up the blurb for the crime novel, which gives it a more exciting pace and enhances the sense of mystery. All you may do with the review quotes is make the quotation marks consistent and correct the spelling. You can make the information about the prizes more effective: emphasizing 'three ... in one year' and adding 'prestigious' may have the necessary impact on the consumer who is unfamiliar with the individual awards.

6 Tables, technical figures and copy-fitting

Knowing how to edit and mark up tables and technical figures, and how to create them when necessary, are skills required mainly – but not exclusively – when you work on non-fiction. Copy-fitting – cutting or expanding text to fit the space available without changing the author's meaning – is relevant only to non-fiction. Regardless of the area in which you plan to work, or are working, acquiring all of these skills will give you the widest choice and the greatest flexibility in your career.

Tables

I have noticed from time to time that some people become anxious at the mere mention of tables, as though they were about to face a terrible ordeal. If you have approached this chapter with that sinking feeling, relax: tables are not difficult. They are used to present verbal or statistical information more concisely and with more visual clarity than narrative text, so that each element and the relationships between, or comparisons of, them are easier to understand. They use minimal text and follow simple patterns, two factors that make them relatively easy to edit.

Structure and layout

Figure 6.1 shows the basic structure of a table, almost all parts of which you would be able to name even if they weren't labelled. No matter how complex a table might seem, it will simply be an extension of this pattern. We'll look at statistical tables primarily, and mention important differences in verbal tables.

RULES

Tables are intended to facilitate comparison of information. Because rules create a barrier between the elements, no vertical rules and a minimum number of horizontal ones are used. There is a relatively thick rule under the heading and one below the body, separating the table into distinct parts. Thin rules are used under column headings and subheadings. Space, rather than a rule, separates the line of totals from the rest of the body.

Word tables in language textbooks for young readers are sometimes designed with horizontal and vertical rules, creating a matrix. To ensure that the rules help rather than hinder the reader, it is a good idea to make them very thin or print them in a shade of grey (50–60% black, for example).

table heading **Table 12.1 Local elections in Fantasyland, 2000**

column headings

Party	Votes cast	No. seats won	%age seats won
Cats	1,200	30 [a]	20
Dogs	2,280	57	38
Gadgets	480	12	8
Pigs	1,440	36 [b]	24
Toys	600	15	10
Total	**6,000**	**150**	**100**

stub — *cell* — *body*

general note Note: the turnout was 89 per cent of the total electorate.

specific notes **a** One seat was lost at a by-election in the following year.
b One seat was won at a by-election in the following year.

source *Source:* T. Counter (ed.), *Vital Imagination Yearbook*, Erehwon: Poli Publishers, 2001.

Figure 6.1 The basic structure of a table

TABLE HEADING

Tables have headings, whereas figures and other illustrations have captions. Captions can be positioned anywhere in relation to an illustration; headings, as the word indicates, are always above the table.

Headings can consist of a number and a title. Numbers are not always necessary. For example, they can be omitted when there are very few tables in a document or when the tables are mentioned in the text only on the page or spread where they appear, as is often the case in books for children. Numbers are essential when there are many tables in the document, when their position relative to relevant text cannot be guaranteed, or when they are compared or cross-referenced in the text. In a journal the tables will be numbered from 1 within each article. In a book the tables may be numbered with the chapter number preceding the number of the table: Table 6.1 is the first table in Chapter 6.

Like newspaper headlines, table headings summarize the content of the table as concisely as possible, and include any information that applies to the entire table, such as a date or period. Only the first word and proper nouns are capitalized, and, as in all displayed headings, there is no full stop at the end.

Units that apply to the entire table – currency, measurements or percentage, for example – are placed in parentheses after the title:

Table 22 Production of selected crops, 1955 (thousands of tonnes)

In Britain the parenthetical information is usually run on after the title, but house style or conventions for publications in other countries might require it to be on a separate line.

COLUMN HEADINGS

Every column in a table represents a category of information and has a heading. The columns are numbered only when they need to be referred to in this way in the text, in which case the numbers (or lower-case letters) appear in parentheses preceding the title. The column titles should be as concise as possible; use capitals for only the first word and proper nouns, omit full points at the end, and be consistent in content and style. When the column titles are number ranges, the spans must not overlap: for example,

1–9, 10–19, *not* 1–10, 10–20.

The heading for the first column (the 'stub' – perhaps the only term that you didn't know) is always in the singular; the others are all singular or all plural as sense demands. Sometimes authors omit the heading for the stub because they think it is obvious. Even if it is, consider whether inserting it will be helpful to the reader and enhance the consistency of presentation of all the tables in the document.

When the column headings have turnovers, the headings range down: the last line of all headings aligns with the last line of the longest one, as in Figures 6.1–6.3. Be careful: the last line of a *heading* in one column does not align with a *subheading* in another. Subheadings, which usually indicate units of measurement, are often symbols or abbreviations (%, £, mm, kg, etc.) and appear in parentheses on a separate line from the heading, usually centred under it.

When two or more levels of column headings are needed, they are separated by a rule spanning the columns (spanner rules) to which they apply. Figure 6.2 shows how these 'decked' headings allow information that could be presented as two tables to be combined in one. Figure 6.3 shows three levels of column headings. At each level the heading is centred over the columns to which it applies, and may also be distinguished typographically. Such merged tables are likely to be appropriate only in publications intended for the academic and professional markets, but even then individual tables are better when the discussions of each are widely separated in the text.

THE STUB

This first column lists the items for which information is being given. As in column headings, numbers or letters are used with verbal entries only if they need to be referred to in that way in the text, and then the number or lower-case letter appears in parentheses preceding the item. Only the first word and proper nouns are capitalized, and there is no terminal punctuation. When the stub items are numerical ranges, they must not overlap.

Although there may be many categories of data in a table, one is always the focal point – it's called the dependent variable and is usually the column nearest the stub. The dependent variable *may* determine the sequence in the stub. If this were the case in Figure 6.1, the stub could be organized according to ascending or descending order of the votes cast. However, because the author wanted to compare information at different dates and the dependent variables would not necessarily be the same relative values, she has ordered the stub alphabetically. Thus the stub remains consistent whether the information for different dates is presented in separate tables or combined in one. The nature of the items in the stub might also determine the order: for example, if data were being compared by age, the order in the stub would be determined by the sequence of age ranges.

The stub can have subheadings too, as shown in Figures 6.2 and 6.3. Like the column heading, they are in the singular. They are ranged left in the column and may be distinguished typographically. The items in the stub are indented under the subheadings.

Table 12.2 Local elections in Fantasyland

spanner rule

	2000			2010		
Party	Votes cast	No. seats won	%age seats won	Votes cast	No. seats won	%age seats won
Animal						
Cats	1,200	30 [a]	20	1,232	24	16
Dogs	2,280	57	38	2,310	45	30
Pigs	1,440	36 [b]	24	2,464	48	32 [c]
Mechanical						
Toys	600	15	10	924	18	12
Gadgets	480	12	8	770	15	10
Total	**6,000**	**150**	**100**	**7,700**	**150**	**100**

decked heading

a One seat was lost at a by-election in the following year.
b One seat was won at a by-election in the following year.
c Local campaigning on environmental issues was a major factor in increased share of vote.

Source: T. Counter (ed.), *Vital Imagination Yearbook*, Erehwon: Poli Publishers, 2001, 2011.

Figure 6.2 A table with two levels of column headings and subheadings in the stub

Tables, technical figures and copy-fitting 193

Table 12.3 Elections to the legislature in Fantasyland

Party	2000 Votes cast	2000 No. Seats won	2000 %age seats won	2010 Votes cast	2010 No. seats won	2010 %age seats won
			Local			
Animal						
Cats	1,200	30 [a]	20	1,232	24	16
Dogs	2,280	57	38	2,310	45	30
Pigs	1,440	36 [b]	24	2,464	48	32 [c]
Mechanical						
Toys	600	15	10	924	18	12
Gadgets & Gizmos	480	12	8	770	15	10
Total	**6,000**	**150**	**100**	**7,700**	**150**	**100**
			National			
Animal						
Cats	10,920	182	26	12,420	189	27
Dogs	11,760	196	28	11,960	182	26
Pigs	9,240	154	22	9,200	140	20
Mechanical						
Toys	5,880	98	14	7,360	112	16
Gadgets & Gizmos	4,200	70	10	5,060	77	11
Total	**42,000**	**700**	**100**	**46,000**	**700**	**100**

a   One seat was lost at a by-election in the following year.
b   One seat was won at a by-election in the following year.
c   Local campaigning on environmental issues was a major factor in increased share of vote.

Source: T. Counter (ed.), *Vital Imagination Yearbook*, Erehwon: Poli Publishers, 2001, 2011.

Figure 6.3 A table with three levels of column headings

THE BODY

As you would expect, an item in the stub aligns horizontally with the entries that relate to it. That's easy when each one is a single line. Here's what happens when there are turnovers. The stub and entry align on the first line of the stub when they both have turnovers, *and* when only the entry has turnovers. However, when an item in the stub has a turnover but an entry in a column does not, they align on the last line of the stub (see Figure 6.3) so you can read straight across into the data.

When the information in a column is all of the same kind, numbers range right on the units or align on the decimal point. You will remember from Chapter 4 that even when house style is for four-digit numbers in the text to be closed up, in tables they must still be separated by a comma or a thin space between the hundreds and thousands to maintain vertical alignment.

The figures should all have the same number of decimal places if possible. You must not simply add zeros to fill in the gaps: zero is a number. The gap might be there because the information does not exist, in which case it may be left blank, or because it exists but is not available, in which case an en rule is used, particularly in publications aimed at high-level readers, such as academics and professionals. Ask authors to supply missing information and to state their system in the notes, if they haven't already done so.

When the information in a column is unrelated, the numerals might range left or be centred for visual clarity, and do not need to have the same number of decimal places. When the statistics are ranges or an arithmetical equation, they are aligned on the en rule or arithmetical symbol. If there is a large discrepancy between the length of the column headings and the entries in the body, the shorter one is usually centred *as a block* over/under the longer one.

Entries in verbal tables usually range left if they are long, but can be centred if they are short. Figure 6.4 shows how turnovers might be treated in a verbal table with narrow columns.

TOTALS

As mentioned above, totals should be separated from the rest of the body of information by space. If this would make the table too deep, the line of type can be emboldened instead. However, if there are also subtotals, averages and/or means, there must be space between the lines. The words in these parts of the stub are usually styled differently from the other items in the stub, so that the reader does not even momentarily confuse them.

THE NOTES

Notes to text and notes to tables must always be cued differently and kept separate from each other. Notes to tables always appear under the table to which they refer. There are four kinds of notes to tables:
1 General notes apply to all the entries and are preceded by the word 'Note' or 'Notes'. Each note starts on a separate line.
2 Notes to specific points in the table are cued in the table by superior lower-case letters. Obviously, numerals cannot be used in statistical tables, because they would make a mathematical statement. Asterisks are reserved for the next category, and other symbols might be used for notes in the text; remember, different systems must be used for notes in the tables and notes in the text. Again, each note starts on a separate line.
3 Levels of probability are represented by asterisks. The lowest level is represented by one asterisk, the next level up by two, and so on. The notes indicate the specific level of each symbol.
4 Source notes follow the format for bibliographic notes used elsewhere in the publication and are preceded by 'Source:' or 'Sources:', which is usually in italics but can be in bold instead. When the source note includes a page reference, it might mean that the author is using a table that appeared in the source. In this case copyright permission must be cleared, because a table is an entire work, regardless of the extent of the publication in which it appeared. However, a page reference might also mean that the author has created the table from information on that page in the source, in which case an acknowledgement to the source is required, but not permission. Another alternative is that the author wants to reproduce an existing table with some changes. Permission is required to do this. The source will want to see the amendments and the source note will state 'Adapted from …'. Some tables do not need source notes because the author has created them with information in the public domain; the table in Figure 6.4 is an example.

Table 4 Verb endings: present tense

Verb	Singular			Plural		
	First person	Second person	Third person	First person	Second person	Third person
Avoir	j'ai	tu as	il a	nous avons	vous avez	ils ont
Donner	je donne	tu donnes	il donne	nous donnons	vous donnez	ils donnent
Recevoir	je reçois	tu reçois	il reçoit	nous recevons	vous recevez	ils reçoivent

Figure 6.4 A verbal table, showing alignment when there are turnovers in the column headings and body

The order of the notes is not always as given here. Some house styles prefer 1, 2, 4, 3 and others 1, 4, 2, 3. The most important point is that the order of the notes should be consistent throughout a publication. Notes are usually set 1 or 2 points smaller than the table text.

Editing

The tables should be supplied separately from the text, in hard copy and electronically, because they will be typeset separately as a group and then positioned. There is also no guarantee that they will be in the same relative position on the page as they are in the author's word-processed document. When you work on hard copy, place the table folios to one side of the main manuscript so you can read across to them when they are mentioned in the text. Depending on the size of your monitor, you might be able to position your open files similarly when you work on-screen.

The accompanying text can highlight particular data or draw attention to certain points or comparisons in tables. As you edit the text, check that each table is referred to correctly by number and that the content is consistent with the text. When the tables are not numbered, they are referred to by location (for example, above, below, opposite). At proof stage the proofreader should check that the text reference is accurate. If it needs correcting, the proofreader should try to prevent the change from altering the number of lines on the page, or draw your attention to where it has occurred.

Telling the typesetter where to position a table or figure is called 'keying in'. Do not assume that typesetters know where to position a table because it is mentioned in the text, and do not circle the text reference. Using red ink, write 'Table' and the number in the left margin next to the text that the table should accompany. (This is frequently the first reference to the table in the text, but do not automatically assume this.) This is an instruction to the typesetter, so square it (differentiating it at a glance from heading codes) in red too. In an e-file, you can add a text box with this information in the margin, in red.

When the tables are not numbered in the publication, number them just for identification: write the number or letter in red at the top right of the hard copy; on an e-file, put the number or letter within square brackets or in a separate text box, all in red, above the table and in your written instructions tell the typesetter that this is for identification only. When you have finished editing the document, read down the margins to check that you have keyed in all the tables, only once and in the correct sequence.

When you are working on a journal, edit the tables in detail as a group when you have finished editing each article or report, because it is easier to spot inconsistencies this way. Similarly, when you are working on a book, edit the tables per chapter so that the author can see the queries on tables and text together. Mark up all the tables in a publication at one time after you have finished editing (see 'Marking up' below), as this makes maintaining consistency easier.

Break down the editing of a table into a series of tasks. Check that:
* the title summarizes the main point of the table, as concisely as possible
* each column has a heading, the stub heading is singular, and the other headings are all singular or all plural, according to sense
* the stub is ordered as indicated by the dependent variable or alphabetically
* all figures in a column have the same number of decimal places
* any arithmetical results – totals, percentages, averages, means – are accurate

- note cues are appropriate and refer to a corresponding note
- there is a source note, if appropriate
- the information in all notes is complete and in the correct order
- the spelling of all words in the table is correct

Correct what you can and query the author where necessary. When figures in a column do not add up to the total given, it might be because there is a mistake in either the figures or the total or because the figures have been rounded. If it is the latter, ask the author to explain this in a note to the table. Finally, check that the numbering of the tables runs correctly in sequence in the text as well as in the keying in.

Marking up

Look through the tables as a group to see what style decisions you might have to make. If there are only a few tables, mark them up individually. If there are many tables, you might find it useful to create a template showing all the style points, or you might find one in the house style. As well as using it to help you maintain consistency in marking up, you can supply it to the typesetter as a guide for global issues such as the use of rules, italics, bold, and horizontal and vertical alignment. Mark exceptions to global style on the individual tables.

When you are not supplying a template, cross out unwanted rules. Do it neatly, with just a few well-spaced diagonal strokes through the rule. **Do not** use a squiggle: horizontally, it can be mistaken for 'bold', and vertically, it's an irritating mess. Use a ruler to draw essential rules that are missing. Label them, or create a code for, 'thick' and 'thin', or give the specific thicknesses if you know them.

If a table has turnover lines, mark them up to show indentation or lack of it. It might be necessary to do this even when you have supplied a template, to distinguish ranged-left turnovers from individual stub entries.

Use ⊐ and ⊏ to correct alignment in columns when only a few items are affected. Otherwise, use two vertical parallel lines at the appropriate side of a column to indicate range right or range left.

In all cases, mark up the headings and stub entries for minimal capitalization, and code parts of the table for typography. Make the codes distinct from those used for the main text. For example, you might use TH for the table heading, TA for the column heads and TB

Tables, technical figures and copy-fitting 199

for subheadings in the stub. The stub and the body do not need any other coding – they are the 'main text' of the table. You might use TN for notes, marking italics, caps and small caps (if used) individually.

Exercise 6.1, editing tables

Brief
Edit and mark up the following text extract and tables, and list any queries for the author for each one.

House style
- metric measurements
- numbers written as words up to and including nine
- four-digit numbers closed up in text
- commas separating numerals where required

European Investment and Aid in the 1990's

Financial aid

The European Investment Bank (EIB), established in 1958 under Article 30 of the Treaty of Rome, is the European Union's (EU) bank for providing capital investment promoting the balanced   5
development of the Union. In 1991–92 there were only 12 members of what was still the European Community. Up to the end of 1992 the EIB had raised 126 billion ecus (the European Currency Unit at that time) and lent 17 billion ecus. Starting in 1990 the Eib also loaned money to counties in Eastern Europe that were making the   10
transition to market economies, to non-member states in the Mediterranean region, and to the African, Caribbean and Pacific (ACP) states (see table 1 below).

Food aid

The EU sends foodstuffs to countries which request assistance in coping with serious food shortages. Emergency aid is also sent to countries devastated by natural disasters or other crises. In 1990 over 1,200,000 tons of grain, as well as dairy products and vegetable oils, were sent to sub-Saharan Africa, Asia and Mediterranean countries (see Table 2).

Geographical breakdown of loans granted, 1991–92

	1991 m ecus	1991 %	% of total	1992 m ecus	1992 %	% of total
Within EC						
Belgium	115.6	.8		396.6	2.5	
Denmark	538.6	3.7		690.8	4.3	
Greece	366.9	2.5		377.5	2.3	
Germany	1300.1	9.0		1663.9	10.3	
France	1924.4	13.3		1895.1	11.7	
Ireland	236.9	1.6		303.5	1.9	
Italy	4000.7	27.7		3796.9	23.5	
Luxembourg	28.9	.2		42.8	.3	
Netherlands	175.4	1.2		154.4	1	
Portugal	1002	6.9		1230.4	7.6	
Spain	2342.5	16.2		3020.6	18.7	
Total within EC	14,422,4	100	94	16,139.7	100	94.8
Outside EC						
ACP states	389.5	42.5		252	28.2	
Mediterranean countries	241.5	26.4		320.8	35.9	
Eastern Europe	285.	31.1		320	35.8	
Total outside EC	916	100	6	891.8	100	
Total loans	15,338.8			17,032.5		

Source: European Investment Bank

Allocation of food aid, 1993 (tons)

Region	Cereals	Milk powder	Butter oil	Vegetable oil	Sugar	Other products[1]
Africa	165,780	927	105	4.900	466	2.615
Caribbean	1540	-	-	-	-	-
Latin America	66,920	5945	-	7345	-	3.380
Mediterranean	110,000	3000	-	8000	-	1
Asia	155,000	-	-	1000		
Total direct aid	499.250	9872	105	21,245	466	6.994
Total indirect aid	845,300	36,890	105	51,639	14,534	39.550
Grand total	1,344,540	46,762	105	72,884	15,000	46,550

1 m ecus

Source: European Commission

Adapted from Dick Leonard, *The Economist Guide to the European Union*, rev. edn, London: The Economist Books Ltd, 1992, pp. 65, 67, 208, 209.

EXERCISE FOLLOW-UP

There were just a few editorial points to correct in the text, and although there was a lot to do on the tables, it should have been easy if you did it a step at a time. When you indent the stub under the subheadings in Table 1, there is no need for the totals within each section to repeat the subheading. When correcting the alphabetical order in the stub, be sure that the transposition mark extends the entire length of the lines being moved. Perhaps you noticed that the United Kingdom was missing from the list when you read it, or perhaps it occurred to you only when you compared the 11 countries listed with the text stating '12 members', or maybe you realized it when you found that the totals for all the columns in this section were not consistent with the entries given for each country. That's three chances to spot the mistake. When you checked the percentages on each line – you did, didn't you? – you found that they were correct, indicating that the totals were not completely wrong, which, in turn, confirms that information is missing. Of course, until you have the missing information, you can't know whether there are further errors in the entries for each country or the totals.

The numbers in the columns in the second section have to align with those above them. You can work out the missing percentage in the last column and ask the author to confirm it.

Remember:
1 Always check the number of the items in a list or table with the number stated in the text.
2 Always check all the arithmetical functions.
3 When the arithmetical check indicates an error, ask the author to check whether it is in the entries or in the arithmetic.

There were mismatches between the totals and two of the columns in Table 2, and a note that should have been a column subheading.

The nature of the source note in both tables should have prompted queries to the author about missing details and permissions.

Creating tables

As well as editing tables that authors have supplied, you can advise authors when text would be better as a table. It's a relatively simple process:
1 Look for the common elements that are being compared to create the stub.
2 Look at the nature of the comparisons to create the column headings.
3 Fill in the data in the cells.
4 Create a heading.
5 Identify the source or ask the author to do this.

Always consult authors before making such a change to text final, and send them a copy of the table to confirm the details.

Exercise 6.2, creating a table

Brief

Create a table from part of the following text, and revise the remaining text to accompany it. In creating the table you will find it helpful to cross out each element in the text as you add it to the table.

House style
- four-digit numerals closed up in text
- commas used to separate numbers where necessary
- 'Source:' italicized

―――――――――

At the time of the Boer War there were four military organizations in Britain that men could join: the regular army, the militia, the volunteers and the yeomanry. By 1898 there were 250,000 men in the regular army. Closely connected to it was the militia, a part-time army for home defence. The men in both armies were mainly unskilled workers. However, the yeomanry, which was the cavalry of the militia, drew its members from the rural middle class and aristocracy: men who would know how to ride and might supply their own horses. The volunteers were also part-time but differed from men in the other organizations in two ways: they were mainly skilled working class or lower middle class, and they did not get paid.

In analysing the support for the political parties during the war, it is interesting to see the scale of recruitment to the regular army between 1899, the year the war began, and 1902, when it ended. According to the statistics in the *General Annual Return of the British Army, 1902* and *1903*, in 1899 the army recruited 23,259 men with no previous military experience, 16,396 from the militia, and 3045 from the volunteers. Throughout 1900 recruitment rose dramatically: 43,992 raw recruits joined, 23,165 joined from the militia, and 20, 962 joined from the volunteers. In 1901 the numbers fell back with only 15, 662 coming from the militia, but there were still more recruits with no experience (28, 516) and from the volunteers (14,221) than in 1899. The figures for raw recruits was 30,507 in 1902; recruits from the militia rose to 18,992 but only 8300 joined the regular army from the volunteers.

To understand the impact of the war, we need to ask how many more men joined the army between 1899 and 1902 than would have in peacetime. Calculating on the basis of figures for the preceding two decades, it is estimated that the regular army would have recruited a total of 128,000 men without previous military experience and from the militia.

From M. D. Blanch, 'British Society and the War' in Peter Warwick (ed.), *The South African War: The Anglo–Boer War 1899–1902*, Harlow, Essex: Longman, 1980.

EXERCISE FOLLOW-UP

The model answer shows that the table replaces a lot of verbiage and makes the information more accessible. You may not have used the same words in revising the text, but you should have at least referred to the table. The calculation at the end of line 31 would be helpful to readers, but the author must, of course, approve adding it to the text. The author has used lower case for terms to describe the military organizations; unless you know the answers to the queries shown, you should direct them to the author so that you can impose correct and consistent capitalization. In the table, the years are placed in the stub because the comparison is between the number of men recruited each year rather than the nature of their previous experience.

Technical figures

Technical figures are diagrams, charts, graphs and maps, any of which might appear in fiction or non-fiction. Like tables, they are intended to convey information more concisely and, because of their visual clarity, in a more accessible way than words. If they do not achieve this goal, you should consider whether they are the most appropriate type of figure or whether words would be better than any figure. Also like tables, figures should be in a separate file from the text (as hard copy and electronically) when they are sent to the typesetter, so that they can be inserted in an appropriate position in the typeset pages; remember, they won't necessarily be in the same position as in the author's word-processed document.

You may receive figures as finished artwork from authors, particularly those preparing material for academic publishers and journals, or as sketches or rough drawings ('roughs')to be typeset or redrawn by professional illustrators. Check the book spec for the use of colour. If you cannot use full colour for the figures, you need to think carefully about how to show differences with gradations of one or two colours. Always ask the designer or illustrator for advice.

Next, edit the figures: check them against the text, style them in discrete groups to help maintain consistency, and key them in. If finished artwork prepared by authors needs alteration, return it to them with clear instructions. Otherwise, treat roughs as you would text: query authors as necessary and ask them to confirm your editorial changes before the figures are sent to the typesetter or illustrator. Type the annotation (often referred to as 'anno') – all the text or labels on figures – for each figure because:

- it is not the typesetter's job to decipher the author's handwriting;
- it is not the illustrator's job to decipher the author's handwriting or to type anno;
- it enables you to ensure consistency of spelling and style on all the figures;
- it is the clearest way of presenting anno with a complex mark-up;
- it allows the author to check everything before incurring proof-correction charges;
- it makes checking the proofs or final artwork easier for you or the proofreader.

Indicate whether the anno is to be positioned on the part of the image to which it refers, or next to it, with or without a line or an arrow pointing to the part. When a key is needed, include all the words – including 'Key' – in the typed list of anno.

Edit the captions, which should also be in a separate file so that they can be typeset together and then inserted in the appropriate position in the pages. Like tables, figures can be numbered per article or per chapter, or left unnumbered when they are to be positioned right next to the text, for example in books for younger readers.

206 *Copy-editing*

When authors provide a copy of a figure from another work, make sure the source is acknowledged and that permission is obtained to reproduce or adapt the figure.

Diagrams

A diagram is a simplified drawing of an object, as Figure 6.5, or of a process, as Figure 6.6. To edit diagrams, check that the text agrees with the information in each, ensure that all the lines of the same general or specific nature are the same weight respectively, that all arrows are the same style, and that all the anno is marked for the same capitalization, if any.

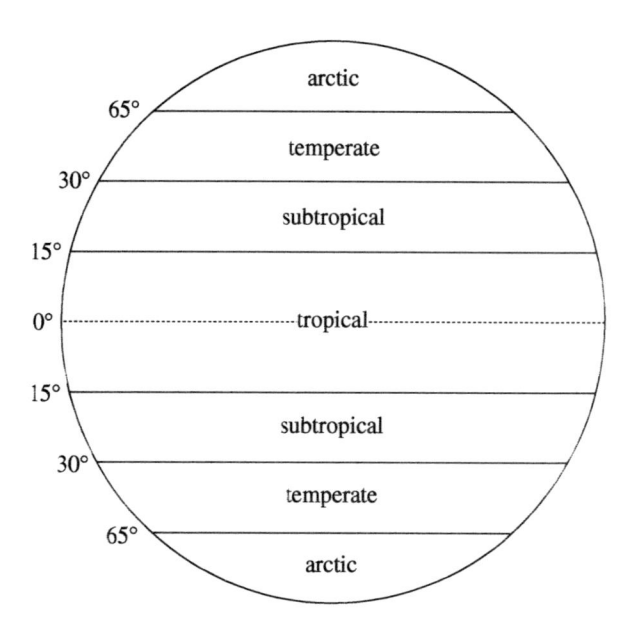

Figure 6.5 A diagram of an object

Sometimes all the information will be in the figure and the text will simply refer to it: for example 'Figure 6.5 shows the world's climatic regions'. Then you are expected to use your common sense and general knowledge in examining the proposed diagram. In specialist texts outside your own field of knowledge, if something does not seem right – say, because it is inconsistent with another diagram or another part of

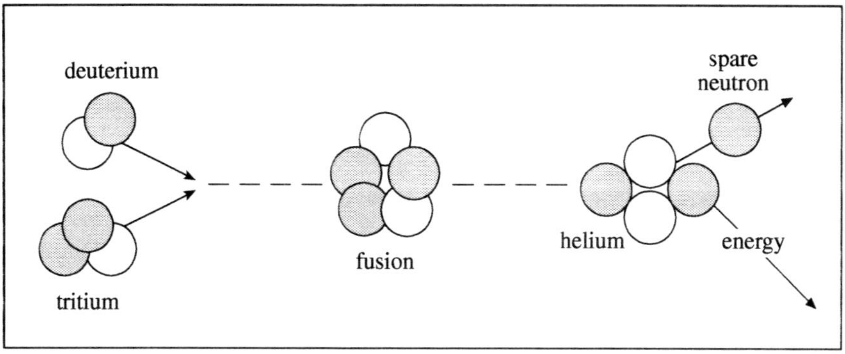

Tables, technical figures and copy-fitting 207

Figure 6.6 A diagram of a process

the text – raise a query with the author. When a diagram representing something within a non-specialist area seems wrong, check a reference. For example, I could check an atlas to see that the temperature zones of the world are accurate in Figure 6.5. However, I have no knowledge of nuclear fusion, so if I suspected there were mistakes in Figure 6.6, I would ask the author questions about the specific point(s).

Exercise 6.3, editing diagrams

Brief
Edit and mark up the following technical figures and their text, and, of course, list any queries for the author.

Every demand guarantee involves at least three parties, the principal, the beneficiary and the guarantor and may involve a fourth, the instructing party. The principal is the contractor at whose request the guarantee is issued. The beneficiary is the person in whose favour the guarantee is issued. The guarantor is the bank or other person issuing the guarantee. Almost invariably the principal and the beneficiary will carry on business in different countries. In a direct (or three party) guarantee the principle's bank, located in the

5

country where the principle has his place of business, issues the
guarantee direct to the beneficiary. Figure 35.11 shows the triangular
relationship arising where P, an English contractor, enters into a
contract with B in Saudi Arabia for the construction of a plant in
Saudi Arabia and arranges for its bank, G Bank, to issue a guarantee
direct to B.

But B may wish to have a guarantee from a bank he knows in his own
country, and that bank, G Bank, will itself wish to be protected by a
counter-guarantee from P's bank, which in this case is termed the
instructing bank (IP Bank). This is the indirect (four–party)
guarantee. At P's request, IP Bank communicates with G Bank and
requests it to issue a gurantee in favour of B against IP Bank's
counter-guarantee. The counter-guarantee will follow the same
pattern as the guarantee and will require IP Bank to pay G Bank on
the lattter's first written demand and any other specified documents.
This four-party structure is shown in figure 35.12

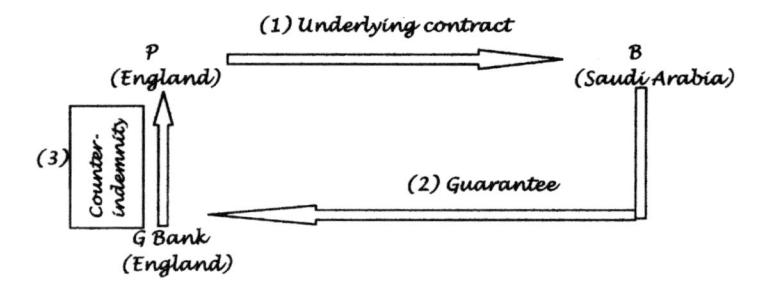

Fig. 35.11 Structure of a three-party demand guarantee

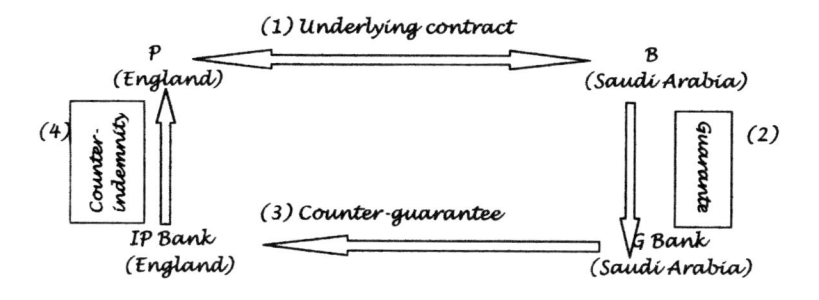

Fig. 35.11

Adapted from Roy Goode, *Commercial Law*, 3rd edn, London, LexisNexis UK, 2004, p. 1021.

EXERCISE FOLLOW-UP

You do have to read the text carefully to get the directions of the arrows right. Then it is a simple matter of *neatly* crossing out the arrow head pointing in the wrong direction and drawing in one pointing in the right direction. When you type the anno and the captions so that they can be typeset, you can also check them for consistency, correct the number of the second figure and add the missing information to its caption. Then all you need to do is get the author to check the changes you have made, and confirm or alter them as necessary.

Graphs

Graphs are diagrams that show the relationship between two (sometimes more) variables, which are represented on vertical and horizontal axes that meet at right angles. The data are plotted on a grid, and authors supplying roughs to be redrawn or set should provide the grid so that the data can be positioned accurately. However, it is not always necessary to reproduce the grid in the final artwork. Consider the purpose of the graph and the needs of the intended reader, and then decide whether or not the grid should appear. When a grid is necessary or helpful, consider whether it should be shown as a lighter tint, so that it does not confuse or obscure the data.

Both axes must be labelled. Like column headings in tables, the label identifying the axis might be accompanied by an abbreviation of a unit of measurement, which would follow it or be on the line under it in parentheses. If it is short enough, the label for the vertical axis can be set at the top of the axis; then the label for the horizontal axis is set to the left of that axis. Otherwise, the label for the vertical axis can be set centred running up the side of the axis, and the label for the horizontal axis can be centred under its axis. Be sure to look at all the graphs in a publication before deciding on a style (by now the word 'consistency' has sprung to your lips). The axes may start with 0, another number, or O (for 'origin'). If they do not start with anything, ask the author to confirm what you think should be there; if you don't know, don't guess – ask. It is the author's job to provide the information.

The data being measured against the variables can be shown as dots on the graph (Figure 6.7), or these points can be joined by a line (a line graph, Figure 6.8). When more than one item is represented on a graph, the points need to be differentiated in some way – by shading, colour or shape – and a key to the differences supplied in the graph or the caption. Lines can be differentiated in the same ways and keyed or annotated. Keys to figures should never obscure any information in the figures themselves.

A bar chart is a graph on which the data are represented by lines or rectangles (Figure 6.9). When more than one item is represented, the

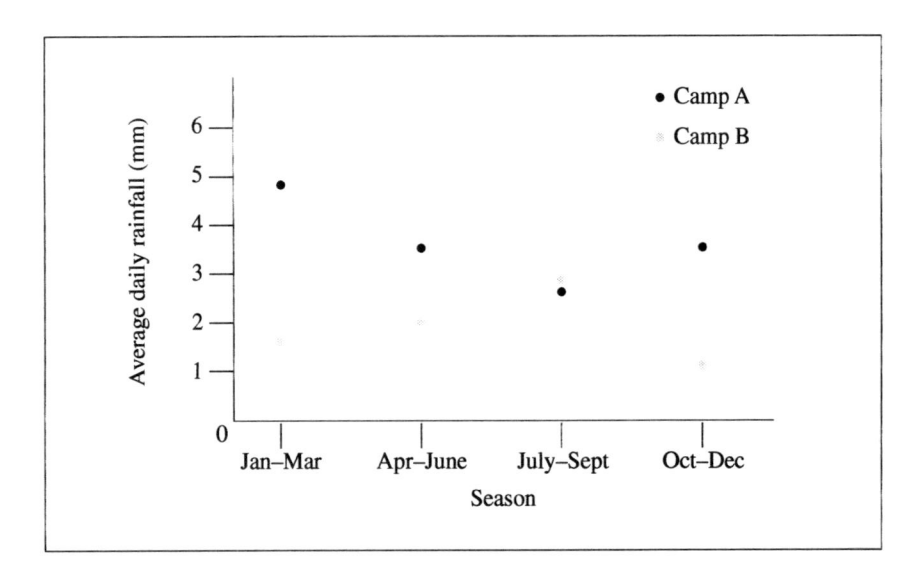

Figure 6.7 A graph showing data represented by points

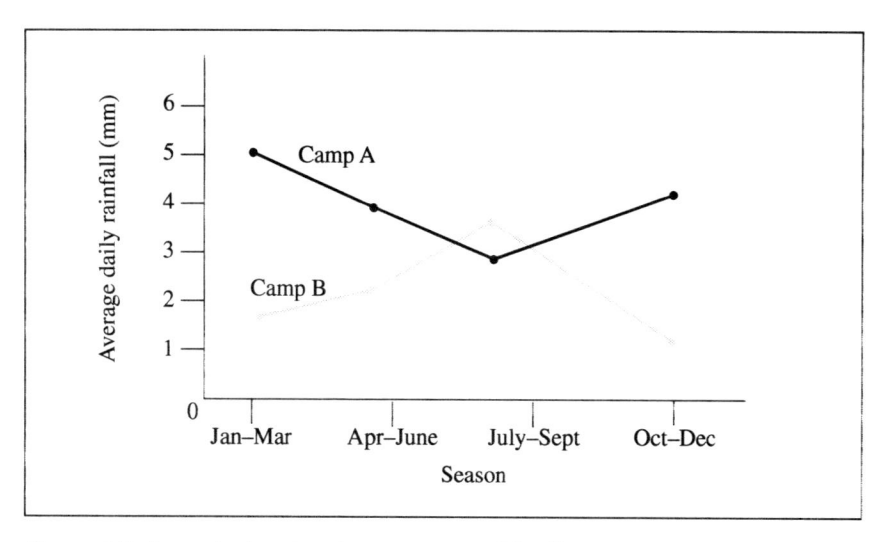

Figure 6.8 A graph showing data represented by lines

lines or bars can be distinguished by colour or shading, with an accompanying key. Bars can be used horizontally or vertically. The bars are spaced when the data represent different categories, and not spaced when the data are grouped.

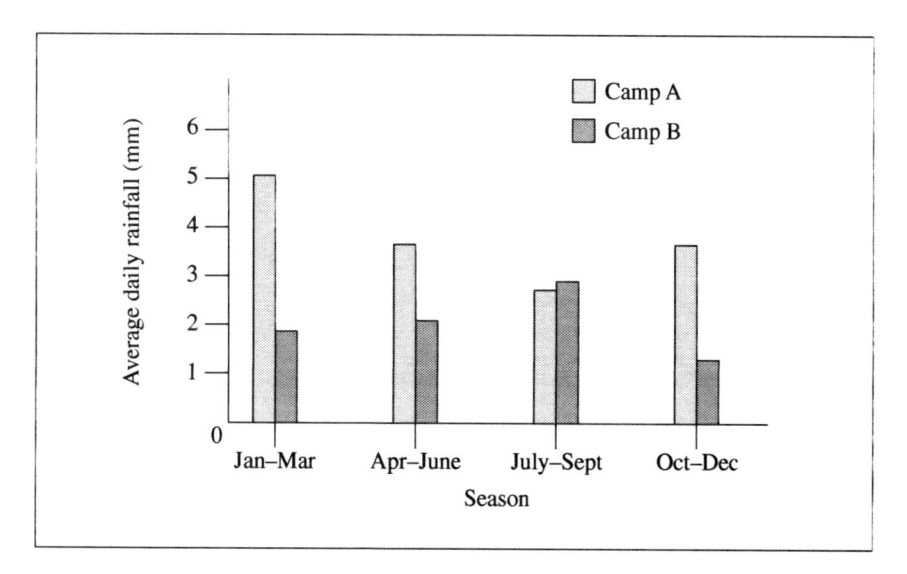

Figure 6.9 A bar chart of the data in figure 6.7

212 *Copy-editing*

Exercise 6.4, editing graphs

Brief
Edit and mark up the following texts and graphs, and list any queries for the authors. Each extract is from a textbook, the first for undergraduates, printed 1/1 (monochrome throughout), and the second for 11–12-year-olds, printed 4/4 (full colour available throughout).

1

The researchers first step was to compare the birth rates in 1976 with those in 1986 to see if there had been any major changes. As shown in the figure below, they found that the birth rate for women below the age of twenty had actually increased from 30,000 to 35,000. There had been a slight fall in the rate — from 108,000 to 96,000 — in women between the ages of 20 and 24, while there had been a rise from 116,000 to 120,000 in the same period for women aged 25–29. The largest rise, from 54,000 to 72,000, was seen in the group between the ages of 29 and 34, with a smaller but still substantial rise from 17,000 to 22,000 in women 35 to 39 years old. Women aged forty and older had an unchanged rate of 4000.

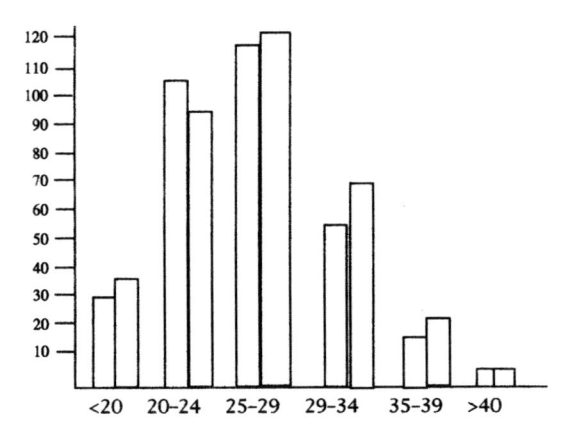

Fig. 7.3

2

Elspeth, Becca and Tiina are pen pals, or maybe that should be e-mail pals, as that is how they communicate with each other most of the time. They are too young to have been able to visit each other yet but are each curious about where the others live. Elspeth decided to make a graph showing the average number of hours of sunshine a day each month in Edinburgh. She asked Becca, who lives in London, and Tiina, who lives in Helsinki, to send her the same information about their cities. Below is the graph Elspeth Elspeth made. Use the information on the graph to answer the questions below.

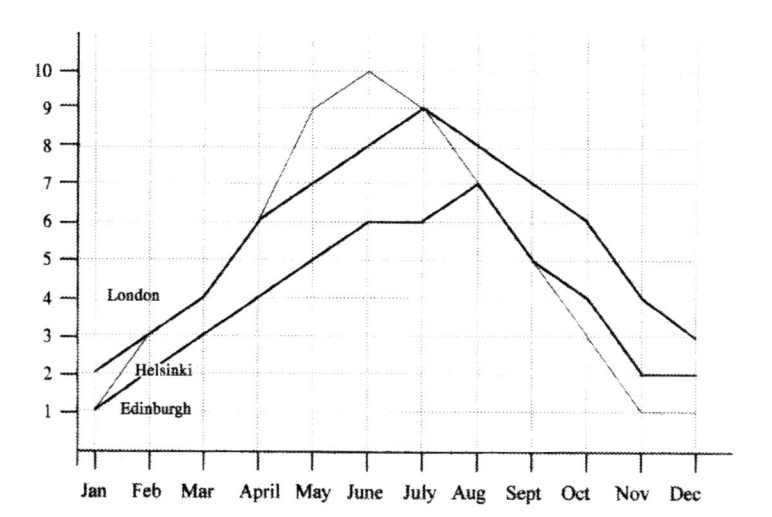

1 Which city gets the most sunshine in a year?
2 Which city gets the least?
3 What is the range of the number of hours of sunshine over the year for each city.
4 What is the total number of hours of sunshine for each city in a year.

EXERCISE FOLLOW-UP

There is no point in repeating in the text all the statistical information shown in the first graph, so you can delete it after cross-checking. However, the text needs to be linked to the graph and can call attention to particular points, as the model answer shows; obviously, the wording can vary. The bars can be made more distinct, even though the printing is 1/1, by using patterns or shading. The numerals in the vertical axis should be ranged right. The axes needed labels and they are both short enough to go at the top and side, respectively, as shown. The figure needed a caption, too: the one shown is concise, descriptive and provides the key to the shading of the bars. Did you remember to key in the chart to the text?

The second graph presented some issues to make you think. First, you needed to differentiate the lines. The book is printing 4/4, so you could choose any colours you like, but make sure they contrast well with each other. Then you needed to work out which line represents Helsinki; even though the result is logical, you should ask the author to confirm it. The obvious tasks were to check the alignment of the numbers in the vertical axis, label both axes and create a caption – it is unlikely that the X.Y style for numbering captions would be used in a book for this age group. Although you could have put the anno next to the lines on the graph, perhaps you thought, as I do, that it might interfere with the clarity of the grid, and therefore positioned the key on a part of the graph where there is no other information.

Did you query the spelling of 'Tiina' or just change it? Even if you had no idea that this is a Finnish spelling, you should ask the author about it: since it was spelled the same way both times, you need to check whether it is deliberate.

The text does not make clear whether the point of the exercise is to teach the reader about line graphs in particular, or about any kind of graph. The query to the author calls attention to the difficulty readers might have with the overlapping lines. The choices are to alter the information or the types of graph. The point here is to make you aware that it is your job as a copy-editor to consider the clarity and usefulness of the visual image in the same way you think about the text. You have to determine not only whether some text would be better – easier for the reader to understand – as an image, but whether some images would be better in a different format and, indeed, whether some images would be better as text.

Maps

Maps can be used to show many kinds of information – climatic, economic, geographical, industrial, political, topographical – about the world in the past, the present and the future. Like any text or illustration, the information on a map should be relevant and clear. However, when authors supply copies of maps produced elsewhere as a convenient reference, they don't always delete unnecessary detail, and sometimes they add more. In checking the reference, bear in mind the purpose of the map, the size it will be when reproduced, and the needs of the reader. Then consider, for example, whether

- all the essential information is given;
- too many topics are included, and they would be clearer on separate maps;
- lines and degrees of latitude and longitude are needed;
- every topographical feature – places of habitation, roads and railways, mountains and waterways – needs to be shown or identified;
- the map is copied and copyright permissions need to be cleared.

From continents to towns, oceans to rivers, motorways to footpaths, maps have more scope for a diversity and hierarchy of anno than most other figures. Check place names that are unfamiliar, transliterated from another alphabet, or in a part of the world that has undergone or is undergoing change to ensure that you have the correctly spelled appropriate name for the period the map represents – should it be Ceylon or Sri Lanka, Burma or Myanmar, Peking or Beijing? Type out the anno in groups – for example, continents, countries, capital cities, oceans, lakes, rivers – to make the mark-up neat, and maintaining consistency throughout a group of maps easy. Each group will be set in a particular size and style so that the reader can quickly identify what kind of feature each name represents.

Check finished artwork to make sure that

- each annotation is correctly spelled and styled;
- each annotation clearly identifies the right place without obscuring any boundaries;
- all vertical or near-vertical annotation runs the same way, and no names (for example, rivers) are upside down;
- boundaries of different kinds – for example, between countries and between divisions within countries – are differentiated;
- there is a linear scale, if relevant;

- there is a north point only when north is not at the top of the map;
- a key, if required, does not cover up any information.

When shades of grey, rather than colours or patterns, are used to show gradations of height, temperature or rainfall, the lightest tone is used for the lowest level, and each level up is progressively darker. Check that the key follows this progression, that the tones are easy to distinguish from each other and that they match the ones used on the map. And, of course, check the maps as a group for consistency. You knew I was going to say that.

Exercise 6.5, working with a map

Brief

The author has provided a sketch map of France to accompany the following extract. Edit the text as usual, checking it against the map as you proceed. A cartographer will draw an accurate map and you will use the sketch to brief him or her, so decide whether information needs to be added, deleted or altered and prepare the list of annotations. Consult the author about your suggested changes.

He screwed the letter into a ball and threw it angrily to the floor. All right, that was that. Now he had a month, possibly two, to kill. He laughed at the phrase, at its ironic aptness. Throwing his clothes into a suitcase and grabbing his passport, he left. By the time he got to his car he had decided: He would go to France. He'd always wanted to see more of it and now there was nothing else to do. Taking the ferry at Dover, he arrived in Calais in time for lunch, but found little else there to detain him. Accordingly he proceeded to Lille where he found a room in a cheap pension and spent a couple of days looking around, eating and trying out his knowledge of the language on the patient locals. Feeling calmer, he decided it might be useful to plan an itinerary, even if he decided to deviate from it as he journeyed.

He bought a map and found he actually enjoyed plotting his proposed
route. He was very near the border with Belgium and was
momentarily tempted to cross over to enjoy a meal of moules and
frites. He could even go border-hopping as he moved arund France,
taking in Germany, Switzerlandand Italy, and later Spain. No, no, no!
Damn it, there wasn't *that* much time. Keep it simple. From Lille, he
would zig south-west to Amiens, then zag south-east to Rheims, and
zig east again to Paris. It was the only place in France he'd been to
before and he had always though it was the perfect place to live, love
and die. He would stay at least a week and then take a day to dawdle
down to Dijon. He would continue south through Besancon and
Lyons, taking his time to enjoy each place and particularly its food.
Following the course of the Rhone as it made a near-straight path
between the Massiff Centrale and the Alps, then heading east, Aix-
en-provence would be his next stop. He was not sure how long he
would stay in that area or which other towns he would visit; it would
depend on how he felt at the time. Certainly, he would avoid the
Riviera - those flashy resorts from St Tropez to Niece held no allure
for him now. No, when he was ready to move on, he would go first
to Marsielle, then follow the rising sun along the coast to Montpelier.
Toulouse, on the Garrone north of the Pyrrenees, had a nice ring to
it; he would go there, then up the river to Bordeaux. From there to
Nantes, passing through Limoges for a look at the porcelain museum,
then along the Loire to Tours and Orleans. Now he would be
following the setting sun. If he timed it right, he could visit Versailles
before returning to Paris, that perfect place. Who could tell how
long twilight would last.

218 *Copy-editing*

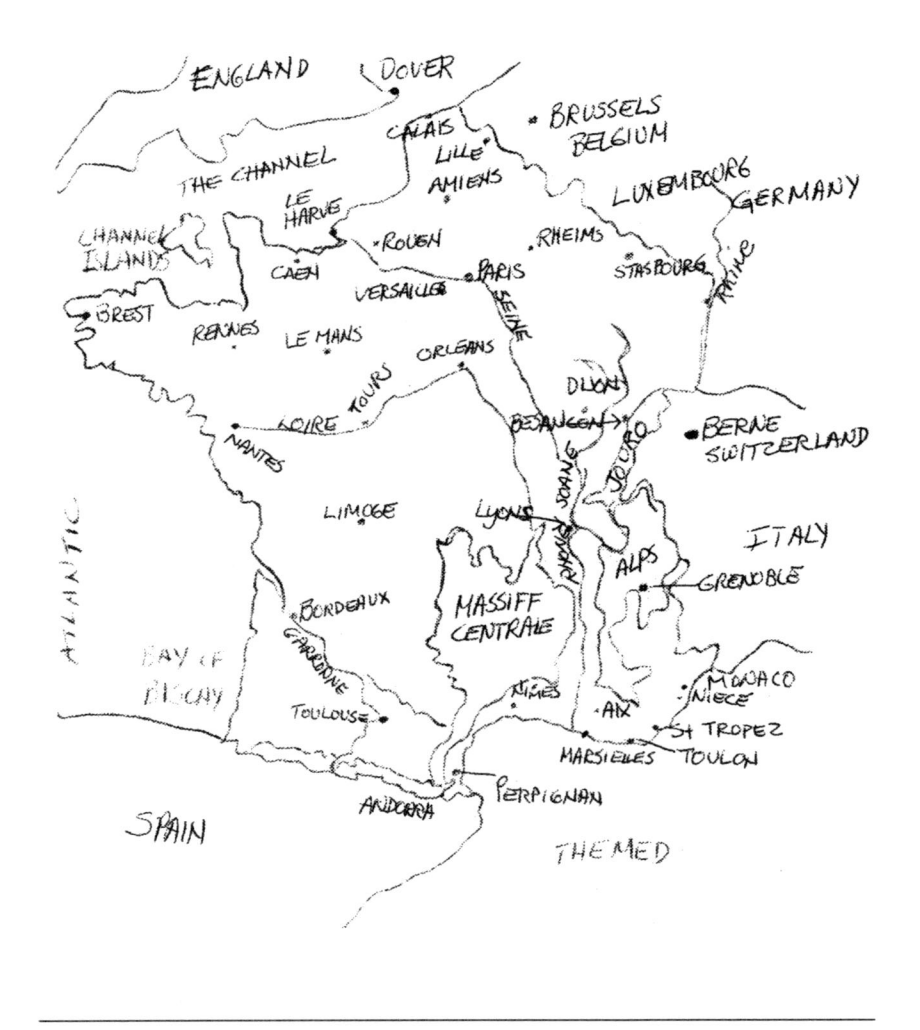

EXERCISE FOLLOW-UP

Checking the map as you read the text would help you find the directional error in the text – Paris is south-west of Reims – and should have alerted you to the problem with the metaphor. If you did not recognize this as a metaphor for death, you would still have had to query the author about the direction of travel and the setting sun.

Deleting 'decided to' in line 12 avoids unnecessary repetition, and the change in lines 25–7 corrects a dangling participle. It is not important whether you resolved these errors in the same way as the model answer – you may have found another, even better way – as long as you *did* correct them. The most efficient way of checking the spelling of the place names is to do it as a single job, using an atlas gazetteer.

The sketch map would become very messy if you were to make changes on it, and since any professional cartographer can draw a map of France, the simplest way to brief him or her is to list what the map must show. You need to type and mark up the annotation anyway, so then the brief requires only a few more lines of instruction. On a small map like this you might list the annotation in each group north to south or west to east to make checking easy. On a more complex map you might list the countries alphabetically and the place names within them directionally. There is no absolute rule: in each case, decide what is the most efficient way to work for both you and the cartographer. Your mark-up code could have been different from the one shown and be as good, as long as it clearly and accurately showed the different levels of the annotation.

Cutting and expanding

There are two points at which text might need to be cut or expanded: before it goes for setting and at first page proof, and we'll look at these in turn.

Before setting

Authors are usually contracted to write a specific number of words, although cookery writers may instead be commissioned to supply a particular number of recipes, and authors of some documents, such as company reports, might be told the number of pages available. The length of the text, along with a specified number and types of illustration if relevant, forms the basis of the budget for a publication.

Before you begin work on a project, check the brief you have been given. Does it say anything about the length? If not, ask your project manager whether the text is the contracted length or needs cutting or expanding, and, if so, by how much. There may be occasions when a publisher will accept a longer than expected text – for example, because the content is so important – but the following explanations should make clear why this is the exception to the rule.

A publication, whether it is a report, journal or book, cannot be extended by a page or two to accommodate extra text. However, fiction is not usually cut or stretched to make an even working (use all the pages in all the signatures) – picture books for children being a notable exception. Instead, extra pages at the back of a novel may be filled with ads for other books by the same author – sometimes even a preview of his or her next book – or published by the same house, rather than left blank. Why? Because it costs relatively little to typeset the ads, which help to promote other books, and thus make good use of the pages that would otherwise be wasted space.

Non-fiction, on the other hand, *can*, and must, be made to fit. While typesetting is relatively inexpensive, paper is a major cost, often proportionally the largest cost in a publication. Journals have an annual subscription price, so they would lose money if some issues had more signatures than planned, and they would lose subscribers if they had fewer. Books are priced to be acceptable to the target market and to provide a certain amount of profit. Adding pages will increase the costs and, therefore, lower the profit unless the price is raised. But the price is determined when the proposal is accepted, and the jacket or cover is usually printed and the book marketed months in advance of publication. Increasing the extent means redoing the jacket or cover, as the spine measurement will be different. Raising the price might make the book unacceptable to the intended audience, and, by failing to live up to expectations, annoy retailers as well as consumers.

Similarly, having fewer pages will require the cover to be revised and the book might not look like value for the price. The publisher is not going to lower the price, because that would affect income. Increasing or decreasing the size of text and illustrations can sometimes work if the alteration is not too great – otherwise, the document might look cramped or oversize, and either can be visually unappealing. Such changes from the original design must be planned before typesetting begins, otherwise the costs in time and money will also eat into profits.

Like printed publications, website pages have a fixed size and capacity, and type size and spacing are vital to visual success. So the message is clear: whatever kind of publication you are working on, make sure the material is the intended length for the extent.

A copy-editor can usually cut or expand an average quality text by up to 10 per cent in the normal course of the job, although it might be easy to cut more if the text is poorly written and generally verbose. However, if a text requires more substance (rather than just verbosity) to be cut or added, it should be returned to its author with advice on where or what kind of material to add or delete. Whether you are cutting or expanding, always ask the author to confirm the changes.

TECHNIQUES FOR CUTTING

Most copy-editing involves some cutting. Tightening up the text – making it more concise and better organized – helps to make it clearer. Get rid of unnecessary modifiers, long phrases where short ones will do, irrelevancies, tautologies and other unnecessary repetition. Make sure that whatever you are cutting *is* unnecessary. Some text might need only the correct transition to reveal its relevance. Repetition of information may be essential, particularly in educational work, and there are times when, although not essential, it might be desirable. In both cases, rephrasing the information may be the best way of reinforcing the message without boring the reader. Remember, too, that sometimes wordy text can be transformed into a space-saving table, graph or diagram. Be sure to give your author the opportunity to confirm, alter or decline your suggested changes.

Exercise 6.6, cutting text

Brief
The following extract was drafted in a rush and the author, a journalist, is aware that it will be cut. Editing it to produce a clear, well-structured article, you should easily be able to cut as much as 20 per cent. Mark up the heading and list any queries

House style
- an informal literary style that permits contractions
- abbreviations for technical terms are capitalized even when the term is a generic description.

NEW SCREEN TECHNOLOGIES ON THE HORIZON

Over the last few years we've all seen quite a formidable boost in

monitor technology. The Liquid Crystal Display based screens have come from a point where they were terribly expensive with rather poor performance, to one where they have excellent picture quality and at a reasonable price. The colour gamut of the better LCD screens exceeds that even of a Barco Calibrator CRT (cathode ray tube), the 'Rolls Royce' of monitors within the graphic arts industry. If the Adobe RGB 1998 colour gamut (one of the suggested working colour spaces in Adobe Photoshop) is used as a reference the gamut of a Barco Callibrator only achieves about 77% of the Adobe RGB.

Some of the high end LCDs from for example NEC-Mitsubishi and Eizo reach close to 90 percent of the Adobe RGB gamut today. Both of these manufacturers have hinted at LCD monitors capable of reaching the full Adobe colour gamut, and due to come onto the market early in the new year. So the era of CRT's seems to be over, What will become of the Barco monitors, still widely used within the printing and publishing industry remains to be seen. Barco showed a prototype LCD screen at Drupa, possibly intended as a successor to the Barco Calibrator, but the project is rumoured to be cancelled.

It seems as if the future lays at the feet of the LCDs, since CRT technology doesn't have a whole lot of scope to go any further, but there are other technologies evolving besides LCDs and Crts. In fact even the LCDS differ quite a lot in terms of the technology they use. Most quality colour LCD s use TFT technology (Thin Film Transistor) since this offers a viewing angle of close to 180 degrees, and they are back-lit using CCFL (cold cathode fluorescent lanp). There will, possibly, be a move towards using a light-emitting diode (LED) in the LCD monitors because this may offer even higher luminance an a better spectral distribution of the light for m ore accurate colours and a larger gamut.

But one should not only consider LCDs when looking for upcoming display technology. Canon and Toshiba have cooperated for several years now and one of the display technologies they are about to launch is called SED, short for surface-conduction electron-emitter display. While closer to Crts in design, these screens can be built very slim and they use less energy. Like CRTs they don't grow deep when they are built wide. An SED based display can be made just centimtres deep at 42" sizes or bigger.

A third (or is it possibly a fourth, plasma displays set aside) technology should also be checked out if you desire a high performance display. It's the DLP based monitors or projectors. The DLP (digital light processing) technology was invented by Texas Instruments and DLP based TVs and projectors are said to offer fast refresh rates (faster than LCDs) and a very large colour gamut. While popular in cinema projection systems and big television sets, the DLT technology doesn't seem to have made its way into computer monitors yet.

Returning to plasma technology, this has an interesting advantage over LCDs. These screens are said to have a larger colour gamut than LCDs but what's perhaps more interestig for proofing applications is that they ma y have better colour uniformity over the whole monitor surface. The drawback is that they require a fairly low ambient light.

_{Adapted from 'New Screen Technologies on the Horizon', *Spindrift*, vol. 2, no. 8, Dec/Jan 2004–5, pp. 5–6, by kind permission of the publisher.}

EXERCISE FOLLOW-UP

Tightening sentences by ridding them of unnecessary words and phrases, and deleting transitional sentences that confused rather than clarified the flow of information, cut this piece drastically and made it clearer. Of course, you also made capitalization consistent, corrected spelling errors, inserted required punctuation, and asked for confirmation if you changed, or planned to change, any of the repeated 'gamut's.

TECHNIQUES FOR EXPANDING

It is easy to pad text with unnecessary repetition and irrelevance, but obviously that is not your aim. Look for places where the text would benefit from explanations, definitions, additional information or examples, and transitions to emphasize or clarify relationships. You might need to ask the author to supply additional information, but when you can make the additions yourself, try to write in the author's style and always ask him or her to confirm or alter what you have done.

Exercise 6.7, expanding text

Brief

This extract is from an article based on research and interviews, and is written by a staffer on the journal, as indicated in the strapline (subsidiary heading). Here the strapline is used as a introductory blurb, and should be marked up as a structure outside the usual heading hierarchy. The extract is roughly 60–70 words short. Edit and mark up the text as usual, and look for ways to expand the text without adding irrelevance, repetition or meaningless verbiage.

House style:
- no contractions
- abbreviations for UK, RSPB
- abbreviations for metric measurements used with numerals
- spell out numbers below 10
- single quotes

Larks recovering?

Numbers of skylarks have halved but thanks to you support, we have been able to look at ways to halt their decline. Our news editor Kate Smith reports.

'Skylark numbers are going to recover, there's no doubt about it' says RSPB research biologist Richard Bradbury. These words are almost as welcome as the skylark's continuous melody that, to me, signifies the true arrival of Spring, for the number of skylarks in the UK has fallen by more than half since I was a child.

Despite the fall in numbers, the skylark is still one of the most widely distributed birds in the British Isles. These birds nest on the ground and prefer open areas of grassland and farmland. One study on arable farmland in eastern England in the mid-1970's, found up to 49 males per square kilometre. 'The difference today, says Richard Bradbury ' is that it is possible to go to a field or a farm and not hear one. That wouldn't have happened before.'

Why have Skylarks disappeared?

'It's something you can't explain simply' says Paul Donald. 'It is essentially due to changes in the way cereals are grown in some parts of the UK.' Cereals support half of the UK's skylarks and traditionally they were planted in the Spring, but now they are often sown in Autumn. This means that by the time the skylarks are nesting, the crops are tall and dense.

'Winter wheat is too tall by June and this hampers the second and third breeding attempts that are needed to maintain numbers,' Peter Robertson tells me. Some skylarks will not nest for a second or third time, while others are forced into more dangerous areas, such as the tramlines where tractors are driven. The nests are at risk of being run over and are more at risk from predators that use tramlines as paths to cross a field.

Skylarks feed their chicks mainly on insects, but pants and seeds become their main food in the winter. If crops are sown in the Spring, then the stubble often remains in the field throughout the winter. This is an important source of food for skylarks and many other farmland birds, as they can extract waste grain and seeds growing within the stubble. With the change in planting from Spring to Autumn, there are not as many stubble fields in the Winter now.

What Are We Doing To Help?
In April 2000, thanks to the generosity of you, our members, we bought a working farm in Cambridgeshire to try out ways to help skylarks and other farmland birds. 'It is a typical East Anglian cereal farm,' say Roger Buisson, the project manager at Hope Farm.

'It is set in a rolling, open landscape, with some small fields, some large fields and a few ponds and copses. We haven't changed the field size of the number of hedgerows as we wanted to show how you could help wildlife while running a typical commercial farm.

'Its unreasonable to expect farmers to go back to Spring sowing, says Peter Robertson. 'They plant crops in the Autumn because it gives the plants longer to grow, producing larger yields and generating more income. What we wanted to do was to look at a way of tweaking Winter cropping so that it would help skylarks but not cost farmers lots of money.'

The team at Hope Farm decided to try leaving bare patches of ground in a wheat field so that skylarks would have room to nest. "This also helps with feeding,' says Roger. 'Skylarks can see around more easily and find food faster, so the chicks will be better fed.'

To leave unsown patches of a few metres wide, all the farmer needs to do when sowing the seed is to turn the drill off for a few seconds at various points. Our research at Hope Farm has shown that these unsown patches have a small affect on the total crop yield. The biggest impact for farmers is a bit of extra paperwork, as they have to subtract the area of these patches from the area of wheat field for which they are paid a government subsidy. We are working with the government to make the paperwork easier and to prevent farmers from losing subsidy payments.

The results from the fields with unsown patches are looking very promising,' says Roger. The number of skylark territories are looking good too. In the Summer of 2000 there were ten territories on the 180 hectare farm; this summer on the same cropping pattern there were 27. Similar results are being seen on other farms, where we are working with industry and government funders, other researchers and farmers to assess the effects of leaving bare patches.

We used unsown patches from the 2001 season onwards. We also tried using wider spaced rows, leaving a gap of 25 cm between each row of wheat rather than the normal 12.5. 'the results for the wider spaced rows are not conclusive,' says Roger. 'It's not looking so beneficial, but its not been disproved either.'

Adapted from Kate Lewis, 'Larks Recovering?', *Birds*, vol. 19, no. 8, Winter 2003, pp. 26–32, by kind permission of the publisher.

EXERCISE FOLLOW-UP

A couple of the people mentioned in the draft were identified by their jobs, so adding this information for the others will make the text consistent on this point. The background information requested in the queries will clarify the size of the problem and how researchers were able to assess it. Repeating some points in different words helps readers to absorb and retain the information, and adding definitions shows an awareness of the audience. Although each query might lead to an addition of only a few words, together they will bring the text up to the right extent.

At page proof

Even when we get the script to the right length for setting, we might need to delete and add (also referred to as 'save and make' and 'cut and fill') at proof to avoid having a very few lines on a page at the end of a chapter or an imbalance in facing pages or adjoining columns, or to get rid of widows or orphans. Often, proofreaders are asked to do this cutting and filling, and if you have trained or worked as a proofreader, you might have experience in resolving these problems. At other times it is the copy-editor, who has worked closely with the author and knows the text intimately, who cuts and fills at page proof or, at least, checks what the proofreader has done.

It is, of course, important that deletions and additions do not alter the meaning or the consistent style of the text. At this stage it is also important to minimize changes to the text to keep costs down, reduce the possibility of new errors – such as bad word breaks, repetition, widows and orphans – being introduced, and limit the effects to as few columns or pages as possible.

I have assumed that you have been trained or worked as a proofreader, so the following information is just a reminder of the basic cut-and-fill techniques.

TECHNIQUES FOR CUTTING

Look for paragraphs that end with very short lines. Count the number of characters in such a line. Check the spacing in the line or two above to see whether it can accommodate any more characters. Then, working from the end of the paragraph back, cut as little as needed to take back the characters on the last line. Look for places where you can make one cut – modifiers, subordinate clauses or examples that the reader will not miss – or change, perhaps replacing a phrase with a single word that will do the job completely or to a large extent. The aim is to minimize the number of corrections.

TECHNIQUES FOR EXPANDING

These really are the reverse of cutting techniques. Choose paragraphs that end with very long or full lines. Working back from the end of the paragraph, look for words that can be expanded into longer words or phrases and for places where relevant information or examples can be added. You must take over at least a few words (only one would create a widow), although the goal is to make the new line about a third full.

7 Endmatter

Although we tend to associate notes and references with works of non-fiction, they can also appear in annotated editions of fiction, so all copy-editors need to understand the main referencing systems. This chapter explains how references and bibliographies are structured, and how to work with them as you edit text. Most non-fiction publications have an index, so this chapter also explains how to brief an indexer and edit an index.

As usual, there is a lot of information in each section, so take your time and be sure you have absorbed the details in each paragraph before continuing.

Notes and reference systems

Notes contain editorial comments that the author does not want to include in the main text. They can appear in any kind of publication, whether or not there are also references. References contain acknowledgement of, or directions to see, other sources. There are three main systems of references:
* author–title
* author–date
* author–number

Each system has its own style of bibliography. The following text guides you through the basics of each system. You will find more specialized information in style manuals such as *Butcher's Copy-editing*, *New Hart's Rules* and the *Chicago Manual of Style*. Academic and professional associations may have their own referencing systems, which can be variations on the three main ones. House style can also affect the way in which the elements in citations are treated.

Author–title system

Author–title references are used mainly in the humanities. Figure 7.1 shows all the elements in references to various kinds of publications.

Read through them first to familiarize yourself with the type of information and how it is presented. Because they follow these simple patterns, references are easy to work with, although they require a lot of attention to detail. There are a few points to notice in particular:

- The author or editor's name is given in the normal order: first name or initial(s) followed by surname. There is no reason to invert names, as the reader does not have to search for them in an alphabetical list.
- If there are *more* than three authors of a single work, it is usual to use only the first author's name and '*et al.*', which means 'and others'.
- The abbreviation for editor(s) follows the name(s) in parentheses, but abbreviations for editor of an edition, translator or reviser, without parentheses, precede the name given later in the citation.
- For references to articles, the place of publication is not included, as the names of journals and newspapers tend to be unique.
- The examples are punctuated very simply, but house style might stipulate a different pattern.
- A single note can contain references to multiple sources.

IBID

All the relevant information is given the first time a work is mentioned in an article or chapter, but it could waste a lot of space to repeat all the information each time the same reference is cited. When the reference is to the single work cited in the immediately preceding note, 'Ibid.', the abbreviation for *ibidem* (in the same place – so never 'in ibid.'), is used; it cannot be used when the preceding note contains more than one title. Volume, chapter and page details can be added if they differ from the first mention. For example:

3 R. W. Burchfield (ed.), *The New Fowler's Modern English Usage*, 3rd edn, Oxford: Clarendon Press, 1996, p. 32.
4 Ibid., p. 517.

'Ibid.' – with or without a full stop, according to house style for abbreviations, and always in roman type – can be repeated as many times as necessary, but when the author has a long string of ibids, check whether they can be consolidated into a single note at the end of the paragraph.

232 *Copy-editing*

Books
1 author's/general editor's first name or initial(s)
2 author's/general editor's surname
3 *title*
4 number of volumes
5 number of edition other than the first
6 name of translator/editor
7 place of publication
8 publisher
9 year of publication (first and last dates for a number of volumes published over a period of time)
10 number of the volume relevant to the reference
11 page number(s)

Examples
Marija Gimbutas, *The Goddesses and Gods of Old Europe, 6500–3500 B.C.* London: Thames and Hudson, 1982, p. 205.
H. W. Fowler, *A Dictionary of Modern English Usage*, 2nd edn, rev. Sir Ernest Gowers. Oxford: Clarendon Press, 1965, pp. 40–1.
Mircea Eliade, *A History of Religious Ideas*, 3 vols., trs. Willard R. Trask. Chicago: University of Chicago Press, 1978–85, vol. 1, pp. 40–1.

Chapters
1 author's first name or initial(s)
2 author's surname
3 'Chapter title'
4 'in' 1–11 above

Example
Brian Willan, 'The Siege of Mafeking', in Peter Warwick (ed.), *The South African War: The Anglo-Boer War 1899–1902*. Harlow, Essex: Longman, 1980, pp. 139–60.

Articles
1 author's first name or initial(s)
2 author's surname
3 'Article title'
4 *Journal title*
5 volume number
6 issue number
7 date of publication
8 page number(s)

Examples
Danuta Kean, 'A suitable place for a woman', *Bookseller*, 17 December 1999, p. 10.
G. Leech and A. Beale, 'Computers in English language research'. *Language Teaching*, 17, 3, 1984, 216–29.

Poems and songs
1 author's first name or initial(s)
2 author's surname
3 'title' for aria, song or short poem; *poem title* for epic poem
4 *opera, musical* or *collection of poems* in which work appeared
5 book/canto/stanza
6 line number(s)
7 place of publication
8 publisher
9 year of publication
10 page number(s) for poems or songs in a collection

Examples
Sara Teasdale, 'August Moonrise', *Flame and Shadow*. New York: Macmillan, 1930, pp. 9–11.
John Donne, 'Air and Angels', *John Donne: The Complete Poems*, ed. A. J. Smith. Harmondsworth, Middlesex: Penguin, 1971, p. 41.

Virgil, *The Aeneid*, trs. C. Day Lewis. Bk IV, 141–79, London: Hogarth Press, 1966.
Marvin Hamlisch and Edward Kleban, 'I Hope I Get It', *A Chorus Line*, New York: Hal Leonard Publishing, 1975.

Plays
1 author's first name or initial(s)
2 author's surname
3 *title*
4 place of publication
5 publisher
6 act, scene, line(s) *or* act/part, page number(s) *or* scene only (TV)

Examples
William Shakespeare, *The Winter's Tale*, I, ii, 268–78 (*or* 1.2.268–78).
David Hare, *Saigon*. London: Faber & Faber, 1983, sc. 37, p. 51.

The Bible
1 book
2 chapter
3 verse

Examples
Deut. 6:3
2 Kgs 6:8–10, 14; 9:3, 5–8

Parliamentary and other official papers
1 initiating government office or most prominent member/chair of committee
2 title, in italics or roman, according to good practice or author
3 description of document
4 command number: use C, Cd, Cmd, Cmnd, Cm, as given by author; each abbreviation refers to a different series
5 place of publication
6 publisher
7 date of publication
8 column, paragraph, section or page number(s)

Example
Committee on Currency and Foreign Exchanges, *First Interim Report*. Cd 9182. London: HMSO, 1918, para 4.

Law cases
1 *parties*, plaintiff first
2 date, in round or square brackets according to source
3 the judicial forum in which the case was heard or reported
4 reference number

Examples
Bunge Corporation v. Tradax Export S.A. [1981] 2 All ER 513.
Boyd v. Emerson (1834) 2 Ad & El 184.
Danecroft Jersey Mills Ltd v. Criegee, The Times, 14 April 1987.

Websites
1 author's first name
2 author's surname
3 'title of article'
4 complete website address, unbroken if possible, or broken after a solidus; in *italics* if the site is a journal, a newspaper or an e-book
5 date
6 (date last viewed)

Example
Benedicte Page, 'How we made our fortune', http://www.*theBookseller*.com. 2000 (accessed 27 March 2000)

Figure 7.1 Elements in references. Use all the elements that exist for the first citation of a reference. The punctuation between elements is a matter of house style.

Sources: Judith Butcher *et al.*, *Copy-Editing: The Cambridge Handbook for Editors, Copy-editors and Proofreaders*, 4th edn, Cambridge: CUP, 2006. *Chicago Manual of Style*, 15th edn, Chicago: The University of Chicago Press, 2003. Janice R. Walker and Todd Taylor, *Columbia Guide to Online Style*, http://www.columbia.edu/cu/cup/cgos/idx_basic.html.

SHORT-TITLE

In the past when a reference was repeated and 'ibid.' was not appropriate, 'op. cit.' was used. The note would give only the surname of the author(s), the words 'op. cit.' (*opere citato*, in the work quoted) and page numbers if they differed from the previous reference. So all the hapless reader had to do was trawl back through all the preceding notes in the chapter to find the title. Not very helpful, especially if there was no bibliography. Of course, if more than one title by the author(s) had been cited, the title would have to be repeated to indicate which source was being referred to. And so we shall be forever grateful to whomever is responsible for the short-title system.

Here, the author or editor is referred to only by surname, unless the first name or initials are needed to distinguish authors of the same surname whose works have been cited. The identification '(ed.)' is also dropped. The title is shortened by dropping the initial article, subtitle, or other words not essential to identify it. Like an 'ibid.' reference, a short-title reference can include different details about the volume, chapter or page. The title in the example above is so well known that a short reference to it would be simply

Burchfield, *Fowler's*.

PRESENTATION: FOOTNOTES AND ENDNOTES

Notes containing only editorial comments can be presented as footnotes or endnotes in any referencing system. They are most helpful to readers when they are presented as footnotes if none of the problems mentioned below exist. Author–title and short-title references can also be presented as footnotes or endnotes, and are the only types of references that can include editorial notes.

As their name indicates, footnotes appear at the foot of the page, within the text area. When there are few footnotes in a chapter or a work, they can be signalled in the text by the following symbols: * † ‡ § ‖ ¶. The symbols are usually placed at the end of a displayed quotation and at the end of a sentence in the text, although they are placed within a sentence if the reference is to a specific word or phrase. They are outside punctuation (see Figure 7.2), except for dashes and when the reference is to text within parentheses. The sequence starts afresh on each page.

The education of youth was taken very seriously in England in the sixteenth and seventeenth centuries for those who could afford it.* Although the teaching was free in the so-called free schools, the cost of entrance fees, books and writing materials excluded the children of the poor.† Money was the key, as Philip Stubbes complained, to gaining a place at university.‡ Girls did not attend school, but in well-to-do families were educated at home by tutors. A continental tour was often a recognized part of a young gentleman's education.§

* William Harrison, *Description of England*, in Raphael Holinshed, *Chronicles*, 3 vols, London: John Harrison, 1577, vol. 1, bk II, chap. 3.
† Joan Simon, *Education and Society in Tudor England*, Cambridge: CUP, 1966, pp. 369–70.
‡ *The Second Part of the Anatomie of Abuses*, London: W. Wright, 1583. His views might be considered part of the modern debate on university fees.
§ J. W. Stoye, *English Travellers Abroad, 1604–1667*, rev. edn, New Haven, Conn.: Yale University Press, 1989.

Figure 7.2 Footnotes cued by symbols. The third note does not include the author's name because it is in the text. Both the cues in the text and the symbols with the notes are superior characters.

The education of youth was taken very seriously in England in the sixteenth and seventeenth centuries for those who could afford it.[1] Although the teaching was free in the so-called free schools, the cost of entrance fees, books and writing materials excluded the children of the poor.[2] Money was the key, as Philip Stubbes complained, to gaining a place at university.[3] Girls did not attend school, but in well-to-do families were educated at home by tutors. A continental tour was often a recognized part of a young gentleman's education.[4]

1 William Harrison, *Description of England*, in Raphael Holinshed, *Chronicles*, 3 vols, London: John Harrison, 1577, vol .1, bk II, chap. 3.
2 Joan Simon, *Education and Society in Tudor England*, Cambridge: CUP, 1966, pp. 369–70.
3 *The Second Part of the Anatomie of Abuses*, London: W. Wright, 1583. His views might be considered part of the modern debate on university fees.
4 J. W. Stoye, *English Travellers Abroad, 1604–1667*, rev. edn, New Haven, Conn.: Yale University Press, 1989.

Figure 7.3 Footnotes cued by number. Notice that the cues in the text are superior figures, and those with the notes are on the line.

The symbols can be doubled if more than the six shown are needed, but it is very confusing for the reader, so when there are more than occasional notes, it is usual to number them instead, starting from 1 in each chapter (see Figure 7.3). The note indicators in the text, whether they are symbols or numbers, are called 'cues'.

The number of lines of text on a page is reduced when footnotes are added, which can give a book with many notes and/or long individual notes an unbalanced appearance. In addition, because footnotes must start – and, ideally, finish – on the page where they are cued in the text, and are in a smaller size than the main text, the pages affected may have to be composed individually, which is time-consuming and expensive. To avoid these disadvantages, when there is more than the occasional note in a publication the notes are usually gathered at the end of articles in journals, and at the end of chapters or the end of a book. The exception is law books that cite case law, where the high number of references per page can make it impractical for readers to turn back and forth to the end of a weighty volume.

The heading 'References' or 'Notes and references', as appropriate, is used for notes at the end of articles or chapters and is marked up with a code such as 'N' or 'R', *not* one from the A, B, C hierarchy (Figure 7.4), unless the house style stipulates differently. However, the same heading for notes at the end of a book is marked up with the code for a chapter, and then the notes or references for each chapter are listed under the full chapter title, which is coded A (Figure 7.4).

EDITING THE NOTES

There are a number of tasks and they need to be done separately for maximum efficiency. Putting a checklist where you can see it easily will help you to:
* match cue and note
* check bibliography
* edit note
* create short title
* check cue numbers
* check note numbers
* style references

Authors are generally asked to present their notes separately from the text regardless of how they are to be presented in the final

> (B) References
>
>   1 William Harrison, *Description of England*, in Raphael Holinshed, *Chronicles*, 3 vols, London: John Harrison, 1577, vol. 1, bk II, chap. 3.
>   2 Joan Simon, *Education and Society in Tudor England*, Cambridge: CUP, 1966, pp. 369–70.
>   3 *The Second Part of the Anatomie of Abuses*, London: W. Wright, 1583. His views might be considered part of the modern debate on university fees.
>   4 J. W. Stoye, *English Travellers Abroad, 1604–1667*, rev. edn, New Haven, Conn.: Yale University Press, 1989.
>
> (CH) Notes and references
>
> (A) Chapter 3: Education in England
>   1 William Harrison, *Description of England*, in Raphael Holinshed, *Chronicles*, 3 vols, London: John Harrison, 1577, vol. 1, bk II, chap. 3.
>   2 Joan Simon, *Education and Society in Tudor England*, Cambridge: CUP, 1966, pp. 369–70.
>   3 *The Second Part of the Anatomie of Abuses*, London: W. Wright, 1583. His views might be considered part of the modern debate on university fees.
>   4 J. W. Stoye, *English Travellers Abroad, 1604–1667*, rev. edn, New Haven, Conn.: Yale University Press, 1989.

Figure 7.4 Mark-up for end-of-chapter notes (top) and end-of-book notes (above)

publication. This means placing them at the end of the chapter or article, or inserting numbers manually and typing the notes in a separate file. Sometimes authors do as asked, and it makes everyone's job easier. If, however, you should receive a text with automatic numbering and embedded notes, and you are going to edit on-screen, ask your project manager or whoever oversees typesetting for advice on what to do. Whether the notes have to be stripped out and put in separate files, whether you or the typesetter will be the best person to do it, and at what stage it needs to be done might depend on the software the typesetter uses.

Let's assume the notes and references have been presented separately. Place the text, references and bibliography side by side in separate piles on your desk, or open the separate files on your computer. Although your screen might not be big enough to view three pages side by side, the advantages are in being able to use the search-and-replace facility to check and, if necessary, correct repeated references, and in using the bibliography to create the list of short titles.

Edit the text in the usual way. On hard copy, when you come to a cue, put a red V under it: cue$\overset{\vee}{\vphantom{x}}$. This helps you later in checking the sequence, and highlights it as a superior figure for a typesetter working from hard copy. On the e-file, you can highlight the cue to make checking the sequence easier, removing the highlighting before you send the files to the typesetter. Check that the cue is in the correct position relative to the punctuation and the material it is commenting on. Then check that there is a matching note: that it not only has the same number but also that the comment or references seem appropriate to the text.

When an editorial comment or a reference does not appear to match, check the next note. If that is the matching note, do not immediately renumber: ask the author whether a cue is missing in the text or the non-matching note should be dropped. Otherwise, if a note does not match, raise a query with the author. Be specific, as in all queries: indicate as concisely as possible why the comment or reference doesn't seem relevant to the text.

When the note matches, edit editorial comment as you would any text. Check that references appear in the bibliography, if there is one (there usually isn't for a journal article), and do not contain conflicting information. On hard copy, tick them there or write the chapter number next to them in pencil so that the next time they are mentioned in the same chapter you know to use the short form. Later, you will also be able to see whether any titles are not referred to in the text. Working on e-files, it is easy to check whether a reference has been repeated or not mentioned. If a source or some of its information in a note is missing from the bibliography, add it; if information in the reference and the bibliography are inconsistent, list the differences in the queries for the author.

You can use a pencil on hard copy to bracket or underline the parts to include in the short form; on-screen, you can edit a duplicate of the bibliography to create the list. If you don't have a bibliography, make lists – on-screen or on hard copy – of each full reference *and* its short form so that you can maintain consistency throughout the document. At a second or subsequent mention of a source, delete unnecessary elements from a full reference to leave the short form, but do not edit the references for house style at this time.

Journal titles can be abbreviated, particularly if they will appear in many references. House style or the brief should indicate whether titles should appear in full, or all, or only the best-known, should be abbreviated. When there is no guidance, ask the project manager how to proceed. When abbreviations are used – particularly in academic and science publications – they must be those stipulated by the individual journals. To resolve discrepancies you find in the references, ask the author; check the house style, which may include or refer to a list of standard abbreviations; or look online. Write the agreed abbreviations on your project style sheet or create a separate style sheet for this purpose to ensure consistency as you work. The latter is best if there are many titles and if a list of the abbreviations is to be included in the prelims or at the beginning of the bibliography.

When you have finished the article or chapter, go back and check only the superior figures in the text to make sure the sequence is correct, that no numbers have been omitted or repeated; the red V or highlighting makes the cues easy to spot quickly. If there are queries about missing or repeated notes, wait until you have the author's answers before renumbering.

When you have to alter note cues and numbers, work out the simplest way. **Do not** obliterate – erase, white out or write over – the original number on the hard copy. Draw a line through it so you can still see it, then write the new number next to it. If there are a great many notes, renumber the cues and the notes page by page. It would be faster to renumber all the cues and then all the notes, but by doing it page by page you can limit the effect of any mistakes. Now check the renumbering: no duplication or omissions. On an e-file, track your changes so that you can check the alterations. In some word-processing programs you can change all the numbers using the automatic renumbering system. Remember to keep a copy of the original file in case something goes wrong when making changes.

STYLING THE REFERENCES

Styling all the references for a chapter or article at one time enables you to do them more quickly and more consistently. Start by consulting the house style. Making a simple template of the most common elements in the main types of citation helps to maintain consistency of order and punctuation. For example, for the first mention, when a full citation is usually given:

> A. N. Surname, *Book*, total vols, edn, Place: Publisher, date, this vol., page(s).

> A. N. Surname, 'Article title', *Journal*, vol. no., issue no., date, page(s).

For subsequent citations:

> Surname, short title, page(s)

House style should state whether to use the abbreviations 'p' (page) and 'pp' (pages), with or without full stops, and closed up or spaced from the numerals. When the abbreviations are not used, the numerals appear alone:

> Burchfield, *Fowler's*, 48–54

Some house styles do not require references to state the place of publication for books, and others allow the omission of the publisher instead. The point of including both is to lead the reader to the source quickly and accurately. Omitting the place of publication ignores the fact that a title might be published in only one of the countries in which a multinational company has offices. Although giving only the place overlooks the possibility that there can be more than one work with the same title published in a given year in that place (yes, it does happen), at least it won't be by the same author or published by the same firm (I'd like to say 'obviously' …). In helping authors get their messages across to readers, we are always testing whether the presentation 'works' for the reader. Well, it's not a perfect world and we have to work with what we have, so here are some guidelines.

When authors include useful information not required by the house style, and do so consistently, do not delete it. In my experience, this does not happen very often. When authors omit information or don't follow the stated order for the elements, and do so consistently, you must consider whether the nature of these errors makes the reference difficult or impossible for the reader to use. For example, if the citations have the place of publication and the publisher reversed, it's not necessary to change them: the reader can tell what each element is. But if the page references are put before the date, the reader might not find them easily, because they are not where they are expected to be, and if 'p' or 'pp' is omitted, which is a common style, the reader might not recognize them at all.

If the place and/or publisher have been left out only occasionally, ask the author to supply them unless you can find them more quickly using the Internet; then ask the author to confirm them. If this information has been omitted consistently, you have to consider the ramifications of asking the author to supply it: if the references are extensive, it might take longer than the schedule allows or be impossible because the author no longer has all the source materials; or the author might refuse. for other reasons. Without this information, the usefulness of the references, and therefore the quality of the publication, is reduced. In such a case, always ask the advice of your project manager or the commissioning editor. The restraints of the schedule and budget will probably preclude you from doing the research too.

Check that all notes end with a full stop, which tells the reader all the information is complete.

EDITING THE BIBLIOGRAPHY

A bibliography is the list of works authors used in writing their texts. It has a chapter-weight heading and appears in the endmatter following end-of-book notes or preceding the index. All the works cited in the individual references should appear in the bibliography. When a bibliography is incomplete, query the author; if he or she wishes it to remain incomplete, title it 'Select bibliography'. Works that are not cited in the notes can appear in the bibliography or, in non-academic books, may be in a list of further reading, which would also have a chapter-weight heading and follow the bibliography in the endmatter. Always check with authors before removing titles from a bibliography; they might have consulted the works even though there are no specific references to them in the text.

The first difference between citing a source in a note and in a bibliography is the order in which the author or editor's names appear: in a bibliography the names are inverted so that the list can be organized alphabetically by the surnames. (Other names that occur in the body of a reference, such as a translator's, are not inverted, because they are not involved in the alphabetization.) In cases of multiple

> Harrison, William. *Description of England*, in Raphael Holinshed, *Chronicles*, 3 vols, London: John Harrison, 1577.
> Mystair, Edwin. *School Life in Mediaeval Britain*, London: Slate, 1952.
> —— (ed.). *Studies in Education: the seventeenth century*, London: Slate, 1953.
> —— and Jones, Fred. *Schools in Eighteenth-century Britain*, London: Slate, 1957.
> —— and Steeps, John. *Discipline in Schools, 1650–1850*, London: Boarden, 1955.
> Simon, Joan. *Education and Society in Tudor England*, Cambridge: CUP, 1966.
> ——. *The Schools Today and Tomorrow*, London: Association for Education in Citizenship, 1943.
> Stoye, J.W. *English Travellers Abroad, 1604–1667*, rev. edn, New Haven, Conn.: Yale University Press, 1989.
> Stubbes, Philip. *The Second Part of the Anatomie of Abuses*, London: W. Wright, 1583.

Figure 7.5 An example of entries in an author–title bibliography

authorship, house style dictates whether all the names are inverted or only the first. I prefer all names to be inverted because it makes works easier to find when the second or subsequent author's names have to be used in deciding alphabetical order (Figure 7.5). Consistency is essential, and the way in which the author has prepared the bibliography might be a deciding factor.

The second difference is in citing page numbers. Citations of articles in periodicals must include page numbers in both notes and bibliography to identify where in the publication the article appears; in notes, they might also include, or state only, the page on which a quotation, illustration or discussion of a subject appears. Page numbers in references to books in the notes may be used to identify a particular chapter, and appear in the bibliography only when the source is a multi-author publication and the author of the chapter is listed as the entry in the bibliography. Page numbers in references to books in the notes may also identify where specific material – a quotation, illustration or discussion – is found within the work, and are omitted from the bibliography.

Style the bibliography when you have worked through the entire book. By this time you will have the details of any titles that were missing and can ask the author about deleting any sources that

were not included in the references. Using templates for the information, this time with the surnames first, ensure that each entry has:
* all the required elements,
* in the required order,
* with the punctuation required by the house style.

Ensure that titles of compilations or edited editions and abbreviations of journal titles, both of which can appear in more than one entry, are consistent. However, do not impose house style on the spelling of titles; they must be quoted as they appear on the source.

Finally, check the alphabetical order of the bibliography. Anonymous works are placed according to the first word of their title, excluding an initial article. There is more than one way to list multiple works by the same author. One is to list the works written (books before articles), compiled, edited or translated by an individual, in that order, followed by the works written (again, books before articles), compiled, edited or translated in collaboration with others.

A 2- or 3-em rule (according to house style) can be used to replace the name of an author (or editor, etc.) after the first mention. 'Anon' cannot be replaced in this way, as it cannot be known to represent the same person each time. The names are repeated when another author's name is added.

When there is more than one entry for the first-named author in multi-author works, the subsequent authors' surnames are used for further alphabetizing. Sources with more than three authors or editors might be listed as 'first author's name *et al.*' in notes but with all the names given in the bibliography. If house style requires an '*et al.*' listing in the bibliography too, it is placed at the end of the alphabetical list of the appropriate multi-author category.

Multiple works within all the categories can be organized alphabetically by title, ignoring the initial article, or chronologically. The former is easier for the reader; the latter is useful if the purpose is to show the cited author's development.

Exercise 7.1, editing text with references and bibliography using the short-title system

Brief
Edit the following text, notes and bibliography.

House style
- -ise verbs
- single quotes, double within
- source notes and references: Name. Title. trs Name. Place: Publisher, date, p. XX.

Highsmith admired Dostoevsky for his rejection of conventional naturalism in favour of a more shocking psychological realism and there is no doubt that the nineteenth century author, particularly in his novel Crime and Punishment, had an enormous impact on her work. After reading the novel, she wrote in her diary that Dostoevsky was her 'master.' She said that that novel could be read as a story of suspense, an opinion shared by Thomas Mann, who wrote in his introduction to the short novels of Doestoevsky that the book was 'the greatest detective novel of all time'.[1]

The parallels between Crime and Punishmen and Highsmith's first published novel, Strangers on A Train, are striking. Like Dostoevsky's anti-hero, Raskolnikov, the two strangers on a train, Bruno and Guy, fantasize about the murders in their minds befoe carrying out the acts. Indeed, the psychological rehearsals for the killings are so fully imagined that they almost serve as substitutes for the actual killings. As Raskolnikov thinks himself into a state of nears hysteria he asks himself 'If I feel so timid now, what will it be when I come to put my plan into execution?'[2] Similarly, Bruno, while shadowing Guy's wife Miriam, runs through all the different ways he could kill her before eventually deciding to strangle her. Guy, unable to sleep and eaten away by guilt, viualises how he would murder Bruno's father, leaving a clue so as to incriminate the son: 'he enacted the murder, and it soothed him like a drug'.[3]

Rather than serving as a caricature or stereotype, a flat signal for one aspect of human behaviour, Raskolnikov is an example of the contradictions in everyman – 'One might almost say that there exist in him two natures, which alternately get the upper hand.[4] Hghsmith, who was similarly fascinated by dualism, explores the issue further in Strangers on a Train. Guy, archetype of reason and order, initially views evil as an external force, something distinctly apart and outside of him. He rejects Bruno's belief in the universality of criminal desires – that each of us harbours a potential murderer – but after killing Bruno's father he realizes the truth, that 'love and hate ... good and evil, lived side by side in the human heart.'[5] Just as Svidrigailov exists in relation to Raskolnikov, so Bruno serves as Guy's 'cast-off self, what he thought he hated but perhaps in reality he loved'.[6]

Taking her lead from the Russian novelist, Highmith explored these ambiguities and contradictions, these paradoxes of human consciousness with skill and subtlety. For instance, in Strangers on A Rain, when Bruno breaks into an apartment – just for the thrill of it – he takes a table model, a piece of coloured glass, a cigarette lighter. ' I especially took what I didn't want,' he says.[7] At the end of the novel Guy, after his confession to Owen, turns to Gerrd, the detective who has heard his every word, and starts to speak, 'saying something entirely different from what he had intended'[8] The scene alludes to one in Crime an Punishment when Raskolnikov feels he has to unburden himself to Sonya. Like Guy, after his outburst, he realizes 'the event upset all his calculations, for it certainly was not *thus* that had intended to confess his crime.'[9]

Highsmith anchors her novels and stories in reality by listing a cloying number of details – the minutiae of life which carries the reader seamlessly over into the world of the uncanny. Jean-Paul Sartre, in his essay on the fantastic, describes such a technique as one of semiotic excess – 'the innumerable signs that line the roads and that mean nothing' – [10] a method particularly suitable for describing and critiquing the modern world.

Tavetan Todorov, in his influential book on the fantastic in literature, shows how modern detective stories have replaced the ghostly tales of the past. All works of fantasy literature, he says, share a number of common elements: fractured identity; the brekdown of boundaries between an individual and their environement; and the blurring of external reality and internal consciousness. These features, he concludes, ' collect the essential elements of the basic network of fantastic themes'.[12] Hihsmith's characters, like Dostoevsky's, occupy a paraxial realm, one described by Mikhail Bakhtin in the following terms 'In Dostoevsky the participants in the performance stand on the threshold (the threshold of life and death, truth and falsehood, danity and insanity) ... 'today's corpses,' capable of neither dying, nor of being born anew'.[13] Highsmith compels the reader to align his point of view with the hero, whose task is to sail us, like Charon, across the dark waters to the other-world of Hades. 'We know that the reader begins his reading by identifying with the hero of the novel, ' says Jean-Paul Sartre.[14] 'Thus the hero, by lending us his point of view, constitutes the sole access to the fantastic.

Notes

1. Thomas Mann. Intrduction, *The Short Novels of Dostoevsky*. New York: Dial Press, 1946
2. Fyodor Dostoevsky. *Crime and Punishment*, trs. Frederick Whishaw, London, J. M. Dent, 1911, p. 8.
3. Patricia Highsmith, *Strangers on a Train*, Cresset Press, 1950, p 149.
4. Dostoevsky. *Crime and Punishment*, p.167.
5. Highsmith, *Strangers*, p.193.
6. Highsmith, *Strangers*, p. 194.
7. Highsmith, *Strangers*, p. 20
8. Highsmith, *Strangers*, p. 307.
9. F, Dostoevsky. *Crime and Punishment*, 343.
10. Jean Paul Sartre, *Literary and Philosophical Essays,* trs Annette Michelson, London, 1955, p.62 This theme is also developed in Sartre's own fiction.
11. Tzvetan Todorov. *The Fantastic: A Structural Approach to a Literary Genre*, trs. R Howard. Ithaca, NY: Cornell University Press. p120.

12 Bakhtin, Mikhail *Problems f Dostoevsky's Poetics*, trans. R. W, Rotsel, NY: Ardis, 1973, p. 122.

13 Jean-Paul Sartre, *Literary and Philosophical Essays,* trs Annette Michelson, London, 1955, p.65

Bibliography

Bakhtin, Mikhail. *Problems f Dostoevsky's Poetics*, trans R. W, Rotsel, NY: Ardis, 1973.

Dostoevsky, Fyodor. *Crime and Punishment*, trs Frederick Whishaw, London, J. M. Dent, 1911.

Highsmith, Patricia. *Strangers on a Train*, London, Cresset Press, 1950.

Mann, Thomas. Introduction, *The Short Novels of Dostoevsky*, New York, Dial Press, 1947.

Sartre, Jean-Paul. *Literary and Philosophical Essays,* trs Annette Michelson, London, Rider & Co, 1955.

Tavetan Todorov. *The Fantastic: A Structural Approach to a Literary Genre*, trs R Howard. Ithaca, NY, Cornell University Press, p120.

Adapted from Andrew Wilson, *Beautiful Shadow: A Life of Patricia Highsmith*, London: Bloomsbury, 2003.

EXERCISE FOLLOW-UP

This short extract included reminders about hyphenation, relative pronouns, noun–verb agreement, quotation marks, and the use of italics for titles. In para 2 you may have chosen another way to do it but the point was to avoid unnecessary repetition by replacing one of the 'killings'. In line 26 it was easy to find a non-gender-specific substitute for 'everyman', a term that must be capitalized when used.

There were only a few queries on the text, although you might have had more. You should not query spellings you can easily check yourself, like 'Doestoevsky', but it is fair to ask about Todorov, who will not be in *NODWE* or a companion to English literature. If there were an inconsistency in the spelling of a character's name that you could not resolve from the author's text, you would ask the author for the correct version – you are not expected to try to find it in the source or on the Internet. A danger of using the Internet for checking names that have been transliterated from another alphabet – such as Raskolnikov and Svidrigailov – is that there may be more than one version, and the text must use the version in the author's source.

There was only one misnumbering of the note cues, but many instances of wrong positioning relative to punctuation.

If Thomas Mann is the editor of the edition, you would put '(ed.)' after his name, delete 'Introduction' and add the page references, or move 'Introduction' to the end of the note and omit the page numbers. However, if he is not the editor, the information remains as shown; to move 'Introduction' to another position would give the impression that Mann is the author of a book *about* the short novels of Dostoevsky.

You can find the information missing from notes 3 and 10 in the bibliography, but you have to ask the date for the source in note 11, as it is missing from the bibliography too. You may say 'I can look up the missing date/publisher/place on the Internet.' You may be able to find it, but you are not expected to look unless your project manager specifically briefs you to do so – it is time-consuming and the budget may not allow for this level of checking. It is the author's responsibility to supply all the bibliographic data. However, in the unlikely event that you have no other queries for the author, it might be quicker to check one or two bibliographic details than to wait for the author to do it. In such a case use the online catalogues of national libraries – such as the British Library and the American Library of Congress (see Resources) – for books, and authorized individual or collective sites for journals.

Capitals and other major cities do not need supplementary information unless there is a risk of confusion. For example, if a book is published in Cambridge in England, the source note will say only 'Cambridge' – the first place of that name. If the place of publication is any other Cambridge, the source note must include the next level of identification – county, state or country; for example there are a dozen places named Cambridge in North America alone. Thus 'NY' follows 'Ithaca' in the Todorov source, because the first place of that name is in Greece. Use the appropriate abbreviation for the secondary place name, but always spell out the primary name, which is why you should have spelled out 'New York' in the Bakhtin reference.

Author–date system

The author–date system, often referred to as the Harvard system, is used mainly in the natural and social sciences. Because it is for source citations only, two systems have to be used if authors wish to make editorial comments too. The references are not cued by symbols or numbers. Instead, abbreviated information appears in parentheses in the text (Figure 7.6). Each such cue is positioned where it will least disturb the flow of the text: at the end of a sentence whenever possible, otherwise where logic demands, and within the nearest relevant punctuation. The key elements are:

- The authors' or editors' surnames; first names or initials are given only when there is reference in the work to more than one author with the same surname. The abbreviation for editor(s) is not included, but appears in the list of references, the equivalent of the bibliography in the author–title system. When authors are mentioned in the text, their names are not repeated in the parenthetical cue. House style will determine whether *et al.* is used when there are more than two or more than three authors.
- The year of publication. When authors are cited for more than one publication in the same year, the date is suffixed 'a' for the first title, then 'b', 'c', etc. When the in-text reference is to works in different years, the dates are separated by a comma:

Humbleton 1993, 2001.

The figure from 6500 years ago is an image of growth (Gimbutas 1982a, 205). Women were thought to assist the earth symbolically in its productivity (Campbell 1976, 139) and may have been the first to sow and reap grain (Briffault 1959, ch. 8; C. Jung 1963, 98–101). Eliade (1978–85, 1: 40–1) suggests that women may have been the owners of the cultivated fields, which would give them a high status.

Figure 7.6 An example of text using the author–date system

- Volume and page references, if relevant, without the abbreviations 'vol(s)' or 'p(p)'

Punctuation is, of course, subject to house style, but it is common practice to omit any between the authors' names and the date, to use a comma between the date and further details, and to use a colon between the volume or issue and page numbers. Multiple sources are separated by semicolons.

It is not possible to use 'ibid.', but there are some similarities to the author–title system in the way multiple references are treated. When there are multiple references in a single paragraph to the *same* page(s) in a single source, and no other sources are mentioned between them, the parenthetical indicator should be put at either the first or the last relevant position. So the similarities are that it has to be a single source in the initial reference and there cannot be a different source between mentions. If the subsequent references in the same paragraph are to different chapters or pages, then the different chapters or pages can be given alone.

LIST OF REFERENCES

Obviously, there has to be a list of references and it must give the complete information for every source. (It can include sources that are not mentioned in the text, and might then be called 'Bibliography'; if it lists only the sources cited, it will be headed 'References'.) As in the author–title system, the entries are listed alphabetically by authors' surnames. All the elements in the citation are the same too, but the order is different: the date follows the authors' or editors' names, as shown in Figure 7.7.

All words in journal titles except articles (unless the first word of the title), prepositions and conjunctions are capitalized. House style decides whether book titles follow the same pattern or have only the first word and proper nouns capitalized, which is usually the style for article and chapter titles.

As in the author–title system, multiple works can be organized in the order written, compiled, edited or translated by an individual, followed by the works written, compiled, edited or translated in collaboration with others. The important difference is that they are listed chronologically in each category. When authors are cited for more than one work published in the same year, the titles are alphabetized

> Briffault, Robert (1959). *The Mother: A Study of the Origins of Sentiments and Institutions*, London: Allen & Unwin.
> Campbell, Joseph (1976). *The Masks of God: Primitive Mythology*, Harmondsworth: Penguin Books.
> —— ed. (1951). *Philosophies of India*, Bollingen Series XXXVI, Princeton: Princeton University Press.
> Campbell, Joseph with Moyers, Bill (1988). *The Power of Myth*, New York: Doubleday.
> Cashford, Jules (1990). 'Joseph Campbell and the grail myth' in John Matthews, ed., *The Household of the Grail*, Wellingborough, Northants.: Aquarian Press.
> Eliade, Mircea (1978–85). *A History of Religious Ideas*, 3 vols, trs. Willard R. Trask, Chicago: University of Chicago Press.
> Gimbutas, Marija (1982a). *The Goddesses and Gods of Old Europe, 6500–3500 B.C.*, London: Thames and Hudson.
> —— (1982b). 'Three waves of the Kurgan people into Old Europe, 4500–2500 B.C.', *Archives Suisses d'Anthropologie Générale*, 43:2.
> Jung, C. G. (1963). *Memories, Dreams and Reflections*, London: Routledge and Kegan Paul.
> Jung, Emma (1971). *The Grail Legend*, London: Hodder & Stoughton.

Figure 7.7 An example of an author–date bibliography or list of references

(ignoring the initial article) first and then the date is suffixed 'a', 'b', 'c', etc., as shown in the entries for Gimbutas in Figure 7.7. Sometimes authors use the suffixes in order of the mention in the text (i.e. the first title mentioned for a particular year is 'a', the second is 'b'). When the author has been consistent, it is not worth changing the order unless the publisher insists.

The 3-em rule can be used to replace repeated names. The use of parentheses for the date following the name (or rule) is common, but always check house style for the use of this and other punctuation.

EDITING

Although you don't want to edit it fully until after you have edited the text, it is a good idea to check the list of references first. Make sure that it is properly alphabetized by author and the year of publication follows the name(s). See that multiple titles by a single author in a single year are alphabetized and the years properly suffixed. Check particularly to see whether there are different entries for parts of the same edited or compiled work and, if so, that the details are consistent. This preliminary work will save you time and avoid the horror of discovering discrepancies in the dates after you have edited a substantial amount of the text. And if it is necessary to add entries, it will be easier to put them in the right place.

Have the text and the list of references side by side on your desk or screen. As you edit the text, check each citation against the list. As with all systems of reference, see whether the reference seems appropriate and, if so, use a pencil to tick it. When you have a single list of references for a book, in the margin pencil the chapter numbers in which each work appears in case a change of any kind affects the references at a later stage. As you work, make a list of discrepancies and missing citations in each article or chapter for the author to resolve. When you finish editing, go back over the pages: the ticks help you to see quickly whether you have checked all the references.

Now go back again and style all the references in the text. Make a template showing the house style of punctuation to help you maintain consistency, for example:

> Surname date, vol. number: page number.

Then style the references at the end of an article or chapter. If all the references are at the end of a book, style them when you have finished all the editing, to make imposing consistency easier and faster. Consult the house style for punctuation and capitalization; for example, some houses do not put chapter or article titles in quotation marks and capitalize only the first word and proper nouns in titles. As before, making a simple template of the most common elements in the main types of citation helps to maintain consistency of order and punctuation:

> Author, A. N. (date) 'Chapter title' in Other Name, ed., *Book*, total vols, edn, Place: Publisher, this vol., page(s)

> Author, A. N. (date) 'Article title', *Journal*, vol. no., issue no., page(s)

Use a style sheet to ensure consistency in repeated titles of compilations or editions and journal title abbreviations. Query discrepancies of any kind with the author. If there are a few citations in the list of references that are not referred to in the text, ask the author whether the reference has been omitted accidentally or the citation should be removed. If there are many citations that are not mentioned in the text, ask the author whether this is intentional.

Exercise 7.2, working with author–date references

Brief
Edit the following text, which has been peer-reviewed for accuracy. Check the in-text references, style the list of references and keep a list of queries for the author.

House style
- -ize for verbs
- minimal caps for book and article/chapter titles
- minimum number of digits in ranges

Individual scores and group scores

Finding a sufficient number of tokens of a variable for each speaker did not apparently emerge as a problem in the early urban surveys which followed Labov's 1966 model. This is because figures were usually calculated for groups of speaks rather than for individuals, a 5
practice which seemed to fit in neatly with Labov's theoretical position that the locus of systematic variation was the group rather than the individual. But following Macaulay's (Macaulay 1977) example, linguists have frequently presented figures for individuals, and a number of objections have been raised to the practice of 10
grouping speakers (see particularly Hudson (1980: 163–67; Romaine (1980: 190).)

There are certainly a number of obvious difficulties that need to be acknowledged: first of all, some groups are extremely small, and where divisions are made on the basis of two speaker variables (such 15 as social class and sex) it may seem a little unreal to label the persons who fall into one of the resulting categories as something along the lines of the 'upper middle class female group.' It is hard to see what kind of claims might reasonably be made about linguistic variation expressed as average scores of groups such as these (an additional difficulty being the abstract and contentious nature of social class labels).

A more general statistical point is that the *mean*, which is the type of average most often used by socialinguists, is not always the most suitable measure of central tendency within a group; under some conditions the *median* or the *mode* are more appropriate. Measures of central tendency need to be interpreted along with measures of within group variability - that is, the clustering of individual scores around a typical value. The statistic most often used to measure within-group variability is the *standard deviation*, although there are other possibilities. Accessible discussions both of measures of central tendency and of variability can be found in Butler (19985b, ch 3) and Erickson and Nosanchuk (1977, ch 3). Since the linguistic homogeneity of groups can vary considerably it is important for sociolinguists who aggregate individual scores to use these measures carefully. In particular, group means need to be used rather more circumspectly than was though necessary in the early studies (Erickson and Nosanchuk 1977, ch 4).

Another reason to be cautious of over reliance on the mean is that there are certain important '*between group*' differences that a simple comparison of group means cannot reveal. Sometimes there is little or no overlap between the scores of individuals in Group A and the individuals in Group B (see Milroy, 1980: 161 for an example), but more often there is considerable overlap. This distribution, considered along with with in-group variability, tells us quite a lot about the relationship of *group* scores to *individual scores* a matter of some interest to sociolinguiists.

Macauly has concluded from his Glasgow study that individual scores do in fact fall into groups in such a way as to allow Glasgow speech to be characterised as three major social dialects. (Macaulay 1978) Guy has concluded from his own study of final stop deletion (1980) that the individual follows the group norm very closely; but since we know that scores for different liguistic variables are not distributed within or between groups in a comparable way, we cannot conclude that all variables will behave in the dame way as the syllable-final alveolar stop. In Belfast (Milroy 1980, 121–49) an analysis of variance technique highlighted differences in the distribution of eight difference linguistic variables.

References

Butler, C. (1985a) *Statistics in linguistics*, Oxford: Blackwell.

Butler, C. (1985b), *Computers in Linguistics*, Oxford: Blackwells.

Dixon, R. M. W. (1971) *The Dyirbal language of North Queensland*, Cambridge: CUP.

Dixon, R. M. W. and Blake, B. J., eds. (1979) *Handbook of Australian languages*, ANU Press.

Dixon, R. M. W. (1980) *The languages of Australia*, Cambridge: CUP.

Erickson, B. H. and T. A. Nosanchuk (1977) *Understanding data*, Toronto: McGraw-Hill Ryerson.

Guy, G. (1980) 'Variation in the group and the individual: the case of the final-stop deletion', in W. Labov, ed., *Locating language in space and time*, New York: Academic Press.

Hudson, R.A. (1980) *Sociolinguistics*, Cambridge: CUP.

Labov, W. (1966) The social stratification of English in New York City, Washington D.C.: Center for Applied Linguistics.

—— (1972a) *Sociolinguistic Patterns*, Philadelphia: Pennsylvania University Press.

—— (1972b) Some principles of linguistic methodology, *Language in Society*, 1: 97–120.

—— (1972c) *Language in the Inner City*, Philadelphia: Pennsylvania University Press.

—— ed. (1980) *Locating Language in time and Space*, New York: Academic Press

—— (1982) Objectivity and commitment in linguistic science: the case of the Black English trial in Ann Arbor, *Language in Society*, 11: 165-201.

Macaulay, R. K. S (1977) *Language, social class, and education*, Edinburgh: Edinburgh Univ Press.

Macaulay, R. K. S (1978) *Variation and Consistency in Galswegian English*, London: Arnold.

Milroy, J. (1980) *Regional Accents of English: Belfast*, Blackstaff: Belfast.

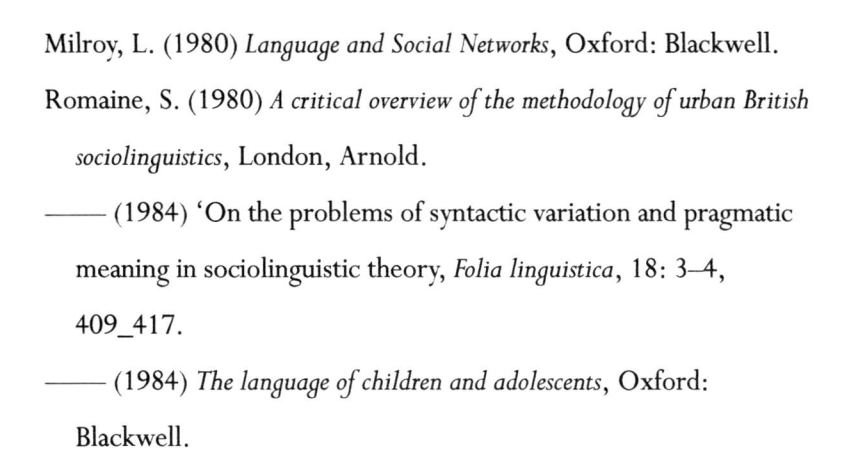

Milroy, L. (1980) *Language and Social Networks*, Oxford: Blackwell.

Romaine, S. (1980) *A critical overview of the methodology of urban British sociolinguistics*, London, Arnold.

—— (1984) 'On the problems of syntactic variation and pragmatic meaning in sociolinguistic theory, *Folia linguistica*, 18: 3–4, 409_417.

—— (1984) *The language of children and adolescents*, Oxford: Blackwell.

Adapted from Lesley Milroy, *Observing and Analysing Natural Language: A Critical Account of Sociolinguistic Method*, Oxford, Blackwell, 1987.

EXERCISE FOLLOW-UP

Peer reviews are concerned with the quality of the information, not spelling, grammar or punctuation. Most of the corrections required in the text were included to make sure you always remember to check the smallest details, from hyphens to relative pronouns. The change in lines 11–12 improves the flow and precludes the need for double parentheses. In line 40 'between group' needs a hyphen but not the quotation marks, and triggers the question about italics for some terms and not others.

The entries for Butler and Labov show that it is important to check the list of references before editing the text: imagine getting through 256 pages only to have to go back and change 'a's, 'b's and 'c's. Did you jump to the conclusion that the reference to Milroy in line 56 was to J. Milroy because the text referred to Belfast? If so, you could have fallen into a big hole; unless you know the contents of the sources, or a title excludes the possibility that it includes content about a specific subject, always check with the author. In this case, in fact, the L. Milroy reference for that year is the correct one – just thought you'd like to know.

Author–number system

Also called 'Vancouver', the author–number system, which is for references only, is widely used in medical and biomedical publishing.

There are some similarities to the other systems, but also important differences. For example, cues appear as numbers in the text but refer only to a list of bibliographic references. In books, each chapter is referenced separately; the lists can appear at the end of chapters or at the end of the book. While all the elements in the references are the same as in the other two systems, the way in which they are styled differs. Here's how it works:

- Sources are numbered in the order in which they appear in the article or chapter. Subsequent references to the same source in the article or chapter repeat the number given at first mention.
- Each number refers to only one source, but more than one number can be used at a location when it is necessary to refer to multiple sources.
- In the text the cues may appear in parentheses or square brackets, on the line or as superior figures, and inside or outside the punctuation, all according to house style.

Obviously, a copy-editor has to be exceptionally careful in changing the numbers when an author deletes or adds a reference at any point in the text (see 'Editing' below).

LIST OF REFERENCES

The full bibliographic details are given in a list of numbered references at the end of articles or chapters, or, arranged by chapters, at the end of the book. Here's how the elements are styled:

- Authors' surnames followed by initials only – unpunctuated by commas, full stops or spaces – are given for the first three or six authors, according to house style, followed by *et al.* when there are more than the stipulated number.
- All source titles have minimal capitalization (first word and proper nouns only). Book and journal titles are usually italicized; article titles are in roman type without quotation marks. No words or abbreviations are used with the numerals representing volume, issue or page numbers.
- Punctuation is usually as shown in Figure 7.8, but can vary according to house style.

> Screening for Down's syndrome in early pregnancy is now standard practice [1] and has a dramatic effect [2]. Patel and Mukherjee [3] have shown, for example, that older mothers' anxiety levels drop significantly once they know the results. Where results are positive, it's important to provide counselling [2], preferably for both parents together [3, 4].
>
> References
> 1   Wald NJ, Cuckle HS, Densen JW. Maternal serum screening for the Down's syndrome in early pregnancy. *BMJ*, 1988; 4: 883–7.
> 2   Oster AG. *Medicine today*. Englewood Cliffs, NJ: Prentice Hall, 1976; 47–59.
> 3   Patel AKH, Mukherjee PR. Ante-natal monitoring. *J. Physiol.*, 1989; 3: 610–19.
> 4   Foster G. *Parental counselling*. Chichester: Wiley, 1990; 124–8.

Figure 7.8 An example of the author–number system

EDITING

Have the text and the list of references side by side on your desk, or open on-screen. Edit the text in the usual way. When you come to cues, highlight them; this is better than the red V when there are multiple numbers and will not mean 'superior' to the typesetter when the numerals are intended to appear on the line. As with all systems of references, check each cue against the list to see whether the reference seems appropriate and, if so, use a pencil to tick it on hard copy or make a note of it on your project style sheet. When you finish editing, go back over the pages and check that the *first mention* of each number is in the correct sequence, that is, the first 1 appears before the first 2, the first 2 before the first 3 and so on. Then go back again and check that the brackets are the correct shape and in the appropriate position in relation to the line and the punctuation.

Wait until all the queries are resolved before changing reference numbers, in case the author decides to add or remove references at this stage.

Style the list of references. In this system there is no alphabetization, but it is possible that different references can be to the same journal or book, so you still need to check for consistency. List any discrepancies for each article or chapter for the author to resolve.

Remember, when you have to alter reference numbers, **do not** obliterate the original number on the hard copy. Draw a line through it so you can still see it and thus check later that each change is accurate. On the list of references write the new numbers to the left of the old ones in a neat column. Check the renumbering: no duplication or omissions. Then work through the text, writing the new numbers neatly above or next to the old ones. On an e-file, use Track Changes so that you can check the alterations. You may find that there is a software program that can help you to alter the numbers automatically; if so, try it out on a copy of the e-file first.

Exercise 7.3, working with author–number references

Brief

The following text has been peer-reviewed, and the content is accurate. There are a lot of abbreviations, and putting them on your style sheet will make it easier for you to maintain consistency. Edit the text, style the references and list any queries for the authors. This extract is from an article in a journal, so house style must be followed rigorously.

House style
- -ize verbs
- use numerals for numbers over nine
- thin space in numerals more than four digits
- symbol rather than words for percentages
- single quotes
- cues in square brackets on the line inside the punctuation
- citations include three authors and then *et al.* where necessary, no elision in page numbers
- journal title abbreviations as in Index Medicus (http://www.nlm.nih.gov)

The role of c-Jun and c-Fos expression in androgen-dependent prostate cancer

In 2001, prostate cancer was responsible for approximately 10,000

deaths in the UK, making it the second most common cause of male
cancer related death [1]. Treatment for advanced or metastatic prostate
cancer has relied on androgen deprivation therapy for the past 55 years
[2]. Initial response rates to andogen deprivation therapy are high but
patients generally relapse within 12-24 months. [2, 3] When this
occurs, the patient is said to have developed androgen-independent
prostate cancer (AIPC). Few treatment options offer effective relief for
patients who develop AIPC [2.4]. The lack of novel and effective
therapies to treat APIC reflects a poor understanding of the mechanisms
underlying development of both the primary disease and, more
particularly, those events that drive the development of AIPC,

The activated protein 1 (AP-1) transcription factor, which is involved in
the control of cell growth and diffrentiation, has previously been
implicated *in vitro* in the development of AIPC (5-9). AP-1 is composed
of c-Jun and/or c-Fos nuclear proteins, which form either c-Jun/c-Jun
or c-Jun/c-Fos dimers. Formation of these dimers requires activation,
via phosphorylation, for c-Jun. Cell line studies suggest that this is
mediated by protein kinase C (KC) or MAP kinase [5].

AP-1 can bind the androgen receptor (AR) and this interaction
prevents either protein from binding to DNA and hence inhibits both
AR and AP-1-mediated gene transcription [5, 10], providing these
molecules are present in equal concentrations. Evidence also suggests
that AP-1 can bind to and activate transcription of some adnrogen-
regulated genes independently of the AR [5]. The effect of both Ar
and Ap-1 in APIC is therefore likely to be dependent both on the

ratio of AP-1 to AP and on the ability of Ap–1 to bind independently to specific promoter regions within the andogen-related gene [4, 10]. Thus the relative concentration of Ap-1 to Ar may represent a cellular mechanism for 'switching' between Ar and Ap-1-regualted gene expression. Where AP 1 is present at higher concentrations than AR, it is foreseeable that all AR is bound to AP-1, allowing excess AP-1 to bind to DNA and influence gene expression.

In vitro studies have demonstrated that the intracellular concentration of c-Jun and cFos is sevenfold greater in androgen-insensitive PC3 cells than in androgen-insensitive LNCaP cells [5], suggesting that Ap-1 might influence APIC [4, 11]. However, little work has been conducted to investigate the significance of this action *in vivo*.

In addition to interactions between AP-1 and AR, there is evidence that the c-Jun monomer may also influence the development of AIPC by functioning independently of AP-1. c-Jun acts as an AR co-activator binding ro the N-terminal domain at amino acids 503–555, [12] promoting AR dimerization and gene transcription [6]. This action of c-June is independent of c-jun phosphorylation, c-Fos, Ap-1 DNA binding, and AR ligand binding [6, 13]. In AIPC cell lines, transcriptional activation of AR is increased by over-expression of c-Jun (14, 15).

References

1 Cancer Research UK Website. Cancer Stats. Mortality-UK. www.cancerresearchuk.org (2004).

2 Trachtenberg J, Blackledge G. Looking to the future: advances

in the management of hormone-refractory prostate cancer. *Eur Urol Suppl* 2002: 1: 44–53.

3   Sumitomo M, Milowsky MI, Shen R, *et al.* Neutral endopeptidase inhibits neuropeptide-mediated transactivation of the insulin-like growth factor receptor–Akt cell survival pathway. *Cancer Res* 2001; 61: 3294–3298

4   Bonaccorsi L, Muratori M, Carloni, *et al.* Androgen receptor and prostate cancer invasion. *Int J Androl* 2003; 26: 21–25.

5   Sato N, Sadar MD, Bruchovsky N. *et al.* Androgenic induction of prostate-specific antigen gene is repressed by protein–protein interaction between the androgen receptor and AP-1/c-Jun in the human prostate cancer cell line LNCaP. *J Biol Chem* 1997; 272: 17485–17494.

6   Bubulya A, Chen SY, Fisher CJ, Zheng Z, Shen XQ, Shemshedini L. c-Jun potentiates the functional interaction between the amino and carboxyl termini of the androgen receptor. *Journal Biol Chem* 2001; 276: 44,704–44,711.

7   Lubahn DB, Brown TR, Simental JA, et al. Sequence of the intron exon junctions of the coding region of the human androgen receptor genes and identification of a point mutation in a family with complete androgen insensitivity. *Proc Natl Acad Sci U S A* 1989; 86: 9534–38.

8   Behrens A, Jochum W, Sibilia M, Wagner EF. Oncogenic transformation by Ras and Fos is mediated by c-Jun N-terminal phosphoryalation. Oncogene 2000; 19: 2657–2663.

9   Shimada K, Nakamura M, Ishida E, Kishi M, *et al.* Requirement

of c-Jun for testosterone-induced sensitisation to N-(4-hydroxphenyl)retinamide-induced apoptosis. *Mol Carcinog* 2003; 36:115–122.

10 Sadar MD, Hussain M, Bruchovsky N. Prostate cancer: molecular biology of early progression to androgen independence. *Endocr Relat Cancer* 1999; 6: 487–502.

11 Wang Q, Lu J, Yong EL. Ligand- and coactivator-mediated transactivation function (AF2) of the androgen receptor ligand-binding domain is inhibited by the cognate hinge region. *Jour Biol Chem* 2001; 276: 7 493–7 499.

12 Wise SC, Burmister LA, Zhou XF, *et al.* Identification of domains of c-Jun mediating androgen receptor transactivation. *Oncogene* 1998; 16: 2001–2009.

13 Bulbuuya A, Wise SC, Shen XQ *et al.* c-Jun can mediate androgen receptor-induced transactivation. *J Biol Chem* 1996; 271: 24583–24 589.

14 Frondal K, Engedal N, Slagsvold T, Saatcioglu F. CREB binding protein is a coactivator for the androgen receptor and mediates cross-talk with AP-1. *J Biol Chem* 1996; 271: 24583–24 589.

15 Tilllman, K, Oberfeld JL, Shen XQ *et al.* c-Fos dimerization with c-Jun represses c-Jun enhancement of androgen receptor transactivation. Endocrine J 1998; 9: 193–200.

Adapted from Joanne Edwards, N. Sarath Krishna, Rono Mukherjee and John M. S. Bartlett, 'The role of c-Jun and c-Fos expression in androgen-dependent prostate cancer', *Journal of Pathology*, 2004; 204: 153–8.

EXERCISE FOLLOW-UP

Unless this is your field of knowledge, you may have found the text difficult to understand fully. Nonetheless, you know the information is accurate, so your main task is to impose consistency and house style, and raise queries where logic or grammar demands.

If the answer to the first query is yes, AR would be followed by a hanging hyphen. The annoying typing errors in AP-1 and AR could be corrected globally.

There were a few more queries for the list of references. It is a good idea to draw attention to the deletion of authors in the sources, because the authors of your text may have a special reason for asking you to bend the rules – a decision best made after consulting your manager. There was only one journal title that was inconsistent; you could have checked it online or changed it to the way it was presented most of the time.

Changing systems

It sometimes happens that an author submits work that does not comply with the system of referencing the publisher requires, and the copy-editor might be asked to change the system while editing. It's not difficult. Always edit the text first, checking the cues as usual. Then, as a separate task, go back over the text to change the style.

- When changing to the short-title system, number all the cues first. Next, compile the notes. Then compile or revise the bibliography. Finally, compare the notes to the bibliography for consistency.
- When changing to the author–date system, revise the bibliography or list of references first, then write in the new cues.
- When changing to the Vancouver system, go through the text and number the titles in the list of references in order of appearance. Then reorder the titles in the list of references and style them. Finally, revise the cues in the text.
  Go on, try it.

Exercise 7.4, changing the system of references

Brief

The extract is from an article in a specialist yearbook. Edit the text and change the references from the author–date system to the short-title system, setting them out as end-of-article notes and amending the bibliography accordingly. Then mark up the text and key in the figures.

House style
- single quotes, double within
- spaced en rules for dashes
- small caps for letters or words inscribed on weapons

For the references:
- English-language titles: books, u.c.l.c; articles, initial cap only
- foreign-language titles: caps as shown
- use 'p.' and 'pp.' followed by a space for page references
- elide numerals in a range to the fewest digits
- use a full stop after the names of authors, a colon between the place of publication and the publisher, and a comma after all other elements

The references in the cues to 'no.' and 'pl.' are to items in the catalogue and pages of illustration (plates), respectively; include them in the position shown.

Two maces from Henry VIIIs aresenal?

Philip J Lankester

It is well known to students of arms and armour that the Royal Armouries contains a large number of hafted weapons remaining from the armoury assembled by King Henry VIII. Comparison with the inventory drawn up in 1547 reveals that the significant numbers of weapons surviving in the collection today are but a small fraction of the original quantity listed in the various royal palaces. Although some of the sections of the 1547 Inventory

5

dealing with arms and armour were published some time ago (Dillon 1888) coverage was incomplete and the recent publication of the whole inventory (Starkey 1998) has provided an invaluable aid to the study f the whole text and the rich quantity of information it contains.

Staff weapons from Italy

It is known that Henry VIII purchased some (long hafted) staff weapons from Italian merchants (Norman & Wilson 1982: 65, no.47; 70–1, no.56; Wilson 1985: 16, 17) and these weapons are likely to have been of Italian manufacture as is suggested by some of their form and their decoration. Quite a number of those surviving in the collections of the Royal Armouries retain their decoration. Some simply have foliage (figure 2); others have human heads (figure 4), animals, secular and sacred human figures or scenes. The decoration is mot commonly formed of lines composed of tiny punched dots (pointillé) but in some cases solid line decoration is used.

While the decoration on a few was evidently specially commissioned, such as the four partisans decorated with the Tudor royal arms (Norman and Wilson 1982: 65, no. 47, pl. XII (center); Rimmer & Richardson 1997:52–3, 174, no. 13, illus.) and a bill with a cipher of letters spelling the name HENRI (Norman & Wilson 1982: 68–9, no. 53, pl. XII (right)), the vast majority were probably purchased from merchants as standard items. A few weapons have been identified in other collections that have decoration that is so similar in form and execution to that found on significant numbers of the weapons from Henry's arsenal in the Royal Armouries that they must at least have been decorated in the same workshop, also the forms of the weapons themselves are often sufficiently close to point strongly to a common place of manufacture. Guy Wilson (1985: 20, note 3) has drawn attention to a weapom of unusual form (not found in the Royal Armouries collection) in the Museo Civico Medievale in Bologna (Boccia & Coelho 1975: 417, no. 739, pl.; Boccia 1991, no.388, illus.; see figure 1), which is inscribed LAUS DEO. The foliage decoration compares closely with that on, for example, two partisans in the Royal Armouries, inv. Nos VII.154 (see figure 2) and VII.210 (Wilson 1985: 17, pl. 5). The 'steeple' projecting from the centre of the top border on the Bologna weapon and the wavy lines on the socket are present on VII.154 (though worn) and on many other similar weapons in the Royal Armouries.

It appears that the Holy Roman Emperor, Charles V purchased weapons with similar decorations: in the Rijksmuseum, Amsterdam, is a corsèque with outward cuving wongs, which is similar to several in the Royal Armouries which have been identified as probably corresponding with 'three-grained staves' in the 1574 *Inventory*. It is decorated in pointillé with Charles's badge and motto: the pillars of Hercules and PLUS ULTRA (Norman & Wilson 1982: 67, no. 49). Henry VIII may even have inadvertently received one of these weapons intended for Charles V because another corséque of the same type in the Royal Armouries (VII.838) is decorated with the Imperial eagle, though it has been suggested that this weapon entered the collection at a later date (Normal and Wilson 1982: 67, no. 49). Further examples of weapons with this type of decoration no doubt exist. A partisan in the Muso Civico Correr in Venice is another possible candidate, thought the published illustration does not permit a certain view (Boccia and Coehlo 1975: 363, no. 306, ills.) It bears and unidentified mark – somewhat resembling a letter I with a crenellated or saw-toothed top – which is found on a number of Italian edged weapons (e.g. Boccia & Coelho 1975: 357 nos 259, 260; 362, no. 297; 364, no 308) including some of those from Henry VIII'a arsenal in the Royal Armouries, for example on the corsèques or 'three grained staves' (Norman and Wilson 1982: 67, no. 50, illus.)

References

Boccia, L. G. 1984 *Armi antichi dele raccolte civiche* Reggiane. Reggio Emilia, Commune di Reggio Nell'Emilia Civici Musei

Boccia, L.G. and E. T. Coelho 1975 *Armi Bianchi Italiane.* Milan, Bramante Editrici

Dillon, H. A. 1888 'Arms and armour at Westminster, the Tower, and Greenwich, 1547', *Archaeologia* 51: 219–80

Norman, A.V.B and Wilson, G. M. 1982 *Treasures from the Tower of London.* University of East Anglia

Richardson, T and Rimer, G 1997 *Treasures from the Tower in the Kremlin* Moscow, State Museum of the Moscow Kremlin

Starkey, D (ed.) 1998 *The Inventory of King Henry VIII: I.* Harvey Miller Publishers for the Society of Antiquaries of London, London

Wilson. G. M. 1985 'A halberd head form the River Thames'. *The Second Park Lane Arms Fair, 14–16 February.* London:15–20

Adapted from Philip J. Lankester, 'Two maces from Henry VIII's arsenal?', *Royal Armouries Yearbook*, vol. 5, 2000

EXERCISE FOLLOW-UP

If you worked through the exercise in a series of steps as described above, it should not have been difficult. It is, of course, essential to check the details carefully. Did you get all the punctuation right? All the names and initials in the correct order in the notes and the bibliography? Remember, it's easier if you make yourself a template for the bibliographic style and check all the entries as a single task. I hope you remembered to mark up the headings and key in the figures. Doing the latter might have revealed to you the need to query the author about the order of the figures and the lack of a reference to figure 3. It always pays to double-check the brief when you think you have finished the job.

Indexes

I fervently hope that any index will be compiled by a professional indexer. Some publishers, particularly academic ones, require authors to *provide* the index. This means the publisher does not want, or perhaps cannot afford, to pay for the index, but it does not mean that authors must create the index themselves; they can pay someone to do it for them. There are authors who are competent – even excellent – indexers but, for those who are not, it would be better for the publisher to help them to find an appropriate professional indexer (see Resources) rather than risk having a poor index ruin an otherwise good book. Commissioning the indexer – choosing the appropriate person and negotiating the schedule and fee – is often the responsibility of the project manager, and this subject in covered in *Editorial Project Management*. However, copy-editors are often asked to prepare the brief, which is sent to the indexer with the proofs.

The purpose of an index is to enable readers to find precise information easily and quickly. All non-fiction book-length publications, with the exception of dictionaries, should have at least one; even some alphabetically arranged encyclopedias are indexed. Journals are usually indexed annually. The copy-editor's role is to brief the indexer and edit the index. The type, organization, length and style of an index should be appropriate to the subject and purpose of the text and the level of the intended reader. As a copy-editor you are not expected to compile indexes, but to edit them you need to understand the principles.

Types

The nature of the publication indicates what type(s) of index(es) might be appropriate. Any publication can be served to some extent by a simple subject index, but some need an index that identifies concepts too, and others are served by indexes specific to the subject matter. For example, a book of poetry will have an index of first lines; an anthology will have an author index; a gardening book might have an index of Latin plant names and one of common names, or a single index combining the two, as well as an index of plant types or gardening techniques; a cookery book could have an index of recipes, ingredients, cooking methods, national origin or type of dish (starter, main course, etc.); law books have indexes of legislation and cases (as you might remember from Chapter 3, these are called 'tables') in addition to a subject index. When the subject matter could have more than one index, consider whether

* more than one is helpful to the intended reader or would be confusing;
* two or more types of index could be combined;
* there is sufficient space.

In deciding how many and what type(s) of index will be most helpful, think about what kind of precise information readers are most likely to want to look up.

Organization

Consider the complexity of the text, and the age and level of the reader, in deciding whether to have subentries and sub-subentries. All books for readers below the reading age of about 12 and simple ones for adults are likely to have only main entries. More complex texts for readers in the same categories might have subentries. Complex texts for readers at the academic and professional level might include sub-subentries, but further subdivisions are to be avoided.

Most indexes are organized alphabetically, either letter by letter or word by word. In the former the alphabetization goes across hyphens and spaces; in the latter it goes up to the hyphen or space (see Figure 7.9). Articles, prepositions and conjunctions may be needed in all levels of subentry to relate the subentry to the main entry, but they are ignored in alphabetizing. Subentries in history books and biographies can be arranged chronologically (see Figure 7.10).

272 *Copy-editing*

Letter by letter	Word by word
ball	ball
ballade	ball-bearing
ball-bearing	ball game
ballet	ball gown
ball game	ball valve
ball gown	ballade
ballistic	ballet
ball valve	ballistic
ballyhoo	ballyhoo

Figure 7.9 Letter-by-letter and word-by-word alphabetization compared

Chronological order	Alphabetical order
William III, King	William III, King
lands at Torbay	arrives in Whitehall
arrives in Whitehall	assassination plot against
declares war on France	death of
assassination plot against	declares war on France
surveillance system of	lands at Torbay
death of	surveillance system of

Figure 7.10 Chronological and alphabetical ordering of subentries compared

Entries at any level are followed by locators: page, paragraph, clause or section numbers that tell where the information is to be found (the use of '*see*' instead of locators is explained on p. 273). Locators *separated* by commas mean that the subject is to be found in those places but the discussion is not continuous, even when the places are sequential. Locators *connected* by an en rule mean that there is a continuous discussion of the subject through that range of places. Since the purpose of an index is to help readers find information, it is pointless to have entries that follow locators with 'f' ('and following page'), 'ff' ('and following pages') or 'passim' ('at various places'). Similarly, it is maddening, as well as a waste of space, to include a 'passing mention': to have locators to the appearance of the word rather than information about the subject.

More than six locators after an entry reduce the efficiency of the index, so if space allows, indexers will break down such entries into subentries, or, if only one level is wanted, into more precise main entries. There is no point in a subentry that does no more than repeat the references in the main entry or adjoining subentries. If a main entry has an inclusive reference covering many pages – e.g. 80–9 – and/or fewer than six references, but precision of information is preferred over concision, the inclusive reference can be omitted and the entry broken down.

A topic might be entered under two (or more) headings, for example 'agriculture, organic' and 'organic agriculture', because readers might expect to find it in either place. This can be acceptable for short entries, but for long ones and those with many locators, cross-referencing to a single entry will save space. It is important that the wording as well as the locators in multiple entries match. Similarly, the same form of wording – inverted or not – should be used for different entries. For example:

brief for indexers   indexers, brief for

not

brief for indexers   indexers, briefing

There are two kinds of cross-reference: *see* and *see also*. The former follows an entry that has no page references or other locators and directs readers to an entry or entries that do have them. The latter can precede or follow the list of locators for main or subentries, and directs readers to related entries (see Figure 7.11). In both cases multiple cross-references are separated by semicolons.

All cross-references should use the exact wording of the entry: for example, '*see* fences' should lead to an entry 'fences', not 'fencing' or 'fences and gates' or any other variation. *See also* cross-references tend to go from the specific to the general, and in that case are not reciprocal. However, they should be reciprocal when they are to the same level of specificity: for example, if an entry on fences includes '*see also* gates', the entry on gates should include a *see also* cross-reference to fences.

A *see* cross-reference that leads back to itself – rocks *see* stones; stones *see* rocks – is called circular, and is a mistake. A cross-reference to an entry that does not exist is called blind, and is a mistake too.

Everyone makes mistakes; good copy-editors spot the mistakes and correct them.

Length

The amount of space available for the index can be determined, at the latest, by the time the text goes for setting, and is easy to confirm when you have the proofs. Add the number on the last page of the proofs – which should include everything from the first page of text to the bibliography, if there is one – to the number of prelim pages if they are numbered in roman numerals. For example, let's say the proofs end on page 235 and the prelims end on page xii: 235 + 12 = 247. Allow for acknowledgements or picture credits, if relevant. In our example we'll allow one page for picture credits: 247 + 1 = 248. Subtract the total from the stipulated extent and the remainder is the space for the index. So, if our publication is intended to be 256 pages, there will be 8 pages for the index.

If the extent has not been fixed (this should not happen, but it does), you may have to check with production what the nearest larger even working (complete signature) is. Remember that most book-length publications are printed in signatures of 16, 32 or 64, and there is no point in guessing which one is being used. The nearest larger even working to 248 in any of these multiples is 256.

Designers or typesetters can work out the number of lines available for the index by multiplying the number of lines on a page by the number of columns, and multiplying the result by the number of pages. They can tell you the number of characters in a line, too, based on the chosen typeface and size.

Style

The main issues are capitalization, punctuation, elision and layout. We can deal with the first three fairly quickly. There is no more reason to capitalize every entry in an index than there is to capitalize every word of text; save the capitals for proper nouns only. House style should state whether entries are to be followed by a comma, a colon or a space; the space is the best choice, as it helps to keep the page visually clear. When there are entries that end in numerals, highlight them for the designer/typesetter so that he or she can find a

> **Broken off**
> revolution 283–5, 288, 290,
>   306–11
>   French 283, 289, 301, 302,
>   311–12
>   green 336–7, 338, 340, 342,
>   343–4
>   and influence on food supply
>   306–31
>   *see also* English Civil War
> rice 180, 185
>   Arabs and 142, 144, 147,
>   241
>   in Bulgaria 245
>   in China 40, 125, 129, 135,
>   136, 137–8
>   dried cooked 225
>   flour 138
>   in India 113, 114, 115, 225,
>   271
>   new strains of 336–7
> roasting 25
>   in animal stomachs 36–8
>   in clay 39–40, 41
>   in ovens 45, 47, 83
>   on spits 41, 42–3
>
> **Run on**
> revolution 283–5, 288, 290, 306–11; French 283, 289, 301, 302, 311–12; green 336–7, 338, 340, 342, 343–4; and influence on food supply 306–31; *see also* English Civil War
> rice 180, 185; Arabs and 142, 144, 147, 241; in Bulgaria 245; in China 40, 125, 129, 135, 136, 137–8; dried cooked 225; flour 138; in India 113, 114, 115, 225, 271; new strains of 336–7
> roasting 25; in animal stomachs 36–8; in clay 39–40, 41; in ovens 45, 47, 83; on spits 41, 42–3

Figure 7.11 Broken-off and run-on styles of index layout compared. Notice the alignment of turnover lines in the broken-off style, and how, in both styles, prepositions and conjunctions are used to make the subentries read back to the main entries but are ignored in alphabetization.

typographical means to avoid confusion with the page references. House style should also cover the issue of elision, which you will recall is discussed in Chapter 4.

Depending on the amount of space available, the index can be continuous, or separated into alphabetical sections by a line space or a display initial. When an index includes subentries, there are two main layout styles: broken off (also called 'set out') and run on (see Figure 7.11). In the broken-off style, each level of subentry is indented under the preceding level. In the run-on style, subentries are run on after the main entry and its locators and separated from other subentries by semicolons; when no locators follow a main entry, a colon is needed to introduce the first subentry. The standard run-on style does not accommodate sub-subentries, but in a hybrid style sub-subentries can be run on under subentries that are broken off. The broken-off style is clearer and certainly best for younger readers, but the run-on style takes up less space.

In the run-on style, all turnover lines are indented to the same measurement, which can be determined by the designer. In the broken-off style it is important that the subentries stand out from the turnover lines. This is easily achieved by indenting all the turnover lines twice as much as the subentries. For example, if the subentries are indented 1 en from the margin, turnover lines for main and subentries are indented 1 em from the margin, as shown in Figure 7.11. Turnover lines would be indented a further 1 en if there were sub-subentries.

Briefing

The ideal brief is just that: brief. It provides the information the individual needs in order to complete the job in the way and to the standard you require. The brief should be written, although you might want to discuss the details beforehand or confirm them afterwards. If you are going to brief indexers regularly, create a standard letter or form on which you can change the details as necessary.

Make sure the brief includes the basic information about the enclosed or attached proofs – title, author, ISBN – in case they get separated. State the type of index and the total number of *lines* (not entries) available. Ask the designer the number of characters to a line, so that the indexer can type to the correct line measure by simply setting the margin tabs. It does not matter whether indexers type in a larger size than the indexes will be set as long as they set their document margins to the number of characters in a line and an unjustified format. Some editors and indexers might tell you that they have never worked this way before. Well, there's a first time for everything, and working this way is as simple as any other, with the advantage of producing an index that will fit within the space allowed. And if it is what you ask for in the brief, it is what you should get.

If the style is the same as that of an existing index, send a copy of some pages from that index. In the case of a new edition of a book,

supply a copy of the original index and comment on it as necessary. (A new, rather than revised, index will have to be produced unless the publisher has bought the copyright in the index or the current indexer is also the original indexer and copyright holder.) Otherwise send the house style for indexes or, if there isn't one, a list of relevant style points:
- levels of subentry
- position of *see also* cross-references
- layout
- alphabetization
- capitalization
- punctuation or space after entries
- elision of numerals
- locators

Obviously, if there are no subentries, you don't have to specify the type of layout; and if the publication has only page numbers, you don't have to specify the type of locator. If the house style has no preference for the style of alphabetization, ask the indexer which he or she will be using.

State the degree of indentation for all turnover lines and subentries, so that it is clear which is which; check with design and production on how this should be done. For illustrated publications, indicate whether images should be indexed when they appear on the same page as relevant text and whether the locators should appear in italics or bold.

Unless it is the type of index where 'passing mentions' aren't possible – for example, an index of first lines – tell the indexer to avoid them. Good indexers will know this, but it is better to confirm it than assume it.

State how the index should be presented and delivered: double-spaced hard copy and/or e-file in a specific software, by e-mail or on a CD. Be sure to check technical details with production first.

Confirm the schedule and fee, and remind the indexer to contact you with any queries or problems, particularly anything that might affect the schedule or fee. Reread the brief carefully. Make sure you have covered all the necessary points. Making changes to an index because the brief is at fault will cost extra and can delay the schedule.

It is a good idea to phone the indexer a few days later to make sure that he or she has received the materials and checked that they are complete, that the brief covers all points unambiguously, and that there are no software problems. A telephone conversation is more effective and efficient than e-mail when issues need clarifying. A follow-up e-mail should then confirm what was agreed.

Editing

You know when the completed index is due, so plan to edit it immediately. Then if there are any errors that must be corrected by the indexer, you can return the index quickly and prevent or minimize disruption to the schedule.

Almost all indexes will be e-files. If you edit the file rather than hard copy, make sure you do it on a copy of the original.

MACRO CHECKS

When you receive the index, check it against all the points in the brief, *one by one*. It will take only a very few minutes to see whether the instructions on the style of layout and presentation, level of sub-entries, location of *see also*, capitalization, punctuation and locators have been followed. This will also enable you to make a list of global changes that might be necessary, such as en rules instead of hyphens between numerals.

When you use a professional indexer, the index should have been typed consistently as specified in the brief. However, if you do find a mistake, check whether there are any other major errors that need correcting – length, alphabetization, etc. – and then ask the indexer to make the necessary corrections and send a new file immediately. You do not want to waste time editing an index that is not the final version.

Check the length. If the index is much longer than you have stipulated, consider whether reducing the type size or, if it is in the broken-off style, setting it run-on would solve the problem and be visually acceptable. If the style needs to be altered, return the index to the indexer to make the changes. If neither of these alterations will work, return the index to the indexer for cutting. Do not make the cuts yourself, not only because you might interfere with a sound structure and miss cross-references but also because you could infringe the indexer's copyright and moral rights (see Chapter 3).

Read through it. Are the entry words those most likely to occur to readers? Do they identify a reasonable size category, large enough to be meaningful and small enough to avoid long strings of numbers?

Are subentries useful and non-repetitive subdivisions of the main entry? Has the use of cross-referencing been kept to a helpful minimum? Are any topics missing that you would expect to find? Cut repetitive subentries and unnecessary cross-referencing, because they are errors, and show the results to the indexer before setting, as you would show changes to any author.

MICRO CHECKS

Be sure to use the collated corrected text proofs when checking the index. List any changes in the proofs that add or delete substantive text or affect the pagination, and ask the indexer to make the necessary adjustments. As it is not a problem of the indexer's making, expect to pay for such amendments.

Although indexers use software to sort alphabetically and numerically, typing errors and manual alterations mean mistakes are possible. Check the alphabetization of main entries first; usually, you need to look at only the first few letters, so it is a relatively quick task. Then check that the subentries read back to the main entries sensibly and that they are in alphabetical order.

Now check that the numerical order of locators for each entry is correct and that the style of elision, including the use of en rules rather than hyphens, is consistent.

Check that the italicization, the spelling of unusual and foreign names, the titles of works, and words that have alternative spellings – for example, medieval, judgement, archaeology, encyclopedia – are consistent with the text.

Check the accuracy of a random selection of entries and subentries. Similarly, spot-check that illustrations are indexed, and that index references to illustrations are accurate.

Check all cross-references to ensure there are no blind or circular ones, and that in these and double entries the wording and locators match. Do this last in case you have to correct the spelling of any entries.

Marking up

You can create a simple instruction template to accompany all indexes to the typesetter, stating, for example,
- index heading level

280 *Copy-editing*

- run-on or broken-off style
- indents for subentries and turnover lines
- en rules between spans of numerals
- line spaces and/or cap initials between alphabetical sections

It will not matter what degree of indentation has been used in the original, as long as the distinction between entries and subentries is clear in the broken-off style. If the distinction isn't clear, ask the indexer to correct the file or do so yourself. Otherwise, you need to mark up the hard copy in detail, which might be done simply by using one colour to highlight the main entries and another to highlight the subentries.

Exercise 7.5, editing an index

Brief

Edit and mark up this extract from an index. List any queries for the indexer. Of course, you do not have the complete index or the text to which it relates, so also make a list of items that you would cross-check in reality.

House style
- broken-off subentries with run-on sub-subentries
- -ise verbs
- capitalize proper nouns only
- space after entry word
- minimal number of digits in page ranges
- cross-references at end of relevant entry or subentry
- line space between alphabetical sections

Index

Numbers in italics refer to illustrations.

acknowledgements154, 157

    and fair dealing 153

    see also picture credits

artwork
- briefing 89–91, 90
- checking 91
- schedule for 67–8
- *see also* illustrations

assessing
- manuscripts 35, 36–37, 60–63
- projects 44–67
- the list 7, 8, 9–11

author tours 167

authors 19–23
- accuracy of information from 75
- briefing for 31–2
- budget problems created by and changes to proof 76, 125
- checking roughs 91
- and copy-editing 73-6; *see also* copy-editing
- copyright *see* copyright
- dates for receiving and returning proofs 67
- explaining contract 32–3
- ideas in search of 22–3
- and indexes 78
- nurturing 33–5
- and picture research 105
- query response time 65–6
- and revisions to draft manuscripts 23, 37
- and schedules, 31, 32

submissions from unpublished 20–1

author's publicity questionnaires 163, 167

Berne Convention for the Protection of Literary and Artistic Works 149;

    see also copyright

binding styles 87

blads

    co-edition sales tool 164–5

    and copy-editing schedule 49, 68, 77

    and picture research schedule 107

    and project schedule 49

blurbs 161, 163–4

briefing

    artwork 89–91, *90*

    authors 31–3

    about 37–9

    copy-editors 52–3, 60–3

    on covers 162

    designers, 85–95

    freelancers 137–8

    indexers 78–80

    photographry 91-2

    picture researchers 102–6

    potential authors 22

    proofreaders 53

budgets 58
  creating 25–6. *26*
  for freelance work 138–41
  principles of 11–14, *12, 13*
  revising 27–9
  and schedules 13
changes
  author's, on proofs 55–6
  consult with production before making 123–4
  editorial, and authors moral rights 74–5
  effecting production 121, 126
co-editions 12, 76–7
  coordinating schedules for 49, 77
  editing text for 77
  planning of 24
copy-editing 3, 59–80
  coeditions 76–7
  principles of 76–7
  and proofreading 3
copyright 145-52
  Berne Convention 149
  duration of, in different countries   149, 153
  duration of literary, dramatic and artistic work in the UK and USA *146–7*
  fair use 151–3
  giving notice of 148

>   infringement of copyright 150, 153
>
>   ownership and rights 149–52
>
>   Universal Copyright Convention (UCC) 149
>
> copyright act 1997 (USA) 145
>
> copyright, designs and patents act 1988 (UK) 145
>
>   moral rights and 151
>
> covers and jackets 92–5, 161–5
>
>   briefing for 162
>
>   information on 163
>
>   and marketing and sales 161–3
>
>   schedule for 49
>
> cover approval meetings 161–2
>
> credits, picture *see* acknowledgements

EXERCISE FOLLOW-UP

The subentries for 'acknowledgements' and 'artwork' are deleted because the main entry had fewer than six references, and those for 'copy-editing' because most of their references were within the range for the main entry. For 'covers and jackets', even when you add the single unique reference in the subentry, the main entry has fewer than six references. The separate entry for 'cover approval meetings' could have been a subentry in 'covers' and is in the same location as the main entry, and so it too can be deleted.

You might have started by thinking that 'author tours' could be included under 'authors'. Maybe then, or later, you thought the same about 'author's publicity questionnaires'. It is only a small step further to realize these two could be combined as an 'and publicity' subheading, or something similar. The subentry for 'budget problems' can be shortened as shown, because the reason does not need to be distinguished from another. The 'dates' subentry can be deleted when the reference is added to the 'and schedules' subentry.

The 'about' subentry to 'briefing' indicates general information and therefore it can be deleted and the references placed after the main entry. The reference for 'potential authors' belongs with the subentry 'authors', as the latter is not distinguished as meaning a particular type, such as 'contracted' or 'experienced'.

The subentry 'Berne Convention' in 'copyright' should have the same wording as the main entry. The two copyright acts could be subentries under 'copyright', as shown. Alternatively, they, Berne and the Universal Copyright Convention could be main entries and only *see also* cross-references in 'copyright'.

The page reference '59–80' for 'copy-editing' is too wide a range to be useful to the reader and needs to be broken down into subentries.

The cross-reference for 'credits, picture' should send the reader directly to the correct entry, not by way of 'acknowledgements'.

Have toolkit, can travel

Copy-editing is a very satisfying job in whatever field you work. I hope that you have enjoyed the book, have learned from it, and will continue to find the information in it of practical use. Throughout your career you will have, and should seize, opportunities to build on this foundation, to learn new skills and different ways of applying your existing ones, to learn about new technologies, the publishing process and the work done by your colleagues in other disciplines, and how companies and their publishing programmes work. Each author and project may offer different stylistic elements to work with as well as information about a subject, and make you aware of changes in the language and its applications.

As you gain experience, you will find that you may be able to move, if you wish, not only from one job to another but also from one kind of publishing to another. And because we live in an electronic age, you may be able to choose to work from home, even when it is in a different country from your employer or clients.

Getting started ...

You need experience to consolidate and expand your basic skills. If you already have a job as a copy-editor, this is a given. If you work in another capacity in a company that produces publications of any kind, look for opportunities to move into a copy-editing job and make the Human Resources department, if there is one, aware of your interests.

If you are not yet employed, think about the kind of publishing in which you are interested. Perhaps you have an academic background or a strong interest in a particular subject or endeavour and want to work in an organization or on a journal related to it. Perhaps you want to work in educational books, or children's books, or adult fiction or non-fiction. For work in traditional publishing, look in bookshops and libraries to see which publications appeal to you. Find out more about publishers, and how to contact them, on their websites and in books such as the *Writers' & Artists' Yearbook* and *The Writer's Handbook*. Read industry journals and the media supplements of the quality newspapers. For work in any of these areas, reply to advertisements and apply for jobs that haven't been advertised too.

... and continuing

Throughout your career, take the initiative to get the training you need, and read the trade journals to keep yourself informed about developments and events in the industry. In Britain, the National Occupational Standards in Publishing (which are available on www.train4publishing.co.uk) state what the industry thinks a person should know and be able to do to be considered competent in a variety of publishing jobs. They can help you identify gaps in your skills or knowledge for your current job and show you what is required for another position to which you aspire.

Glossary

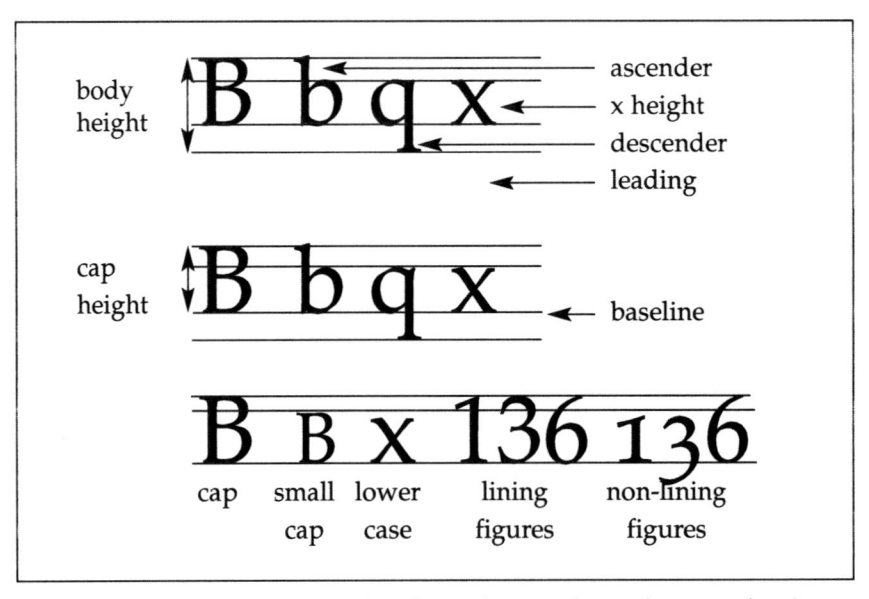

Figure a Parts of type. *See* ascender; descender; non-lining figures; x-height.

ascender The part of a lower-case letter that rises above the height of the letter x; d, h and k are examples of letters with ascenders. *See also* descender, non-lining figures, x-height.

baseline The imaginary line on which the type sits.

binding The style of covering and the way in which the pages are attached to it. Binding styles include: hardback (or cased); paperback, limp and B format (all of which describe soft covers); spiral; looseleaf; sewn; wire- or saddle-stitched; perfect (glued).

bleed When an illustration spreads beyond the text area right to the foredge, gutter, head or foot on the trimmed page.

bold Heavy type. Bold can be applied as an attribute (emboldening), but there are also typefaces that have a variation that is bold, in which case the degree of bold is part of the name, e.g. Stone, Stone Semi-bold, Stone Bold.

book block *See* running sheets.

brief A set of instructions relating to a particular job or task.

bromide Text or illustration reproduced in high definition on glossy paper ready to be photographed by the printer so that the film could be used to make printing plates; also called repro. This once-standard procedure is now used only occasionally.

case The binding of a hardback book, consisting of boards and cloth.

cast-off The calculation of the number of lines or pages a piece of text will make when it is typeset. It is usually based on a word count in relation to the chosen page design, with allowance made for tables and illustrations, if relevant.

club line *See* orphan.

copy Text for setting, e.g. the author's manuscript, or the wording for the cover or jacket.

cover The binding of a periodical or paperback book.

CTP Computer-to-plate: the standard production procedure, in which printing plates are made directly from electronic files.

descender The part of a lower-case letter that falls below the baseline; g, p and q are examples of letters with descenders. *See also* ascender, x-height.

DPI Dots per inch. *See also* screen.

e-file An electronic document, delivered on disk or CD or by e-mail. *See also* hard copy.

em A relative measure of type, the width and height of the letter M in a given font; 1 em is 10 points in 10-point type, 12 points in 12-point type. *See also* point.

en Half an em, the width and height of the letter N in a given font.

endmatter The pages in a book that follow the main text, such as an index.

even working Using all the pages in all the signatures in a book. *See also* signature.

extent The number of pages.

folio The number that appears on a printed page of text; also refers to a sheet written and numbered on one side only, such as a typescript or a manuscript.

font/fount As a result of the general use of computers for word-processing, 'font' is now commonly used to mean a typeface. However, in the print and publishing industries, it means both the typeface and the size of the printing characters.

foredge margin The margin at the outside edge of the page.

format In printing, used variously to mean the dimensions of the printed page, with the first dimension being the longest; to describe whether the height or width is longest; and to indicate the style of binding. *See also* binding, landscape, portrait.

In word-processing, used to describe disks and the styling of textual elements.

In some publishing houses, used to refer not only to the printing format but also to a specific typographic design.

fount *See* font.

galley A proof of continuous text, without illustrations, that has not been divided into pages. Once the standard form of first proof, galleys are now used only occasionally.

gutter The place where two pages of a publication join at the spine. The margin between the spine edge and the text is called the 'back margin', and the gutter area is referred to as 'backs combined'. The term is also used to refer to the vertical space between two columns of type on a single page.

hard copy Document on paper, also called a 'printout' when it is the printed version of an e-file. *See also* e-file.

imposed proofs Proofs on which illustrations are shown in position with text.

imposition Pages arranged so that they will appear consecutively when the printed sheet is folded; proofs of these pages are called imposed page proofs.

italic Slanting type. Italics can be applied as an attribute (italicizing), but there are also typefaces that have a variation that is italic, in which case this is part of the name, e.g. Garamond, Garamond Italic.

jacket Loose paper cover on a case-bound (hardback) book.

justified Setting in which the text is aligned at both margins, which can require some words to be split at the end of the line. The spacing between the words is constant on one line but can differ from line to line, depending on the number of characters that will fit within the measure. *See also* unjustified.

landscape A page that is wider than it is tall. *See also* portrait.

layout The physical arrangement (page design) of the material on the printed page.

leading Pronounced 'ledding', this is the space between printed lines of text. The term comes from the days when type was set in metal, and lines of lead were inserted between the lines of type to create more space. Text that is set solid has no leading. The amount of leading is indicated by the numeral in the denominator: thus 10-point solid setting is written 10/10, and 10-point setting with 1 point of leading is written 10/11.

lining figures Numerals that align with each other at the top and bottom.

manuscript Handwritten or typewritten text intended for publication.

mark-up The codes and tags that specify heading levels and structural elements for design and typesetting.

measure The width of a line of type; 'full measure' is the width of the type area of a page, which can be composed of one or more columns.

non-lining figures Numerals that do not align with each other at top and bottom, appearing to have ascenders and descenders; also called old-style figures.

on-screen Work carried out on the electronic file.

orphan The first line of a paragraph at the foot of a page, often regarded as unacceptable, particularly in non-fiction; also called a club line. *See also* widow.

Ozalid A trademarked name used generally to refer to the final proof of the black film of text and illustrations; also called dyelines, blues, and silvers. Film is rarely used now and these terms are becoming obsolete; *see* CTP; plotter proof.

PDF Portable Document Format: an electronic file that retains all the design elements of the original electronic file and can be viewed on any computer with Acrobat Reader, but can be altered only by using the software that created it. It is used, among other things, to send files to the printer for printing.

pica A measurement of 12 points.

plotter proof A proof on paper of the imposition for printing plates, produced from electronic files when printing will be CTP. The proof shows all colours, but is used for checking position, not quality.

point A measurement of type and space; 72 points = 1 inch.

portrait A page that is taller than it is wide. *See also* landscape.

prelims Short for 'preliminary pages', these are the pages in a book that precede the main text.

production The manufacturing stages of producing a publication, from typesetting to printing or uploading to a website.

progressives A set of colour proofs of each colour in the four-colour set and of combinations of the colours.

proofread   To check a proof of text and/or illustrations for accuracy and consistency. Proofreading against copy means making this check against the material that was the basis of the typesetting; proofreading blind means reading only the proof.

recto   A right-hand page. *See also* verso.

repro   *See* bromide.

reversed-out   Text or lines produced as white on black or another colour.

roman   In typography, used to mean type that is not italic or bold.

running head   The heading set at the top of each page except chapter openings; also called a headline or page head.

running sheets   A set of unbound signatures of a book, generated to allow the publisher to check that the printer is assembling the book in the correct order.

sans serif   A typeface without serifs, e.g., a, m, s. *See also* serifs.

screen   The grid that divides an image into dots to enable printing of photographs or tints. Screen measurements are given in dots per inch (DPI), ranging from 65 (coarse) to 125 (fine) or more.

serifs   The slight projections that finish the strokes in letters, e.g., a, m, s. *See also* sans serif.

signature   A section of a book – usually a multiple of 16 up to a maximum of 128 pages, depending on the number of times the printing sheet is folded.

small caps   Capital letters that align with the x-height.

specification   Usually called 'the spec', this describes the publication in terms of format, extent, number of words, and number and type of illustrations. A type spec includes details about the measure, spacing, and the typefaces and sizes used. A production spec includes information about printing, paper and other materials, and treatments (finishes) applied to covers and jackets.

spine   The back edge of the journal or book where the pages are bound.

spread   Two facing pages; also called a double-page spread.

target market   The intended readers for a publication, who may be defined by age, reading ability, knowledge or academic level, gender, nationality.

text area/type area   The area of the trimmed page occupied by the text; it is surrounded by the margins. Illustrations appear in the text area but can also extend beyond it.

tint A shade of grey or another colour, which may be laid across text or illustrations. It is made up as a series of dots (*see* screen) and expressed as a percentage.

type spec *See* specification.

unjustified Setting where the text is aligned at only one margin, usually the left. The spacing between words is the same throughout the document. The length of each line is determined by the last whole word that fits within the maximum measure. Hyphenated words can be broken at the hyphen in unjustified setting.

verso A left-hand page. *See also* recto.

widow A short last line of a paragraph at the top of a page; also the last word of a paragraph on a line by itself. Both are often regarded as unacceptable, particularly in non-fiction. *See also* orphan.

x-height The height of a lower-case x or other letter without an ascender or descender.

Model answers

The model answers on the following pages have been run on, rather than each one starting on a new page, to save paper. With the exception of plays, real texts do not have line numbers. They are given here so that you can use them to write your queries to authors and to find the same place on the exercise you worked. Only the lines with text are numbered, not the line spaces. Exercise 5.2 uses the actual line numbers from the play.

Line numbers are not given when there is another way to pinpoint the location of a query, such as a note number or a step in a procedure.

Not all the answers shown here are the only ones possible. In some cases there might be other ways to edit the text and phrase the queries, but the principles will be the same.

Exercise 1.1

(CH) Food

(A) Dairy
(B) Milk
(C) Full-fat milk
(C) Semi-skimmed milk
(C) Skimmed milk
(B) Cream
(C) Single cream
(C) Double cream
(C) Whipping cream
(B) Butter
(C) Fresh butter
(C) Salted butter
(C) Clarified butter

(B) Cheese
(C) Hard cheese
(D) Pecorino
(D) Parmesan
(C) Firm cheese
(D) Cheddar
(D) Emmenthal
(D) Leicester
(C) Soft cheese
(D) Brie
(D) Camembert
(D) Gorgonzola
(D) Mozzarella
(A) Fruit
(B) Apples
(C) Dessert apples
(D) Cox

(D) Delicious
(D) McIntosh
(C) Cooking apples
(C) Bramley
(D) Rome Beauty
(D) Royal Russet
(D) Grapes
(B) Green grapes
(C) Red grapes
(C) Black grapes
(C) Berries
(B) Strawberries
(C) Blackberries
(C) Raspberries

Exercise 1.2

(PT) Part IV Herb Profiles

(CH) A Look At The Most Common Herbs

In this chapter you'll read more about the herbs most frequently used for treating a variety of conditions. The herbs are listed alphabetically by their common names, with their Latin names in brackets. You'll find basic information on each herb: its other common names, where it is harvested, the plant parts used, available forms of the herb, the conditions it is used for, and any cautions or reasons why you shouldn't take it. Some herbs are now endangered in their wild form and should be purchased from reputable sources that specify that the herb was harvested from cultivated plants. Therefore, when applicable, there is 'conscientious consumer' information to guide your buying decisions.

There are no dosages in this chapter, which is mainly for readers who want to compare information on different herbs. If you see that a herb is used to treat a particular condition, you should read that chapter before purchasing or taking the herb. Sometimes those chapters offer additional cautions for specific conditions, such as possible bad interactions of herbs and drugs. It's also important not to self-treat some disorders but to be advised by a professional herbalist or doctor.

(A) AGNUS CASTUS (VITEX AGNUS-CASTUS)

(B) Also called

Chaste tree, monk's pepper, vitex.

(B) Source

Native to south-western Europe, naturalized in the south-eastern United States, grown commercially in Europe.

(B) Parts used

Fruit (berries).

(B) Forms available

Capsules, tablets, teas, tinctures, combination products.

(B) Uses

Premenstrual tension, heavy or frequent menstruation, spotting, impaired menstrual flow, swelling and tenderness of breasts, infertility, menopausal symptoms, and other women's conditions requiring hormone regulation.

(B) Caution

Do not use agnus castus if taking hormone replacement therapy or birth-control pills. Generally not recommended for use when pregnant; however, in cases of progesterone deficiency, it has been administered under medical supervision to prevent miscarriages in the first trimester. Some minor skin irritations have been reported.

(A) ALOE (*ALOE VERA*)

(B) Also called

Cape aloe.

(B) Source

Native to Africa; grown commercially in southern Texas and Mexico.

(B) Parts used

Leaf gel, juice.

(B) Forms available

Various concentrations of the gel, powdered dry juice. The gel is incorporated into ointments, creams, lotions and the like. Some of aloe's active compounds deteriorate in storage, so use the fresh gel for maximum potency.

(B) Uses

Externally, aloe gel has long been valued for healing minor burns, wounds and abrasions, and relieving associated pain and inflammation. Aloe juice may hold promise for treating diabetes and reducing the levels of triglycerides and blood sugar.

(B) Caution

Don't use this herb if you have intestinal obstruction, abdominal pain of unknown origin, diarrhoea, inflamed intestines (colitis, Crohn's disease, irritable bowel syndrome). Aloe juice may produce a laxative effect if taken in a higher dose than recommended. Don't use for more than 10 days.

(A) ARNICA (*Arnica*) (AQ)

(B) Also called

Leopard's bane, mountain tobacco.

Source

Native to Europe; most species occur in the mountains of North America.

Parts used

Whole plant, flower.

Forms available

Creams, ointments, gels, tinctures, homeopathic preparations.

Uses

Externally as an anti-inflammatory, pain reliever and antiseptic for sprains, bruises, acne, injuries, and swelling caused by bone fractures, insect bites, rheumatic pains and chilblains. Seldom used internally because its primary active constituents are considered toxic.

Caution

Avoid if you're pregnant. Use only on a short-term basis for acute conditions. May cause allergic dermatitis in sensitive persons or with prolonged use. Do not apply to open wounds or broken skin, except under the advice of a health-care practitioner. Taken internally, low doses can cause gastroenteritis; high doses may damage the heart and in rare cases can induce cardiac arrest.

Conscientious consumer information

Protected in the wild in parts of Europe. May be at risk in the wild elsewhere; needs further study.

ASTRAGALUS (*ASTRAGALUS MEMBRANACEUS*)

(B) Also called

Huang qi.
(B) *Source*
(B) *Parts used* (AQ)
(B) Forms available

Capsules, extracts, tablets, tinctures and in many traditional Chinese formulas.

(B) Uses

Colds, flu, minor infections. Many studies confirm immune-boosting, antiviral, antibacterial and tonic properties. Shows promise in restoring T-cell function in cancer patients and preventing growth of cancerous cells.

(B) Caution

None known.

Adapted from Linda B. White and Steven Foster, *The Herbal Drugstore*, London, Rodale Books, 2000, pp. 546–50.

Queries for author
l. 66   Please state which species of Arnica
btwn ll. 92 & 93   Please provide information for 'Source' and 'Parts used'.

Exercise 1.3

10 Cybele, Great Goddess of Anatolia and Rome

For O, I know, in the dust where we have buried
The silenced races and all their abominations,
We have buried so much of the delicate magic of life.

D. H. Lawrence, 'Cypresses' 5

The Bronze Age myth of the mother goddess and her son–lover did not die out in spite of the formal worship of the great father god. It persisted in various forms in Egypt, Anatolia, Syria, Palestine, Greece and Rome until it found a new expression in the Mystery cults of Egypt, Greece and Rome. As spirit and nature were driven further 10 and further apart in the religions of the Iron Age, this myth continued to hold them together in their original relationship. It is no coincidence that Anatolia and Syria, as well as Alexandria and Rome, were the areas most receptive to both the Orthodox and Gnostic traditions of Christianity. 15

Cybele is far less familiar to us than other goddesses, and the liturgies and hymns addressed to her in the pre-Roman era are very sparse in comparison with the many poems and songs arising from the worship of Inanna and Isis. Nevertheless, it is through her, as well as through the Sumerian and Egyptian goddesses, that the myth of the goddess 20 can be traced from the Neolithic era through the Iron Age and far into the Christian era, for, amazingly, it hardly changes throughout this immense period of time.

The lion is inseparable from the image of the goddess. In Anatolia this relationship can be traced as far back as Çatal Hüyük, where the mother goddess in the act of giving birth sits between two felines, and a miniature lion or leopard rests on the head of the Minoan goddess, who may have come to Crete from Anatolia. In Greece statues of Cybele show her with a lion resting on her lap. After the cult of Cybele moved to Rome early in the third century AD, her chariot, harnessed to lions, was drawn through the streets in her yearly procession.

Like all great goddesses, Cybele was guardian of the dead and goddess of fertility and wild life. Her connection with the goddesses of Greece is clear, for Artemis, the great goddess of wild, untamed nature, was one of her names, and Aphrodite, in the Homeric Hymn, also comes to Mount Ida, with its many springs, followed by wild animals. Another Homeric Hymn, to the nameless 'Mother of the Gods', sings of her in these words:

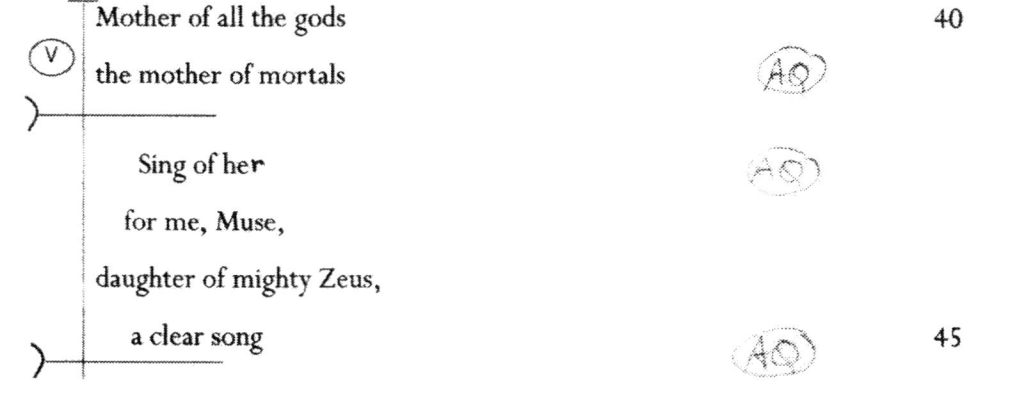

> Mother of all the gods
> the mother of mortals
>
> Sing of her
> for me, Muse,
> daughter of mighty Zeus,
> a clear song

> She knows
>   the clatter of rattles
>   the din of kettle drums
>   and she loves
>   the wailing of flutes.¹   50

Another hymn of the second to third century AD addresses Cybele as the mother of the gods:

> Rightly thou art called the Mother of the Gods
> Because by thy loyalty
> Thou hast conquered the power of the Gods.²   55

The cult of Cybele spread from Anatolia to Greece. In the fifth century BC a magnificent seated statue of Cybele flanked by lions and with a tambourine in her hands was placed in her temple, the Metroon, in Athens. The Emperor Julian in the fourth century AD told the story of how Cybele's temple was first established in Athens: 'The Athenians   60 are said to have insulted and driven away the gallus [priest of Cybele] … not understanding how important the Goddess was … from that followed the wrath of the deity and the attempt to appease it … The Metroon, they say, was set up for this purpose – the place where all the official documents of the Athenians used to be kept.'³   65

The Hittite Invasion

Anatolia endured a devastating series of invasions by Indo-European tribes between 2300 and 1700 BC. At least 300 cities and villages were sacked and buried during this time. The most powerful of these tribes were the Hittites, who conquered Anatolia about 1740 BC and, overthrowing the dynasty of Hammurabi in Babylon about 1600 BC, established an empire that lasted until about 1170 BC, shortly after the Trojan War.

Names and places

The earliest form of Cybele's name may have been Kubaba or Kumbaba. The root of the name may be *kuba*, meaning a cube, which suggests the connection with the cube-shaped stone worshipped as the goddess in Anatolia. The five ideograms of Kubaba's name in Hittite writing were a lozenge or cube, a double-headed axe, a dove, a vase and a door or gate.

1 Translation Jules Cashford, *Harvest*, vol. 35, 1989–90, p. 209.

2 G. B. Pighi, *La Poesia Religiosa Romana*, Bologna, 1958, quoted in M. J. Vermaseren, *Cybele and Attis* (trs. A. M. H. Lemmers), London, Thames and Hudson, 1977, p. 10.

3 Julian, *Orat.* (ed. G. Rochefort), V, 159a, Paris, 1963, quoted in Vermaseren, *Cybele and Attis*, p. 32.

Adapted from Anne Baring and Jules Cashford, *The Myth of the Goddess: Evolution of an Image*, Harmondsworth, Penguin Books, 1991, pp. 391–5.

Queries for author
GENERAL
- Are all verses shown here line for line as in the sources?
- Have permissions been cleared for the epigraph and verses?
- Homeric Hymn: is 'hymn' a proper noun in this context, i.e. must be capitalized?

SPECIFIC
l. 20 Please confirm 'and' rather than 'or'.

306 *Copy-editing*

l. 41   Should there be a full stop or comma after 'mortals'?
l. 42   Please confirm 'her' rather than 'he'.
l. 45   Should there be a full stop after 'song'?
l. 52   Should 'mother' and 'gods' be capitalized, as in ll. 38–9, 53?
l. 73   Would 'after the end of the Trojan War' be clearer?

Instructions for designer/typesetter
- Set all verse line for line
- First paras under headings full out; subsequent paras indented
- Use spaced en rules for dashes
- Small caps: AD, BC

MARK-UP CODES
CH   chapter   A   first level subheading
EPV   verse epigraph   T   special feature
Q   displayed quote   TH   special feature heading
V   verse   FN   footnotes

Exercise 1.4

1 Excerpt from a cookery article

For an elegant sweet at a midsummer party, try this variation on a traditional pavlova. It's easy to make with prepared meringue nests from the supermarket. You will need: 250 g grapes, 250 g raspberries, 2 ripe pears, 2 ripe peaches, 2 oranges, 500 ml whipping cream, 12 meringue nests. Wash the grapes and raspberries and peel the pears, peaches and oranges. Slice the grapes in half and chop all the other fruit except the raspberries. Put the fruit in a bowl and mix. Whip the cream to soft peaks and fold into the fruit. Fill the meringue nests with the mixture. The meringues are so sweet that you don't need any sugar!

2 Excerpt from a computer guide

Setting text attributes

Text attributes determine how characters appear in Browse and when you print. Text attributes include font, size, style and colour; alignment of text characters in a field; text line spacing.

In Layout you can set text attributes for field so data in that field, in all records, appears as you specify. Follow these three steps to set text attributes: 1 in Layout, select the field you want to modify (click once in the field); 2 from the submenus on the Format menu, choose the text attributes you want; 3 choose Browse to resume data entry.

ClarisWorks User's Guide, Santa Clara, CA, Claris Corporation, 1993

3 Excerpt from a guide to copyright

Criminal proceedings The provisions of the Act regarding penalties and summary proceedings in respect of dealings which infringe copyright are set out in sections 107–110. Section 107 provides that any person who (a) makes for sale or hire; or (b) imports into the United Kingdom otherwise than for his private and domestic use; or (c) possesses in the course of business with a view to committing any act infringing the copyright; or (d) in the course of business (i) sells or lets for hire, or (ii) offers or exposes for sale or hire, or (iii) exhibits in public, or (iv) distributes; or (e) distributes otherwise in the course of a business to such an extent as to affect prejudicially the owner of the copyright an article which he knows or has reason to believe is an infringing copy of a copyright work shall be guilty of an offence.

Michael F. Flint, *A User's Guide to Copyright*, 4th edn, London, Butterworths, 1997, p. 82

4 Excerpt from an article on building materials

Photovoltaic (PV) cladding can be considered as a new building material that not only serves as a source of energy but also protects buildings from the elements. It will not be suitable in all situations, such as sensitive historical areas subject to planning restrictions. However, there are many circumstances in which it is appropriate, especially where glass walls are used, such as curtain walling, rainscreen cladding and roofs.

Rainscreen cladding has been identified as a prime site for the exploitation of PV cladding technology. Such a location is particularly useful because rainscreens naturally permit ventilation behind the cladding, which encourages cooling and improves PV performance.

Curtain walling is another location in which PV cladding might be used, but care must be taken to avoid the visual intrusion of wiring and junction boxes.

Pitched roofs offer opportunities for mounting PV arrays, and atria roofs, where the view out is often less important than the general light level, also offer potential sites.

Peter F. Smith and Adrian C. Pitts, *Energy: Building for the Third Millennium*, London, Batsford, 1997

5 Excerpt from a story

Fleet Street was choked with red-headed folk, and Pope's Court looked like a coster's orange barrow. I should not have thought there were so many in the whole country as were brought together by that single advertisement. Every shade of colour they were: straw, lemon, orange, brick, Irish-setter, liver, clay; but, as Spaulding said, there were not many who had the real vivid flame-coloured tint.

Sir Arthur Conan Doyle, 'The Red-Headed League'

Exercise 2.1

The common frog grows up to 8 cm in length and has a smooth moist skin. Usually a yellowish brown, its skin colours vary a lot, and can be oranges, greens, red or even blue. A frog has an obvious hump on its back and moves by hops, jumps and leaps. Toads have rougher, drier, warty skin and tends to crawl. 5

A frogs have distinctive large eyes that stick up so they can see out of the water while their bodies is submerged. They have very good eyesight and can detect even the slightest movement from an unsuspecting creature. Using their long sticky tongue at high speed, frogs their prey is quickly snapped up; they will eat almost anything that 10 moves but their favourite food is snails and slugs. Frogs don't really real have teeth, just small pegs in their jaws to stop their prey escaping. When they have an animal in their mouths, they squash it between their tongue and eyeballs (which can be drawn down into the head) to make ~~them~~ it easier to swallow.

When it's warmer and the days are getting longer, frogs emerge from hibernation, crawling out from the bottom of ponds and from under rocks. In the relative safety of the pond a male tries to attract a mate. Slightly smaller and darker than the females, ~~you can identify~~ the males by the bluish tinge to their throats can also be identified. Males climb on to a female's back and hang on with ~~their~~ its front legs until she is ready to lay her eggs. The wait may be days or even weeks, and the male has special rough black swellings (called 'nuptial pads') on ~~their~~ its thumbs that help ~~them~~ it to hang on. Only a few of the 2,000 eggs the female lays will hatch into tadpoles.

The mass of black eggs, called frogspawn, ~~have~~ has a jelly coating and ~~and are~~ is a very tasty and nutritious meal for fish, water beetles and dragonfly nymphs. The frogspawn floats on the surface of the water, warmed by the sun, and the tadpoles finally hatch after two to four weeks. Insects or fish not only eat frogspawn but also tadpoles, which try to hide among the weeds.

Tadpoles start life as vegetarians, mainly eating algae and plants, but after about seven weeks they start eating insects. ~~It has~~ They have gills so that ~~it~~ they can breathe underwater. Until ~~they~~ tadpoles are about four weeks old, the gills can be seen on the outside of the ~~tadpole's~~ their body. Then the gills are absorbed into the body. ~~The~~ tadpoles grows hind legs, then front ones, and finally looses ~~its~~ their tail. After 12 weeks, with all four legs and

Exercise 2.2

THE STATE OF OUR HEALTH

The NHS is always in the news. There is a cycle of articles about the seemingly endless reorganisations and restructurings; the long hours and the poor pay, which results in people not entering the medical profession or leaving it quickly for private practice or better conditions abroad; the closure of wards because there aren't enough doctors and nurses; the lack of beds; the patients on trolleys in corridors where they lie untended for hours; the waiting lists; the postcode lottery. People can hardly be blamed for wondering whether they can get into a hospital if they need to and whether they'll get good care if they do.

A) Not As Bad As We Feared?

When I visited a close friend in hospital recently, he told me how hard everyone had worked to treat not only his medical condition but also to make him feel comfortable. There was the consultant, who tried to allay his fears before the surgery by explaining what was about to happen. It had been the middle of the night and my friend was very

weak from the loss of blood, he said, and could only remember what
she had said vaguely but her manner had been comforting. She came to see him
the next day to reassure him that the operation had gone well. The
nurses, who, of course, gave him his medications and the aides,
who saw to all his other needs, from smoothing the bedclothes to
bringing his meals, were all efficient and personable. Everything was
great, he told me, until our mutual friend Ted had turned up and
started on about the resurgence of MRSA, an infection that had
been rampant in the early 2000s and could kill you. My friend hadn't
known about it before and now was watching the cleaners like an
eagle, checking that the nurses were wearing gloves when they changed
his bandages, wondering if the plates had been sterilised and the
aides had washed their hands. Instead of believing the hospital was the
right place for his recuperation, he now wanted to go home as soon
as possible. His situation is so far from unique that action is finally
being taken.

Are We Dreaming?

The government, which knows it stands to lose many of its
supporters if it doesn't produce a strategy to cope with the current
problems, has made a number of important decisions. Hospitals
that fail to achieve the minimum standard will be told not only
what their failings are, but also be given funding to remedy them.
Recognising that the rise in the spread of infections is a result of
poor hygiene, the government money will be earmarked for employing additional
cleaners. Other new policies, which apply to all hospitals, were
announced by a man who had earned the public's confidence as

Minister for Scientific Advancement and is the new Minister for
Health: Robin Natiramas. Signs will be placed in appropriate places   45
to remind all staff, including doctors and nurses, to wash their hands,
and to wear and dispose of gowns and gloves appropriately. Senior
staff in all departments will check that the proper procedures are
being followed, particularly by new or temporary staff, who might
not be familiar with the new guidelines. An expert team of public   50
health inspectors will make unannounced visits to inspect kitchens,
where dirty surfaces, inefficient dishwashers and unrefrigerated
food could lead to major disasters. Funds will be provided for
rebuilding every hospital that is more than forty years old this
year, so that they will come up to the standard set out in the NHS   55
Reform Act 2035.

Exercise 2.3

On a fine summer morning, when the leaves were warm under the
sun and the more industrious bees abroad, diving into every blue and
red cup that could possibly be considered a flower, Anne was sitting
at the back window of her mother's portion of the house measuring
out lengths of worsted for a fringed rug that she was making, which   5
lay, about three-quarters finished, beside her; the work, though
chromatically brilliant, was tedious; a hearth-rug was a thing that

nobody worked at from morning to night; it was taken up and put down; it was in the chair, on the floor, across the handrail, under the bed, kicked here, kicked there, rolled away in the closet, brought out again and so on, more capriciously perhaps than any other home-made article. nobody was expected to finish a rug within a calculable period and the wools of the beginning became faded and historical before the end was reached. a sense of this inherent nature of worsted-work rather than idleness led Anne to look rather frequently from the open casement.

The girl glanced at the down and the sheep for no particular reason; the steep margin of turf and daisies rising above the roofs, chimneys, apple trees and church tower of the hamlet around her bounded the view from her position, and it was necessary to look somewhere when she raised her head. While thus engaged in working and stopping, her attention was attracted by the sudden rising and running away of the sheep squatted on the down, and there succeeded sounds of a heavy tramping over the hard sod that the sheep had quitted, the tramp being accompanied by a metallic jingle. turning her eyes further, she beheld two cavalry soldiers on bulky grey chargers, armed and accoutred throughout, ascending the down at a point to the left where the incline was comparatively easy. the burnished chains buckles and plates of their trappings shone like little looking-glasses, and the blue, red and white about them was unsubdued by weather or wear.

The two troopers rode proudly on as if nothing less than crowns and

empires ever concerned their magnificent minds, they reached that
part of the down ~~which~~ *that* lay just in front of her, where they came to a
halt; in another minute there appeared behind them a group   35
containing some half dozen more of the same sort; these came on,
halted and dismounted likewise.

Two of the soldiers then walked some distance onward together,
when one stood still, the other advancing further and stretching a
white line of tape between them; two more of the men marched to   40
another outlying point, where they made marks in the ground; thus
they walked about and took distances according to some
preconcerted scheme.

At the end of this systematic proceeding one solitary horseman – a
commissioned officer if his uniform could be judged rightly at this   45
distance – rode up the down, went over the ground, looked at what
the others had done and seemed to think that it was good; and then
the girl heard yet louder tramps and clankings, and she beheld rising
from where the others had risen a whole column of cavalry in
marching order; at a distance behind these came a cloud of dust   50
enveloping more and more troops, their arms and accoutrements
reflecting the sun through the haze in faint flashes, stars and streaks of
light; the whole body approached slowly towards the plateau at the
top of the down.

Anne threw down her work and, letting her eyes remain on the   55
nearing masses of cavalry, the worsteds getting entangled as they

would, said, 'Mother, mother, come here, here's such a fine sight! what does it mean? what can they be going to do up there.'

From Thomas Hardy, *The Trumpet-Major*

Exercise 2.4

Close to the rude landing stage was a small brick house, with a
wooden placard slung out through the second window. 'Mordecai
Smith' was printed across it in large letters and, underneath, 'Boats to
hire by the hour or day. A second inscription above the door
informed us that a steam launch was kept - a statement that was   5
confirmed by a great pile of coke upon the jetty. Sherlock Holmes
looked slowly round and his face assumed an ominous expression.
'This looks bad,' said he. 'These fellows are sharper than I expected.
They seem to have covered their tracks. There has, I fear, been
preconcerted management here.'   10
He was approaching the door of the house, when it opened and a
little curly-headed lad of six came running out, followed by a stoutish
red-faced woman with a large sponge in her hand.
'You come back and be washed, Jack,' she shouted. 'Come back, you
young imp, for if your father comes home and finds you like that,   15
he'll let us hear of it.'
'Dear little chap!' cried Holmes, strategically. 'What a rosy-cheeked
young rascal! Now, Jack, is there anything you would like?'
The youth pondered for a moment.

'I'd like a shillin',' he said.

'Nothing you would like better?'

'I'd like two shillin' better,' the prodigy answered after some thought.

'Here you are then! Catch! A fine child, Mrs Smith!'

'Lor' bless you, sir, he is that, and forward. He gets a'most too much for me to manage, 'specialy when my man is away days at a time.'

'Away, is he?' said Holmes in a disappointed voice. 'I am sorry for that, for I wanted to speak to Mr Smith.'

'He's been away since yesterday morning, sir, and, truth to tell, I am beginning to feel frightened about him. But if it was about a boat, sir, maybe I could serve as well.'

'I wanted to hire his steam launch.'

'Why, bless you, sir, it is in the steam launch that he has gone. That's what puzzles me, for I know there ain't more coals in her than would take her to about Woolwich and back. If he'd been away in the barge I'd ha' thought nothin', for many a time a job has taken him as far as Gravesend, and if there was much doin' there he might ha' stayed over. But what good is a steam launch without coals?'

'He might have bought some at a wharf down the river.'

'He might, sir, but it weren't his way. Many a time I've heard him call out at prices they charge for a few odd bags. Besides, I don't like that wooden legged man, wi' his ugly face and outlandish talk. What did he want always knocking about here for?'

'A wooden legged man?' said Holmes, with bland surprise.

'Yes, sir, a brown, monkey-faced chap that's called more 'n once for my old man. It was him that roused him up yesternight and, what's more, my man knew he was comin', for he had steam up in the launch. I tell you straight, sir, I don't feel easy in my mind about it.'

'But my dear Mrs Smith,' said Holmes, shrugging his shoulders, 'you are frightening yourself about nothing. How could you possibly tell that it was the wooden legged man who came in the night? I don't quite understand how you can be so sure.'

'His voice, sir. I knew his voice, which is kind o'thick and foggy. He tapped at the winder - about three it would be. "Show a leg, matey, says he, "time to turn out guard."'

'And was this wooden-legged man alone?'

'Couldn't say, I am sure, sir. I didn't hear no one else.'

'I am sorry, Mrs Smith, for I wanted a steam launch and I have heard good reports of the of the let me see, what is her name?'

'The Aurora, sir.'

'Ah! She's not that old green launch with a yellow line, very broad in the beam?'

'No, indeed. She's as trim a little thing as on any river. She's been fresh painted, black with two red streaks.'

From Sir Arthur Conan Doyle, *The Sign of Four*.

Instructions for typesetter
GLOBAL
- Spaced en rules for dashes
- wooden legged → wooden-legged

Exercise 3.1

<Half-title, p. i>
Thumbprint

<Half-title verso, p. ii>
Other titles from Bitter Lemon Press
Holy Smoke by Tonino Benacquista
The Russian Passenger by Günter Ohnemus
Tequila Blue by Rolo Diez
Goat Song by Chantal Pelletier
The Snowman by Jörg Fauser

<Title page, p. iii>
Thumbprint
Friedrich Glauser
Translated from the German by Mike Mitchell
[logo]
Bitter Lemon Press
London

<Title-page verso, p. iv>
First published in the United Kingdom in 2004 by Bitter Lemon Press, 37 Arundel Gardens, London W11 2LW.
www.bitterlemonpress.com
First published in German as *Schlumpf Erwin, Mord (Wachtmeister Studer)* by Limmat Verlag, Zurich, 1995.
Originally published as '*Wachtmeister Studer*' in *Zürcher Illustrierte*, 1936.
This edition has been translated with the financial assistance of Pro Helvetica, the Arts Council of Switzerland.
© Limmat Verlag 1995
English translation © Mike Mitchell 2004.
All rights reserved. No part of this publication may be reproduced in any form or by any means without the written permission of the publisher.
The moral right of Mike Mitchell to be identified as the author of the translation has been asserted in accordance with the

Copyright, Designs and Patents Act 1988.
A CIP record for this work is available from the British Library.
ISBN 1-904738-00-1

Typeset by RefineCatch Limited, Bungay, Suffolk.
Printed and bound by W S Bookwell, Finland.

Exercise 3.2

1 *Geriatric Medicine*
(CH) Contents
(CA) Commentary: A new era for statin use in CHD prevention 00
(CB) Alison Boyle
(CA) The social theories of ageing 00
(CB) Dr A. B. Michael, Specialist Registrar in Geriatric Medicine, Queen's Hospital, Burton on Trent, and Dr B. Rowe, Senior Lecturer in Social Gerontology, Department of Geriatric Medicine, University of Keele
(CA) The role of catheter valves in urinary incontinence 00
(CB) Julie Hutton, Nursing Sister, Ramyard Dowe House, Blackheath, London
(CA) CVD and the GMS contract 00
(CB) Dr George Kassianos, General Practitioner, Bracknell Forest, Berkshire
(CA) The challenge of medical management in PD 00
(CB) Dr Christopher Beer, Senior Lecturer, University Department of Geriatric Medicine, Perth
(CA) Writing for Publication in GM 00
(CA) Advance Reports 00

2 *Birds*
(CH) Contents
(CA) Features

(B) Members' weekend 00
(C) A chance for you to enjoy a break in York and learn more about birds and the RSPB
(B) Birds and combines 00
(C) Ornithologist and farmer Mike Shrubb reflects on how agricultural changes have affected British wildlife
(B) Priceless peatlands 00
(C) Rob Hume visits Frosinard as part of a year-long celebration of the RSPB's working for wildlife in Scotland
(B) Beating a retreat 00
(C) Andre Farrar, leader of the RSPB's conservation team at The Lodge, expresses his worry that snipe, lapwings and redshanks are declining in the countryside
(B) Bird art at the SWLA 00
(C) Artist Dafila Scott, who won the RSPB award in the show, comments on her favourite pictures in the Society of Wildlife Artists' Exhibition
(A) Regulars
    The RSPB view 00
(B) Mailbox 00
    The news 00
    Learning about birds 00
    Enjoying your wildlife garden 00
    Action pages 00
    Birdbox 00
    Classified ads 00
    RSPB people 00

3 *Exploring the Weather*
(D) Contents
    Introduction 0
    The Global Circulation 00
    The Atmosphere 00
    Oceans, Currents and Climates 00
    Weather on the Move 00
    Jet Streams 00
    Climates 00
    Seasons 00

Daily Weather 00
Extreme Conditions 000
Energy from the Weather 000
Measuring the Weather 000
Who Uses Forecasts? 000
Weather Lore 000
Weather and Our Bodies 000
Climate and Crops 000
Are We Changing the Weather? 000
The Future of Forecasting 000
Glossary 000
Further Reading 000
Index 000
Picture Credits 000

Exercise 3.3

1 *Geriatric Medicine*
Verso and recto running heads
Contents
Boyle: Statin use in CHD prevention
Michael and Rowe: Social theories of ageing
Hutton: Catheter valves in urinary incontinence
Kassianos: CVD and the GMS contract
Beer: Medical management in PD
Advance Reports

Running feet

verso	*recto*
00 GM August 20—	August 20— GM 00

2 *Birds*
   Verso and recto running heads
   chapter-weight headings

   Running feet
   verso   *recto*
   00 *Birds* Spring 20—   Spring 20— *Birds* 00

3 *Exploring the Weather*
   verso   *recto*
   Exploring the Weather   chapter-weight heading

Exercise 3.4

[Date]

Rights Department
[Publisher's name and address]

Dear …

Re Jones, *Sting in the Tale*

We request permission to reproduce:
   'Revenge' by Isabel Allende, translated by Margaret Sayers
   Peden, which appears in [title, date of publication], on pages
   XX–XX
in the following publication:
   Editor: Stirling Jones
   Title: Sting in the Tale: An Anthology
   Extent: 240 pp.
   Publication date: October 20—
   Proposed price: £8.99 pb.

Proposed print run: 3000
Rights required: World English-language

We will, of course, give full acknowledgement to the author, translator, title and publisher, but please inform us if additional information or a particular form of wording is required. Please also let us know if we must seek permission from another source for any or all of the rights required.

Yours faithfully

Exercise 4.1

the two passions fuelling parliament and the people were religious fervour and the fear that the king, egged on by his catholic wife, was aiming to become an absolute ruler. the religious rollercoaster of the previous century, when successive tudor monarchs first overthrew the catholic church, set up protestantism, restored catholicism and then settled into uneasy compromise under elizabeth, had left a legacy of fierce hatred of the catholics and a burgeoning of protestant sects. the movement came to be called puritanism and the puritans, disliking the established church, with its bishops and tithes that bore harshly on the poor, who had no money to pay them became the allies of the political opponents of the king. margaret pepys, like a great many of her neighbours, seems to have veered towards puritanism, although she still attended st brides church and had her own pew. her boys grew accustomed to hearing puritan preachers in the street. in

1640 a local leather-seller called praisegod barebones set up his baptist congregation right outside in fleet street. baptist ministers saw no need for church buildings, supported themselves by working at other jobs and welcomed women as preachers, and more baptist congregations were begun in other parts of town. the city apprentices who gathered in westminster in 1641 shouted 'no bishops!', and there was some fighting in the days after christmas the same boys blocked the river stairs to prevent bishops newly appointed by the king from taking their seats in the house of lords and went on to attack them in their coaches. when the bishops protested, parliament found grounds for impeaching them and sent them to prison, at which the apprentices rang the city churchbells joyfully and made bonfires in the street. the king then moved to impeach his chief enemies in parliament.

pepys was quite old enough to be on the streets when, on 4 january 1642, the king pursued the five mps he was trying to arrest from the house of commons into the city. The King was mobbed by huge numbers of tradesmen, apprentices and seamen, all shouting 'privilege of parliament, privilege of parliament' — a difficult mouthful for a mob, but they made it sound frightening. although the king was not harmed, he was thoroughly scared. this was a spectacular moment in english history, and a week later charles left london with his family. he was not seen again until his execution in whitehall, seven years later, when an approving pepys was by his own account standing in the crowd.

on the day after the king left, the five mps he had threatened made a triumphal journey on the thames from the city to westminster, escorted by a flotilla of beribboned boats loaded with cheering and waving londoners while citizen soldiers marched along the strand with drums and flags to meet them as they came ashore. these soldiers, known as the trained bands, were ordinary townsmen organized into fighting groups, their effectiveness depending more on enthusiasm than discipline. the next big street show was the execution in late january of two catholic priests in front of an approving crowd. in march parliament began to raise its own army, and in may the city's regiments were reviewed on finsbury fields in front of the assembled mps. in june londoners were asked for money by parliament and they responded generously, even though times were hard for tradesmen in the absence of the court. john pepys's lawyer customers had fewer clients and less to spend, and the prospect of civil war promised worse to come as their one-time neighbour lawyer whitlocke, now in parliament, warned, saying the country was 'at the pit's brink, ready to plunge ourselves into an ocean of troubles and miseries ... what the issue of it will be no man alive can tell'. in july the royalist mayor, gurney, was impeached in parliament and sent to the tower, where he remained almost until his death five years later. a puritan was appointed as mayor in his place. milton called the city 'the mansion house of liberty', and as such it had to prepare to defend itself against the gathering forces of the king, who raised his standard at nottingham on 22 august 1642.

This was the official start of the civil war.

It was brought about essentially by the king's refusal to accept the limitations parliament was determined to set upon his power, and by parliament's refusal to accept his supremacy. The war split the nation, dividing families, cities, counties and social classes as well as the great bodies and institutions, the navy, the universities, and the legal and medical professions; and the religious rift between those who held to the established church of england and those who rejected it sharpened the bitterness of the fight. Within seven years the country would rid itself of king, lords and bishops, and though these reforms were reversed, it was never again ruled for any length of time without the cooperation of the elected house of commons. From the English revolution came much of the inspiration for both the american and the french revolutions of the next century. The intellectual revolution that accompanied the war was as important as the war itself.

Meanwhile, parliament ordered the digging of trenches and building of ramparts and forts to close all the main roads into london. Islington, the fields around st pancras church, mile end, rotherhithe and wapping were the sites of some of the twenty-four forts. A huge workforce was needed. It was found among the people of the city and the suburbs, women and children included. Sam and tom pepys may well have taken part. When announcements were made in the churches, citizens turned out with 'baskets, spades and such-like instruments, for digging of trenches and casting up of breast works from one fort to another'. More than 20,000 people were said to have worked on the defences, a sixth of the population. They were directed by sailors and officers of the trained bands, and their effectiveness was observed with surprise and respect by the venetian ambassador among others. john evelyn, a supporter of the king, also came to view the 'much celebrated line of communication'. the work was in full swing in the autumn of 1642, the season of edward montagu's marriage to jemima crew in westminster and of prince rupert's sacking of brentford, which inspired john milton to write his sonnet 'when the assault was intended to the city'. it was addressed to the expected royalist invaders, and suggested they would be well advised to spare a poet.

milton's plea proved unnecessary. the royalists were kept from london. the london troops had good supplies, including the baskets of food brought to them by their wives and sweethearts. the royalists were tired after a long march, and short of supplies, and their nerve failed. the earl of essex, with 24,000 of the trained bands, held turnham green for parliament.

Adapted from Claire Tomalin, *Samuel Pepys: The Unequalled Self*, London, Viking, 2002.

Queries for author
GENERAL
- Acknowledgements of quotations throughout: are sources to be added to the text or will there be notes at the end of the chapter?
- Capitalize 'City' throughout, for the City of London?

SPECIFIC
l. 10   'who had ... pay them': rather tautological after 'poor', OK to delete?
l. 38   Suggest delete 'in 1649', as date will be clear to readers.
l. 56   What was Whitlocke's first name?

Model answers

l. 59   What was Mayor Gurney's first name?

l. 65   'between opposing factions' unnecessary in context, so have deleted, OK?

l. 99   Is this the title of the poem or the first line? If it is the title, is the capitalization that used by Milton?

l. 104   'The royalists … failed' moved to precede 'The London troops …' in l. 103 for better linking of all sentences in the paragraph.

Instructions for typesetter
GLOBAL
- Check and correct spacing throughout e-file: 1 space between words and after all punctuation unless otherwise marked.
- First paragraph under heading(s) full out, subsequent paras closed up and indented
- Initial caps for the following unless circled/highlighted [ellipsis indicates stem has more than one ending]

August	King
Baptist	London…
Catholic…	Margaret
Charles	Milton…
City	MPs
Elizabeth	Parliament
England	Pepys…
English	Protestant…
House of Commons	Puritan…
House of Lords	Strand
January	Thames
John	Tudor
July	Westminster
June	Whitehall

330 *Copy-editing*

Exercise 4.2

Rita was tired. She had stayed up late the night before practising her shorthand by taking notes as she watched one news programme after another, as she had been doing for two weeks. Her well-thumbed copy of A Career in Journalism told her shorthand was the only way to keep an accurate account of every word and every action, and was an essential skill for a reporter. Rita was more of a general assistant than a reporter at the Five Villages Gazette, occasionally being allowed to write a short report on a village fete or flower show. This evening she had been to a local council meeting. There were no major issues on the agenda, certainly nothing really newsworthy, but her editor said it would be good experience for her to attend and report. And now she was stiff from the tension of sitting in the council chamber straining to hear everything that was said and write it down at the same time, and her hand was cramped from having gripped the pencil so tightly. But tired, stiff and cramped, she was still in high spirits. The meeting had begun in the usual dull way — attendance, apologies for absence, reading and approval of the minutes of the last meeting — and looked like it would continue in that vein with a discussion of a report on road maintenance and repairs. Then Councillor Beauregard had made a comment that Rita didn't hear, and Councillor Stally had screamed at him 'How dare you! Apologise! Apologise at once or I'll—' 'You'll what?' retorted Beauregard, clenching his fists and looking menacing. The other councillors had had to intervene to prevent a fight. The meeting was

adjourned and the two near combatants ushered out separately, each
surrounded by a few colleagues. OK, rita thought, not earth-
shattering, but it would certainly make an interesting article.

She had put her notebook into her shoulder bag, grabbed her jacket
from under the bench and headed out of the council chamber in
pursuit of a strong coffee to revive her before the trip home. La Stella
d'Italia was across the street, cleverly split into a coffee bar
at the front and a traditional Italian trattoria at the back. It had been
there as long as Rita could remember and was as popular as any of the
fancier establishments that had opened more recently. Rita's father, a
regular at La Stella from the early days – his and its, had recently
commented on how the décor had changed but the menu had not.
This was only partly true, and perhaps a reflection of the fact that he
usually ordered exactly the same meal. The dark red walls had been
repainted a mediterranean gold, a scattering of original paintings had
replaced the hanging fishnets and baskets and the faded prints of Guardi's
Santa Maria della Salute and the Dogana and Canaletto's Piazza San
Marco and other views of Venice and the chianti bottles covered in
candle wax had been banished in favour of frosted glass bowls that
radiated the candle light. Dust catching chandeliers had gone and
small downlights now provided bright light when needed during the
day and a warm glow in the evenings. The old menu, however, had
not been discarded. The classics in every category had been retained
while changing tastes had allowed the addition of other Italian dishes
that would once have been too daring for the residents of the town
and surrounding villages. So as well as the familiar minestrone and

zuppa di verdura, the menu now offered ribollita and zuppa garmugia; the pastas included not only spaghetti bolognese and ravioli with tomato sauce but also capelli d'angelo neri con capesante and the vegetarian's delight, maltagliati al sugo di melanzane. When Rita went ~~but~~ for a meal there with her parents, her father always ordered osso buco while her mother could be counted on to choose veal escalopes in mushroom sauce, although they both claimed they would soon try coniglio al forno, or the fagiano in salmi or perhaps the carciofi ripieni, all of which had appeared on the menu in the last couple of years. Rita would always try one new dish and encourage her parents to have a taste but they always declined.

As she made her way through the door and to a small table at the front the aromas were so tantalizing that Rita, who had had only a cheese sandwich — brie and halved grapes, her own invention — before the meeting, knew she would have to have just a little something, perhaps just a couple of biscotti, with her coffee. And which coffee would she have? Ah, it would definitely be a latte. Waiting for her coffee and, oh dear, a little selection of crostini, Rita pretended to read an article in the current week's *Economist*, which someone had left behind, while she eavesdropped on the conversations around her. Actually, she thought it looked like a very interesting article and, if the café had been empty, she really would have read it. As it was, however, the place was rather full, the tables were fairly close together and by concentrating on one or another she could clearly hear everything being said. The two boys and a girl to her left were discussing the songs on *Dumb Noise*, the latest album by The Raw Deal. This was not the kind of music Rita chose to listen to but some of her friends liked it and she had to admit that the lyrics of 'Too Many Drums', the hit single from the album, made her laugh. As she listened to the trio discussing the merits of the lead singer she could hear the 'Winter' movement of Vivaldi's Four Seasons playing quietly in the trattoria at the back. When the coffee and crostini arrived, Rita transferred her attention to two middle-aged women discussing advice they had heard about growing bougainvilleas on Gardeners' Question Time. Rita's Aunt Millie had a fabulous bougainvillea glabra in her little conservatory but before Rita could pick up any tips to pass along she was distracted by an agitated voice speaking just above a whisper at the table slightly behind her.

'... not to phone me. It can be traced.'

'Well, meeting in public's not a great idea either, is it?'

'We just bumped into each other, that's all. Decided to have a coffee in the same place. Now, what's so damned important? And keep your voice down!'

Rita was riveted. Why should two men be worried about being seen together? Why did they need to whisper?

'Drake says the goods are arriving tonight and he wants us to help him move them.'

'Move them? Move them where? When?"

'The Burgo will dock unseen after —'

'Shut up! Haven't either of you got any brains?' Even at a hoarse whisper the familiar voice sounded exasperated.

Rita's curiosity got the better of her. She took out her compact and

334 *Copy-editing*

appeared to be checking her hair as she moved the mirror so she could see the men behind her. It was Dan Reynard, the defendant in Anser v Reynard! She had seen his photo in the national press. "Rusty" Reynard, so called because of his orange-tinted brown hair, was accused of embezzling funds from his business partner, Guillaume Anser. What was he doing here? And who was that rather rough-looking man with him? As the waiter bringing coffees to Reynard's table blocked her from view, Rita took her notepad and pencil out of her handbag as discretely as possible. Feeling like a character in a film – like that old black-and-white one she'd seen on TV last year, The Big Scoop – Rita brushed her hair away from her ear and casually leaned back in her chair, hoping to hear more.

105

110

Queries to author
l. 24 Suggest start new paragraph here; do you agree?
l. 28 Rita has a shoulder bag here, but a handbag at l. 111: which should it be?
l. 42 Have changed 'Florence' to 'Venice'.

Instructions to typesetter
- First para full out; subsequent paras closed up and indented
- Dashes are spaced en rules

Exercise 4.3.

In 1939 the United States had a regular army of only 190,000 men; by the end of the war it would be 8.5 million.

Over the second half of 1943 and the first half of 1944, the D-Day
build-up period in which this story opens, new American soldiers,
sailors and airmen were pouring into Britain in their thousands every
week, to make a total of some 1.7 million British-based American
troops by the eve of the Normandy invasion. A vast quantity of
American life was being committed to the crucible of the war in
North-west Europe and the Second Front, which Russia, to relieve
the pressure upon itself, had asked the western allies to open against
Germany. Every one of those hundreds of thousands of men had
family, friends, or sweethearts back home; naturally there was
unease, and some reassurance was in order.

In the first half of 1944 <u>Time</u>, <u>Life</u> and <u>Newsweek</u> carried profiles of
'the Doughboy's General', Omar Bradley, commander of the US
Army in north-west Europe. 'Most of them', Bradley noted, 'stressed
that I valued the lives of my soldiers and would not spend them
recklessly.' In December 1943 General Dwight D. Eisenhower had
been appointed Supreme Commander of the Allied Expeditionary
Force. Eisenhower's attitude was that his relationship with the
American soldier was 'sacred'.

In the United States there was patriotism and even enthusiasm for the
war. There was scarcely a house that did not display the flag of one of
the services, meaning a husband, brother, father or, most commonly,
son was serving in it. But there were houses, too, in whose windows gold
stars and the words 'Gold Star Mother' were displayed, meaning a
life lost, perhaps in the pacific ocean campaign against Japan or in the

North African or Italian campaigns of 1942–43. More gold stars — many more — could be expected from the opening of the Second Front; but America had the word of its military leaders that deaths would be kept to the minimum possible in war. There would be no unnecessary, wasteful, superficially glorious heroics of the kind that seemed to abound in the military histories of the European countries. No 'noble 600' would ride, as in Tennyson's poem about the charge of the Light Brigade, 'into the valley of death'.

The Plymouth section of Convoy T-4 put to sea at 9.45 on the morning of April 27. The 515 would lead the line of LSTs, and as the ship slipped its mooring in Plymouth Harbour the loud hailer system crackled into life with Doyle's voice saying 'This is a drill, but we're going into enemy waters.' The ships cleared the harbour easterly and then, in Plymouth Sound, formed themselves into a convoy of five, the 515 at its head, followed by the 496, 511, 531 and the 58 towing its two platoons. Also waiting in the Sound was the Royal Navy flower-class corvette Azalea, which would precede the 515 as escort.

With U-boats in mind, the Azalea was equipped with hedgehog and depth charges. But she had other armament too; fewer guns than the average LST but of heavier calibre. Perhaps, as with Commander Skahill, the experience of T-4 would later colour how those on the convoy perceived Azalea. A number of survivors have said that they thought the corvette was an anti-submarine trawler; for example, Elson Hendrick, Doyle's communications officer on the 515: 'As convoy T-4 was forming up off Plymouth I got a look at our escort through binoculars. She looked more like a converted trawler to me than a corvette.' (In what must be a slightly mistaken memory, Henderick recalled that 'as we were forming up outside Plymouth I took a blinker message from her: "My best speed 10 knots.") Likewise, someone on another LST would recall that 'we were reported to have more fire power than the trawler' when, in fact, the Azalea was armed with 4-inch cannon forward and a 2-pounder on the bridge, with two anti-aircraft Oerlikons and a 2-pounder about the bridge and funnel.

But the Azalea was not intended as the T-4's only or chief escort. The bulk of the convoy's fire-power protection was to be provided by the 26-knot destroyer Scimitar; in a common British escort pattern of the time, it would steam along T-4's flank while Azalea took the bow position. Scimitar, however, had a small hole in her side and at 7.52 that morning had signalled Plymouth to that effect.

The Scimitar was ordered into port for dockyard repairs, which could not begin until 28 April. At some point after 10 a.m., as the first five ships of T-4 were lining up in Plymouth Sound, the Scimitar, their second escort ship, steamed past them in the opposite direction. The first five ships of T-4 were about to sail out into 'enemy waters' deaf, dumb, virtually blind (few of the LSTs had radar), and defenceless.

So were the three LSTs in Brixham, but perhaps because they and less far to go before meeting up with the Plymouth section off Berry Head, the eastern tip of Start Bay, they left Harbour later, on the afternoon of the 27th. The first of them in line was the 499, followed by the 289 and 507. 250 of 1048 UDT Company, were, according to records, among the 395 soldiers on the 289.

Now all the ships are at sea, sailing into the dusk of British double summer time, and at 8.30 p.m. meeting off Berry Head to form T-4. In the same order as before, the Brixham section attaches itself to the ships from Plymouth, Azalea a mile ahead, 600 yards between the LSTs – although their station-keeping would prove shaky.

Now it is between 9 and 10 pm. The sky is dark, with a setting quarter moon. Visibility is good. The air is chilly and the ships intake valves are registering sea temperature of 42ºFahrenheit. Led by their solitary escort, the eight large LSTs are about to embark on another of that night's 'endless meanderings'. The idea is that the ships should stay at sea for as long as they will on D-Day. Off Torquay and the promontory called Hope's Nose they start a long, slow turn to starboard. From here their course to the transport area 12 miles off Slapton Sands is shaped like a perfect question mark.

The transport area is full of ships as T-4 starts its turn. Rear-Admiral Moon would report that at the close of 27 April his Force U had 221 ships and boats of all shapes and sizes under its protection in Lyme Bay, 'awaiting unloading and sailing empty at daylight'. There were 21 LSTs, 28 LCIs, 65 LCTs and '14 miscellaneous and 92

small landing craft. Moon also referred to an APA, or attack   100
transport: the USS <u>Bayfield</u>, command ship for Tiger, as it would be
for Utah. On board the <u>Bayfield</u> with Moon were General Collins of
the Seventh Corps and Major-General Raymond O. Barton,
commander of the Fourth Infantry Division, which that morning had
made the assault on Slapton Sands.   105

<small>Adapted from Nigel Lewis, *Channel Firing: the Tragedy of Exercise Tiger*, London, Viking, 1989, pp. 3–4, 73–4, 75, 76, 78–9.</small>

Queries to author
ll. 51,55   Is the correct spelling 'Hendrick' or 'Henderick'?
l. 55   Will readers know significance of '10 knots' or can text indicate that this was too slow for the purpose?

Instructions to typesetter: GLOBAL
- First para full out; subsequent paras closed up and indented
- Italics: Azalea; Scimitar
- Dashes are spaced en rules

Exercise 4.4

(CH)   USING A COMPOST BIN

This booklet will take you through the process of setting up your
compost bin and using it to make high quality compost. It will tell
you how to use the compost in your garden and how to tackle any
composting problems that might arise.   5

(A)   How To Start

Selecting the Best Site

The bin is placed in your selected position in the garden on soil, never on concrete or paving. Ideally, the site is in the shade, far enough from the house to prevent any odours being detected but not so far that it is difficult or tiring to carry kitchen and garden waste to it. is sheltered from the wind and

Installation

to help drainage from the bin and allow worms to enter the compost, break up the soil on which the Y bin is to be placed. Recessing the bottom of the Y bin into the soil seals its, which increases stability and reduces excessive air flow in bins without a base. If vermin area in your area and there is no base, dig in and set the bin on top of it a sheet of narrow gauge wire mesh you will need to replace this if it breaks or corroded. Check that the Y bin is level.

Kitchen Bin

sort kitchen materials into a smaller bin as you work, then keep. The kitchen bin in a convenient place, with the lid shut. Transfer the contents of the kitchen bin to the compost bin every day, or at least every other day.

Which Organic Materials Can Be Composted?

Although in principle any organic material can be composted, for reasons that will be discussed, you should select what you add to your composting mixture with great care. Materials used for composting are called 'feedstock'.

A. Kitchen Materials

Fruit and vegetable peelings and salad scraps are excellent for composting. Cut up or crush large or fibrous stems, such as those of cabbage and brussel sprouts, before use. You can also use bread, teabags, coffee grounds and filters, small amounts of vegetable oils and fats and crushed egg shells.

B. Garden Materials

Grass cuttings are excellent for composting. Do not add large amounts of grass alone mixed them in with other feedstock, such as leaves and shredded woody material, to prevent the cuttings from producing an offensive smell. Shred leaves and cut up dead flowers before use, as they otherwise take a long time to compost.

C. Other materials

Human and pet hair and feathers provide good sources of nitrogen, and manure and the sawdust or wood-chip bedding from rabbit, bird and guinea pig, and horses, which helps composting considerably. For health reasons do not use cat or dog faeces, or cat litter, which absorbs moisture. ~~Horse manure, with wood chips or straw as bedding, can~~ be excellent ~~components~~ in a composting mixture, providing useful ~~nutrients and helpful micro-organisms~~

Newspaper ~~can be~~ added in small quantities ~~as long~~ of as it is ~~first~~ finely shredded, but avoid cardboard, except perhaps for shredded egg boxes. ~~is best avoided~~.

Which Wastes Should Not Be Composted?

~~There are a number of wastes that should never be added to a compost mixture.~~ Do not use for composting, The following wastes ~~should be avoided~~ for the reasons given.

Non-Organic Materials

Glass, plastics, plastic bags and metals will not break down in a compost heap and will reduce the quality of the compost if present. ~~They should be~~ separate them from waste for composting and recycled or reuse them whenever possible.

Meat, Fish And Bones

Although fish and meat will break down in a compost bin, it is best to avoid them ~~their use~~. They can attract dogs, cats, hedgehogs, foxes, rats and flies, and produce offensive smells.

Disease-Carrying Plants ~~Material~~

The micro-organisms causing many plant diseases are not always killed by the typical garden composting process and can cause further problems. ~~should be excluded from the feedstock.~~ Problems can particularly arise if, for example, if

Do not add diseased plants to the compost bin.

compost made from waste including diseased tomato plants is then applied to the next crop of tomatoes. This can lead to a build-up of disease affecting these plants.

B) Other organic wastes

Do not add Leather and rubber, or synthetic textiles, as they will not break down to any significant extent. Exclude Wool, linen and cotton too, as they will only break down very slowly and may contain undesirable dyes. Do not use. The contents of vacuum-cleaner bags, coal ash, soot, cigarette ash and cigarette stubs, or treated or painted wood. Do not add Plants treated with herbicides or pesticides, as these chemicals may prevent composting or make the finished compost unusable in the garden. Never add Mineral oils, such as motor oil, to compost.

Remember – if in doubt leave it out!

A) Making Compost In The Composting Bin

Composting is a natural process carried out by micro-organisms such as bacteria and fungi. An efficient gardener controls this process to produce weed-free, sweet-smelling compost. You can achieve excellent results by following the few simple suggestions outlined below.

B) Use Good feedstock

A list of feedstock suitable for composting is given on pages 00–00.

Not too Wet

Do not allow the mixture of feedstock to be too wet or too soft. If you attempt to make compost from vegetable peelings, salads or grass cuttings only, it will tend to collapse into a sticky mess and produce offensive odours. Some drier, woody or fibrous material with the soft vegetable matter. To prevent the compost from becoming too wet and to give it a good structure, mix in.

Not too Dry

Do not allow the mixture of feedstock to be too dry. If you attempt to make compost from shredded wood or straw or tree trimmings alone, composting will be very slow or may not take place at all. Mixing in grass cuttings, horse manure or some other suitable green materials usually ensures there is sufficient moisture and nitrogen present to encourage the micro-organisms to start composting.

Not too Woody

Do not attempt to make compost with large pieces of material such as unshredded woody branches, large pieces of fibrous roots or stems, or unshredded leaves.

Mix In Batches

Mix the materials to be composted, after shredding if necessary, before placing the mixture into the bin. Do not put in large amounts of a single type of feedstock at any one time.

Keep it Loose

Do not allow the mixture to become compacted. Never stand on or press the compost down, but keep the structure loose so that air can easily penetrate through the composting mixture.

How to fill the Composting Bin

Open the lid of the composting bin and add a first layer of shredded stems and trimmings to a depth of about 5–10 cm. Then, using the principles outlined above, add feedstock on a daily basis until the bin is full. You will find that the level of material will drop considerably in the first few days. Continue to fill with a suitable mixture of material until the bin is full again.

How Long Does it Take to Make Compost?

Depending on the ingredients used to make the compost and how often the compost is turned (see below), composting can take ten to twenty weeks. During this time the weight of the material in the bin will drop by about 50 per cent while the volume will reduce by 33 to 66 per cent.

Turning the compost regularly

The composting process can be accelerated and the quality of the compost considerably improved. When turning, make sure the composting material in the outside of the heap goes into the centre, and that the material in the centre is moved to the outside. Continue this process until all of the compost is uniformly turned, adding moisture if necessary.

Adapted from Peter Ridley Waste Systems, *Using a Compost Bin*, Saxmundham, Suffolk.

346 Copy-editing

Queries to author
GENERAL
Here is a copy of the revised text, which has been edited to make it more direct and easier for the reader to follow, and to remove repetition. Please let me know whether there are any changes you would like to make. There are also some queries below.

SPECIFIC
l. 21   'set the bin on top': is this correct?
ll. 53–5 'For health reasons … moisture': would it be better to move this to the section on wastes that should not be used?
In most cases you explain why a waste should not be used. Can you add similar explanations to 'Not too woody' (l. 119) and 'Mix in batches' (l. 124), please?

Instructions to designer/typesetter: GLOBAL
• All paras full out, space between paras

Exercise 5.1

What was going on? He used to be able to recite the entire poem as easily as say his name. Now all he could recall was 'if thou must love me, let it be for nought except for love's sake only.' He knew that was right, he knew it, but that was cold comfort when there were another twelve lines to the sonnet. Which one was it? It was in the teens – number ~~13~~ thirteen or ~~14~~ fourteen perhaps. Yes, yes, that's right, it was the fourteenth of Elizabeth Barrett Browning's <u>Sonnets from the Portuguese</u>. OK, OK, let's not just give into this stupid business of losing one's memory; think how you're going to fight it. [1]Old Sanjay, now he'd be a great help. What's his phone number? Damn, what *is* his phone number?

'Sanjay? Hi, it's Pete, how are you? Listen, remember a couple of months ago when we were having coffee and talking about the old days? And Abe remembered how you won that competition for reciting poetry?'

'Yeah, I wasn't sure if he'd finally got over coming second. So?'

'It was a long time ago; he's over it. And you'll recall that I came fourth. Anyway, how good are you now?'

'What, at reciting poetry?'

'Poetry or anything. Not so much reciting as just remembering.'

'Hmm, probably not as good as I used to be. You know, I kept it up – memorising poetry – for a long time after school. It really impressed the girls, and Reeta said it was one of the most romantic things about me. But I haven't done it for a long time now. Why?'

'I've been trying to remember that Barrett Browning sonnet, the one that starts "If thou must love me, let it be for nought/Except for love's sake only." Only I can't get any farther than that.'

'Have you tried looking it up in a book? Or on the web? You didn't really ring to see if I remembered it, did you?'

'Yes and no. Do you?'

There was silence, and Pete figured Sanjay was just combing through his memory, so he didn't say anything either. He was right.

'Got a pen?'

Then Sanjay spoke not only the words but also their meaning, pausing occasionally, and Pete wrote them down even as he rejoiced

348 Copy-editing

in ~~its~~ their familiarity. Later, after he'd explained his idea to Sanjay and they'd agreed to meet the following week, he found his anthology of Victorian poetry and looked up the sonnet. Sanjay had been word-perfect, although, since he had spoken so expressively, Pete's version didn't have the line breaks or capital letters as they were on the page:

If thou must love me, let it be for nought
Except for love's sake only. Do not say
'I love her for her smile ... her look ... her way
Of speaking gently ... for a trick of thought
That falls on well with mine, and certes brought
A sense of pleasant ease on such a day' –
For these things in themselves, Belovèd, may
Be changed, or change for thee, – and love, so wrought,
may be unwrought so. Neither love me for
Thine own dear pity's wiping my cheeks dry, –
A creature might forget to weep,
who bore thy comfort long, and lose thy love thereby!
But love me for love's sake, that evermore
Thou mayst love on, through love's eternity.

Pete really loved that poem. In fact, like Sanjay, Abe and Mark, he loved poetry, and he wasn't willing to lose it. He had spoken to Abe and Mark too. They had remained friends since school, when they had worked together to memorise poems and then competed against each other for the school prize. They didn't often meet as a group, but they were all retired now and the revival of their poetry ~~trio~~ quartet seemed a good way to fill some of their time.

'Not a bad idea', Abe had said. 'I don't have anything pressing to do and I suspect Becca will be glad to have me out of the house for a while. You make the coffee and I'll bring some biscuits.'

'Good, but bring some poetry too.'

Mark had not only been enthusiastic, he had also guessed that Abe would offer to bring something to eat. 'Don't you remember how he always brought biscuits or chocolates or a bag of sweets in the old days? Said it helped him to concentrate. Maybe that's why he didn't win,' Mark laughed, 'he didn't have anything to eat during the contest. Sure, I'll come. I'll bring some modern stuff, 'cause I know you'll supply the golden oldies.'

They would each bring a book of poetry or at least a few of their favourite poems: they would read them all and then choose a few to memorise for their next meeting. Sanjay had said that, for this first session at least, none of the poems should be very long or they might get discouraged, so they had agreed on nothing longer than a sonnet. Pete decided to type out two of his favourites in addition to the Barrett Browning. He would do it from memory and then look them up to correct the errors and fill the gaps. He started with Shakespeare's second sonnet:

When forty winters shall besiege thy brow
And dig deep trenches in thy beauty's field

He'd done rather well with that one, missing just a few words here and there. He started to type another: My glass shall not persuade

me that I am old. So long as youth and thou are of one date, but he
decided one poem about old age was enough. Still, he checked what
he had typed so far and then continued to read. He read, dozed, got
up for a cup of tea and found other things to do. A few days later he
pulled some books off the shelf and began to browse. He needed to
find another poem for the meeting. Nothing too obvious. Aha! Here
was Maria's copy of Flame and Shadow, a collection of poems by Sara
Teasdale. There must be something in there. Yes, 'Meadowlarks'
would do: not about old age or death, not gloomy at all, not really.
He typed it out:

In the silver light after a storm
  Under dripping boughs of bright new green,
I take the low path to hear meadowlarks
  Alone and high-hearted as if I were a queen.

What have I to fear in life or death
  Who have known these things: the kiss in the night,
The white flying joy when a song is born
  And meadowlarks whistling in silver light.

Queries to author
l. 44 Missing line has been added to sonnet: does the wording match your edition?
l. 76 Suggest combining sentences as shown to avoid over-emphasis on 'So ...', OK?
l. 84 Do you want to identify this sonnet?

Model answers 351

Instructions to designer/typesetter
- First paras under headings/after marked line spaces to be full out; subsequent paras closed up, indented unless otherwise marked.
- Dashes are spaced en rules
- V = displayed verse: set line for line, space for space
- Embedded verse: spaced solidus for line breaks

Exercise 5.2, marking up a play script

Scene 1v Hall in Capulet's house

Enter **Lady Capulet** and **Nurse**

Lady Capulet: Hold, take these keys, and fetch more spices, nurse.

Nurse: They call for quinces and dates in the pastry.

Enter **Capulet**

Capulet: Come stir, stir, stir! The second cock hath crow'd.

The curfew bell hath rung, 'tis three o'clock:

Look to the baked meats good Angelica:

Spare not for cost.

Nurse: Go you cot-quean, go,

Get you to bed; faith, you'll be sick tomorrow

For this night's watching.

Capulet: No, not a whit: what! I have watch'd ere now

All night for lesser cause, and ne'er been sick.

Lady Capulet: Ay, you have been a mouse-hunt in your time;

But I will watch you from such watching now. [*Exeunt Lady Capulet and Nurse*]

Capulet: A jealous-hood, a jealous-hood! – Now fellow, what's there?

Enter servants, with spits, logs and baskets

First Servant: Things for the cook, sir, but I know not what.

Capulet: Make haste, make haste. [*Exit first Servant*] Sirrah, fetch drier logs:

Call Peter, he will show thee where they are.

Second Servant: I have a head, sir, that will find out logs,

And never trouble Peter for the matter. [*Exit*]

Capulet: 'Mass, and well said; a merry whoreson, ha!

Thou shalt be logger-head. Good faith, 'tis day:

The county will be here with the music straight

For so he said he would. *Music within* I hear him near. –

Nurse! – Wife! – What, ho! – what, nurse, I say!

Re-enter Nurse

Go waken Juliet, go and trim her up;

I'll go and chat with Paris: – hie, make haste,

Make haste: the bridegroom he is come already:

Make haste, I say.   [*Exeunt*]

Scene v Juliet's chamber; Juliet on the bed

Enter **Nurse**

Nurse: Mistress! what, mistress! Juliet! fast, I warrant her, she:
Why, lamb! why, lady! fie, you slug-a-bed!
Why, love, I say! madam! sweet-heart! why, bride!
What, not a word? you take your pennyworths now;
Sleep for a week; for the next night, I warrant,
The County Paris has set up his rest
That you shall rest but little – God forgive me,
Marry, and amen, how sound she is asleep!
I needs must wake her. Madam, madam, madam!
Ay, let the county take you in your bed;   10
He'll fright you up, i'faith. Will it not be?
What, dress'd! and in your clothes! And down again!
I must needs wake you! Lady! lady! lady!
Alas, alas! Help, help! My lady's dead!
O, well-a-day that ever I was born!
Some aqua-vitae, ho! My lord! My lady!

Enter **Lady Capulet**

Lady Capulet: What noise is here?
Nurse: O lamentable day!
Lady Capulet: What is the matter?
Nurse: Look, look, O heavy day!

Lady Capulet: O me, O me! My child, my only life,

Revive, look up, or I will die with thee.

Help, help! Call help!

Enter Capulet

Capulet: For shame, bring Juliet forth; her lord is come.

Nurse: She's dead, deceased, she's dead; alack the day!

Lady Capulet: Alack the day, she's dead, she's dead, she's dead!

Capulet: Ha! Let me see her. Out, alas! she's cold; her blood is settled and her joints are stiff;

Life and these lips have long been separated.

Death lies on her like an untimely frost

Upon the sweetest flower of all the field.

Nurse: O lamentable day!

Lady Capulet: O woeful time!

Capulet: Death, that hath ta'en her hence to make me wail,

ties up my tongue and will not let me speak.

Enter Friar Laurence and Paris, with Musicians

Friar Laurence: Come, is the bride ready to go to church?

Capulet: Ready to go, but never to return.

O son, the night before thy wedding-day

Model answers 355

Hath death lain with thy wife: see, there she lies,

Flower as she was, deflowered by him.
Death is my son-in-law, Death is my heir;
My daughter he hath wedded: I will die

And leave him all; life, living, all is Death's   40

Paris: Have I thought long to see this morning's face,

And does it give me such a sight as this?

Lady Capulet: Accurst, unhappy, wretched, hateful day!

Most miserable hour that e'er time saw

In lasting labour of his pilgrimage!

But one, poor one, one poor and loving child,

But one thing to rejoice and solace in,

And cruel death hath catch'd it from my sight!

Nurse: O woe! O woeful, woeful, woeful day!

Most lamentable day, most woeful day,   50

That ever, ever, I did yet behold!

O day! O day! O day! O hateful day!

Never was seen so black a day as this:

O woeful day, o woeful day!

Paris: Beguiled, divorced, wronged, spited, slain!

Most detestable death, by thee beguiled,

By cruel cruel thee quite overthrown!

O love! O life! not life, but love in death!

Capulet: Despised, distressed, hated, martyr'd, kill'd!

Uncomfortable time, why camest thou now   60

To murder, murder our solemnity?

O child! O child! my soul, and not my child!

Dead art thou! Alack, my child is dead;

And with my child my joys are buried!

Queries for author
Please tell me which edition has been used as the source. There are a number of differences between the sources I have checked, so please advise on the following.

General:	Should words after an exclamation point be lower case, as in IV.v.2 for example, or upper case, as in IV.v.12?
IV.iv.21	Full point and dash or just full point after 'logger-head'?
IV.iv.23	'[Music within]' as shown or on line after 'I hear him near'?
IV.v.11-12	Is there a stage direction here: 'Undraws the curtain'?
IV.v.36, 38, 40, 48, 56	'Death' or 'death' consistently, or as shown?
IV.v.37	My edition shows '… wife. – There she lies.' Please advise which version to use.
IV.v.38	Please confirm missing text is: Death is my son-in-law, Death is my heir;
IV.v.40	Full point or exclamation mark at the end of the line?
IV.v.43	Does your edition show 'Accurst' or 'Accurs'd'?
IV.v.55-6	'Beguiled' or 'beguil'd'?
IV.v.59	'Despised' or 'despis'd'? Note 'martyr'd' in same line.

Instructions for designer/typesetter
SD = stage directions, centred
▓▓ = characters
Turnovers: indent from right

Exercise 5.3

A) Fish risotto

This is one of our family favourites for a light, nourishing, late supper on Fridays after a long and busy week. Sally has the recipe down to a T, and the delicious crunchy texture of the mangetout, with the softness of the rice and fish, blend perfectly with the Asian flavour of curry. Excellent nutrition and a good ORAC recipe too.

Serves 5

2 tbsp rapeseed oil, preferably organic but certainly GM-free

1 garlic clove, finely chopped

1 onion, chopped

2 tsp curry powder

1 small red pepper

225 g (8 oz) arborio rice

450 ml (16 fl oz) Basic Stock (see page 00)

450 ml (16 fl oz) coconut milk

350 g (12 oz) cod fillet or other firm fish such as hake, halibut, monkfish, haddock, fresh tuna or swordfish – or 225 g (8 oz) fish and 110 g (4 oz) cooked, peeled prawns

75 g (3 oz) young mange tout, cut into 1.5 cm (½ in) lengths

225 g (8 oz) canned sweetcorn, rinsed and drained

leaves of 6 sprigs flat-leaf parsley, coarsely chopped

1 Heat the oil in a deep frying pan or saucepan and gently sauté the

358 *Copy-editing*

|onion| and |garlic| until soft – about 5 minutes.

2 Stir in the curry powder, mix thoroughly and cook for 2 minutes.

3 Add the red pepper, stock, |coconut milk| and ~~rice~~ rice, and simmer for 20 minutes, until the rice is tender and nearly all the liquid has been absorbed. Remove from the heat.

4 Break the fish into bite-sized chunks, stir into the rice mixture, mix well and put back on a gentle heat for ~~five~~ 5 minutes, adding more stock if the risotto looks as if it's drying out. Check that the firm fish is cooked: fish with denser flesh, monkfish and tuna particularly, may take a few minutes longer.

5 Add the mange-tout and sweetcorn, and heat through for 2 minutes. Serve the risotto with the parsley on top.

(A) Beef and Couscous Pilaff

Distinct flavours of North Africa enhance this substantial dish. The unique combination of pistachios, beef and spices is what produces the taste, but it's the ~~addition of the~~ peas and dried fruits that bump up the ORAC score. Including generous amounts of fresh mint improves digestion and offsets any fattiness in the beef.

(S) Serves

(L) Scant ½ tsp ground cumin

Scant ½ tsp ground cinnamon

1 tsp ground coriander

225 g (8 oz) lean braising steak, cut into small cubes

2 tbsp rapeseed oil, preferably organic but certainly GM-free

225 g (8 oz) couscous

75 g (3 oz) no-need-to-soak dried apricots, each cut into six pieces

75 g (3 oz) sultanas
700ml (1½ pints) Basic Stock (see page 00)
75 g shelled pistachio nuts
Leaves of 4 large sprigs of mint, chopped

1 Mix the ground cumin and cinnamon and half the coriander.

2 Coat the meat with the spice mixture and set aside.

3 Heat half the oil in a large frying pan, pour in the couscous and cook, stirring continuously, for 2 minutes. Take off the heat and stir in the remaining coriander.

4 Add the dried apricots to the couscous.

5 Boil the stock and add half to the couscous, stir, cover and leave to stand for 10 minutes.

6 Meanwhile, dry-fry the nuts gently for 5 minutes.

7 Fluff up the couscous with a fork and add the rest of the stock.

8 Cook the peas in boiling water for 2 minutes, sprinkle them on top of the couscous and set aside.

9 In another pan, seal the steak, turn down the heat slightly and continue cooking for 8 minutes, or until as well done as you like it, stirring continuously.

10 Add the meat and nuts to the couscous and stir thoroughly.

11 Sprinkle with the mint and serve.

Steamed fish in foil

A brilliantly easy way to cook fish and the healthiest way to cook the vegetables, this recipe produces a finished dish that is high in essential nutrients and has a simple clean flavour.

Serves 4

4 steaks of salmon, halibut or hake

2 small carrots, thinly sliced lengthways with a vegetable peeler

1 orange pepper, deseeded and cut into very fine strips

4 spring onions, sliced lengthways into strands

juice of 1 lemon

150 ml (5 fl oz) dry white wine

50 g (2 oz) unsalted butter

4 sprigs dill

700 g (1½ lb) mixed green leafy vegetables – spinach, chard, cabbage, kale, etc. – coarsely chopped

2 leeks, very finely sliced lengthways

freshly ground black pepper

1 Preheat the oven to 200 °C/400 °F/gas mark 6.

2 Cut 4 pieces of kitchen foil large enough to envelop each piece of fish comfortably. Put each fish steak into the middle of a piece of foil. Add the strips of carrots, pepper and spring onions.

3 Pull up the sides of the foil and pour in the wine and lemon juice. Dot each fish with butter, lay the dill on top, add a twist of freshly ground black pepper and seal the parcels.

4 Place the parcels in the oven and bake for 20 minutes.

5 Meanwhile, put the leafy green vegetables in a steamer and cook until they're just tender but with bite.

6 When the fish is done, pile the green vegetables on individual serving plates. Carefully open one end of each foil parcel and pour the juices over the vegetables. Use a fish slice or spatula to lift the fish, with the vegetables on top, onto the green vegetables, and serve⊙

Recipes adapted from Michael van Straten, *The ORACle Diet*, London, Kyle Cathie, 2002.

Queries for the author
Fish risotto
- Serves how many?
- Is curry powder light, medium or hot?
- How is the red pepper prepared?
- When are the prawns added?

Beef and couscous pilaf
- I have renumbered the steps after 7, but I have used your original step numbers below.
- We will use standard spelling of 'pilaf', OK?
- Serves how many?
- Braising steak: want to change 'small' to 'about X cm'?
- Need peas in the ingredients list: quantity? fresh or frozen?
- Step 3 uses half the oil; when is the remainder used? to seal the steak in step 10?
- Step 5: 'Boil the stock' for how long? or 'Bring the stock to a boil and …'?
- When are the sultanas used? Step 4, or perhaps 11?

Steamed fish in foil
- Preheating the oven is now step 1, and the other steps are renumbered, but I have used your original step numbers below.
- Should the text mention ORAC in the intro, as in other recipes?
- Step 2: Would it be clearer to the reader to say 'dot each fish'?
- Step 3: place parcels on baking tray first or on oven shelf?
- Step 4: How long do the vegetables take to cook? If less time than the fish, shall we say approximately when to start them?
- The leeks are not mentioned in the method: should they be placed in the foil in step 2 or steamed with the other vegetables in step 4?

Instructions for designer/typesetter

GLOBAL
- Fixed space between numerals and abbreviated units in lists; first few marked.
- All paragraphs full out; line space between
- mange tout/mange-tout ⟶ mangetout

CODES
A = recipe title
L = list
S = serves

Exercise 5.4

1

(Front panel:)

The Standard Guide to Cats

Consultant Editor: O. P. Elliott

General Editors: Katrina Brown and Dr Tom Korat

(Spine:)

Elliott, Brown, Korat

The Standard Guide to Cats

Zoo House [and logo]

(Front flap (single photo of cat):)

The Standard Guide to Cats

~~This book has been~~ produced with the cooperation of the Governing

Council of the Cat Fancy in Great Britain and the Cat Fanciers' Association Inc. of the United States.

The first cat reference book that meets the needs of pedigree breeders as well as owners, The *Standard Guide to Cats* has been produced in cooperation with the paramount breed-recognition organizations in the world. The Standards of Points are given for all recognized breeds and colour variations, in the precise wording of the official British and American standards. Each Standard is accompanied by a short history, photographs of top quality show cats and kittens, line drawings to illustrate specific points and coat patterns. A chapter on health care and research, boarding cattery and stud quarters standards a chapter on development and behaviour in the specially commissioned Eye Colour Guide, avoids the distortion of photography and reproduces the correct shades as stated in official standards. Therefore the correct shades artwork, prepared under guidance from the governing bodies. A similar Coat Colour Guide and Coat Pattern Guide are also included.

There is a full index to every breed, colour and veterinary term used in the book.

Ⓐ This unique feature is complemented by

Back flap:

O. P. Elliott is on the Council of the Cat Fanciers' Association Inc., and is a well-known breeder and cat-show judge.

Katrina Brown has been organizing world-class cat shows for more than twenty years, and has written many books and articles, and contributed to many encyclopedias in that time. She is a cat breeder, a stud owner, and an internationally renowned cat-show judge. She is also on the Governing Council of the Cat Fancy, a member of the International Committee of the Cat Fanciers' Association Inc. and a patron of the Cat Clubs in Australia and South Africa.

Dr Tom Korat is a specialist in cat genetics and behaviour and has written several popular books on these subjects, as well as articles for scientific journals. He is also a highly regarded international cat-show judge.

Zoo House

901 The Enclosure

Big City BC1 2EM

www.zoohouse.com

Back panel (5 photos):

The first complete guide to the Standards of Points of more than 300 breeds and colour variations in cats, produced in cooperation with the world's top breed-recognition bodies, the Governing Council of the Cat Fancy in Britain and the Cat Fanciers' Association Inc. of the United States. The 350 illustrations include colour guides to eyes and coats, line drawings of

points and coat patterns, and photos of every breed as a kitten and
adult. This is the essential reference book for pedigree breeders and pet owners.

2

Front cover:

Holy Smoke

Tonino Benacquista

Winner of France's Grand Prix de la Littérature Policière
and the Prix Mystère de la Critique

Spine:

Holy Smoke

Tonino Benacquista

Bitter Lemon Press [and logo]

Back cover:

The Mafia was only the first of Tonio's problems.

Some favours simply cannot be refused. Tonio Polsinelli agrees to write a love letter for Dario, a Paris gigolo. When Dario is found murdered, a single bullet to the head, Tonio finds that his friend has left him a small vineyard east of Naples. The wine is undrinkable but an elaborate scam has been set up. The smell of easy money attracts the attentions of the Mafia and the Vatican and the unbridled hatred of the local people. Mafiosi are not choir boys, monsignors can be very much like Mafiosi.

A darkly comic and iconoclastic tale told by an author of great verve and humour.

'A story of wine, miracles, the mafia, fascists and even love ... Benacquista improves at every outing', *Libération*

'Energy, humour, fast-paced action and florid storytelling', *Le Nouvel Observateur*

Holy Smoke won three prestigious prizes in one year: the Grand Prix de la Littérature Policière, the 813 Trophy and the Prix Mystère de la Critique.

[logo]

Bitter Lemon Press

Crime Paperback Original

£8.99

[barcode attached]

Queries to appropriate colleagues
1 Please supply the ISBN barcode, credit for photos, credit for cover design, price if it is to appear on the jacket.
2 Please supply the credit for the cover design and any images used.

Exercise 6.1

European Investment and Aid in the 1990s

Financial aid

The European Investment Bank (EIB), established in 1958 under Article 30 of the Treaty of Rome, is the European Union's (EU) bank for providing capital investment promoting the balanced development of the Union. In 1991–92 there were only 12 members of what was still the European Community. Up to the end of 1992 the EIB had raised 126 billion ecus (the European Currency Unit at that time) and lent 17 billion ecus. Starting in 1990 the EIB also loaned money to countries in Eastern Europe that were making the transition to market economies, to non-member states in the Mediterranean region, and to the African, Caribbean and Pacific (ACP) states (see Table 1).

Food aid

The EU sends foodstuffs to countries that request assistance in coping with serious food shortages. Emergency aid is also sent to countries devastated by natural disasters or other crises. In 1990 over 1.2 million tons of grain, as well as dairy products and vegetable oils, were sent to sub-Saharan Africa, Asia and Mediterranean countries (see Table 2).

Table 1. Geographical breakdown of loans granted, 1991–92

Area	1991			1992		
	m ecus	%	% of total	m ecus	%	% of total
Within EC						
Belgium	115.6	0.8		396.6	2.5	
Denmark	538.6	3.7		690.8	4.3	
Greece	366.9	2.5		377.5	2.3	
Germany	1,300.1	9.0		1,663.9	10.3	
France	1,924.4	13.3		1,895.1	11.7	
Ireland	236.9	1.6		303.5	1.9	
Italy	4,000.7	27.7		3,796.9	23.5	
Luxembourg	28.9	0.2		42.8	0.3	
Netherlands	175.4	1.2		154.4	1.0	
Portugal	1,002.0	6.9		1,230.4	7.6	
Spain	2,342.5	16.2		3,020.6	18.7	
Total	14,422.4	100.0	94	16,139.7	100.0	94.8
Outside EC						
ACP states	389.5	42.5		252.0	28.2	
Mediterranean countries	241.5	26.4		320.8	35.9	
Eastern Europe	285.0	31.1		320.0	35.8	
Total	916.0	100.0	6	891.8	100.0	
Total loans	15,338.8			17,032.5		

Source: European Investment Bank

Model answers 369

Table 2
Allocation of food aid, 1993 (tons)

Region	Cereals	Milk powder	Butter oil	Vegetable oil	Sugar	Other products (m ecus)
Africa	165,780	927	105	4,900	466	2.615
Caribbean	1,540	-	-	-	-	-
Latin America	66,920	5,945	-	7,345	-	3.380
Mediterranean	110,000	3,000	-	8,000	-	1.0
Asia	155,000	-	-	1,000		
Total direct aid	499,250	9,872	105	21,245	466	6.994
Total indirect aid	845,300	36,890	105	51,639	14,534	39.550
Grand total	1,344,540	46,762	105	72,884	15,000	46,550

(m ecus)
Source: European Commission

Adapted from Dick Leonard, *The Economist Guide to the European Union*, rev. edn, London: The Economist Books Ltd, 1992, pp. 65, 67, 208, 209.

Queries for author
l. 6 More accurate to say 'In 1992'? cf Table 1.
l. 16 Text says 1990, Table 2 says 1993: which is correct?

Table 1
- Please confirm insertion of zeros before decimal points.
- Please supply numerals after decimal points for:
    Portugal 1991
    Netherlands 1992
    ACP states 1992
    Eastern Europe 1991 and 1992
    Total outside EC 1991
- 'Within EC ' 1991 and 1992: figures in columns do not agree with totals or equal 100 per cent. Please check whether there should be entries for UK and/or other countries and provide information
- For 1991 'Total within EC' + 'Total outside EC' does not equal

sum shown in 'total loans'; please check all figures and advise changes.
- 'Total outside EC' 1992: % figures in column = 99.9; add explanation or change figures
  – Should '% of total' be 5.2?

Table 2
- Cereals and other products: in each case the total direct aid is greater than the sum of the column. Please check figures and advise changes.
- Cereals, butter oil, and other products: in each case the sum of total direct aid and total indirect aid does not agree with grand total. Please check figures and advise changes.
- Other products
  – This is only category in ecus; suggest add explanation to text.
  – Mediterranean: please confirm that this is '1.' and add numbers for three decimal places

Table sources: if this is published data, please supply author, title, place of publication, publisher, date, pages

Codes for designer/typesetter
GLOBAL: in tables, change hyphens to en rules

CH = chapter head	TB = table subheads
A = first level subhead	S = source note
T = table	HR = thick rule
TH = table heading	LR = thin rule
TA = table column heads	

Exercise 6.2

At the time of the Boer War there were four military organizations in Britain that men could join: the regular army, the militia, the volunteers and the yeomanry. By 1898 there were 250,000 men in the regular army. Closely connected to it was the militia, a part-time army for home defence. The men in both armies were mainly unskilled workers. However, the yeomanry, which was the cavalry of the militia, drew its members from the rural middle class and aristocracy: men who would know how to ride and might supply their own horses. The volunteers were also part-time but differed from men in the other organizations in two ways: they were mainly skilled working class or lower middle class, and they did not get paid.

In analysing the support for the political parties during the war, it is interesting to see the scale of recruitment to the regular army between 1899, the year the war began, and 1902, when it ended. Table X shows that, following a huge increase in recruitment in 1900, the first full year of the war, the scale of increase was considerably less in 1901 and 1902. ~~According to the statistics in the General Annual Return of the British Army, 1902 and 1903, in 1899 the army recruited 23,259 men with no previous military experience, 16,396 from the militia, and 3045 from the volunteers. Throughout 1900 recruitment rose~~ dramatically: 43,992 raw recruits joined, 23,165 joined from the militia, and 20,962 joined from the volunteers. In 1901 the numbers fell back with only 15,662 coming from the militia, but there were still more recruits with no experience (28,516) and from the volunteers (14,221) than in 1899. The figures for raw recruits was 30,507 in 1902; recruits from the militia rose to 18,992 but only ~~8300 joined the regular army from the volunteers.~~

To understand the impact of the war, we need to ask how many more men joined the army between 1899 and 1902 than would have in peacetime. Calculating on the basis of figures for the preceding two decades, it is estimated that the regular army would have recruited a total of 128,000 men without previous military experience and from the militia, *an increase of 72,489, or just over 36 per cent.* [30]

From M. D. Blanch, 'British Society and the War' in Peter Warwick (ed.), *The South African War: The Anglo–Boer War 1899–1902*, Harlow, Essex: Longman, 1980.

Queries for author
- Capitalize 'Regular Army' or refer to it as 'regular army'?
- Capitalize 'Militia', 'Yeomanry', 'Volunteers'? Are these official names of the organizations or just descriptions?
- Please check new Table X below and suggested changes at end of paras 2 and 3.
- Please supply place of publication, publisher and date of publication for Table X.

[TH] Table X Recruitment to the regular army, 1899–1902 [HR]

[TA] Year	No military experience	From the militia	From the volunteers
1899	23,259	16,396	3,045
1900	43,992	23,165	20,962
1901	28,516	15,662	14,221
1902	30,507	18,992	8,300
Total	126,274	74,125	46,528

[LR] [HR]

[S] Source: *General Annual Return of the British Army, 1902* and *1903*...

Codes for designer/typesetter
TH = table heading
TA = table column heading
HR = thick rule
LR = thin rule
S = source note

Exercise 6.3

Every demand guarantee involves at least three parties, the principal, the beneficiary and the guarantor, and may involve a fourth, the instructing party. The principal is the contractor at whose request the guarantee is issued. The beneficiary is the person or organization in whose favour the guarantee is issued. The guarantor is the bank or other person issuing the guarantee. Almost invariably, the principal and the beneficiary will carry on business in different countries. In a direct (or three-party) guarantee the principal's bank, located in the country where the principal has his place of business, issues the guarantee direct to the beneficiary. Figure 35.11 shows the triangular relationship arising where P, an English contractor, enters into a contract with B in Saudi Arabia for the construction of a plant in Saudi Arabia and arranges for its bank, G Bank, to issue a guarantee direct to B.

But B may wish to have a guarantee from a bank he knows in his own country, and that bank, G Bank, will itself wish to be protected by a counter-guarantee from P's bank, which in this case is termed the instructing bank (IP Bank). This is the indirect or four-party guarantee. At P's request, IP Bank communicates with G Bank and requests it to issue a guarantee in favour of B against IP Bank's counter-guarantee. The counter-guarantee will follow the same pattern as the guarantee and will require IP Bank to pay G Bank on the latter's first written demand and any other specified documents. This four-party structure is shown in figure 35.12.

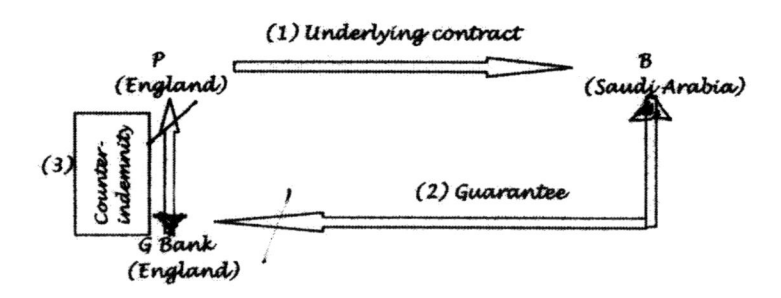

Fig. 35.11 Structure of a three-party demand guarantee

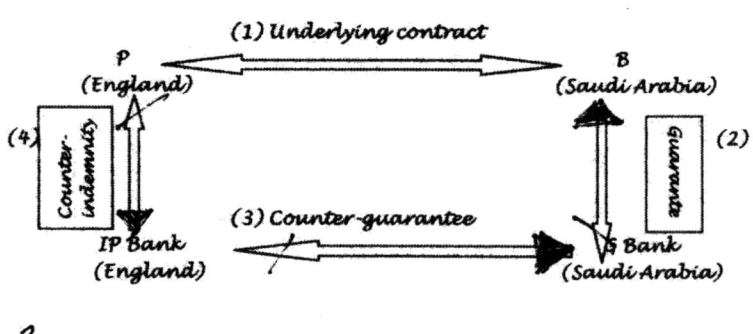

Fig. 35.12

Adapted from Roy Goode, *Commercial Law*, 3rd edn, London, LexisNexis UK, 2004, p. 1021.

Annotation

Fig 35.11
(1) Underlying contract
(2) Guarantee
(3) Counter-indemnity

P (England)
B (Saudi Arabia)
G Bank (England)

Fig. 35.12
(1) Underlying contract
(2) Guarantee
(3) Counter-guarantee
(4) Counter-indemnity
P (England)
B (Saudi Arabia)
G Bank (Saudi Arabia)
IP Bank (England)

Captions
Figure 35.11 Structure of a three-party demand guarantee
Figure 35.12 Structure of a four-party demand guarantee

Queries for author
- Figs 35.11 (3) and 35.12 (4): Is 'counter-indemnity' correct in both cases?

Exercise 6.4

1

The researchers first step was to compare the birth rates in 1976 with those in 1986 to see if there had been any major changes. As Figure 7.3 shows, they found that the annual birth rate for women in most groups had increased, with the largest rise in the group between the ages of 30 and 34. There had been a slight fall in the rate from 108,000 to 96,000 in women between the ages of 20 and 24, and no change in women aged 40 and over. The largest rise, from 54,000 to 72,000, was seen in the group between the ages of 29 and 34, with a smaller but still substantial rise from 17,000 to 22,000 in women 35 to 39 years old.

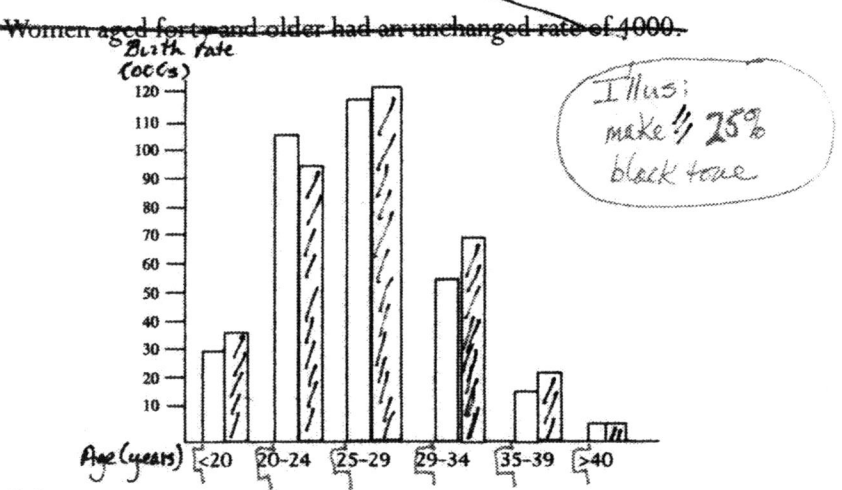

Fig. 7.3

376 Copy-editing

2

Elspeth, Becca and Tiina are pen pals, or maybe that should be e-mail pals, as that is how they communicate with each other most of the time. They are too young to have been able to visit each other yet but each of them is curious about where the others live. Elspeth decided to make a graph showing the average number of hours of sunshine a day each month in Edinburgh. She asked Becca, who lives in London, and Tiina, who lives in Helsinki, to send her the same information about their cities. Look at the graph Elspeth made. Use the information on it to answer the questions below.

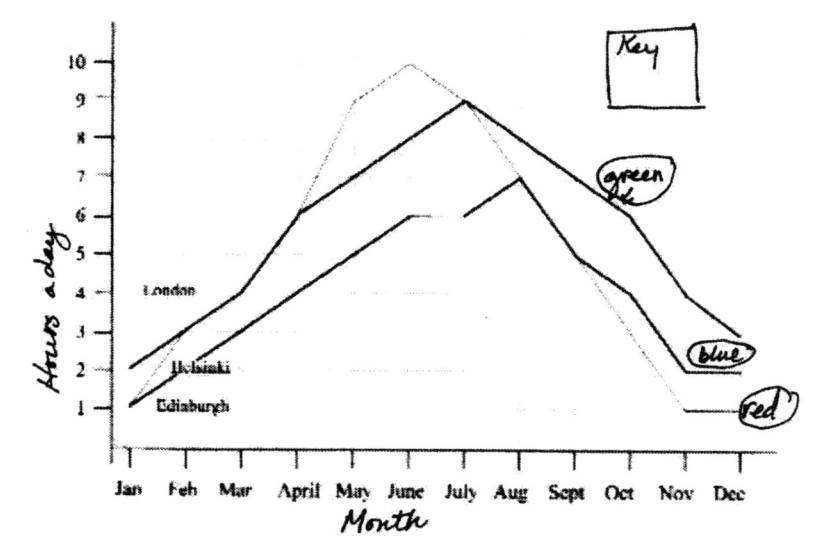

1 Which city gets the most sunshine in a year?
2 Which city gets the least?
3 What is the range of the number of hours of sunshine over the year for each city?
4 What is the total number of hours of sunshine for each city in a year?

Model answers 377

1
(Annotation)
(AA) Birth rate (000s)
(AB) 120 110 100 90 80 70 60 50 40 30 20 10
(AA) Age (years)
(AB) <20 20–24 25–29 30–34 35–39 >40

(Caption)
Figure 7.3 Comparison of birth rates of women in 1976 (light) and 1986 (dark)

Codes for designer/typesetter
AA = axis heading   AB = axis text

2
(Annotation)
(AA) Key
(blue) ——— Edinburgh
(red) ——— Helsinki
(green) ——— London
(AA) Hours a day
(AB) 10 9 8 7 6 5 4 3 2 1 0
(AA) Month
(AB) Jan Feb Mar April May June July Aug Sept Oct Nov Dec

(Caption)
Elspeth's graph

Codes for designer/typesetter
AA = category label   AB = category text

Queries for author
- Please check that line for Helsinki is accurate.
- Suggest using English spelling 'Tina', as text does not make clear that 'Tiina' is Finnish spelling, or use another Finnish name.
- Would a bar chart be clearer? Or is it possible to substitute another place for Helsinki to avoid overlaps, which might be difficult for reader?

Exercise 6.5

He screwed the letter into a ball and threw it angrily to the floor. All right, that was that. Now he had a month, possibly two, to kill. He laughed at the phrase, at its ironic aptness. Throwing his clothes into a suitcase and grabbing his passport, he left. By the time he got to his car he had decided: he would go to France. He'd always wanted to see more of it and now there was nothing else to do. Taking the ferry at Dover, he arrived in Calais in time for lunch, but found little else there to detain him. Accordingly, he proceeded to Lille, where he found a room in a cheap <u>pension</u> and spent a couple of days looking around, eating and trying out his knowledge of the language on the patient locals. Feeling calmer, he decided it might be useful to plan an itinerary, even if he deviated from it as he journeyed. He bought a map and found he actually enjoyed plotting his proposed route. He was very near the border with Belgium and was momentarily tempted to cross over to enjoy a meal of <u>moules et frites</u>. He could even go border-hopping as he moved around France, taking in Germany, Switzerland, and Italy, and later Spain. No, no, no! Damn it, there wasn't *that* much time. Keep it simple. From Lille, he would zig south-west to Amiens, then zag south-east to Rheims, and zig south-west again to Paris. It was the only place in France he'd been to before and he had always thought it was the perfect place to live, love and die. He would stay at least a week and then take a day to dawdle down to Dijon. He would continue south through Besançon and Lyons, taking his time to enjoy each place and particularly its food. Following the course of the Rhône as it made a near-straight path

Model answers 379

between the Massif Central and the Alps, then heading east, *he would stop next in* Aix-en-provence ~~would be his next stop~~. He was not sure how long he would stay in that area or which other towns he would visit; it would depend on how he felt at the time. Certainly, he would avoid the Riviera – those flashy resorts from St-Tropez to Nice held no allure   30
for him now. No, when he was ready to move on, he would go first to Marseille, then follow the rising sun along the coast to Montpellier. Toulouse, on the Garonne north of the Pyrenees, had a nice ring to it; he would go there, then up the river to Bordeaux. From there to Nantes, passing through Limoges for a look at the porcelain museum,   35
then along the Loire to Tours and Orléans. Now he would be following the setting sun. If he timed it right, he could visit Versailles before returning to Paris, that perfect place. Who could tell how long twilight would last?

Queries for author
General   Would it be helpful to use a name for the character in the few places where there is a third-person narrative, e.g. the opening sentence?
ll. 15–16   Suggest 'et' rather than 'and' so that name of dish is entirely in French.
ll. 36–39   Is this intended as a metaphor for death? The character is moving in the opposite direction of the setting sun, so suggest change metaphor or change the route so that the character is moving west.
Map   • Should we change all the place names to French, as he buys the map in France?
            • Cities: suggest show only those character will visit
            • Topographical features: suggest we show only those in France, as others are not relevant to the story.

Brief for cartographer
Map of France showing:
- boundaries with countries to the east and south
- south coast of England
- metric and imperial scale
- only places and features listed in attached annotation

Codes for cartographer
MA = countries   R = rivers
MB = cities   WA = oceans
MT = mountains   WB = bays and channels
                       S = scale

Model answers 381

(Annotation)

(MA) ⎡ England
    ⎢ France
    ⎢ Belgium
    ⎢ Luxembourg
    ⎢ Germany
    ⎢ Switzerland
    ⎢ Italy
    ⎢ Spain
    ⎢ Andorra
    ⎣ Monaco

⎡ Dover
⎢ (MB) Calais
⎢ Lille
⎢ Amiens
⎢ Reims
⎢ Paris
⎢ Dijon
⎢ Besançon
⎢ Lyons
⎢ Aix-en-Provence
⎢ St-Tropez
⎢ Nice
⎢ Marseilles
⎢ Montpellier
⎢ Orléans
⎢ Toulouse
⎢ Bordeaux
⎢ Limoges
⎢ Nantes
⎢ Tours
⎣ Versailles

(WA) ⎡ Atlantic Ocean
     ⎣ Mediterranean Sea

(WB) ⎡ English Channel
     ⎣ Bay of Biscay

(R) ⎡ Seine
    ⎢ Saône
    ⎢ Rhône
    ⎢ Garonne
    ⎣ Loire

(MT) ⎡ Jura
     ⎢ Alps
     ⎢ Massif Central
     ⎣ Pyrenees

(S) ⎡ Scale 0   100 km
    ⎣   0   100 miles

Exercise 6.6

(CH) NEW SCREEN TECHNOLOGIES ON THE HORIZON

Over the last few years we've ~~all~~ seen quite a formidable boost in
monitor technology. The (Liquid Crystal Display) ~~based~~ screens ~~have~~
    LCD   originally
had rather poor picture quality and,   but now
~~come from a point where they~~ were terribly expensive ~~with rather~~

have excellent picture quality and are reasonably priced. The colour gamut of the better LCD screens exceeds that even of a Barco Calibrator CRT (cathode ray tube), the 'Rolls Royce' of monitors within the graphic arts industry. Using the Adobe RGB 1998 colour gamut (one of the suggested working colour spaces in Adobe Photoshop) as a reference, the gamut of a Barco Calibrator only achieves about 77 per cent.

Some of the high-end LCDs from, for example, NEC-Mitsubishi and Eizo reach close to 90 per cent of the Adobe RGB gamut. Both of these manufacturers have hinted that LCD monitors capable of reaching the full Adobe colour gamut will come onto the market early in the new year. So the era of CRTs seems to be over, and the future of the Barco monitors, still widely used within the printing and publishing industry, is uncertain. The Barco showed a prototype LCD screen at Drupa, possibly intended as a successor to the Barco Calibrator, is rumoured to be cancelled.

It seems as if the future lies with the LCDs, since CRT technology doesn't have much scope to go further, but there are other technologies evolving. In fact, even the LCDs differ quite a lot in terms of the technology they use. Most quality colour LCD's use TFT (Thin Film Transistor) technology, which offers a viewing angle of close to 180°, and are back-lit using CCFL (cold cathode fluorescent lamp). There could be a move towards using an LED (light-emitting diode) in the LCD monitors because it may offer even higher luminance and a better spectral distribution of the light for more accurate colours and a larger gamut.

Canon and Toshiba who have cooperated for several years are about to launch a new display technology, SED (surface-conduction electron-emitter display). While closer to CRTs in design, these screens are very slim and they use less energy. An SED-based display can be made just centimetres deep at 42" or more.

Another technology should also be checked if you desire a high performance display. The DLP (digital light processing) technology invented by Texas Instruments, DLP TVs and projectors are said to offer refresh rates that are faster than LCDs and a very large colour gamut. While popular in cinema projection systems and large TVs, the DLT technology hasn't made its way into computer monitors yet.

Plasma screens have an interesting advantage over LCDs. They are said to have a larger colour gamut than LCDs and, perhaps more interesting for proofing

384 *Copy-editing*

applications~~ is that~~ they ma|y have better colour uniformity over the whole monitor surface. The drawback is that they require a fairly low ambient light.

Adapted from 'New Screen Technologies on the Horizon', *Spindrift*, vol. 2, no. 8, Dec/Jan 2004–5, pp. 5–6, by kind permission of the publisher.

Queries for author
- General   OK to vary 'gamut' throughout, e.g. 'range', 'spectrum', or very technical use here?
- l. 13   'high-end LCDs': high in quality or high in price?
- l. 41   'centimetres deep at 42" ': how many centimetres or what is the range?
    OK to change cm to inches to avoid this mixture of imperial and metric measurements?

Exercise 6.7.

(CH) Larks recovering?

Numbers of skylarks have halved but, thanks to your support, we have been able to look at ways to halt their decline. Our news editor Kate Smith reports.

'Skylark numbers are going to recover, there's no doubt about it,' says RSPB research biologist Richard Bradbury. These words are almost as welcome as the skylark's continuous melody, *which,* ~~that~~ to me, signifies the true arrival of Spring, for the number of skylarks in the UK has fallen by more than half since I was a child.

Despite the fall in numbers, the skylark is still one of the most

widely distributed birds in the British Isles. These birds nest on the
ground and prefer open areas of grassland and farmland. One study
on arable farmland in eastern England in the mid-1970's, found up
to 49 males per square kilometre. 'The difference today,' says
Richard Bradbury, ' is that it is possible to go to a field or a farm and
not hear one. That wouldn't have happened before.'

Why have Skylarks disappeared?

'It's something you can't explain simply,' says Paul Donald. 'It is
essentially due to changes in the way cereals are grown in some
parts of the UK.' Cereals support half of the UK's skylarks and
traditionally, they were planted in the Spring, but now they are
often sown in Autumn. This means that by the time the skylarks are
nesting, the crops are tall and dense, the opposite of what skylarks need.

'Winter wheat is too tall by June and this hampers the second and
third breeding attempts that are needed to maintain numbers,' Peter
Robertson tells me. Some skylarks will not nest for a second or
third time, while others are forced into more dangerous areas, such
as the tramlines where tractors are driven. The nests are at risk of
being run over and are more at risk from predators that use
tramlines as paths to cross a field.

Skylarks feed their chicks mainly on insects, but plants and seeds
become their main food in the winter. If crops are sown in the
Spring, then the stubble often remains in the field throughout the
winter. This is an important source of food for skylarks and many
the stalks left after the crop has been harvested

other farmland birds, as they can extract waste grain and seeds growing within the stubble. With the change in planting from Spring to Autumn, there are not as many stubble fields in the Winter now, so food for skylarks might be in short supply.

What Are We Doing To Help?

In April 2000, thanks to the generosity of you, our members, we bought a working farm in Cambridgeshire to try out ways to help skylarks and other farmland birds. 'It is a typical East Anglian cereal farm,' says Roger Buisson, the project manager at Hope Farm. 'It is set in a rolling, open landscape, with some small fields, some large fields and a few ponds and copses. We haven't changed the field size or the number of hedgerows as we wanted to show how you could help wildlife while running a typical commercial farm.'

'It's unreasonable to expect farmers to go back to Spring sowing,' says Peter, 'They plant crops in the Autumn because it gives the plants longer to grow, producing larger yields and generating more income. What we wanted to do was to look at a way of tweaking Winter cropping so that it would help skylarks but not cost farmers lots of money.'

The team at Hope Farm decided to try leaving bare patches of ground in a wheat field so that skylarks would have room to nest. 'This also helps with feeding,' says Roger. 'Skylarks can see around more easily and find food faster, so the chicks will be better fed.'

To leave unsown patches a few metres wide, all the farmer needs to do when sowing the seed is to turn the drill off for a few seconds at various points. Our research at Hope Farm has shown that these unsown patches have a small effect on the total crop yield. The biggest impact for farmers is a bit of extra paperwork, as they have to subtract the area of these patches from the area of wheat field for which they are paid a government subsidy. We are working with the government to make the paperwork easier and to prevent farmers from losing subsidy payments.

'The results from the fields with unsown patches are looking very promising,' says Roger. The number of skylark territories is looking good too. In the Summer of 2000 there were 10 territories on the 180 ha farm; this summer on the same cropping pattern there were 27. Similar results are being seen on other farms, where we are working with industry and government funders, other researchers and farmers to assess the effects of leaving bare patches.

We used unsown patches from the 2001 season onwards. We also tried using wider-spaced rows, leaving a gap of 25 cm between each row of wheat rather than the normal 12.5 cm. 'The results for the wider-spaced rows are not conclusive,' says Roger. 'It's not looking so beneficial, but it's not been disproved either.'

Adapted from Kate Lewis, 'Larks Recovering?', *Birds*, vol. 19, no. 8, Winter 2003, pp 26–32, by kind permission of the publisher.

Queries for author

l. 9	Please indicate numbers then, and date referred to.
ll. 12–13	Please add background information, e.g., research carried out and by whom.
l. 18	Please provide brief description of Paul Donald, as

	for Bradbury
l. 22	Please specify month(s). Is additional copy OK to emphasize point?
ll. 25–6	Please give short description of Peter Robertson.
l. 28	'tramlines': meaning paths created by tractors during sowing?
l. 29	Please give examples of a few predators.
l. 33	Suggest added text is useful addition for our urban readers, OK?
l. 37	Suggest add text like this for reinforcement, OK?

Instructions for designer/typesetter
CODES
CH = chapter head
A   = subhead
S   = strapline

GLOBAL CHANGES (exceptions marked)
Spring → spring
Autumn → autumn
Winter → winter

Exercise 7.1

Highsmith admired Dostoevsky for his rejection of conventional naturalism in favour of a more shocking psychological realism, and there is no doubt that the nineteenth-century author, particularly in his novel Crime and Punishment, had an enormous impact on her work. After reading the novel, she wrote in her diary that Dostoevsky was her 'master'. She said that Crime and Punishment could be read as a story of suspense, an opinion shared by Thomas Mann, who wrote in his introduction to the short novels of Dostoevsky that the book was 'the greatest detective novel of all time'.

The parallels between Crime and Punishment and Highsmith's first published novel, Strangers on A Train, are striking. Like Dostoevsky's anti-hero, Raskolnikov, the two strangers on a train, Bruno and Guy, fantasise about the murders in their minds before carrying out the acts. Indeed, the psychological rehearsals for the killings are so fully imagined that they almost serve as substitutes for the actual murders. As Raskolnikov thinks himself into a state of near hysteria he asks himself, 'If I feel so timid now, what will it be when I come to put my plan into execution?' Similarly, Bruno, while shadowing Guy's wife, Miriam, runs through all the different ways he could kill her before eventually deciding to strangle her. Guy, unable to sleep and eaten away by guilt, visualises how he would murder Bruno's father, leaving a clue so as to incriminate the son: 'he enacted the murder, and it soothed him like a drug.'

Rather than serving as a caricature or stereotype, a flat signal for one aspect of human behaviour, Raskolnikov is an example of the contradictions in everyone – 'One might almost say that there exist in him two natures, which alternately get the upper hand.' Highsmith, who was similarly fascinated by dualism, explores the issue further in Strangers on a Train. Guy, archetype of reason and order, initially views evil as an external force, something distinctly apart and outside of him. He rejects Bruno's belief in the universality of criminal desires – that each of us harbours a potential murderer – but after killing Bruno's father he realises the truth, that 'love and hate ... good and evil, lived side by side in the human heart.' Just as Svidrigailov exists in relation to Raskolnikov, so Bruno serves as Guy's 'cast-off self, what he thought he hated but perhaps in reality he loved'.

Taking her lead from the Russian novelist, Highsmith explored these ambiguities and contradictions, these paradoxes of human consciousness with skill and subtlety. For instance, in Strangers on a Train, when Bruno breaks into an apartment – just for the thrill of it – he takes a table model, a piece of coloured glass, a cigarette lighter. 'I especially took what I didn't want,' he says. At the end of the novel Guy, after his confession to Owen, turns to Gerard, the detective who has heard his every word, and starts to speak, 'saying something entirely different from what he had intended'. The scene alludes to one in Crime and Punishment when Raskolnikov feels he has to unburden himself to Sonya. Like Guy, after his outburst, he realises 'the event upset all his calculations, for it certainly was not *thus that* he had intended to confess his crime'.

Highsmith anchors her novels and stories in reality by listing a cloying number of details – the minutiae of life that carry the reader seamlessly over into the world of the uncanny. Jean-Paul Sartre, in his essay on the fantastic, describes such a technique as one of semiotic excess – 'the innumerable signs that line the roads and that mean nothing' – a method particularly suitable for describing and critiquing the modern world.

Tzvetan Todorov, in his influential book on the fantastic in literature, shows how modern detective stories have replaced the ghostly tales of the past. All works of fantasy literature, he says, share a number of elements: fractured identity, the breakdown of boundaries between an individual and his or her environment, and the blurring of external reality and internal consciousness. These features, he concludes, 'collect the essential elements of the basic network of fantastic themes'.[11] Highsmith's characters, like Dostoevsky's, occupy a paraxial realm, one described by Mikhail Bakhtin in the following terms: 'In Dostoevsky the participants in the performance stand on the threshold (the threshold of life and death, truth and falsehood, sanity and insanity) ... "today's corpse", capable of neither dying, nor of being born anew".[12] Highsmith compels reader to align their point of view with the hero, whose task is to sail us, like Charon, across the dark waters to the other-world of Hades. 'We know that the reader begins his reading by identifying with the hero of the novel,' says Jean-Paul Sartre. 'Thus the hero, by lending us his point of view, constitutes the sole access to the fantastic.'[13]

Notes

1. Thomas Mann. 'Introduction', *The Short Novels of Dostoevsky*. New York: Dial Press, 1946.
2. Fyodor Dostoevsky. *Crime and Punishment*, trs. Frederick Whishaw. London: J. M. Dent, 1911, p. 8.
3. Patricia Highsmith. *Strangers on a Train*. London: Cresset Press, 1950, p. 149.
4. Dostoevsky. *Crime and Punishment*, p. 167.
5. Highsmith. *Strangers*, p. 193.
6. Ibid. p. 194.

7 Ibid., p. 20.
8 Ibid., p. 307.
9 F. Dostoevsky, *Crime and Punishment*, p. 343.
10 Jean-Paul Sartre, *Literary and Philosophical Essays*, trs Annette Michelson, Rider & Co., London, 1955, p. 62. This theme is also developed in Sartre's own fiction.
11 Tzvetan Todorov, *The Fantastic: A Structural Approach to a Literary Genre*, trs R. Howard, Ithaca, NY: Cornell University Press, 19.., p. 120.
12 Bakhtin, Mikhail, *Problems of Dostoevsky's Poetics*, trans. R. W. Rotsel, New York: Ardis, 1973, p. 122.
13 Sartre, *Philosophical Essays*, p. 65.

Bibliography

Bakhtin, Mikhail. *Problems of Dostoevsky's Poetics*, trans R. W. Rotsel, New York: Ardis, 1973.

Dostoevsky, Fyodor. *Crime and Punishment*, trs Frederick Whishaw, London: J. M. Dent, 1911.

Highshmith, Patricia. *Strangers on a Train*, London: Cresset Press, 1950.

Mann, Thomas. 'Introduction', *The Short Novels of Dostoevsky*, New York: Dial Press, 1947.

Sartre, Jean-Paul. *Literary and Philosophical Essays*, trs Annette Michelson, London: Rider & Co., 1955.

Model answers 393

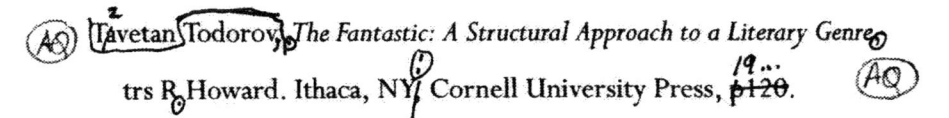

(AQ) Tavetan Todorov, *The Fantastic: A Structural Approach to a Literary Genre*, trs R. Howard. Ithaca, NY: Cornell University Press, 1975. (AQ)

Adapted from Andrew Wilson, *Beautiful Shadow: A Life of Patricia Highsmith*, London: Bloomsbury, 2003.

Queries for author
l. 17   Is there a word missing between 'be' and 'when', such as 'like'?
l. 43   Who is Gerrd? perhaps Gerrard?
l. 53   Include title of essay here or in note?
l. 57   'Tavetan' or 'Tzvetan', as in Notes?

Notes
1   Is Mann the editor of the volume?
    What is the name of the translator?
    Please supply page refs for the Introduction.
11 What is the date of publication?

Instructions for designer/typesetter
• First paragraph full out; subsequent paras closed up and indented.

CODES
R = references heading

Exercise 7.2

(CH) Individual scores and group scores

Finding a sufficient number of tokens of a variable for each speaker did not apparently emerge as a problem in the early urban surveys that followed Labov's 1966 model. This is because figures were usually calculated for groups of speakers rather than for individuals, a practice that seemed to fit in neatly with Labov's theoretical position that the locus of systematic variation was the group rather than the individual. But following Macaulay's (1977) example, linguists have frequently presented figures for individuals, and a number of objections have been raised to the practice of grouping speakers (see particularly Hudson (1980: 163–67) and Romaine (1980: 190)).

There are certainly a number of obvious difficulties that need to be acknowledged: first of all, some groups are extremely small, and where divisions are made on the basis of two speaker variables (such as social class and sex) it may seem a little unreal to label the persons who fall into one of the resulting categories as something along the lines of the 'upper-middle-class female group'. It is hard to see what kind of claims might reasonably be made about linguistic variation expressed as average scores of groups such as these (an additional difficulty being the abstract and contentious nature of social-class labels).

A more general statistical point is that the *mean*, which is the type of average most often used by sociolinguists, is not always the most suitable measure of central tendency within a group; under some conditions the *median* or the *mode* is more appropriate. Measures of central tendency need to be interpreted along with measures of within-group variability — that is, the clustering of individual scores around a typical value. The statistic most often used to measure

within-group variability is the *standard deviation*, although there are
other possibilities. Accessible discussions both of measures of central
tendency and of variability can be found in Butler (1985a, ch 3) and
Erickson and Nosanchuk (1977, ch 3). Since the linguistic
homogeneity of groups can vary considerably it is important for
sociolinguists who aggregate individual scores to use these measures
carefully. In particular, group means need to be used rather more
circumspectly than was thought necessary in the early studies
(Erickson and Nosanchuk 1977, ch 4).

Another reason to be cautious of over-reliance on the mean is that
there are certain important *between-group* differences that a simple
comparison of group means cannot reveal. Sometimes there is little
or no overlap between the scores of individuals in Group A and the
individuals in Group B (see Milroy 1980: 161 for an example), but
more often there is considerable overlap. This distribution,
considered along with within-group variability, tells us quite a lot
about the relationship of *group* scores to *individual scores*, a matter of
some interest to sociolinguists.

Macaulay (1978) has concluded from his Glasgow study that individual scores
do in fact fall into groups in such a way as to allow Glasgow speech to
be characterized as three major social dialects. Guy (1980)
has concluded from his own study of final-stop deletion that
the individual follows the group norm very closely; but since we
know that scores for different linguistic variables are not distributed
within or between groups in a comparable way, we cannot conclude

that all variables will behave in the same way as the syllable-final alveolar stop. In Belfast (Milroy 1980, 121–49) an analysis of variance technique highlighted differences in the distribution of eight different linguistic variables.

References

Butler, C. (1985a) *Computers in linguistics*, Oxford: Blackwell.

Butler, C. (1985b) *Statistics in Linguistics*, Oxford: Blackwell.

Dixon, R. M. W. (1971) *The Dyirbal language of North Queensland*, Cambridge: CUP.

Dixon, R. M. W. and Blake, B. J., eds. (1979) *Handbook of Australian languages*, ANU Press.

—— (1980) *The languages of Australia*, Cambridge: CUP.

Erickson, B. H. and T. A. Nosanchuk (1977) *Understanding data*, Toronto: McGraw-Hill Ryerson.

Guy, G. (1980) 'Variation in the group and the individual: the case of the final-stop deletion', in W. Labov, ed., *Locating language in space and time*, New York: Academic Press.

Hudson, R. A. (1980) *Sociolinguistics*, Cambridge: CUP.

Labov, W. (1966) *The social stratification of English in New York City*, Washington D.C.: Center for Applied Linguistics.

—— (1972b) *Sociolinguistic Patterns*, Philadelphia: Pennsylvania University Press.

—— (1972c) 'Some principles of linguistic methodology', *Language in Society*, 1: 97–120.

—— (1972a) *Language in the Inner City*, Philadelphia: Pennsylvania University Press.

Labov, W. (ed.) (1980) *Locating Language in time and Space*, New York: Academic Press.

—— (1982) 'Objectivity and commitment in linguistic science: the case of the Black English trial in Ann Arbor', *Language in Society*, 11: 165–201.

Macaulay, R. K. S. (1977) *Language, social class, and education*, Edinburgh: Edinburgh University Press.

Macaulay, R. K. S. (1978) *Variation and Consistency in Glaswegian English*, London: Arnold.

Milroy, J. (1980) *Regional Accents of English: Belfast*, Blackstaff, Belfast.

Milroy, L. (1980) *Language and Social Networks*, Oxford: Blackwell.

Romaine, S. (1980) *A critical overview of the methodology of urban British sociolinguistics*, London: Arnold.

—— (1984a) 'On the problems of syntactic variation and pragmatic meaning in sociolinguistic theory, *Folia linguistica*, 18: 3–4, 409–17.

—— (1984b) *The language of children and adolescents*, Oxford: Blackwell.

Adapted from Lesley Milroy, *Observing and Analysing Natural Language: A Critical Account of Sociolinguistic Method*, Oxford, Blackwell, 1987.

Queries for author
l. 40   If italics are used here for 'between-group', should they be used in l. 28 for 'within-group'?
l. 43   Is the reference to L or J Milroy?
l. 46   It is usual to use italics for introducing terms only at first mention, so suggest italicizing 'group' and 'individual' in ll. 7, 8 rather than here.

398 Copy-editing

l. 56   Is the reference to L or J Milroy?

References
Dixon and Blake (1975)   Please provide place of publication.
Guy (1980)   Please provide page references.
Labov (ed.) (1980)   'Locating language in time and space'
                          or 'in space and time', as in Guy
                          (1980) ref?

Instructions for designer/typesetter
- First paragraph full out; subsequent paras closed up and indented.
- Dashes are spaced en rules
- Rules at beginning of lines in references = 3 ems

CODES
CH= chapter heading
R = references heading

Exercise 7.3

[CH] The role of c-Jun and c-Fos expression in androgen-dependent prostate cancer

In 2001, prostate cancer was responsible for approximately 10,000 deaths in the UK, making it the second most common cause of male cancer-related death [1]. Treatment for advanced or metastatic prostate cancer has relied on androgen-deprivation therapy for the past 55 years [2]. Initial response rates to andogen-deprivation therapy are high but patients generally relapse within 12-24 months. [2, 3] When this occurs, the patient is said to have developed androgen-independent

5

prostate cancer (AIPC). Few treatment options offer effective relief for patients who develop AIPC [2, 4]. The lack of novel and effective therapies to treat APIC reflects a poor understanding of the mechanisms underlying development of both the primary disease and, more particularly, those events that drive the development of AIPC.

The activated protein 1 (AP-1) transcription factor, which is involved in the control of cell growth and differentiation, has previously been implicated *in vitro* in the development of AIPC [5-9]. AP-1 is composed of c-Jun and/or c-Fos nuclear proteins, which form either c-Jun/c-Jun or c-Jun/c-Fos dimers. Formation of these dimers requires activation, via phosphorylation, of c-Jun. Cell line studies suggest that this is mediated by protein kinase C (PKC) or MAP kinase [5].

AP-1 can bind the androgen receptor (AR) and this interaction prevents either protein from binding to DNA and hence inhibits both AR and AP-1-mediated gene transcription [5, 10], providing these molecules are present in equal concentrations. Evidence also suggests that AP-1 can bind to and activate transcription of some androgen-regulated genes independently of the AR [5]. The effect of both Ar and Ap-1 in APIC is therefore likely to be dependent both on the ratio of AP-1 to AP and on the ability of Ap-1 to bind independently to specific promoter regions within the androgen-related gene [4, 10]. Thus the relative concentration of Ap-1 to Ar may represent a cellular mechanism for 'switching' between Ar and Ap-1-regulated gene expression. Where AP-1 is present at higher concentrations than AR, it is foreseeable that all AR is bound to AP-1, allowing excess AP-1 to bind to DNA and influence gene expression. 35

In vitro studies have demonstrated that the intracellular concentration of c-Jun and cFos is sevenfold greater in androgen-insensitive PC3 cells than in androgen-insensitive LNCaP cells [5], suggesting that Ap-1 might influence APIC [4, 11]. However, little work has been conducted to investigate the significance of this action *in vivo*. 40

In addition to interactions between AP-1 and AR, there is evidence that the c-Jun monomer may also influence the development of AIPC by functioning independently of AP-1. c-Jun acts as an AR co-activator binding to the N-terminal domain at amino acids 503–555 [12], promoting AR dimerization and gene transcription [6]. This action of c- 45 Jun is independent of c-jun phosphorylation, c-Fos, Ap-1 DNA binding, and AR ligand binding [6, 13]. In AIPC cell lines, transcriptional activation of AR is increased by over-expression of c-Jun [14, 15].

References

1 Cancer Research UK Website. Cancer Stats. Mortality-UK. www.cancerresearchuk.org (2004).

2 Trachtenberg J, Blackledge G. Looking to the future: advances in the management of hormone-refractory prostate cancer. *Eur Urol Suppl* 2002; 1: 44–53.

3 Sumitomo M, Milowsky MI, Shen R, *et al*. Neutral endopeptidase inhibits neuropeptide-mediated transactivation of the insulin-like growth factor receptor–Akt cell survival pathway. *Cancer Res* 2001; 61: 3294–3298.

4   Bonaccorsi L, Muratori M, Carloni, *et al*. Androgen receptor and prostate cancer invasion. *Int J Androl* 2003; 26: 21–25.

5   Sato N, Sadar MD, Bruchovsky N, *et al*. Androgenic induction of prostate-specific antigen gene is repressed by protein–protein interaction between the androgen receptor and AP-1/c-Jun in the human prostate cancer cell line LNCaP. *J Biol Chem* 1997; 272: 17485–17494.

6   Bubulya A, Chen SY, Fisher CJ, *et al*. c-Jun potentiates the functional interaction between the amino and carboxyl termini of the androgen receptor. *Biol Chem* 2001; 276: 44704–44711.

7   Lubahn DB, Brown TR, Simental JA, et al. Sequence of the intron exon junctions of the coding region of the human androgen receptor genes and identification of a point mutation in a family with complete androgen insensitivity. *Proc Natl Acad Sci U S A* 1989; 86: 9534–95̄38.

8   Behrens A, Jochum W, Sibilia M, *et al*. Oncogenic transformation by Ras and Fos is mediated by c-Jun N-terminal phosphorylation. Oncogene 2000; 19: 2657–2663.

9   Shimada K, Nakamura M, Ishida E, *et al*. Requirement of c-Jun for testosterone-induced sensitisation to N-(4-hydroxyphenyl)retinamide-induced apoptosis. *Mol Carcinog* 2003; 36:115–122.

10 Sadar MD, Hussain M, Bruchovsky N. Prostate cancer: molecular biology of early progression to androgen independence. *Endocr Relat Cancer* 1999; 6: 487–502.

11 Wang Q, Lu J, Yong EL. Ligand- and coactivator-mediated transactivation function (AF2) of the androgen receptor ligand-binding domain is inhibited by the cognate hinge region. *J Biol Chem* 2001; 276: 7493–7499.

12 Wise SC, Burmister LA, Zhou XF, *et al*. Identification of domains of c-Jun mediating androgen receptor transactivation. *Oncogene* 1998; 16: 2001–2009.

13 Bulbuuya A, Wise SC, Shen XQ *et al*. c-Jun can mediate androgen receptor-induced transactivation. *J Biol Chem* 1996; 271: 24 583–24 589.

14 Frondal K, Engedal N, Slagsvold T, *et al*. CREB binding protein is a coactivator for the androgen receptor and mediates cross-talk with AP-1. *J Biol Chem* 1996; 271: 24 583–24 589.

15 Tillman K, Oberfeld JL, Shen XQ, *et al*. c-Fos dimerization with c-Jun represses c-Jun enhancement of androgen receptor transactivation. *Endocrine* 1998; 9: 193–200.

Adapted from Joanne Edwards, N. Sarath Krishna, Rono Mukherjee and John M. S. Bartlett, 'The role of c-Jun and c-Fos expression in androgen-dependent prostate cancer', *Journal of Pathology*, 2004; 204: 153–8.

Queries to author
l. 24 　　　　Is AR also mediated?
ll. 38–9　　　Should text read 'greater in androgen-insensitive PC3 cells than in androgen-sensitive LNCaP cells' or is 'androgen-insensitive LNCaP' correct?
References
1　　　　　Is there a specific date accessed?
4　　　　　Please provide initial(s) for Carloni.
6, 8, 9, 14　Have shortened list of authors per house style.

Model answers   403

6, 13   Is author's name 'Bubulya' or 'Bubuuya'?
7   'intron exon' or 'intron-exon'?
13, 14 Different articles but same journal, date, page and line numbers; please check both and provide corrections.

Instructions to designer/typesetter
- First paragraph full out, subsequent paras closed up and indented.
- En rules between numerals; first few marked
- Thin space marked in numerals of more than 4 digits

CODES
CH = chapter title
R = references heading

GLOBAL CHANGES
Ar   ⟶ AR
Ap-1   ⟶ AP-1
APIC   ⟶ AIPC

Exercise 7.4

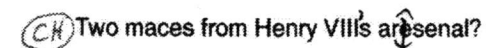

(CH) Two maces from Henry VIII's arsenal?
(CHA) Philip J Lankester

It is well known to students of arms and armour that the Royal Armouries contains a large number of hafted weapons remaining from the armoury assembled by King Henry VIII. Comparison with the inventory drawn up in 1547 reveals that the significant numbers of weapons surviving in the collection today are but a small fraction of the original quantity listed in the

5

various royal palaces. Although some of the sections of the 1547 Inventory dealing with arms and armour were published some time ago, coverage was incomplete, and the recent publication of the whole inventory has provided an invaluable aid to the study of the whole text and the rich quantity of information it contains.

Staff weapons from Italy

It is known that Henry VIII purchased some (long hafted) staff weapons from Italian merchants, that they are likely to have been of Italian manufacture as is suggested by some of their form and their decoration. Quite a number of those surviving in the collections of the Royal Armouries retain their decoration. Some simply have foliage (figure 2); others have human heads (figure 4), animals, secular and sacred human figures or scenes. The decoration is most commonly formed of lines composed of tiny punched dots (pointillé) but in some cases solid line decoration is used.

While the decoration on a few was evidently specially commissioned, such as the four partisans decorated with the Tudor royal arms and a bill with a cipher of letters spelling the name HENRI, the vast majority were probably purchased from merchants as standard items. A few weapons in other collections have decoration that is so similar in form and execution to that found on significant numbers of the weapons from Henry's arsenal in the Royal Armouries that they must at least have been decorated in the same workshop, and the forms of the weapons themselves are often sufficiently close to point strongly to a common place of manufacture. Guy Wilson has drawn attention to a weapon of unusual form (not found in the Royal Armouries collection) in the Museo Civico Medievale in Bologna (see figure 1), which is inscribed LAUS DEO. The foliage decoration compares closely with that on, for example, two partisans in the Royal Armouries, inv. Nos VII.154 (see figure 2) and VII.210. The 'steeple' projecting from the centre of the top border on the Bologna weapon and the wavy lines on the socket are present on VII.154 (though worn) and on many other similar weapons in the Royal Armouries.

It appears that the Holy Roman Emperor, Charles V, purchased weapons with similar decorations: in the Rijksmuseum, Amsterdam, is a corsèque with outward-curving wings, which is similar to several in the Royal Armouries that have been identified as probably corresponding with 'three-grained staves' in the 1574 *Inventory*. It is decorated in pointillé with Charles's badge and motto: the pillars of Hercules and PLUS ULTRA. Henry VIII may even have inadvertently received one of these weapons intended for Charles V, because another corsèque of the same type in the Royal Armouries (VII.838) is decorated with the Imperial eagle, though it has been suggested that this weapon entered the collection at a later date. Further examples of weapons with this type of decoration no doubt exist. A partisan in the Museo Civico Correr in Venice is another possible candidate, though the published illustration does not permit a certain view. It bears and unidentified mark – somewhat resembling a letter I with a crenellated or saw-toothed top – which is found on a number of Italian edged weapons, including some of those from Henry VIII's arsenal in the Royal Armouries, for example on the corsèques or 'three-grained staves'.

Bibliography

Boccia, L. G. Armi antichi dele raccolte civiche Reggiane, Reggio Emilia, Commune di Reggio Nell'Emilia Civici Musei, 1984.

Boccia, L. G. and Coelho, E. T. Armi Bianchi Italiane, Milan, Bramante Editrici, 1975.

Dillon, H. A. 'Arms and armour at Westminster, the Tower, and Greenwich, 1547', Archaeologia, 51, 1888, pp. 219–80.

Norman, A. V. B. and Wilson, G. M. 1982 Treasures from the Tower of London, Norwich, University of East Anglia.

Richardson, T. and Rimer, G. Treasures from the Tower in the Kremlin, Moscow, State Museum of the Moscow Kremlin, 1997, London.

Starkey, D. (ed.) The Inventory of King Henry VIII: I. Harvey Miller Publishers for the Society of Antiquaries of London, 1998.

Wilson, G. M. 'A halberd head from the River Thames', The Second Park Lane Arms Fair, 14–16 February, London, 1985, pp. 15–20.

Adapted from Philip J. Lankester, 'Two maces from Henry VIII's arsenal?', *Royal Armouries Yearbook*, vol. 5, 2000

Notes
1 H. A. Dillon. 'Arms and armour at Westminster, the Tower, and Greenwich, 1547', *Archaeologia*, 51, 1888, pp. 219–80.
2 D. Starkey (ed.). *The Inventory of King Henry VIII: 1*, London: Harvey Miller Publishers for the Society of Antiquaries of London, 1998.
3 A. V. B. Norman and G. M. Wilson. *Treasures from the Tower of London*, Norwich: University of East Anglia, 1982, p. 65, no. 47; pp. 70–1, no. 56; G. M. Wilson. 'A halberd head from the River Thames', *The Second Park Lane Arms Fair, 14–16 February*, London, 1985, pp. 16, 17.
4 Norman and Wilson. *Treasures*, p. 65, no. 47, pl. XII (centre); T. Richardson and G. Rimer. *Treasures from the Tower in the Kremlin*, Moscow: State Museum of the Moscow Kremlin, 1997, pp. 52–3, 174, no. 13, illus.
5 Norman and Wilson, *Treasures*, pp. 68–9, no. 53, pl. XII (right).
6 Wilson, 'A halberd head', p. 20, n. 3; L. G. Boccia and E. T. Coelho. *Armi Bianchi Italiane*, Milan: Bramante Editrici, 1975, p. 417, no. 739, pl.; L. G. Boccia, *Armi antichi dele raccolte civiche Reggiane*, Reggio Emilia: Commune di Reggio Nell'Emilia Civici Musei, 1984, no. 388, illus.
7 Wilson. 'A halberd head', p. 17, pl. 5.
8 Norman and Wilson. *Treasures*, p. 67, no. 49.
9 Ibid.
10 Boccia and Coelho. *Armi Bianchi Italiane*, p. 363, no. 306, illus.
11 For example, ibid., p. 357, nos. 259, 260; p. 362, no. 297; p. 364, no. 308.
12 Norman and Wilson. *Treasures*, p. 67, no. 50, illus.

Queries for author
ll. 19–20   It is usual to have the figures numbered in order of their appearance in the text. Shall we renumber 2 as 1, and 4 as 2?
• What is figure 3 and where should it be inserted?
l. 22   Is 'pointillé' considered an English term in this field, or is it usually italicized?

l. 37   See second query for ll. 19–20: if we renumber the figures, will 1 be 3 or 4?

l. 45   Is 'corseque' considered an English term in this field, or is it usually italicized?
- Which is correct, 'corséque' or 'corsèque' (l. 52)?

l. 58   'a certain view': does this mean 'a particular view' or 'the view in the published illustration is not conclusive'?

l. 59   'a letter I: is this a capital I or a lower-case L?

References

Norman and Wilson	Please confirm Norwich is place of publication.
Richardson and Rimer	Should authors be cited in this order or as Rimer and Richardson? • Is the name 'Rimer' or 'Rimmer'?
Wilson, 'A halberd head'	Is there a named editor of the publication? A named publisher?

Instructions for designer/typsetter
- En rules between ranges of numerals

CODES
CH   = article title
CHA = author
A   = subhead
R   = references heading

Model answers 409

Exercise 7.5

(CH) Index

(N) Numbers in italics refer to illustrations.

acknowledgements 4 153, 154, 157

~~and fair dealing 153~~

see also picture credits

artwork 67-8, 89-91, 90

~~briefing 89-91, 90~~

~~checking 91~~

~~schedule for 67-8~~

see also illustrations

assessing

manuscripts 35, 36-37, 60-63

projects 44-67

the list 7, 8, 9-11

~~author tours 167~~

authors 19-23

accuracy of information from 75

(A&) briefing for 31-2

budget problems created by ~~and changes to proof~~ 76, 125

checking roughs 91

and copy-editing 73-6; see also copy-editing

and copyright see copyright

~~dates for receiving and returning proofs 67~~

explaining contract to 32-3

ideas in search of 22–3

and indexes 78

nurturing 33–5

and picture research 105

query response time 65–6

and revisions to draft manuscripts 23, 37

and schedules 31, 32, 67

submissions from unpublished 20–1

authors and publicity 163, 167

Berne Convention for the Protection of Literary and Artistic Works 149

   see also copyright

binding styles 87

blads

   co-edition sales tool 164–5

   and copy-editing schedule 49, 68, 77

   and picture research schedule 107

   and project schedule 49

blurbs 161, 163–4

briefing 37–9

   artwork 89–91, 90

   authors 22, 31–3

   copy-editors 52–3, 60–3

   covers 162

designers, 85–95

freelancers 137–8

indexers 78–80

photography 91-2

picture researchers 102–6

~~potential authors 22~~

proofreaders 53

budgets 58

creating 25–6. *26*

for freelance work 138–41

principles of 11–14, *12, 13*

revising 27–9

and schedules 13

changes

author's, on proofs 55–6

consult with production before making 123–4

editorial, and authors moral rights 74–5

affecting production 121, 123–4, 126

co-editions 12, 76–7

blads and 164-5

coordinating schedules for 49, 77

editing text for 77

planning of 24

copy-editing 59–80

briefing 52-3, 60-3

co-editions 76–7

principles of 76–7

and proofreading 3

412 Copy-editing

copyright 145-52
　Berne Convention for the Protection of Literary and Artistic Works 149
　duration of, in different countries 146-7, 149, 153
　~~duration of literary, dramatic and artistic work in the UK and USA 146-7~~
　and fair use 151–3
　giving notice of 148
　infringement of ~~copyright~~ 150, 153
　ownership of rights 149–52
　Universal Copyright Convention (UCC) 149
　copyright act 1997 (USA) 145
　copyright, designs and patents act 1988 (UK) 145
　moral rights and 151
covers and jackets 49, 92–5, 161–5
　~~briefing for 162~~
　information on 163
　and marketing and sales 161–3
　schedule for 49
　~~cover approval meetings 161–2~~
credits, picture *see* picture credits

Cross checks
illustrations
picture credits
Universal Copyright Convention

Queries for indexer
• authors: need subentry for 'potential'
• ref for 'authors, briefing' = 31–2; refs for 'authors' under

'briefing' = 31–3; please check.
- 'budgets': add subentry 'problems'? cf. under 'authors'
- 'changes, author's': add 76, 125, as 'authors, budget problems'?
- 'co-editions': delete existing sunentries or add subentries to specify topic on pp. 12, 76-7, and add subentry 'blads and'?
- 'copy-editing': add page refs from 'briefing'?
  – break down '59–80' intomore specific subentries.

Instructions for designer/typesetter
- Main entries full out
- Subentries on new line, as typed; indented 1N from margin
- All turnovers indented 1M from margin
- Line space between alphabetical sections

CODES
CH = chapter-weight heading
N   = note

Resources

General

These are the minimum resources you need. Depending on the field in which you work, you might also require specialist reference works. Everyone should have their own copy of a dictionary and, ideally, *NODWE (see below)*. Copies of other books can be shared if they are kept within easy reach of everyone who needs them; if you work alone, invest in your own copies. Some resources are available online, but might not be cost-effective for your needs.

English dictionary
You need it to check spellings and definitions. Most organizations designate a specific dictionary, so that all their publications use the same spellings. The English language is always growing and changing, so make sure you have an up-to-date edition.

Foreign-language dictionaries
Authors often include words and phrases from other languages. A few will be found in English-language dictionaries and in *NODWE* (see next title), but it is very useful to have, at least, concise French and German dictionaries for checking spelling and accents.

The New Oxford Dictionary for Writers and Editors. Oxford, Oxford University Press, 2005
Use *NODWE* to check more specialized information, such as hyphenation, abbreviations, use of italics, foreign words and phrases, spelling of names of people and places.

Dictionary of word division/spelling dictionary
A quick way to check spelling, hyphenation, and where to break words when necessary at the end of a line of type. Handy for copyeditors and writers, and essential for proofreaders.

Thesaurus
Helps you to help the author avoid undesirable repetition of words. Printed versions are more wide-ranging than the ones supplied with word-processing programs.

Biographical dictionary
Does the text refer to the right person? Check the spelling, the dates and the description. You can search for names online, but it's probably faster to use a book, which will also show you other people with the same or similar names and thus help you resolve your query.

Dictionary of phrase and fable
In 2005 Oxford University Press published the second edition of *The Oxford Dictionary of Phrase and Fable*, and Weidenfeld & Nicolson published the seventeenth edition of *Brewer's Dictionary of Phrase and Fable*. Both provide the meaning and history of thousands of words and phrases not found in a conventional dictionary, and biographical sketches of real people and fictional characters throughout history. There are other volumes that concentrate on a particular country or time period. All of these books are entertaining to read as well as useful for research.

Companion to English literature
Make sure the title of the work is quoted accurately, that the author's name is spelled correctly, and that the dates for both are right. If you search online, make sure your source is authoritative.

World atlas
Use the gazetteer to check spelling, and the maps to check location, distances and directions. The spelling of place names transliterated from non-Latin alphabets can vary, so a particular atlas is usually specified for a consistent house style.

Encyclopedia
Depending on what kind of material you are editing, you might need a specialist or a general encyclopedia, and either might be paper-based or online. Use it to check basic information about which you are not sure. Make sure online sources are authoritative, not merely a collection of opinions posing as facts. When the information differs from

that in your author's text, remember to ask the author to confirm or reject it; the author might be more accurate or up to date than your source.

Dictionary of quotations
Complete works of Shakespeare
The Bible
These are the sources of frequent quotations in books on any subject, in fiction and non-fiction. Some authors quote from memory. When you suspect an inaccuracy, you can use these to check the quote itself and the attribution to the source. When you check quotes from the last two sources, make sure you are using the same edition or version the author has used. As always, ask the author to confirm any change you plan to make to the text as a result of your research.

Style manuals

All copy-editors have at least one of the following manuals. Many editors and proofreaders have more than one, so that they get consensus where it exists and different points of view otherwise. I certainly recommend this approach. These are not the only manuals, but the ones I can personally recommend. There are also specialist manuals for different subject areas.

Butcher, Judith, Drake, Caroline and Leach, Maureen,
Butcher's Copy-editing: The Cambridge Handbook for Editors, Copy-editors and Proofreaders, 4th edn, Cambridge, Cambridge University Press, 2006.
Butcher's began as a house-style guide and soon became a general style guide for copy-editors working in British English. I do not know a copy-editor who doesn't own it and rely on it.

Chicago Manual of Style, 15th edn, Chicago, University of Chicago Press, 2003.
The pre-eminent American style guide, it has a wealth of informative detail and is valuable for those editing works in American English. It

includes a chapter on American English grammar and usage by Bryan A. Garner (see below).

The Economist Style Guide, 9th edn, London, Profile Books, 2005.
The first part of this volume is a dictionary of usage and style based on the house style of *The Economist*. The second part compares American and British English, and the third part is an alphabetical directory of information, ranging from abbreviations to the time of day around the world.

New Hart's Rules, Oxford, Oxford University Press, 2005.
Originally for compositors, this little book became the first style guide for editors. It was temporarily replaced by *The Oxford Guide to Style*, but has now resurfaced in its original format. It has been completely revised, and for this reason is styled 'new' rather than being the fortieth edition.

English usage and writing style

The following books are just a few of the many available. The titles are self-explanatory. I think that *The New Fowler's Modern English Usage* and *The Elements of Style* are essential, and I wouldn't want to be without *Troublesome Words*. Take the time to make the acquaintance of the others, as well as the many grammar reference books available, and then decide which ones suit your needs and speak to you clearly. If you are reading this book many years after its publication, look for the most recent edition of each title.

Bryson, Bill, *Troublesome Words*, 3rd edn, London, Penguin, 2002.
A concise, straightforward guide to usage, it has an appendix on punctuation and a glossary of grammatical terms.

Burchfield, R. W. (ed.), *The New Fowler's Modern English Usage*, 3rd edn, Oxford, Clarendon Press, 1996.
Not only explanations of accepted usage of words now but also the history of that usage, examples of correct and incorrect ussage, and, sometimes, comments on what the usage is likely to be in the future.

Carey, G. V., *Mind the Stop: A Brief Guide to Punctuation*, new edn, Harmondsworth, Penguin, 1971.

Garner, Bryan A., *A Dictionary of Modern American Usage*, New York and Oxford, Oxford University Press, 1998.
It *is* another language in many ways. You might have learned a lot about American English from watching American films and TV programmes and reading American publications, but if it's not your native language and you are editing for the American market, you really want this book.

Gowers, Ernest, *The Complete Plain Words*, 3rd edn, rev. Sidney Greenbaum and Janet Whitcut, Harmondsworth, Penguin, 1986.

Partridge, Eric, *Usage and Abusage: A Guide to Good English*, 3rd edn, rev. Janet Whitcut, London, Hamish Hamilton, 1994.

Strunk, William and White, E. B., *The Elements of Style*, 4th edn, London, Longman, 2000.
This delightful little book is a great guide to clarity of composition and ways to avoid grammatical pitfalls.

Copyright guides

Flint, Michael F., Thorne, Clive D. and Fitzpatrick, Nicholas, *A User's Guide to Copyright*, 6th edn, Haywards Heath, Tottel Publishing, 2006.

Jones, Hugh and Benson, Christopher, *Publishing Law*, 3rd edn, Routledge, 2006.

Production

Bann, David, *The All-New Print Production Handbook*, RotoVision, 2006.
An excellent book that will tell you about the entire production process, from pre-press through finishing. The illustrations will show you some things you might otherwise not have an opportunity to see, and the very useful glossary is extensive.

Organizations for editors in Europe

Association of Freelance Editors, Proofreaders and Indexers

www.afepi.ie
For individuals in Ireland.

European Association of Science Editors (EASE)

www.ease.org.uk
Despite its name, EASE has members throughout the world and in many different publishing-related disciplines. It offers a quarterly journal, an editor's handbook, an electronic forum, a conference every three years, and seminars and workshops.

National Union of Journalists (NUJ)

www.nujbook.org/freeln01.htm

Society for Editors and Proofreaders

www.sfep.org.uk
This non-profit-distributing organization has the twin aims of promoting high editorial standards and achieving recognition of the professional status of its members. Membership is open to freelancers and employees. The benefits include regular newsletters, local group meetings, an annual national conference, training courses, an accreditation scheme, an electronic forum, and an online directory.

Society of English-Native-Speaking Editors (SENSE)

www.sense-online.nl
For editors working in the Netherlands. The more accurate phrase 'Native-English-Speaking' would not make as neat an acronym.

Society of Indexers

www.indexers.org.uk
The professional body for British and Irish indexers. Contact the

Society to find appropriate indexers, for information about indexing and for links to related sites.

Organizations for editors outside Europe

Australia

Society of Editors (NSW) Inc.: www.editorsnsw.com
Society of Editors (Queensland) Inc.: www.editorsqld.com
Society of Editors (South Australia) Inc.: www.editors-sa.org.au
Society of Editors (Tasmania) Inc.: www.tas-editors.org.au
Society of Editors (Victoria) Inc.: www.socedvic.org
Society of Editors (Western Australia) Inc.: www.editorswa.com

Canada

Editors' Association of Canada (EAC): www.editors.ca
Association canadienne des réviseurs: www.reviseurs.ca

Hong Kong

Women in Publishing Society: www.hkwips.org

South Africa

Professional Editors' Group: www.editors.org.za

United States of America

Editorial Freelancers Association (EFA): www.the-efa.org

Training organizations in Britain and Ireland

Clé: the Irish Book Publishers' Association

www.publishingireland.com
A cross-border organization providing services and training. Membership is open to publishers, and associate membership to individuals working in the industry.

Publishing Scotland

www.publishingscotland.org
Provides services, training, events and a forum for discussion for companies, organizations and individuals in the publishing industry in Scotland.

The Publishing Training Centre at Book House

www.train4publishing.co.uk
PTC offers a wide range of open and distance-learning courses that will help you continue to develop your career. The website also provides a link to the National Occupational Standards, where you will find out what the industry thinks people in the various publishing disciplines need to know and be able to do to be considered competent.

Other useful websites

http://whatis.techtarget.com
A website providing, amongst other things, definitions of computer technology terms.

http://blpc.bl.uk/catalogues/listings.html
Online access to the British Library catalogues.

http://copac.ac.uk
Copac® is a union catalogue. It provides free access to the merged online catalogues of 24 major university research libraries in the UK and Ireland plus the British Library, the National Library of Scotland, and the National Library of Wales.

www.loc.gov/z3950/gateway.html
Online access to the American Library of Congress catalogue.

www.paperlessproofs.com
Software for marking PDFs with standard symbols.

Index

Page references in *italics* refer to illustrations.
Page references with 'g' after the number refer to the glossary.

A
abbreviations 57, 103, 221
  of journal titles 238, 242, 252
  list of 93, 238
  in notes 231
  p. and pp. 239
  of plant names 128
  in references 231, 258
  in tables 191
  for units of measurement 136, 175
acknowledgements
  of copyright material 106, 109, 206
  position of, for displayed poetry 159
  in prelims 93
  see also credits; picture credits
active vs passive voice 147–8, 155
addressees, style for 54–5
addresses, numbers in 137
  see also numbers; numerals
adjectives
  capitals for 118
  and commas 51
  compound, style of 62
adverbs 52, 54
affiliations, authors' 89, 90, 92
agency notice 85
agreement in number *see* subject–verb agreement
aircraft names, style for 126
'all rights reserved' clause 84, 88
  see also copyright; imprint page
alphabetization
  in bibliography 242

  in indexes 271, 272, 279
American style
  for abbreviations and contractions 57
  for collective nouns 38
  for dash 65
  for dates 137–8
  for use of quotation marks 68
animals, classification of 127–8
annotation (anno), presentation of 205, 215
annual reports *see* company reports
anthologies
  copyright in 107
  indexes for 271
  of poetry 158
apostrophe, use of 65–6, 138
appendices 95, 100
apposites 53–4
  see also clauses; sentences
art works, style for titles of 118, 119
articles, titles of
  capitals for 119
  quotation marks for 126
  in references 232
artwork *see* illustrations; technical figures
ASCII files, marking up 4–5
asterisks, use of 195, 233, *234*
atlas 207, 219, 412
author
  attribution to 19, 82, 89, 90–1, 92
  and copyright ownership 104–6
  moral rights of 84–5, 105

423

author – *continued*
  names in bibliography 240–1
  queries to *see* queries to author
  voice of 35–6, 37, 40, 148; *see also* voice
author–date system (Harvard system) 249–57, *249*
  see also reference systems
author–number system (Vancouver system) 257–60, *259*
  see also reference systems
author–title system 230–49, *241*, 250
  see also reference systems; short-title system
axes on graphs 209–10

B
B format 78
bacteria, style for names of 128
bar chart 210–11, *211*
  see also diagrams; graphs; illustrations; maps
Berne Convention for the Protection of Literary and Artistic Works 104
  see also copyright
Bible, references to *232*
biblio *see* imprint page
bibliography
  editing 240–2, 251–3, 259–60
  using em rules in 65
  see also reference systems
binding, types of 77–80, 108, 288g
biological names, style for 125, 127–8
blasphemy 114
bleed 2, 288g
blurb 78, 81, 99, 146, 181–2
board books 77, 82
book block 79–80
book style xxiv
brackets *see* parentheses; square brackets
brand names 116

briefs 288g
  for cartographer 219
  following and preparing xiv, xvi, 35, 147, 219
  for indexer 270, 276–8
  and references 238, 248
British Standard *Marks for copy preparation and proof correction* (BS 5261-2: 2005) ix, xxi
broadcast programmes, style for 68, 128
brochures 36, 79
BS 5261-2: 2005 *see* British Standard *Marks for copy preparation and proof correction*
budget 219, 240, 248
bullets for lists 27, 28–9, 29, 33, 175
  see also lists

C
capitals
  for adjectives and verbs 118
  for chapter titles 119, 250
  for compass points 119
  on contents page 89, 99
  in indexes 274
  marking up for 9–10, *10*
  for pronouns 118
  for proper nouns 115–17
  for rank and title 117
  in titles of works 118, 124–5
caps *see* capitals; small caps
captions 92, 93, 126, 190, 206, 209
cardinal numbers 137–8
  see also numbers; numerals; ordinal numbers
cast list 165
catalogues, purpose of 146
Cataloguing in Publication Data (CIP) 85, 88
chapter titles
  capitals for 119, 250

on contents page 89, 99
  in references 232
characters in fiction
  and libel 113
  and passing off 112
  in plays, style for 165–7
  and punctuation 54–5, 57
  sample style sheet for *xxv*
  voice of 34–5, 37, 41, 42, 64
children's books 77, 220
  numbers in 140
  prelims in 81, 82, 99
chronology, position of, in prelims 93
CIP *see* Cataloguing in Publication Data
clarity
  in tables and figures 188, 194, 204, 214
  of text 37, 38, 64, 125, 126
clauses 51–3
club line *see* orphan
code sheet 16, 17, 29
codes 3–4
  for displayed quotations 4, 16–18
  in electronic copy 4–5
  for headings 91
  for lists 29
  for poetry 19, 158–9
  in stage directions 167, 173
  for tables 198–9
  see also code sheet
colon 56, 64
  in index 274, 276
  in references 250
  in speech 55, 165
colophon *see* logo
columns
  alignment of, in tables 3
  on grids 3
  headings for, in tables 190–1
comb-bound books 77, 80
commas
  with adjectives 51
  with adverbs 54

apposites set off by 53–4
between clauses 51–2
interjections and 54
inverted *see* quotation marks
serial 50–1
with speakers and addressees 54–5
commissioning editor xv, 1
company reports 26, 34, 137, 146, 219
compass points, style for 119
conditions of sale paragraph 87
conjunctions
  at the beginning of sentences 37
  in indexes 271, 275
  style for, in titles 9, 119, 250
  and subject–verb agreement 38–9
contacts, network of xv–xvi, *xv*
contents page
  and folios 80
  information on 89–91, 92, 93, 95, 96
  in journals 83
  and running heads 100
contracts, author xviii
cookery books
  indexes in 271
  and intended readers 146
  lists in 26, 33, 174
  style for instructions in 175
  units of measurement in 174
  see also manuals
copy-editing marks xxi, xxii
  see also British Standard *Marks for copy preparation and proof correction*
copyright 80, 93, 103–14
  duration of 103–4, 105–6
  infringement of 109–10
  notice 84
  ownership 104
  see also Berne Convention for the Protection of Literary and Artistic Works; Copyright, Design and Patents Act (1988); passing off;

426 Copy-editing

copyright – *continued*
  Universal Copyright Convention
  Copyright, Designs and Patents Act (1988) 84–5
  see also copyright
covers xx, 77–80, 289g
  design of, and passing off 112
  editing copy for 181–2
  ISBN on 86, 181
credits 78, 86–7
  see also acknowledgements; picture credits
cross-references
  in indexes 273–4
  italicization of 125
  numbers and 7, 190
cultivars, style for names of 128
cutting and expanding 219–21, 224, 228–9

D
dangling participle 41–2, 218
dashes
  and note cues 238
  in quotations 67
  style of 64–5
  and subordinate clauses 52
dates, style for 137–8, 140
decimal numbers 139
decked headings 191, *192*
  see also tables
dedication 88, 89
  see also prelims
definite article, capitalization of 119
degree symbol, use of 136
design xiv, 78
designers xvi, 1–2
diagrams 93, 206–7, *206*, *207*
  see also graphs; illustrations; maps
dialogue *see* speech
dictionaries 115, 146
  biographical 62
  contributors to 92

foreign words in 128–9
running heads in 100
disclaimers 109
diseases, style for names of 128
displayed
  headings 190
  lists 25–7, 29, 33
  marking up for, matter *18*, 76
  note cues and, quotations 233
  poetry 19, 158–9
  quotations 16–19
document map 5
drawings *see* technical figures
dust jacket 78

E
e-file(s) xviii, 289g
  and global changes 124
  indexes as 278
  keying in on 197
  marking up prelims in 81–3, 88–9, 91
  marking up text in 4–5, 18, 19, 94
  marking up verse in 19, 159, 166
  and references 236–7, 238, 260
  style menus for 167
edition number 78, 82
electronic copy *see* e-file(s)
ellipsis 72–3, 158
em 289g
  rule 61, 65, 76, 242, 251
en 289g
  rule 61, 63–4, 76, 140
encyclopedias 36, 92, 100, 270
endmatter 289g
  contents of 95–6
  running heads in 100
  see also endnotes; index; notes; reference systems
endnotes 233, *236*
  running heads for 100–1
  see also endmatter; notes; reference systems
endpapers 79

epigraphs 19
  location of 89, 94
  marking up 20
even working 80, 220, 274, 289g
exclamation mark 56, 57
extracts *see* quotations

F
fair dealing 106
false attribution 105
fiction 34–5, 204
  capitalization in 116, 118
  characters in 37
  consistency in167
  lists in 25
  notes and references in 230
  numbers in 134
  page extent in 220
  running heads in 101
  style sheet for xxiv, *xxvi*
  voices in 35, 37
figures *see* illustrations; technical figures
films, style for titles of 119
flaps on jacket 78, 79
folios 2, 100, 289g
  in prelims 80–1
  see also page numbers; pagination
font/fount 2, 17, 87, 289g
foods, capitals for 118
footnotes 233–5, *234*
  marking up 20
  see also endnotes; notes in tables; reference systems
foredge margin 2, 289g
foreign words, style for 125, 128–9
foreword 78, 82, 90–1, 92
formal style 26, 34, 37, 148
format 78, 214, 276, 290g
format publishing 2
fount *see* font
fractions 137
front matter *see* prelims
frontispiece 81, 89

full stop 56–7, 60, 72–3
further reading 96, 99, 240

G
gardening books, index for 271
gender problems in third person singular 39–40
genealogical diagrams 93
  see also technical figures
generic names 118
genus, style for name of 127
grammar 34–50
graphs 134, 137, 209–14, *210*, *211*
  see also diagrams; illustrations; maps
grid in page design 1, 2, 3

H
half-title 81
  see also prelims
half-title verso 81, 88
  see also prelims
hardback covers 77–8
Harvard system *see* author–date system
headings
  for acts and scenes in plays 165
  and contents page 89
  decked, in tables 191
  hierarchy of 5–8
  levels of 5–8, 147, 148
  marking up 5
  numbering 7–8
  type spec for 9
  see also tables, headings for
headline *see* running heads
historical eras, capitals for 115
homographs 63
hormones, style for names of 128
house style xxiii–xxiv, 16, 27, 35, 36, 51, 117, 129, 158
hyphens 61–3, 76, 265

I
ibid. 231, 250

illustrations
  bleed of 2
  copyright in 84, 105, 107
  credits for 78, 89, 91–2
  see also photographs; technical figures
illustrators, name of, in prelims 82
images *see* illustrations; photographs; technical figures
imperial units *see* units of measurement
imprint page 82–3, 86, 88
  see also prelims
indecency in publications 113
indexers xvi, 270, 276–7, 278
indexes xiv, xix
  to anthologies 271
  changes affecting 277
  checking 278–9
  commissioning 276–8
  in contents page 90
  copyright in 84–5, 105, 278
  cross-references in 273–4, 278–9
  editing 278
  to journals 279
  layout of 275–6, *275*
  length of 274, 278
  marking up 279–80
  organization of 271–4, *272*
  passing mentions in 277
  style issues in 274–6
  subentries in 271, 272–3, 276–80
  types of 271
informal style 34, 35, 134, 148, 221
infringement of copyright 109–10
  see also copyright
ingredient lists 33, 174, 180
instruction books *see* manuals
interjections, punctuation of 54
International Organization for Standardization (ISO) 85
International Standard Book Number (ISBN) 78, 79, 80, 85–6, 88

International Standard Music Number (ISMN) 86
International Standard Serial Number (ISSN) 79, 80, 86
Introduction, pagination of 94
inverted commas *see* quotation marks
ISBN *see* International Standard Book Number
ISMN *see* International Standard Music Number
ISO 5776 (international standard) xxi
ISO *see* International Organization for Standardization
ISSN *see* International Standard Serial Number
issue number of journal 79, 80, 82, *232*
italics 68, *127*, 134, 290g
  added to quotation 67
  for biological names 127–8
  for foreign words 128–9
  for legal cases 126
  for names of means of transport 125, 126
  for stage directions 166
  for titles of works 119, 126

J
jacket xx, 77, 78, 86, 290g
  editing copy for 181–2
journals 1, 5, 7, 9
  binding of 79
  contents page in 83, 90, 91
  cover of 79
  imprint page in 83
  indexing of 279
  ISSN for 79, 80, 86
  issue number of 79, 80, 82, *232*
  and passing off 112
  prelims in 80
  running heads and feet in 101
  titles of 238, 250
justified text 290g

and fixed space 136
and hyphenation 61

K
key for artwork 205
keying in figures 197, 205

L
labels on artwork *see* annotation
languages, capitalization for 118
Latin names in classifications, style for 10, 127
law books 235, 271
layout 290g
  of indexes 275–6, *275*
  of lists 26, 28-9
  of poetry 157–9, 166
  of quotations 17, 19
  of tables 189, *189*, 191–2, *192*, *193*, 194–6, *196*
leaflets 36, 146
legal cases, style for 125, 126, *232*
legal matters 112–14
  see also copyright
level
  lowering and raising 147–8
  purpose and 145–6
libel xiv, 113
  see also legal matters
limp-bound books 78, 79
  see also binding, types of
line breaks in poetry 158, 166
  see also poetry
lining figures (numerals) 139, 291g
lists
  of contributors 92
  embedded 25–6
  of illustrations 91–2
  of ingredients 174
  marking up 25–33, *29*
  numbered 26
  punctuation of 50–1, 56
  serial comma in 50
  style of displayed 26–9, *28*–*9*

symbols in 27
of tools and materials 174
locators in indexes 272–4
see also indexes
logo 77, 78, 82, 87, 181
looseleaf binding 77, 80, 173
  see also binding, types of

M
magazines *see* journals
main clauses 51–2
  see also apposites; sentences; subordinate clauses
manuals 26, 173–5
  see also cookery books
maps 110, 215–19
  see also diagrams; graphs; illustrations
margins 2
marking up xviii, xix, *xxii*, *xxiii*, 1–2, 291g
  capitals 9–10, *10*
  code sheet 16, *17*
  contents page 91
  electronic copy 4–5, 81
  footnotes 20
  hard copy 3–4
  headings 3, 5–7
  lists 25–7, 29, *29*
  plays 167
  poetry 158–9
  prelims 81–7
  quotations 4, 17–20, *18*
  running heads 102
masthead 80, 83
  see also imprint
measurements *see* units of measurement
metric units *see* units of measurement
modifiers, misplaced 42
moral rights 84–5, 88, 105
  see also copyright
multi-contributor books 89, 240–1, 250

N

newsletters 1, 5, 36, 146
newspapers, styke for titles of 119
nobility, style for titles of 117, 138
non-lining figures (numerals) 139, 291g
notes
　editing 235–8
　editorial 230, 233
　mark up for 236
　presentation of 234–5
　references in *see* reference systems
　in tables 195–6
　see also endnotes; footnotes; reference systems
nouns
　agreement in number with verbs 38–40
　capitals for 115–17
　indefinite 39–40
numbering
　acts and scenes 165
　captions 214
　chapters 89, 91, 94
　headings 7–8
　notes 234, 236
　pages 94
　paragraphs 137
　parts of a book 89, 90, 94
　prelims 80–1
　of tables 198
　see also pagination
numbers
　cardinal 137–8
　imprecise 135
　ordinal 138–9
　for periods of time 138
　precise 136
　ranges of *see* ranges of numbers
　style and punctuation of 139
　as words or numerals 134–5
　see also folios; page numbers
numerals
　elision of, in ranges 63–4, 140, 272
　four-digit, and over 139–40
　lining and non-lining 139, *288*, 291g
　in tables 194
　see also numbers; ranges of numbers; tables

O

objectivity, vocabulary and 148
obscenity 113
op. cit., use of, in notes 233
ordinal numbers 138–9
　see also cardinal numbers; numbers; numerals
orphan 229, 291g
Oxford comma 50–1

P

page numbers
　on contents page 91
　in references 241
　see also folios; pagination
pagination 94, 279
　see also folios; page numbers
paper costs 220
paperback
　binding 77
　covers 78–9
　half-title in 81
paragraphs
　conventions for, in dialogue 68–9
　numbering of 137
　setting instructions for 5
parentheses
　in lists 26, 27
　for subordinate clauses 52, 64
　see also square brackets
parliamentary papers, in references 232
participle, dangling 41–2
passing mentions 277
　see also indexes
passing off 105, 112–13
　see also copyright
passive vs active voice 147–8, 155

patient anonymity 113
peoples, capitals for 118
percentages, style for 137
perfect binding 77, 79
periodicals *see* journals
permissions xiv
  acknowledged in prelims 92, 93
  and fair dealing 106
  and illustrations 107, 206
  for poetry 158
  requesting 108–9
  see also acknowledgements; copyright
personal names
  capitals for 124
  compound 62–4
photographs
  copyright in 84, 105, 107
  privacy issues and 113
picture credits 93, 274
  see also acknowledgements; credits
place names 116, 215, 219
place of publication
  in prelims 82–4
  in references 239–40
plagiarism 109–10
  see also copyright
plant names *see* biological names; cultivar names; genus names; species names
plays
  agency notice for 85
  characters' names in, style for 165
  dialogue in, layout of 166
  extracts of, in text 167
  marking up 167
  numbering of acts and scenes in 165
  references to, style for *232*
  stage directions in 166
  style for line numbers in 167
  titles of, style for 119
poetry 157

anthologies of 158
displayed 19, 158–9
embedded 158
indexes of 271
line breaks in 158, 166
references to, style for 159, *232*
possessive pronouns 66
PPC *see* printed-paper covers
pre-press stages xvi–xviii, *xvii*
preface 90, 92–3
prelims xiv, , 291g
  acknowledgments in 93
  contents page in 89–91
  dedication in 88
  epigraph in 89
  foreword in 92
  half-title in 81
  imprint page in 82–7
  introduction in 94
  lists in 91–2, 93
  preface in 92–3
  printing history in 83–4
  title page in 82
prepositional phrase, dangling 42, 45
prepositions
  and commas 52–3
  at end of sentence 37
  no capitalization for 9, 119, 250
  omission of 174, 175
  with subentries in indexes 271, 275
  and 'whom' 46
price on cover 78, 79
printed-paper covers (PPC) 78
printing history in prelims 83–4
probability, levels of
  omission of zero in 137
  represented by asterisks 195
production xiv, 291g
  stages of xvi–xx, *xvii*
project manager, role of xx
pronouns
  capitals for 118
  indefinite 39–40

pronouns – *continued*
  possessive 66
  relative 45–6, 53
proofreader, role of 91, 197, 229
proofreading marks *see* British Standard *Marks for copy preparation and proof correction*
proofs xix–xxi
  changes in, affecting index 277
  cutting and expanding text in 228–9
publication
  history in prelims 83–4
  place of 82, 83, 231, 232
  year of 83–4, 104, 232, 249, 251
publisher
  identification in ISBN 86
  name on cover 78, 79
  see also publication history in prelims
punctuation
  in citing plays 167
  in index entries 274
  italics and 125
  in references 167, 231, 233, 242
  and tone of voice 57, 71
  see also colon; commas; exclamation mark; ellipsis; full stop; question mark; quotation marks; semicolon

Q
qualifications, author's, on contents page 90, 92
QuarkXpress, marking up for 4
queries for author, writing xxiv–xxviii
question mark 57
quotation marks
  double and single 68, 76
  functions of 67–8
  with internal punctuation 71–2
  and poetry 158, 159
  with terminal punctuation 69–71

quotations
  displayed 16–19
  editorial treatment of 66–7
  embedded 67, 70
  marking up 4, 17–20, *18*
  permissions for use of 24, 106–9
  from plays 167
  of poetry 19, 157–9
  see also acknowledgements; copyright; epigraph

R
racial hatred, incitement to 114
  see also legal matters
ranges of numbers
  alignment of, in tables 194
  elision in 140
  en rule in 63–4, 272
  no overlap in 190, 191
  see also numbers; numerals; tables
ranks and titles, style for 116–17
reference systems
  author–date (Harvard) 249–57, *249*, *251*
  author–number (Vancouver) 257–60, *259*
  author–title 230–49, *250*
  changing 265
  short-title 233
references
  elements in 230–1, *232*
  list of 250–2, *251*, 258, 259–60, *259*
  styling of 238–40, *234*, *236*
  see also bibliography; notes; reference systems
relative pronouns 45–6
religious denominations, capitals for 115
repetition 147, 148, 229
reports, company 26, 34, 137, 146, 219
reprint information 84
review quotes 187

rhetorical questions 57
right of integrity 105
  see also moral rights
rights see copyright; moral rights; permissions
road numbers, style of 137
  see also numbers; numerals
rules, to be disregarded 37
rules in tables 189
  see also tables
run-on
  index style 275–6, *275*, 278, 279
  marking up 159
running feet 100, 101
running heads 2, 100–3, 292g

S
saddle-stitching 79
save and make see cutting and expanding
scare quotes 68
semicolon 55–6, 60
sentences 37–8
  see also apposites; clauses; dangling participle; modifiers, misplaced; punctuation; relative pronouns; subject–verb agreement
serial comma 50–1
series title
  style for, in text 126, *127*
  on title page 82
sewn binding 79
  see also binding, types of
ships, style for names of 125
short-title system 233
  see also reference systems
sic 67
side-stitching 79
  see also binding, types of
signature 79, 80, 274, 292g
singular vs plural 38–40
small caps 9, 90, 125, 165, *288*, 292g

sneer quotes 68
softback 78
  see also binding, types of
songs
  references to *232*
  style for titles of 118, 119
source notes in tables 195
spacecraft, style for names of 126
speakers, commas offsetting 54–5
species, style for name of 127
specification 1, 292g
speech
  capitals for addressees in 117
  colon introducing 56
  commas offsetting 54, 55, 70–1
  differences in 35
  ellipsis in 72
  em rule in 65
  natural style of 37, 39, 41
  in plays 166–7
  quotation marks for 67, 68–9
spine 77–8, 79, 292g
spiral-bound books 77, 80
  see also binding, types of
sponsorship of book 78, 86–7, 88
square brackets
  with quotations 67, 70
  in stage directions 166
  in Vancouver system 258
  see also parentheses
stab-stitching 79
  see also binding, types of
stage directions 166
  see also plays
strapline 224
structures in text, marking up for 3–4, 5, 16
stub in tables *189*, 191–2, *192*, 194, 197
style see capitals; italics; numbers
style manuals 230
style sheet xxiv, *xxv*, *xxvi*
subject–verb agreement 38–40
subjectivity, vocabulary and 148

subjunctive mood 41
subordinate clauses 52
   see also apposites; main clauses; sentences
subspecies, style for name of 128
subtitle
   dropped in short-title reference 233
   italics for citing 125, 126, *126*
   on jackets/covers 181
   on title page 82
symbols
   alignment of, in tables 194
   for cueing notes 195, 233–5, *234*, 249
   for levels of probability 195
   for lists 27
   no elision with 140
   for percentages 137
   proof-correction *see* British Standard *Marks for copy preparation and proof correction*
   in table subheadings 191
   see also degree

T
table of contents *see* contents page
tablers 93
tables
   body of *189*, 194
   creating 202
   editing 196–8
   headings for *189*, 190–2, *192*, *193*
   marking up 197, 198–9
   notes to 193, *195*–6
   preparation of 191
   rules in 189
   structure and layout of 188–96, *189*
   stub in 191–2, *192*
   totals in 194–5
   verbal 194, *196*
tables (law books) 93, 126, 271

technical figures 204–19
   see also diagrams; illustrations
temperature, degrees of 136
text area/type area 2, 292g
'that' vs 'which' 456
thin space 136, 139, 194
title identifier in ISBN 86
title page 82
   see also prelims
titles of people, capitals for 116–17
titles of works
   capitals in 119
   italics for 125, 126, *127*
   other, in prelims 81
   and passing off 112
tone of voice, changing 148–9
trade paperback 78
   see also binding, types of
trade-marked names 118
trains, style for names of 126
translation, publication history of 84, 88
translator's name in prelims 82
transport, style for names of means of 125, 126
turnover lines
   in indexes 276, 277
   in plays 166
   in poetry 159
   in tables 194, 198, *275*
type spec *see* specification
typeface *see* font
typesetters 1–2, 86
typographic design 1–2

U
units of measurement 134, 136, 174, 175
Universal Copyright Convention (UCC) 84, 104
   see also copyright

V
Vancouver system 257–60, 265
   see also reference systems

variables, dependent 192, 209–10
  see also tables
varietal name, style for 128
verbs
  and agreement with subjects 38, 39
  capitals for 118
verse *see* poetry
vocabulary 35, 146, 147, 148
voice
  active and passive 147, 148
  author's 35–6, 37, 40, 148
  changing tone of 148–9
  creating a character's 35–6
  house 36
  punctuation and tone of 57, 71
volume number 80, 82
volume rights 108
  see also permissions

W
'was' vs 'were' 40–1
website
  address in prelims 83
  pages 220
  style for, in references 232
'which' vs 'that' 456
'who' vs 'whom' 37, 46
widow 229, 293g
wire-stitching 77, 79
  see also binding, types of
word break 61, 229

x-height 293g